WOOF-A-PEDIA

The Ultimate Dog Breed Guide

A Comprehensive Guide to Tips and Tricks for Choosing
the Perfect Dog for Your Lifestyle

Copyright © 2024 by K9 Chatter and Rowan's Publishing, LLC.

All rights reserved.

This book is copyright-protected. Unauthorized reproduction, duplication, or transmission of its content is strictly prohibited and may result in legal action.

By reading this book, the reader agrees that under no circumstances is the author responsible for any losses, direct or indirect, which are incurred as a result of the use of the information contained within this book, including, but not limited to, errors, omissions, or inaccuracies. It's licensed for your personal enjoyment only. This book may not be resold or given away to other people. If you would like to share this book with another person, please purchase an additional copy for each reader. If you're reading this book and did not purchase it, or it was not purchased for your use only, please visit your favorite book retailer to purchase your copy. Thank you for respecting the hard work of this author.

TABLE OF CONTENTS

Welcome to Woof-a-pedia	1
The Basics of Dog Breeds	5
The Importance of Kennel Clubs	8
Choosing the Right Breed	14
Adopting vs. Buying	17
Bringing Your New Pup Home	23
Health and Nutrition	26
Exercise and Enrichment	30
Training and Socialization	32
Dogs for Special Needs	35
Traveling with Your Dog	41
Dog Breed Profiles	44
Appendix A: Resources for Ongoing Support and Education	III
Appendix B: Breed Group Quick Reference	V
Appendix C: Glossary of Terms	VII
Appendix D: Resources and Further Reading	XIV
Bibliography	XVI
Dog Breed Index	XXV

WELCOME TO WOOF-A-PEDIA

Hey there, fellow dog lover! So, whether you're totally new to the whole wagging-tail scene or you've had a bunch of canine besties over the years (you know, the kind that hog the bed and pretend they don't know what "stay" means), picking the right breed is a big deal. I've been there myself—like, no joke, I once spent a whole weekend scrolling through puppy pics, debating if I was actually ready for the non-stop, bouncy energy of a Border Collie. Spoiler alert: I wasn't. Turns out, I'm more of a "couch-loving Bulldog" type, and trust me, my couch has never been happier.

The truth is, the breed you choose can totally shape your home life and happiness—both yours and your furry friend's. I mean, think about it: do you really want to be training a high-energy pup when all you want is a chill movie buddy? That's why this guide—yep, we're calling it Woof-a-pedia—is here to walk you through every step of the way.

Okay, so here's the thing. Here at K9 Chatter, we are kinda over those textbook-style breed guides. You know the ones, they're all "textbook" info that basically reads like someone copy-pasted stats from a breed website. Honestly, it's a snoozefest. And maybe it's just us, but we never seem to remember any of it anyway. (Except the cute pictures…those we remember.) Osmosis is supposed to be a thing, but we've yet to soak up anything other than a nap after reading those guides. So, yeah, we're doing something different here.

Between us, we've racked up over 150 years of hands-on, fur-covered, treat-filled experience in the dog world. We're not just your average pet professionals, we're a crew made up of veterinarians, vet techs, trainers, and boarding experts. From the nitty-gritty of medical care to the wild (and often hilarious) world of dog behavior, we've seen it all. Each of us has a unique specialty, and you'll notice that as we each take you through the parts of this guide that play to our strengths. You might get a story from a trainer who once turned a wild, sock-stealing pup into a well-mannered star. Or maybe a vet tech will share that unforgettable moment when a once-scared rescue dog looked up at them with pure trust.

We've been through the highs and lows of pet care, and trust me, we've learned a few lessons along the way…sometimes the hard way (who knew a five-pound chihuahua could outsmart four grown adults?).

Finding the right breed for you isn't just about ticking boxes on a list—it's about understanding your lifestyle, your energy, and maybe even your quirks. Are you someone who dreams of long hikes with a loyal companion by your side? Or are you more of a "curl-up-on-the-couch-with-my-coffee" type? Either way, there's a breed that will not only fit into your life but make it brighter.

When we sat down to write this guide, we knew we didn't want to give you just dry facts. We wanted to weave in personal stories—those little moments that made us fall in love with dogs in the first place. Imagine *Woof-a-pedia* as your trusty sidekick—the dog encyclopedia with a twist. We're not just offering advice; we're giving you our personal stories, our hard-earned wisdom, and yes, even a few of our mistakes (like that time someone underestimated a Beagle's determination to follow his nose… through a locked door). By the end of this guide, you'll have a much clearer picture of which breed will not just fit into your home, but into your heart.

And here's the thing: finding the right breed is also about finding a dog that matches you. You may be drawn to a high-energy herding dog because of their intelligence, but if you're not ready for their need to work and move, you'll both be frustrated. On the other hand, a low-maintenance breed might sound perfect until you realize you crave the challenge of training and exercising a more demanding pup. We've all been there, second-guessing ourselves, but that's why we're here to share what we've learned.

We've got you covered with detailed profiles of every breed recognized by the American Kennel Club (AKC). We'll break down everything you need to know—personalities, quirks, care needs—basically, all the things the typical guides should tell you but, like, in a way that actually makes sense. Whether you're on the hunt for a jogging partner (no judgment if you're braver than I am) or you're all about finding that perfect movie-night snuggle buddy, we've got the lowdown.

So grab a coffee (or maybe a squeaky toy if your pup's nearby), and settle in. Let us guide you through the maze of breeds, shedding light on what truly makes each one special. You'll get insights from a trainer who's wrangled the wildest of pups, advice from a vet tech who's dealt with more post-surgery cuddles than you can count, and tips from boarding pros who've seen firsthand what happens when dogs are left in the wrong environment.

WHAT YOU'LL SNIFF OUT IN THIS GUIDE:

Part 1: Understanding Dog Breeds (AKA: Doggie 101)

Let's kick things off with the basics. Ever wondered why some breeds look like they belong on a royal throne (looking at you, Afghan Hound), while others seem born to herd sheep or dig up your backyard? We'll dig into the fascinating history of different breeds and why organizations like the AKC even exist. Think of this as the backstory for all those doggie traits we know and love—or sometimes, just put up with. Plus, we'll help you figure out which dog personalities vibe best with your lifestyle. Are you a hiking enthusiast? A homebody? A family with kids who can't sit still? We'll match you up.

Pro Tip: Take a moment to think about your daily routine and energy level. A friend of mine, Lucy, fell in love with a high-energy Australian Shepherd pup. But as much as she loved that dog, she wasn't ready for the hours of exercise and attention he needed. Sometimes, the cutest dogs are the most high-maintenance!

Part 2: Breed Profiles A-Z (The Real Woof & Wag Show)

This is where things get exciting! We've compiled a massive collection of breed profiles, detailing everything from the history and personality of each breed to their grooming needs and how they'll fit into your family. If you've ever wondered what it's like to live with a Poodle versus a Basset Hound (spoiler: very different), this section is your go-to.

Oh, and here's a fun fact: Did you know Dalmatians are known for their "smile"? Yep, when they're happy, they curl their lips back into a grin. Adorable, right? But also, they can be pretty stubborn, so you'll need some patience (and lots of treats) when training them.

Part 3: Living with Your Dog (AKA: It's Not Just Walks in the Park)

Okay, you've picked your breed—woohoo! But now what? This part of the guide walks you through bringing your new buddy home, from setting up their cozy space to making the first few weeks as smooth as possible. We'll chat about training tips (like what to do when your pup thinks your shoe is a chew toy) and dive into health care basics, nutrition, and even a few fun games to play. Did you know playing tug-of-war can actually help with training? Yep, it's all about bonding and building trust.

A quick story: When I first brought my Golden Retriever, Charlie, home, I was convinced he'd be the perfect fetch partner. Turns out, he had other plans—like chasing squirrels and refusing to bring the ball back. But hey, we figured out our own groove, and now, tug-of-war is our jam. The point is, every dog has their own quirks. Embrace them, and you'll find joy in the little things.

Part 4: Special Considerations (Adoption, Puppies, and Senior Pups—Oh My!)

Thinking of adopting instead of shopping for a breeder? This section has all the info you need. We cover everything from finding reputable breeders and adoption agencies to understanding what it takes to care for senior dogs or raising puppies. Trust me, raising a puppy is like having a toddler that never grows up—they're cute and all, but they'll test your patience!

Also, if you've ever dreamed of traveling with your dog, we've got some tips for that too. (Hint: If your dog's anything like my friend Jess's Cocker Spaniel, who freaks out in cars, you'll want to ease into those road trips with short drives and plenty of treats!)

Bonus: Quick Tips, Fun Facts, and a Handy Checklist

We know how overwhelming it can be to choose the right breed, so we've put together a few extras. Our appendices are packed with quick reference guides, a glossary (because what even is a "double coat"?), and a checklist to keep you on track during your breed selection process. Oh, and we've thrown in some fun dog trivia—because who doesn't want to impress their friends with random facts like how Greyhounds are faster than racehorses (at least for short distances)?

Choosing the right dog isn't just about finding one that's cute (although, let's be honest, they're all cute). It's about making sure you and your pup are a match made in doggie heaven. Different breeds have their own needs when it comes to exercise, grooming, training, and companionship. A mismatch between what a dog needs and what you can provide can lead to frustration—both for you and your furry friend. I've seen it happen, and it's not fun. But when you get it right? Oh, it's magic.

So take your time, explore your options, and remember, this is about finding a buddy who'll fit into your life seamlessly, whether that means morning runs, movie nights on the couch, or weekend camping trips. Woof-a-pedia is here to make sure your journey to finding the perfect pup is as rewarding and joyful as the years you'll spend together.

PART 1: The Basics

CHAPTER 1:
The Basics of Dog Breeds

You know, if you've ever met a Labrador or a tiny, feisty Chihuahua, you've probably noticed how different dog breeds can be—both in looks and personality. A dog breed isn't just about fur color or size; it's like a family with its own set of traits passed down from generation to generation. Some breeds are known for their playful nature, while others might be more protective or independent. I remember meeting a Golden Retriever once, and it was like being greeted by an old friend—those big, friendly eyes and that wagging tail just melt your heart, right? Breeds like this come about through careful, selective breeding, where dogs with specific qualities—like that loyal, gentle nature—are paired together to create pups that carry on those traits. Over time, this process creates a breed that's easily recognizable, whether it's the majestic German Shepherd or the fluffy Pomeranian. And, of course, kennel clubs around the world set breed standards to make sure these unique qualities are preserved, guiding breeders to raise pups that match those expectations. It's pretty amazing how much thought goes into maintaining the personality and look of each breed!

THE HISTORY AND EVOLUTION OF DOG BREEDS

Did you know that the history of dog breeds is actually wrapped up in the story of humanity itself? It's true—dogs were some of the very first animals we managed to domesticate. And when I say "some of the first," I mean way back—like somewhere between 15,000 and 40,000 years ago! Imagine early humans hanging out with wolves and thinking, "Hey, these guys could be helpful." And so, they started taming them. Over centuries (and a lot of selective breeding later), those wolves gradually transformed into the diverse dog breeds we know and love today. Pretty wild, right?

The real doggy evolution party kicked off when humans stopped wandering and set up permanent homes in agricultural communities. Suddenly, dogs had jobs! With hunting, herding, and guarding becoming part of daily life, people began to breed dogs specifically to be superstars in these roles. That's how we ended up with breeds that are practically custom-made for certain tasks. Let's dive into a few of these amazing categories:

Herding Dogs: Ever seen a Border Collie in action? If not, picture a dog so smart and focused it almost looks like it's herding sheep with telepathy. Herding dogs like the Border Collie or the Australian Shepherd were bred to manage livestock. They needed to be quick thinkers, independent workers, and obedient enough to listen to their owners' commands. These breeds didn't just 'manage' livestock—they practically ran the show. Fun fact: Some experts even say that the Border Collie is the smartest dog breed out there. No big deal.

Hunting Dogs: Okay, so hunting dogs had a different kind of mission. These pups were all about helping humans track, point, retrieve, or even chase down prey. Take the Beagle, for instance, with its adorable, floppy ears. Cute, right? But those ears actually help them stir up scents from the ground, making them fantastic trackers. Then there's the Labrador Retriever—a dog that's basically the MVP of hunting and retrieving (and maybe cuddling too). And let's not forget the Greyhound, a breed that was born to chase. These dogs are so fast, they could probably outrun a car (okay, maybe not a sports car, but you get what I mean).

Guard Dogs: Now, if you needed protection back in the day, you couldn't just set up a security camera—you needed a loyal, watchful dog with some serious strength. That's where guard dogs like the Rottweiler and

German Shepherd come in. These breeds were trained to defend their human families and properties, and they took their jobs seriously. Rottweilers, for example, have been used since Roman times as guard dogs and cattle protectors. Meanwhile, German Shepherds are basically the action movie heroes of the dog world—strong, brave, and super loyal.

Companion Dogs: Not every dog had to be a hardworking hero, though. Some breeds were bred purely for their friendly, loving nature, and they excelled at being companions. Cavalier King Charles Spaniels, for instance, were literal lapdogs for European nobility. Can you imagine lounging around in a palace with one of these adorable pups on your lap? They're just that cute and cuddly. Or take the Pomeranian—small, fluffy, and full of personality, these dogs became all the rage among royals and commoners alike.

As human societies changed, so did the roles dogs played. The Industrial Revolution, for example, brought more people into cities, which meant less need for working dogs and a boom in the popularity of companion breeds. Suddenly, dogs weren't just tools for work—they became family members and best friends. And honestly, I think we can all agree that they've done a fantastic job in that role.

Fast forward to today, and dog breeds continue to evolve. New breeds pop up, and existing ones adapt to fit our modern lifestyles. Some breeds that were once hunters or herders are now more like jogging partners or therapy animals. It's a reminder that as humans change, dogs change with us. And honestly, that's what makes them so incredible—they're not just man's best friend; they've been our partners through the entire journey of civilization.

So, the next time you see your dog lying on the couch, remember: They come from a long line of hunters, herders, or guardians. And while they may not be chasing down prey or guarding a flock of sheep these days, they've still got that history written into their DNA. Pretty cool, huh?

THE ROLE OF BREED STANDARDS IN DOG OWNERSHIP

Ever wondered why some dogs are perfectly suited for cozy apartment living while others seem born for endless days of outdoor adventures? Or why some pups are as laid-back as an old slipper, while others have energy levels that make you think they run on jet fuel? It all comes down to breed standards—a set of guidelines that shape everything from a dog's physical traits to its behavior. And trust me, they're more important than you might think!

When I was looking for my own pup, I had my heart set on a Golden Retriever. I wanted a family-friendly dog, the kind you see in movies playing fetch and greeting everyone with that big goofy smile. But I didn't know about breed standards at the time. I just thought, "Golden Retrievers are cute; they'll be perfect." It wasn't until I started talking to a breeder that I realized how much detail goes into maintaining a breed's unique characteristics. She explained that every aspect of a Golden's appearance and temperament—from its dense, water-resistant coat to its naturally friendly demeanor—is written down and preserved through careful breeding practices.
It was fascinating (and a little overwhelming), but knowing these standards helped me feel confident that I was choosing a breed that would fit my lifestyle and expectations.

Let's dive in. Breed standards aren't just about looks; they provide a detailed guide on what makes each breed special. These standards, set by kennel clubs and breed organizations, act like a blueprint for breeders to follow. Here's what they typically include:
   1. **Physical Traits** Think size, weight, coat type, color, ear shape, and even tail length. If you've ever wondered why a Bulldog has that stocky, muscular build or why a Greyhound is all sleek lines and speed, it's because their breed standards spell it out. For instance, a Golden Retriever's standard describes its coat as dense and water-resistant—perfect for a dog that was bred for retrieving game from water. And those soulful, friendly eyes? Not a coincidence; it's all part of the standard to ensure they have a warm, intelligent expression.
   2. **Behavioral Traits** But it's not just about appearance. Standards also describe the typical behavior and personality traits of each breed. Ever noticed how a Border Collie is practically bouncing off the walls with energy, ready to work or play at any moment? That's because their breed standard emphasizes intelligence, high energy levels, and a strong work ethic. The goal is to help breeders maintain these behaviors, so if you're getting a Border Collie, you know you're in for an active, smart, and eager-to-learn companion.
   3. **Health Considerations** Here's where it gets really important. Breed standards also address health issues common within each breed, guiding breeders to prioritize healthier dogs and reduce genetic problems.

This can be a lifesaver—literally. For example, Bulldogs are prone to respiratory issues because of their short snouts, so ethical breeders are encouraged to choose dogs that exhibit fewer of these traits, ensuring healthier pups. It's a way of safeguarding the breed's well-being while preserving its distinctive look and personality. Okay, so now you know what breed standards cover, but why should you care? Well, if you're thinking about bringing a new dog into your life, these standards can be your best friend (pun intended). They give you a snapshot of what to expect when it comes to a dog's appearance, behavior, and health. That's valuable information when you're trying to find a dog that matches your lifestyle.

Take my friend Sara, for example. She lives in a small apartment in the city and loves to chill at home. When she was considering getting a dog, she originally thought about a high-energy breed like a Husky (I know, right?). Luckily, she checked the breed standards and realized that Huskies thrive with tons of exercise and space to roam—definitely not the best match for city living. Instead, she opted for a French Bulldog, a breed known for its smaller size, low energy levels, and adaptability to apartment life. Now, she and her pup are a perfect match, enjoying their cozy evenings together without the stress of unmet needs.

If you've ever watched a dog show, you've seen breed standards in action. Judges meticulously evaluate each dog to see how closely it aligns with its breed's ideal characteristics. It's not just about how pretty a dog looks (though, let's be honest, they are adorable); it's about how well the dog embodies everything the breed is supposed to represent, from its physical build to its behavior.
So, when you see a Dalmatian strutting confidently in the ring with its sleek, spotted coat, know that it's not just random luck. It's the result of breeders working to uphold the standard set for that breed—ensuring the dog looks and acts like a classic Dalmatian should. And those judges? They're not just there to hand out ribbons; they're guardians of these breed standards, helping to keep each breed's legacy intact.

Choosing a dog isn't just about finding one that's cute (though, let's be honest, they're all cute). It's about finding a breed that matches your personality, lifestyle, and environment. Do you love going on long hikes and exploring the great outdoors? A high-energy breed like an Australian Shepherd or a Labrador might be the way to go. Or maybe you prefer relaxing weekends at home with a cup of coffee and a book—breeds like the Cavalier King Charles Spaniel or the Bichon Frise could be a perfect fit.
When you take the time to learn about breed standards, you set yourself up for success. You know what to expect, and you can make an informed decision that ensures both you and your new furry friend are happy together. After all, the joy of owning a dog that perfectly matches your lifestyle is unmatched—there's something incredibly special about finding a pup that just "gets" you, right from the start.

Breed standards might sound technical, but they're the secret to understanding why dogs are the way they are. They preserve the rich history and unique qualities of each breed, helping us appreciate everything from a Dachshund's long body (designed for burrowing) to a Poodle's intelligence and elegance. So, if you're considering bringing a dog into your life, take a closer look at these standards. They're a valuable tool in finding the canine companion who'll become your new best friend—and trust me, it's worth every moment of research to find that perfect match.
In the end, understanding breed standards isn't just about picking a dog; it's about embracing a breed's legacy and ensuring a harmonious, fulfilling relationship. And who wouldn't want that with their furry companion?

CHAPTER 2:
The Importance of Kennel Clubs

Ever been to a dog show? If not, let me tell you—there's a whole world of wagging tails, proud owners, and dogs strutting their stuff like they're on a runway. And behind all this excitement? That's where kennel clubs come in. These clubs aren't just about fancy ribbons and titles (although they're pretty fun too!); they're like the ultimate hub for everything dog breed-related. From keeping tabs on pedigrees to hosting events, these clubs are where dog lovers and their furry companions come together to celebrate all things canine.

I remember the first time I stumbled into the world of kennel clubs. I had just adopted a scrappy little terrier mix, and I was clueless about dog training beyond "sit" and "stay." But then, I met a breeder at a local club event who introduced me to the club's training classes. Trust me, it was a game-changer. Not only did I learn the ropes, but I also discovered a whole community of people as obsessed with dogs as I was. Kennel clubs, I realized, are more than just organizations; they're like a second family for dog enthusiasts.

Kennel clubs have been around since the late 1800s (crazy, right?), and they started off with the mission to set up some structure in the wild world of dog shows. You know, making sure everyone's on the same page when it comes to breed standards. But nowadays, they do way more than that. Here's a quick rundown:

Breed Registration: They keep tabs on purebred dogs, kind of like tracking the family tree. If your pup has a fancy pedigree, they're the ones who give you the official papers to prove it.

Setting Breed Standards: Think of them as the rulebook makers. They decide what makes a golden retriever, well, golden, or a dachshund's body just the right amount of long and low. And they update these standards as needed to keep things in line with each breed's history and traits.

Organizing Events: If you've ever seen those agility courses where dogs are zooming through tunnels or gracefully jumping hurdles, that's all kennel club magic. From obedience trials to conformation shows (basically, dog beauty contests), they host a ton of events where dogs and owners can show off their stuff.

Education and Resources: Here's where they really shine. Kennel clubs offer guidance on everything—training tips, responsible breeding practices, and how to keep your dog healthy and happy. They were a lifesaver when I was figuring out my terrier's endless energy levels.

Promoting Health and Welfare: It's not just about the looks. Kennel clubs are all about making sure dogs are healthy too. They run health tests and genetic screenings to tackle breed-specific health issues. It's nice to know that they're working to make sure our furry pals live their best lives.

Now, I know some folks think kennel clubs are all about purebreds and fancy dogs, but honestly, they offer a lot for everyone—whether you've got a prize-winning poodle or a lovable mutt like mine. Sure, there's a focus on preserving breed standards, but they also promote responsible pet ownership and community events that welcome all dogs. And let's be real, there's something heartwarming about a place where people come together just because they love dogs.

If you've never checked out a kennel club, I'd say give it a shot. You might find yourself surrounded by folks who get as excited as you do when a dog pulls off the perfect sit-stay—or maybe you'll get inspired to enter your dog in the next agility trial. Who knows? It's all part of the fun!

DIFFERENCES IN KENNEL CLUBS WORLDWIDE

When it comes to kennel clubs, it's not a one-size-fits-all scenario. These organizations, scattered all over the globe, each have their own way of doing things. Whether you're a breeder, a dog owner, or just a dog enthusiast like me, knowing a bit about what makes each club tick can be super helpful. Let's dive into some of the biggest ones and see what they're all about!

The American Kennel Club (AKC)
Founded: 1884
Location: United States
Mission Statement: "We are committed to advancing the sport of the purebred dog. We are dedicated to maintaining the integrity of our Registry. We protect the health and well-being of all dogs. We cherish dogs as companions."
Now, the AKC is a big deal—like, really big. It's the largest registry of purebred dogs in the U.S., and I've even seen their events on TV, where the dogs look like absolute royalty. One year, I attended their National Championship (which is basically the Oscars for dogs), and it was jaw-dropping. Picture this: perfectly groomed pups, strutting down the arena, tails up and eyes sparkling. It's more than just a beauty contest, though. The AKC hosts over 22,000 events annually, from agility trials to obedience competitions. These events are all about showcasing not just the dog's looks but their skills and personalities too.
What I really appreciate about the AKC is their dedication to keeping each breed true to its roots. They set high standards, ensuring each dog retains the traits and characteristics that make them special. And they don't just stop there. The AKC has a Canine Health Foundation that pours resources into research—everything from genetic diseases to common health issues—because they genuinely care about these dogs' well-being. Oh, and if you're a dog lover who's big on advocacy, they've got your back. The AKC works on legislation to protect dog owners' rights, making sure you and your furry friend are covered.

The Canadian Kennel Club (CKC)
Founded: 1888
Location: Canada
Mission Statement: "As the prime registry of purebred dogs in Canada, our purpose is to serve our members and the public with education, support, guidance, and sanctioning of events for all their canine endeavors. Our goal is the preservation of purebred dogs and the health, well-being, and enjoyment of all dogs."
Ah, the CKC—Canada's answer to the AKC but with a dash of maple syrup charm. I remember meeting a CKC breeder at an event a few years back. She was passionate about her work, and the pride she took in her line of Labrador Retrievers was infectious. The CKC is all about keeping detailed pedigrees and tracking lineage, which is crucial for those who want to know the background of their future pup.
Every year, they hold the Canadian National Dog Show, which attracts the best of the best from all over. It's the event where dogs strut their stuff, and it's a blast to watch—especially when a cheeky pup decides to go off-script and do their own thing. Beyond the shows, the CKC is a treasure trove of resources for breeders and dog owners alike. They promote responsible dog ownership, ethical breeding, and overall canine health. They really want to make sure every dog in Canada gets the love and care they deserve, which is something I think any dog lover can get behind.

The Fédération Cynologique Internationale (FCI)
Founded: 1911
Location: Belgium
Mission Statement: "To promote and protect purebred dogs globally, and to foster cooperation among national kennel clubs."
Okay, so the FCI is like the United Nations for dogs. It's all about creating one giant, global registry for purebred dogs and ensuring that everyone follows the same rules—no matter where you are in the world. I find this super fascinating because it means that if you're competing in a dog show in Europe, Asia, or South America, the standards are consistent. It's this universal approach that sets the FCI apart, and it's comforting to know that they're working with clubs everywhere to keep breed standards in check.

The FCI doesn't just stop at shows; they're big on education too. They offer a ton of resources about dog health, breeding practices, and welfare. So if you're curious about what goes into raising a happy, healthy pup or want to know how breeders make sure their dogs are the best they can be, the FCI has got the scoop. They're all about making sure the information is shared globally, so no matter where you and your pup are, you've got access to the best practices.

The Kennel Club (UK)
Founded: 1873
Location: United Kingdom
Mission Statement: "To improve the health, welfare, and general well-being of dogs throughout their lives."
Now, when I think of dog shows, I think of Crufts. It's like the Super Bowl of dog events, and yep, it's organized by the UK's Kennel Club. These folks are all about making sure dogs are happy and healthy, which I absolutely love. They're the ones who set the breed standards and work closely with breeders to keep everything on track, ensuring that each dog stays true to what makes their breed special.
One thing that stands out about the Kennel Club is their focus on health and welfare. They've got initiatives like the Assured Breeder Scheme, where breeders must meet certain standards before they can participate. It's all about raising dogs the right way, and honestly, I think that's something every kennel club should aim for. Plus, the Kennel Club Charitable Trust backs a bunch of health research and welfare projects, so you know they're walking the walk, not just talking the talk.

The United Kennel Club (UKC)
Founded: 1898
Location: United States
Mission Statement: Aims to promote "Real Dogs for Real People" through a variety of programs and services.
The UKC is like the AKC's fun, laid-back cousin. They're all about celebrating dogs for their personalities and skills rather than just their looks. I've seen dogs show off their talents at UKC events—everything from hunting tests to weight pulls. It's wild to watch these dogs in action, especially when you see them light up, doing what they were born to do.
The UKC places a big emphasis on a dog's working abilities and temperament. Their motto is "Real Dogs for Real People," and honestly, I love that. It feels less about perfection and more about what makes each dog unique. If you've got a dog with some serious talent or an incredible personality, the UKC's events are the place to show it off. From conformation shows to obedience trials, they cover everything, and they focus on the whole dog, not just its appearance. It's refreshing and makes for a much more engaging experience if you ask me.

So, whether you're into the AKC's all-American style, the CKC's cozy Canadian vibe, the FCI's international flair, or the UKC's laid-back fun, there's a kennel club out there for everyone. The best part? They all share the same passion: making sure dogs live their best lives. And honestly, what more could we ask for?

DIFFERENCES IN PHILOSOPHY AND PRACTICE

Philosophy
AKC: Ever heard of the American Kennel Club (AKC)? It's all about celebrating purebred dogs as amazing family members. They go above and beyond to make sure our furry pals stay healthy and happy, and they're huge on promoting responsible pet ownership. You know, the kind where your dog isn't just a pet but a true part of the family.

UKC: Now, if you're into dogs that do a bit of everything, the United Kennel Club (UKC) might just be your jam. They push this whole "total dog" philosophy, which is basically about dogs that not only look good but also have the brains and skills to match. Think of it as dogs that are total overachievers—agility champs, hunting experts, and all-around versatile pals. Who wouldn't love that?

CKC: Over in Canada, the Canadian Kennel Club (CKC) really champions the idea of purebred dogs, focusing on their welfare and development. They're all about responsible breeding and making sure these pups get the best start in life. If you're a fan of Canadian pride (and who isn't?), then knowing CKC is committed to these high standards is a pretty cool thing.

The Kennel Club (UK): Ah, the Kennel Club in the UK! If you've ever been to Crufts, you know how seriously they take dog welfare. This club is dedicated to advancing the ethical breeding of dogs and emphasizes their health and well-being like you wouldn't believe. They've got that proper British approach, making sure every pup is treated like royalty!

FCI: And let's not forget about the FCI, or Fédération Cynologique Internationale if you're feeling fancy. This international federation works hard to bring dog lovers together from all corners of the world. Their goal? To foster harmony in breed standards and host epic dog shows that connect purebred enthusiasts globally. It's like one big worldwide celebration of dogs!

Registration Policies

AKC: When it comes to registering purebred dogs, the AKC is the go-to place. They have a super detailed lineage process, ensuring that every pup's family tree is rock-solid. They even offer limited registration options for dogs not intended for breeding—talk about covering all bases!

UKC: The UKC, on the other hand, is all about performance. Sure, they register purebreds, but they also recognize mixed breeds that excel in events. Weight pulling, hunting trials, you name it! They believe if your dog's got the skills, it deserves to be part of the club. I mean, who wouldn't want to celebrate a hardworking dog?

CKC: Up in Canada, the CKC takes purebred documentation super seriously. Their pedigree requirements are strict, but that's how they maintain top-notch standards for Canadian canines. It's all about quality over quantity, and they do a fantastic job of ensuring that each pup meets those high standards. Gotta love that dedication!

The Kennel Club (UK): The UK's Kennel Club keeps things interesting. Besides registering purebred dogs, they've also got an Activity Register for those pups that are nailing it in performance events. It's like giving these dogs a little extra flair on their canine credentials—pretty cool, right?

FCI: The FCI, with its international vibe, works with national kennel clubs around the globe to keep everything in sync. They make sure standards and documentation match up no matter where you are. It's a massive task, but hey, someone's gotta keep all those breed enthusiasts on the same page!

Events and Competitions

AKC: If you're looking for dog events in the U.S., the AKC has something for every canine fan. From the elegance of conformation shows to the excitement of agility trials and the challenge of obedience competitions, they really know how to keep things interesting. Ever seen a dog nail an agility course? It's like watching an Olympic athlete—so much fun!

UKC: Now, if you want to see dogs in action, the UKC has you covered. They host everything from weight pulling and hunting trials to classic conformation shows. It's like a showcase of all the cool skills dogs can have, and it's so much more than just looking pretty. These events really highlight the diverse talents of our furry friends—talk about impressive!

CKC: The CKC in Canada keeps the dog-loving spirit alive with its variety of events, from conformation shows to obedience trials and agility competitions. It's amazing to see the bond between dogs and their owners on display. Ever been to one of these events? You can feel the energy—everyone's cheering on their pups, and it's such a blast to watch them shine!

The Kennel Club (UK): And of course, the Kennel Club in the UK is famous for Crufts—probably the world's most legendary dog show. If you've ever been, you know how electrifying the atmosphere is—dogs of every size and skill competing for that top spot! But it's not just about Crufts; they've got tons of other events throughout the year, making it a hub for dog lovers.

FCI: Finally, the FCI takes the international stage like no other. They oversee dog shows and competitions all around the world, making sure that judging is consistent and fair. It's pretty impressive how they manage to bring together dog lovers from different cultures and keep everyone united under the same set of standards. A true global community for dog enthusiasts!

SIGNIFICANCE OF KENNEL CLUB RECOGNITION

For Dog Breeders:
Have you ever wondered what sets some breeders apart from the rest? It's all about that official nod from a kennel club. When breeders earn that recognition, it's like getting a golden seal of approval. I've personally seen breeders transform their entire operations after becoming affiliated. Suddenly, potential buyers see that stamp and think, "This breeder must know their stuff!" It's a credibility boost that instantly builds trust and assures folks that they're getting a pup with a quality pedigree.

But that's not all. Recognized breeders gain access to a treasure trove of resources—everything from advanced health testing programs to educational seminars and networking events. Imagine being part of a community that shares the same passion for dogs and learning from the best in the business! It's a chance to elevate your skills, learn new tricks (pun intended), and connect with others who can help grow your reputation even further.

And, let's be real—puppies from recognized breeders? They're like the superstars of the dog world. Buyers are actively searching for dogs backed by reputable kennel clubs, and having that association instantly makes your puppies more marketable. It's like going from a local band to a sold-out concert tour!

For Dog Breeds:
Kennel club recognition isn't just a win for breeders; it's a game-changer for the breeds themselves. Think about it: when a breed is officially recognized, it's like preserving a little piece of history. That club helps safeguard the unique traits and characteristics that make each breed special. Whether it's the playful personality of a Labrador or the dignified stance of a Dalmatian, these clubs ensure that these qualities are passed down, generation after generation, keeping each breed's legacy alive.

Plus, kennel clubs go beyond just recognition; they're on a mission to get people excited about different breeds. Through events, publications, and outreach, they shine a spotlight on breeds that might otherwise go unnoticed. Ever seen a dog show and thought, "Wow, I didn't even know that breed existed!" That's the magic of promotion and awareness in action!

And when it comes to health and well-being, kennel clubs are like the superheroes of the dog world. They champion responsible breeding practices, focusing on genetic testing and health screenings to address any issues early on. It's not just about maintaining a breed's looks; it's about ensuring that each pup grows up strong, happy, and healthy. You could say kennel clubs act like guardians, protecting the future of these dogs so that every wagging tail and playful bark echoes for generations to come.

CREATION AND SIGNIFICANCE OF DOG BREED GROUPS

You ever wondered why dogs come in so many shapes and sizes—some tiny enough to fit in your purse, while others look like they could pull a small car? Well, it all boils down to breed groups! These groups were created to classify dogs based on their original jobs and unique traits, and honestly, they're like the Hogwarts houses of the canine world. Each breed group has its own personality, skills, and quirks that explain why they've been around for centuries. Understanding this system not only gives us a glimpse into why different breeds were developed, but it also makes organizing dog shows and competitions way easier (because seriously, you can't compare a Pomeranian to a Great Dane—it's just not fair!).

Dogs are grouped based on their history, physical traits, and behaviors. Imagine it like sorting them into squads based on their superpowers. Here's the scoop:

- Herding Group: These guys are the overachievers, the type-A dogs who can't stand seeing a mess. Think Border Collies and Australian Shepherds—they were bred to herd livestock and are known for their insane agility and smarts. Fun fact: some of these dogs are so intelligent, they can predict your next move before you even make it. I once watched a Border Collie practically choreograph a sheep's dance routine all by itself—talk about talent!

- Hound Group: Ah, the hounds—these are the classic hunters, like Beagles and Greyhounds. They've got noses so powerful, they could probably smell a cookie crumb hidden in your pocket from two blocks away. Seriously, these dogs were bred for hunting, using their keen senses of smell or sight to track down game. If you've ever seen a Greyhound run, you know it's like watching a furry Formula 1 car zip across the track. Fast, focused, and all business—well, until they catch a scent that distracts them!

- Working Group: Now, here's where you find the true multitaskers. Boxers, Siberian Huskies—these dogs are like the blue-collar heroes of the canine world. They're strong, versatile, and up for any challenge, whether it's guarding a home, pulling a sled, or even diving into rescue work. I once met a Husky who looked at me like he was judging whether I'd be any good at sled-pulling. Spoiler: I would not.

- Terrier Group: Terriers are the scrappy, energetic pups that make you think, "Did someone sneak espresso into their water bowl?" Breeds like the Jack Russell and Bull Terrier were originally bred to hunt vermin. They're fearless, tenacious, and have a personality that says, "No mouse, mole, or squirrel is safe." A friend of mine has a Jack Russell, and that little guy bounces around like he's got springs in his paws—relentless, but hey, that's why they're so good at their job.

- Toy Group: Let's talk about the Toy Group. These are the lap dogs, the divas, the ones who know they're cute and aren't afraid to flaunt it. Chihuahuas, Pomeranians—small in size but massive in personality. These breeds were primarily bred for companionship, and they know how to win your heart with those big eyes and tiny paws. And trust me, a Chihuahua can boss around a dog three times its size without even blinking. It's like they know they've got main character energy.

- Non-Sporting Group: Now, this is where things get interesting. The Non-Sporting Group is a bit of a mixed bag, like the "miscellaneous" drawer in your kitchen. Breeds like Dalmatians and Bulldogs fall into this group because they don't fit neatly into other categories but still have their own special flair. Take the Bulldog, for instance—sure, they don't herd or hunt, but they've got that iconic waddle and a face that looks perpetually unimpressed. Who needs a specific job when you've got charisma?

- Sporting Group: Finally, we've got the all-stars of the dog world: the Sporting Group. Golden Retrievers, Labrador Retrievers—these are the friendly, athletic types who are just as happy fetching a ball as they are retrieving game. It's like they were born to make friends and have a good time. Honestly, if they were people, they'd be the ones high-fiving everyone at a party. You ever meet a Golden Retriever who didn't instantly make you smile? Yeah, me neither.

Understanding these breed groups doesn't just make you sound smart at the dog park (though it's a nice bonus). It can actually help you choose a breed that fits your lifestyle. Looking for a loyal companion to keep you company in your city apartment? A Toy Group dog might be perfect. Need a running buddy? A breed from the Sporting Group could be your new best friend.

And while different kennel clubs around the world might have their own way of sorting and naming these groups, they all share a common goal: promoting purebred dogs, upholding breed standards, and ensuring the health and happiness of our furry friends. Knowing these distinctions can help you make informed decisions and practice responsible dog ownership. So, whether you're a die-hard Terrier fan or a lover of the laid-back Labrador, there's a place for every pup in the grand scheme of things.

CHAPTER 3:
Choosing the Right Breed

Owning a dog is honestly one of the best decisions you can make—but it's also a huge commitment. Trust me, it's not just about seeing a cute face and thinking, "I have to have that one!" (although I can't blame you if that's happened). It's really about finding a loyal buddy who clicks with your lifestyle and brings joy to your home without turning your life upside down. I remember when my cousin, Emma, got a high-energy border collie because it was "so cute." Spoiler: her studio apartment was not quite the playground that pup needed, and let's just say her furniture didn't stand a chance.

The bottom line is, choosing the right breed is a big deal. It's like dating, but fluffier and with way less emotional drama (hopefully). You've gotta find a dog whose personality and needs fit your schedule, living space, and overall vibe. So, how do you do that? Don't worry, I've got your back. Let's dive in and figure out how to match the perfect pup to your unique situation!

ASSESSING YOUR LIFESTYLE AND NEEDS

Time Commitment and Work Schedule

Okay, first things first: how much time can you realistically give your furry friend every day? Dogs are like toddlers—they need daily care, attention, and, yes, bathroom breaks that don't magically happen on their own (if only). If you've got a 9-to-5 that often turns into a 9-to-8, it's probably best to consider breeds that are cool with chilling solo for longer stretches. Think of them like the introverts of the dog world—happy doing their own thing. Breeds like basset hounds or greyhounds are pretty laid-back and don't mind snoozing while you're out making a living. But if you've got more time to spare or work from home, you might want a more active breed—like a golden retriever or a lab—that thrives on playtime and belly rubs. They'll become your "work-from-home assistant," guaranteed to nap through Zoom calls.

And hey, if you're someone who's super busy but still determined to be a dog parent, options like hiring a dog walker or using doggy daycare are total lifesavers. It's all about striking that balance between your own life and your pup's needs. Happy human, happy dog, right?

Living Space & Family Dynamics

Your living situation plays a huge role in picking the right breed. I mean, if you're in a cozy apartment downtown, the last thing you want is a Great Dane trying to share your couch (or bed, or kitchen counter). Smaller breeds like French bulldogs or chihuahuas are perfect for tighter spaces; they don't need much room and are usually happy to claim one cozy corner as their own. But if you've got a house with a yard, now you're talkin'! Larger breeds like German shepherds or golden retrievers will love having a space to stretch their legs and zoom around.

Family dynamics matter, too. If you've got young kids running around, breeds known for their patience and playful nature—like labs or beagles—are fantastic. They can handle the chaos and love being part of the action. On the flip side, if it's just you or you and a partner, you might go for a more chill breed like a Shih Tzu or a basset hound. They're basically experts at cozy movie nights. And if you've got older folks in the house, calmer breeds like pugs or senior dogs from a rescue are ideal since they usually enjoy a quieter, relaxed vibe.

Allergies
Oh, allergies. They're the ultimate "but wait" moment when you're falling in love with a pup. If you or someone in your household has a sensitive nose, don't worry, there's hope! You've got hypoallergenic breeds like poodles or Bichon frises that shed less and produce fewer allergens (no dog is completely hypoallergenic, but some are definitely easier on the sinuses). Think of it as finding the perfect match between adorable and sneeze-free.

Activity Levels and Hobbies
Now, here's a fun one—what do you like to do? Your hobbies and activity level are big clues for the kind of dog you'll vibe with. If you're an outdoorsy type—always hiking, running, or biking—breeds that love to move, like Australian shepherds or border collies, could be your perfect match. You'll basically have a four-legged adventure buddy who's as pumped for the next trail as you are.

On the flip side, if your idea of a perfect Saturday is curling up with a good book or binge-watching the latest Netflix series, go for a breed that's more laid-back, like a bulldog or a basset hound. They're content with shorter walks and are total experts in couch naps. Honestly, they might even beat you in the napping department.

If you're into dog sports like agility or obedience training, there are plenty of breeds that excel in these activities (looking at you, border collies and Shetland sheepdogs!). And if you're more about snuggles than sprints, well, there are plenty of cuddle-bugs out there, too, like the good old Cavalier King Charles spaniel.

WHAT TO LOOK FOR IN THE PERFECT BREED
Okay, so once you've got a handle on your lifestyle, it's time to find a breed that's a perfect match. Remember, it's all about finding a dog that fits into your routine and doesn't turn your life upside down. A dog that meshes with your energy level and home situation is way less likely to get into shenanigans (like, say, chewing your shoes because they're bored). Trust me, I've learned that lesson the hard way.

Size matters—no matter how cute that giant St. Bernard puppy looks right now, picture them full-grown in your apartment. Yikes, right? Generally, small dogs (up to 20 pounds) are great for apartments or smaller living spaces, while medium dogs (20-60 pounds) need a bit more room to roam. And large dogs (60+ pounds)? They'll appreciate a yard or regular outdoor playtime to burn off their energy.

A dog's temperament is also a biggie. This is basically their personality blueprint—some dogs are social butterflies, loving every pet and person they meet, while others are more independent or even a little shy. If you've got a big family or other pets, finding a pup that gets along with everyone is key. Meanwhile, if you prefer a quiet, chill lifestyle, a dog that's low-key and doesn't need constant socializing is your best bet.

And let's not forget about energy levels. Some dogs are like Energizer bunnies—always ready for a game of fetch, a run, or any kind of activity. Others are more "let's chill and watch TV" types. Finding a dog whose energy matches yours is the golden ticket to a happy, balanced relationship.

At the end of the day, having a dog that aligns with your routine, your living space, and your personality means fewer headaches and more belly rubs. After all, dogs aren't just pets; they're companions, sidekicks, and sometimes (let's be honest) emotional support animals when you've had a rough day. So, take your time, think about your life, and choose the pup that'll make every day a little bit brighter.

PART 2: Learning to Live with Your New Dog

CHAPTER 4:
Adopting vs. Buying

Whether you're looking for a ball of energy that never stops wagging or a cuddle bug to keep you company during Netflix marathons, finding the right dog is a big deal. I remember when my buddy adopted his golden retriever, Baxter, from a rescue shelter. He swore he wasn't ready for a dog, but the moment he locked eyes with that goofy face, it was game over. Now, they're inseparable. Baxter's even got his own Instagram (and more followers than me, go figure).

But hold up—before you head off to swipe right on your perfect pooch, let's talk about where to actually find your new best friend. You've got options, from adopting at a shelter or rescue organization to buying from a breeder. And while both routes can lead to a lifetime of doggy kisses and tail wags, there are a few things to consider before you make the leap. Let's break it down, shall we?

ADOPTING FROM A LOCAL SHELTER: WHY IT'S MORE THAN JUST GIVING A DOG A HOME

Have you ever thought about what it feels like to lock eyes with a dog who's been waiting for a second chance? It's like that spark when you find a long-lost friend—only this time, the friend's got fur, a wagging tail, and the biggest heart ready to love you forever. That's the magic of adopting a dog from a shelter. It's not just about giving a dog a new home; it's about rewriting their story, giving them a chance to live a life they might've thought they'd lost.

Let me tell you about Max. He was this scruffy little guy sitting in the corner of the shelter, and when I first saw him, I wasn't sure if he was interested in me or just curious about what I had in my pocket. But when we locked eyes, something clicked. He wasn't just another dog in a cage—he was Max, the dog who would soon become my loyal companion, my partner on evening walks, and the one who curls up beside me after a long day. Max had a rough start, no doubt about that, but watching him bloom into the playful, goofy dog he is now was worth every extra bit of effort.

When you adopt from a shelter, you're not just changing one dog's life—you're becoming part of a bigger mission. You're helping alleviate overcrowding, supporting humane practices, and giving dogs like Max a new beginning. Let's break it down:

The Joys of Adopting from a Shelter

1. *Saving a Life* - Bringing a shelter dog into your home is like becoming a hero in their story. You're not just saving a life; you're giving them a second chance to experience love and happiness. Imagine what it feels like for that dog—to go from sitting in a kennel, unsure of their future, to running around in a backyard, chasing squirrels, or just lazing on the couch by your side. You become their everything. How amazing is that? Cost-Effectiveness - Here's a bonus that's hard to ignore: adopting from a shelter can be easier on your wallet. Most shelters cover the initial costs like vaccinations, spaying/neutering, and health checks within the adoption fee. You're essentially walking away with a dog that's ready for a new chapter at a fraction of the cost of buying from a breeder. And if you're anything like me, you know that extra money can go straight into spoiling them with new toys and treats.
2. *Supporting Humane Practices* - Shelters are often full of people with hearts as big as the dogs they're trying to save. They work tirelessly to ensure these animals are treated with kindness and care, and by adopting, you're joining in that mission. Every dog adopted is one more success story, one more life spared, and it feels

pretty good knowing you're helping that movement grow.
3. *The Exciting Variety* - Here's something fun: when you walk into a shelter, you're met with a whole variety of dogs. Small, big, purebred, mixed breed, young, old—it's like walking into a furry treasure trove. Sure, it might take a little patience to find your perfect match, but trust me, when you do, it's like finding that missing puzzle piece you didn't know you'd lost.
4. *Behavioral Insights* - Shelter staff and volunteers often spend a good chunk of time getting to know these dogs, and their insights can be a goldmine. When I adopted Max, the shelter volunteer was able to give me a heads-up about his quirks—like how he's terrified of vacuum cleaners but will happily chase a ball all day. Knowing that in advance helped me prepare and eased his transition into his new home.
5. *Community Impact* - When you adopt locally, you're doing more than just giving a dog a home—you're supporting your community. Every adoption helps reduce overcrowding in shelters and makes space for another animal in need. Plus, there's this sense of pride that comes with knowing you've made a difference right in your own backyard.

The Challenges (Because Every Good Story Has Them)
But hey, let's keep it real. Adopting from a shelter isn't always a walk in the park. Sometimes, it takes patience, and sometimes, it takes a bit of extra work. Let's talk about the less-glamorous side of adoption, because while the journey is rewarding, it's not always easy.

1. *Unknown History* - One of the challenges with adopting a shelter dog is the mystery that comes with them. Unlike buying a dog from a breeder where you get their whole background, with shelter dogs, it's more like adopting a novel that's missing a few chapters. Max came with no backstory—I didn't know where he'd been, what he'd experienced, or even how old he really was. But that was part of the adventure, learning together and figuring things out as we went.
2. *Behavioral Issues* - Sometimes, shelter dogs carry emotional baggage. Max was a bit skittish at first, and I didn't understand why he freaked out whenever I opened an umbrella. Over time, I realized it wasn't just the umbrella—it was anything that opened suddenly. Patience and love helped him work through it, but not every dog adjusts quickly. It might take professional training or just some extra TLC. But when they finally relax and trust you? There's no better feeling.
3. *Health Concerns* - Let's face it: some shelter dogs come with health issues, especially if they've had a rough start. Shelters do their best to provide basic vet care, but sometimes things pop up after you've brought your new buddy home. Be ready for a few unexpected vet visits and know that taking care of their health is just part of the package. Max had a little skin infection when I first adopted him, but after a few treatments and some extra pampering, he was good as new.
4. *Adjustment Period* - Bringing a shelter dog home isn't always an immediate fit. It takes time. Max needed a couple of weeks to really settle in, and there were some bumps along the way—like the time he chewed up my favorite shoes. But with a little patience and understanding, we found our rhythm. Watching him learn to trust and relax was one of the most rewarding parts of the process.
5. *Potential for Misalignment* - Even with the best intentions, sometimes it's hard to find the perfect match right off the bat. Max had way more energy than I expected, which meant more walks and playtime than I had planned for. But we adjusted. It's important to be flexible and willing to adapt because, at the end of the day, you're building a relationship that's worth the effort.

Yes, adopting from a shelter comes with challenges, but the rewards? They far outweigh the bumps in the road. That moment when your new furry friend curls up next to you for the first time, fully trusting and at peace—that's when you know it's all worth it. The bond you build with a shelter dog, knowing you've given them a fresh start, is unlike any other.

FINDING THE RIGHT RESCUE OR SHELTER FOR YOUR NEW BEST FRIEND: A GUIDE WITH HEART
Whether you're looking for a bouncy puppy or a chill older dog who already knows the drill, finding the right shelter or rescue is key to making this adoption journey a success. But hey, don't worry, we've got you. Let's walk through this together, one step at a time. Think of it as your adoption game plan, packed with personal tips, insider info, and maybe a little humor along the way. After all, this is a fun process too!

Start with Research (and a Little Online Stalking)
Okay, so maybe not stalking exactly, but your first stop should definitely be the internet. Trust me, a little research goes a long way here. There are some great websites like Petfinder, Adopt-a-Pet, and the ASPCA's shelter

directory where you can find local shelters or rescue groups. The cool thing? You can see listings of adoptable pets in your area right from your couch. Just a few clicks and you might spot a dog that already feels like "the one."

But don't just stop at browsing photos (even though, yes, the puppy pics will melt your heart). Take some time to read about the shelters. Check their reviews, scroll through their social media, and see if they're sharing those feel-good adoption stories or if they seem active in the community. You want to know they're really invested in animal welfare, not just going through the motions. When I found Luna's shelter, they had this video up on Facebook of a litter of puppies bouncing around a yard, and I knew immediately these people genuinely cared.

Ask Around for Referrals—Your Vet Knows What's Up

One thing that really helped me in my search was asking my vet for recommendations. Your local vet often knows the most reputable shelters and rescue groups in your area. They can also give you the inside scoop—like, which places have a solid reputation for treating animals well and finding them good homes. And hey, don't forget to ask friends and family too! You'll probably be surprised by how many people you know have gone through the adoption process themselves.

A friend of mine recommended the shelter where I eventually found Luna. She said the staff was super supportive and made sure she and her new pup were a perfect match. That's exactly what you want—a place that's focused on long-term success, not just getting the animals out the door as quickly as possible.

Make It Personal: Visit the Shelter

You've gotta see it to believe it. Photos online are great, but there's nothing like visiting the shelter or rescue in person. You want to see the vibe, meet the staff, and, of course, spend some time with the animals. I remember walking into Luna's shelter and immediately being struck by how clean everything was. The kennels were tidy, the animals looked well cared for, and the staff? Super friendly and clearly passionate about what they do.

It's kind of like house hunting—everything can look perfect in the pictures, but you won't really know until you're there. Pay attention to the details. Is the place clean? Do the animals have comfy beds, fresh water, and plenty of space to move around? If the staff seems engaged and knowledgeable, that's a great sign. If the animals seem happy and well cared for, that's an even better sign.

Questions to Ask Like You're a Detective

When you're getting serious about adopting, you'll want to come prepared with some solid questions. Think of it like a job interview, except you're the one doing the hiring. After all, this is a new family member we're talking about!

Here's a short list of things you might want to ask:

1. *What's the dog's backstory?* If they know the dog's history, that's helpful. You want to get a feel for what they've been through.
2. *Any behavior issues?* Has the dog been tested for aggression or anxiety? A good shelter will be upfront about this.
3. *Are they house-trained or crate-trained?* This can be a game-changer, especially if you're not ready to start from scratch with training.
4. *What about health?* Ask about vaccines, spaying/neutering, microchipping, and if there are any existing medical conditions.
5. *What's the adoption process like?* Some places require home visits or interviews to make sure it's a good fit. It might seem like a hassle, but it's really a sign that the shelter cares about where their animals end up.

When I was looking for Luna, I visited one shelter that felt more like a used car dealership than an adoption center. The staff kept pressuring me to take a dog home that day, even though I wasn't ready. I left without looking back, and I'm so glad I waited to find the right fit.

What to Look for During Your Shelter Visit

So, you're on-site and ready to find your new best friend—what should you be keeping an eye out for?

- *Cleanliness and Organization* - You want to feel good about the environment. A clean, well-organized shelter means the animals are in good hands.

K9 Chatter

- *Animal Comfort* - Are the enclosures spacious and comfortable? Are the animals relaxed, with clean coats and bright eyes? Even in a stressful environment like a shelter, the dogs should look cared for.
- *Staff Interaction* - Watch how the staff interacts with the animals. Do they seem loving and attentive? Do they answer your questions willingly and knowledgeably?
- *Community Involvement* - A good shelter will be active in their community, hosting events or fundraisers, and engaging with the public. It shows they're dedicated to their cause.
- *Transparency with Records* - They should be able to provide the dog's medical history, behavioral assessments, and any important documents with no hesitation.

Red Flags: Proceed with Caution
Not every shelter is as great as it seems. If something feels off, don't ignore it. Here are some things that should make you pause:

- *Lack of transparency* - If they're dodging questions or being vague about the animal's background, health, or behavior, that's a red flag. Good shelters will be open and honest with you.
- *Dirty or poorly maintained facilities* - You should never see animals in overcrowded, dirty cages. A clean environment is essential for the animals' health.
- *Pressure to adopt* - A reputable shelter won't push you to make a decision right away. They want to make sure it's the right fit for both you and the dog.

Adopting a pet isn't always easy, but it's one of the most rewarding experiences. When I first brought Luna home, I was nervous, excited, and honestly, a little overwhelmed. But as soon as she curled up in my lap that first night, I knew I'd made the right decision.

Take your time, do your research, and listen to your gut. Somewhere out there, there's a dog with a wagging tail, waiting for you to walk through the door and say, "You're coming home with me." And trust me, when that moment happens, you'll know it was all worth it.

PURCHASING FROM A REPUTABLE BREEDER: THE JOURNEY TO FINDING YOUR PERFECT PUP

I'll never forget the day I met my breeder. It was one of those moments where you just know you're in good hands. I arrived at her place, and right away, you could feel the love and care she poured into her dogs. The parent dogs? Absolutely charming, healthy, and full of life. Meeting them reassured me that my soon-to-be puppy was coming from a home, not just a business.

Picking a dog from a reputable breeder isn't just about getting a dog—it's about forming a relationship, not only with your new fur baby but with the breeder themselves. Trust me, it's an experience that can make a world of difference for you and your future pet.

Why a Reputable Breeder Makes a Difference
Okay, so you're probably wondering: What's the big deal about choosing a breeder? I get it, you might be tempted by the ease of scrolling through listings or visiting the local pet shop. But when you go the extra mile and find a trusted breeder, you're setting yourself (and your pup) up for a much smoother ride in the long run. Let's break it down.

- *Health First, Always* - When you get a puppy from a reputable breeder, you're not just buying a pet—you're investing in peace of mind. These breeders prioritize health in ways you can't imagine. It's like having a family doctor who knows your entire family history. They'll test for genetic disorders and screen for common health issues that could pop up later. That means your puppy is less likely to surprise you with some unexpected health scare.

I remember talking to my breeder about the health screenings, and she showed me stacks of paperwork—no joke—documenting every test. "I want my puppies to live long, healthy lives with their new families," she said. And I believed her.

- *Breeders Know Their Stuff* - A good breeder is like the Wikipedia of their dog breed—only better, and with way more heart. They've been around these dogs for years and know every quirk, behavior, and characteristic. If you're unsure whether a particular breed fits your lifestyle, they'll tell you straight. Do you want a dog that'll lounge around, or one that needs daily adventures? They'll help match you with the right kind of dog.

For instance, when I was choosing between breeds, my breeder asked, "Are you ready for the energy level of this breed? They'll want to keep you on your toes!" She wasn't kidding. Thanks to her advice, I knew exactly what I was getting into and how much coffee I'd need to keep up!

- *Socialization and Early Training* - Here's a secret: good breeders don't just care about the health of their dogs—they care about their behavior, too. By the time you bring your new puppy home, they've already been exposed to different people, sounds, and experiences. It's like giving your dog a head start in the world!

I'll never forget meeting my puppy for the first time. He confidently trotted over to me, wagging his tail like he'd known me forever. That's what early socialization does—it creates confident, well-adjusted dogs. No skittishness, no weird behavioral issues down the road.

- *Ethical Breeding* - It's Not Just a Buzzword - Ethical breeding isn't just about avoiding overbreeding or mistreating dogs—it's about setting a gold standard for the dogs' quality of life. Reputable breeders treat their dogs like family, not just products. They'll show you where the puppies are raised—clean, spacious areas where the dogs are cared for, not cramped or dirty places.

When I visited the breeder's facility, it was spotless. The dogs had plenty of room to play, and the environment felt welcoming. There wasn't a single part of me that felt uneasy. And that's how you should feel when visiting a breeder—a sense of trust and transparency.

The Pros and (Let's Be Real) Cons of Reputable Breeders
The Perks
- *Health Guarantees* - When you get your puppy from a reputable breeder, they'll often provide health guarantees. It's like getting a warranty on a brand-new car—minus the mechanic trips. You'll know your pup comes from healthy lines, which reduces the risk of serious health issues down the road.
- *Breed Knowledge* - Reputable breeders are walking encyclopedias when it comes to their breed. They'll tell you what to expect temperament-wise, how much exercise your dog will need, and even tips on grooming. Honestly, it's like having your own dog mentor.
- *Support for the Long Haul* - A reputable breeder doesn't just say goodbye once you walk out the door. They're there for you, ready to offer advice on training, diet, or any questions that pop up along the way. My breeder and I still chat occasionally, and it feels more like a friendship than a transaction.

The Drawbacks
- *Cost* - Let's be real—reputable breeders aren't cheap. But remember, you're paying for a high standard of care, not just the puppy itself. The health screenings, socialization, and ethical practices all add up. It's worth the investment for the peace of mind and quality you're getting.
- *Wait Time* - Patience is key. Reputable breeders often have waiting lists because they don't churn out puppies like a factory. They plan each litter carefully, focusing on the health and wellbeing of the dogs. It's worth the wait, though. After all, good things come to those who wait, right?

How to Find a Breeder You Can Trust
Now, finding a reputable breeder is like finding the perfect pair of shoes—it might take a little digging, but once you find the right one, you'll know. Here's how to get started:

- *Do Your Research* - Start by searching breeders in your area or for the specific breed you want. Look for breeders affiliated with national or regional breed clubs—they usually uphold high ethical standards.
- *Talk to Breed Clubs and Vets* - Breed clubs are a great resource. They'll have lists of reputable breeders and can offer advice. And don't forget to chat with your vet or a local dog trainer—they're in the loop about breeders in your area.
- *Online Reviews and Testimonials* - This one's a no-brainer. Check out reviews from other puppy parents who've worked with the breeder. Happy clients mean happy pups, and you'll get a sense of what to expect.

Questions to Ask Your Breeder
Once you've found a breeder, it's time for the fun part—asking all the questions! We've included a list of subjects you should be asking about with some sample questions that all responsible breeders should have no issues discussing with you.

1. *Breeding Practices*
- How long have you been breeding this breed?

- What is your breeding philosophy or goal?
- Can you explain your process for selecting breeding pairs?
2. *Health and Genetics*
- What health tests and screenings do the parent dogs undergo?
- Can you provide the health records of the puppies and their parents?
- Are the puppies up-to-date on vaccinations and deworming?
3. *Puppy Care and Socialization*
- How are the puppies socialized and exposed to different stimuli?
- What kind of environment are the puppies raised in?
- Have the puppies been examined by a veterinarian?
4. *Living Conditions*
- Can I see where the puppies are raised?
- How do you ensure the cleanliness and health of the living environment?
5. *Contracts and Guarantees*
- Do you have a written contract or agreement for the sale?
- What kind of health guarantee or warranty do you provide?
- Are there any specific requirements or conditions for the puppy's future care?
6. *Parent Dogs*
- Can I meet the puppy's parents?
- How do the parents behave, and what are their temperaments like?
7. *Puppy Selection*
- How do you determine which puppies are available for sale?
- Can I interact with the puppies to assess their temperament?
8. *References*
- Can you provide references from previous buyers?
- Are there testimonials or reviews available about your breeding program?
9. *Post-Purchase Support*
- What kind of support or guidance do you offer after the sale?
- Are you available for questions or concerns once the puppy is home?
10. *Future Breeding Plans*
- Do you have any upcoming litters or future breeding plans?
- What is your policy on breeding rights or spaying/neutering?

When I sat down with my breeder, I felt like I was interrogating her with all my questions, but she didn't mind at all. In fact, she welcomed it. That's how you know you've found a good one—they want you to feel confident and comfortable.

Watch Out for Red Flags
Not all breeders are created equal, so here's what to watch for:

- *Lack of Transparency* - If they're vague or dodgy about showing you their facility or health records, run the other way.
- *Poor Living Conditions* - If the place looks dirty or overcrowded, that's a big red flag. The dogs should be living in clean, spacious environments.
- *Pushy Sales Tactics* - A good breeder will never pressure you to buy a puppy quickly. They'll let you take your time and make sure you're making the right choice.

Bringing a dog into your life is a big decision—it's not just about finding the right breed but about finding the right breeder, too. Take your time, ask lots of questions, and don't settle for anything less than someone who treats their dogs with the love and care they deserve. By choosing a reputable breeder, you're not just getting a dog—you're welcoming a new family member into your life, one who's happy, healthy, and ready to fill your home with joy.

CHAPTER 5:
Bringing Your New Pup Home

So, you've made the big decision to bring a puppy into your life—whether you're adopting from a shelter or going through a breeder, this moment can feel equally exciting and nerve-wracking. I totally get it! I remember when I was getting ready for my first pup, Bella. One minute I was thrilled about snuggling her all day, and the next, I was in a mild panic because I realized I had NO idea how to "puppy-proof" my home. But hey, don't worry! With the right prep, you'll be good to go. Let's walk through it together.

CREATING A SAFE AND WELCOMING ENVIRONMENT

Dog-Proofing Your Home

Think of your puppy like a furry little explorer. They'll be on a mission to get into everything—and I mean everything. I once found Bella trying to chew on the TV remote, and let me tell you, I've never sprinted across the room so fast in my life. You're going to want to make sure your home is as safe as possible for your curious new friend.

Here are a few key things to consider:

- *Lock Up the Goodies:* Cleaning supplies, medications, or anything remotely chewable should be stored safely away. Childproof locks can be a lifesaver here.
- *Hide Those Cords:* Puppies seem to think that electrical cords are the tastiest snacks. Use cord protectors or tape them down. Bella once tried to gnaw on my laptop charger... not fun.
- *No Small Objects:* Pick up any small items like coins, hair ties, or that random Lego piece that's been hiding under your couch. If it's small enough to fit in their mouth, they'll try to eat it. Puppies have zero chill.
- *Trash Cans are Puppy Buffets:* Secure trash bins or keep them out of reach. Trust me, your pup will see it as an all-you-can-eat buffet if you don't.
- *Block Off Dangerous Zones:* Use baby gates or keep doors closed to places like the stairs or any rooms with "puppy hazards." One time, Bella bolted upstairs and got stuck under the bed. Lesson learned.
- *Furniture Check:* Make sure your furniture is sturdy, especially if your pup's a jumper. And yep, they will jump. Puppies have springs in their legs, I swear.

If you have a yard, make sure it's properly fenced with no gaps. Puppies are like little Houdinis, they'll find a way out if there's one. You don't want to be running down the street in your pajamas at 6 AM yelling for them to come back (been there, done that).

Designating Space & Gathering Essential Supplies

Just like us, puppies need their own little sanctuary. They're leaving their old life behind, and your home is brand new to them, so creating a cozy, safe space will help them settle in.

- *Sleeping Area* - Pick a quiet, low-traffic spot for your puppy's bed or crate. Puppies love routine, and having a designated sleeping area gives them a sense of security. I set up Bella's crate next to my bed when she first arrived, and seeing her doze off, all snuggled up, melted my heart

every single night. *Pro tip*: toss in something with your scent, like an old t-shirt. It's like magic. Your pup will feel a little less lonely and a whole lot more comforted by having your smell nearby.
- *Feeding Area* - Consistency is key here. Choose one spot for food and water bowls and stick with it. Puppies thrive on routine, and they'll learn quickly where to head when it's mealtime. *Pro tip*: use sturdy, non-slip bowls (preferably stainless steel or ceramic). Bella once flipped her plastic bowl, and it turned into an impromptu slip-n-slide in the kitchen. Hilarious but messy.
- *Play and Exercise Area* - Got a yard? Lucky you. If not, designate a space indoors where your pup can burn off all that boundless puppy energy. I'm telling you, they're like little Energizer bunnies. Make sure it's a safe zone where they can't knock over anything fragile. Bella once thought she could fit through a stack of books. Spoiler: she couldn't.
- *Comfort Items* - Crates, playpens, soft bedding—it's all about giving your new furry friend a space to feel secure. When it comes to picking a crate, size matters. You want it big enough for them to stand up, turn around, and get comfy, but not so big that they think one corner's for sleeping and the other is for, well, bathroom breaks. Gross.

And don't forget cozy bedding! Puppies sleep A LOT, so make sure they have something soft to snooze on. I remember the first time Bella curled up in her crate, snuggling her little blanket. I just stood there watching her sleep (borderline stalker behavior, I know, but she was so cute I couldn't help it).

Essential Supplies
Alright, let's talk supplies. Shopping for your new puppy is fun—like getting ready for a baby but with less crying (hopefully).

Here's your must-have list:

- *Feeding Supplies:* Go for non-slip bowls that can handle puppy chaos. High-quality dog food that matches their age and size is crucial. Talk to your vet about the best options for your little furball. Bella had a sensitive stomach, so it took some trial and error before we found the right food.
- *Grooming Supplies:* Brushing is key, especially if you've got a fluffy pup. Dog-specific shampoos, brushes, and nail clippers will keep your puppy looking fresh. Don't forget that dog-friendly toothpaste! Puppy breath is cute, but puppy morning breath? Not so much.
- *Toys, Toys, and More Toys:* Puppies are like toddlers—they need constant entertainment. Chew toys are a must to save your shoes from becoming a snack. Look for durable, safe toys that won't fall apart after a few gnaws. Bella went through toys like a tornado, so I learned to invest in the good stuff.
- *Safety Gates:* These are life-savers, especially if you want to create a puppy-friendly zone or keep them out of certain rooms. My living room turned into a gated fortress for a while, but hey, it kept Bella out of trouble.
- *Camera or Monitor:* If you're like me and a little bit of a helicopter pet parent, a pet camera can be a great way to keep an eye on your puppy when you're not in the room. Sometimes, I'd check the camera just to see Bella curled up in her crate, being the perfect little angel (before waking up and turning into a mischievous ball of energy again).

Bringing a new puppy into your home is an adventure—equal parts fun, chaos, and heart-melting cuteness. With a little preparation, you can create a space where your new pup will feel safe, loved, and ready to take on the world (or at least your living room).

Remember, the goal is to make them feel comfortable and secure, but also to protect your stuff from getting completely destroyed. Puppies are curious, clumsy, and sometimes a bit reckless, but that's what makes the journey so fun. And before you know it, you'll be sitting on the couch, with your pup snuggled up next to you, wondering how you ever lived without them.

Introducing Your Dog to Other Pets: The Doggie Meet-and-Greet
Okay, so you've finally brought home your new furry friend—exciting, right? But wait, there's just one little thing: your other pets are probably wondering who this new kid on the block is. Introducing pets can feel like setting up an awkward blind date. Will they hit it off? Will there be growling? Sniffing? A dramatic exit? Let me tell you, I've been there, and it can be a rollercoaster. But don't worry! With a little patience and planning, your pets will be coexisting in harmony—or at least tolerating each other like distant cousins at Thanksgiving.

Start in Neutral Territory: No One Likes Surprise Roommates
Imagine someone walking into your bedroom, plopping down on your bed, and declaring, "I live here now." You'd be like, "Uh, excuse me?" Well, that's probably how your resident pet feels when you suddenly toss a new dog into their favorite space. It's a major vibe killer! Instead of throwing them together in the living room

(aka the resident pet's turf), take the meeting somewhere neutral. The backyard? Perfect. A room they both barely use? Even better. You want a space where no one has dibs, so it's like both pets are just visitors checking out a new Airbnb.

I remember introducing my dog, Bailey, to my cat, Luna. Let me tell you—it was not love at first sight. I brought them together in the backyard, with Bailey wagging his tail like, "Hey! New friend!" while Luna shot me a look that said, "Are you kidding me?" Spoiler: there was no instant connection. But starting outside, where neither of them felt territorial, helped keep the peace.

Sniffing, Wagging, and... Maybe Some Growling (It's Normal!)

Here's the deal—first impressions are a big deal, but with animals, it's mostly all about sniffing each other's behinds. I know, not the friendliest human greeting, but for them? Totally standard. So, when you bring your new dog home, let them approach slowly and do their thing. Sniffing, tail wagging, maybe even a little growl or two. That's all normal behavior as they're figuring each other out. Think of it as them saying, "Okay, who are you, and why are you here?"

But hey, don't let your guard down completely. Keep a close eye out—watch for any signs of discomfort. If things start getting heated (a.k.a. someone's barking up a storm or there's some serious side-eye from the cat), step in. Gently, of course. It's like being the moderator at a tense family dinner—you want to stop things before anyone throws mashed potatoes. Just keep it chill, and give them space to get used to each other.

Cats and Dogs? Yeah, It's a Process

If you've got a cat, you already know—cats and dogs are like oil and water... at first. Cats are territorial by nature, and your dog's boundless enthusiasm might not win them over right away. When I introduced Bailey to Luna, it wasn't exactly a Hallmark moment. Luna spent the first week perched on top of the fridge, glaring down at Bailey like some kind of feline overlord. Bailey, bless his heart, just sat there wagging his tail, utterly clueless.

The key here? Time and space. Let them interact at their own pace—don't force it. Sometimes cats need to watch from afar before they decide the dog isn't a threat to their kingdom. If your cat spends the first few days hissing from across the room or hiding out like a hermit, don't stress. That's all part of the process. Just keep offering treats (to both of them) and positive reinforcement when they're calm. Before you know it, they might start sharing the same space... even if it's with a solid two feet of distance between them.

Gradual Introductions: Rome Wasn't Built in a Day

Now, if your household is a little more diverse in the pet department (two dogs, a cat, maybe even a rabbit?), you've got to take things slow. Really slow. It's like introducing your friends to each other—they need time to warm up. You wouldn't just throw your introverted buddy into a raging party and expect them to thrive, right? Same goes for your pets.

Start with brief, supervised meet-and-greets. I'm talking five, ten minutes at most. Put your new dog on a leash, and if your resident pet is a dog, leash them up too. If your resident pet is a cat, maybe just make sure there's a quick exit route, because cats tend to prefer the "I'll be over here, thank you" approach. During these meet-ups, watch closely for body language. If you see stiff tails, raised fur, or any side-eye glares that say "I'm not feeling this," step in with a calm voice and maybe a quick redirect with a toy or treat.

Watch for Signs: The Silent Language of Pets

Animals have their own little language, and they're talking to each other constantly through body signals. Your job is to play interpreter. If your dog's wagging its tail like it's auditioning for a windmill commercial, that's usually a good sign. But if the tail's stiff, ears are back, or your cat looks like it's about to pull out some ninja moves, it's time to intervene.

Instead of "paying close attention," think of it as being their silent bodyguard—ready to step in before the fur flies. And hey, give them both an escape route. Every pet needs a little "me time." If the situation feels tense, let them take a break in their own corners, and try again later.

Praise the Heck Out of Them

When your pets manage to get through a meeting without drama—throw a party! Okay, maybe not a literal party, but shower them with praise. "Good job, guys! Look at you being all civilized!" A little treat or belly rub for good behavior goes a long way in reinforcing positive vibes. Trust me, your pets will start to associate each other with good things—like snacks, cuddles, and that weird high-pitched voice you use when you're proud of them.

Keep it Chill, and Don't Be Afraid to Ask for Help

Now, don't feel bad if things don't click right away. Some pets just need more time to warm up to each other. And honestly, it can be frustrating. If your pets are still giving each other the cold shoulder—or worse, the "I'm going to chase you around the house until we both collapse" routine—don't be afraid to call in a pro. Trainers or behaviorists can help guide you through those rough patches. It's like marriage counseling, but for your fur babies.

Bringing a new pet into your home is an adventure, full of excitement and a little bit of chaos. Just remember, introducing your pets is a process, not an event. With patience, humor, and a few treats along the way, they'll get there. And who knows? One day, you might walk into the room and find them snuggled up together like they've been best friends forever. Or, at the very least, coexisting peacefully like two roommates who've agreed to share the Wi-Fi password but nothing else.

CHAPTER 6:
Health and Nutrition

Owning a dog isn't just about taking them for a walk or giving them belly rubs (though, let's be real, those are the fun parts!). Maintaining your dog's health is the foundation of giving them a long, happy life. And honestly? It's a little like parenting—full of love, a bit of worry, and a lot of learning as you go.
Let's dive into the essentials, from keeping your pup's diet on point to making sure they're getting their regular vet checkups and how to avoid those sky-high vet bills that can pop up when you least expect them.

DIET AND NUTRITION: BECAUSE EVEN DOGS DESERVE FINE DINING

Okay, maybe not exactly fine dining, but come on—your dog deserves better than a bowl full of mystery meat, right?
When I first got my dog, Luna, I thought any bag of kibble from the pet store would do the trick. But after a few weeks of constant scratching and weird tummy issues, I realized not all dog food is created equal. So, I did some research (and plenty of vet visits) and found that just like us, our furry friends thrive on a well-balanced diet. That means proteins that would make a Michelin-starred chef smile—salmon, lean chicken, beef. None of that filler stuff like corn or soy.

Picking the right food for your dog is like finding the perfect pair of jeans—it's all about the fit. Puppies need nutrient-packed meals to grow up strong, while older dogs might need food that's gentler on their tummies (and lower in calories, since they're more into couch naps than sprints around the yard).

If your dog is anything like Luna, keep an eye out for food allergies. I didn't realize she was allergic to chicken until I switched her to a salmon-based food. The constant scratching? Gone. Her coat? Shiny. And yes, I totally felt like a proud dog mom for figuring it out.

Quick tip: Always check the label. Make sure a high-quality protein is listed first. And if you're not sure about any of the ingredients, don't hesitate to ask your vet. They'll steer you clear of any unnecessary fillers or ingredients that might not sit well with your dog's system.

Oh, and treats? My advice: keep it fun but balanced. Your dog doesn't need a snack every time they look at you with those puppy-dog eyes (even though it's basically impossible to resist). Treats should make up no more than 10% of their daily calories. I've found that giving Luna crunchy carrots or low-calorie snacks makes her just as happy as the store-bought stuff—and I get to feel good about her not putting on extra pounds!

REGULAR HEALTH CHECKS: PREVENTATIVE CARE IS THE REAL MVP

Here's a little story for you: I almost skipped Luna's yearly vet check-up last year because, well, life got busy. But I'm so glad I didn't. Turns out, she had the beginnings of a dental issue that could've turned ugly (and expensive) if we hadn't caught it early. A simple dental cleaning saved us a ton of stress—and saved her a lot of pain.

This is why regular vet visits are crucial. For most healthy adult dogs, once a year is enough. But if your pup is getting up there in age or has health conditions like arthritis or allergies, you might want to bump it up to every six months. Each visit should include a physical exam, a look at their teeth (because yes, dogs can get cavities too), and a chat with your vet about any changes in your dog's behavior or diet.

Vaccinations are another biggie. Keeping your dog up to date on shots like rabies, distemper, and parvovirus is a non-negotiable. It's like armor against nasty diseases that could seriously harm them. Depending on where you live and your dog's lifestyle, your vet might recommend other vaccines too—like Bordetella for kennel cough (if your dog loves doggy daycare) or Lyme disease if you're in a tick-heavy area.

IS PET INSURANCE REALLY WORTH IT?

So, picture this: You're hanging out on the couch, binging tv with your furry best friend. Life is good. Then suddenly, your pup decides to leap off the couch like he's training for the canine Olympics—and lands wrong. Cue the yelps. You rush to the emergency vet, heart pounding, only to be slapped with a $2,000 bill for X-rays and treatment. Ouch.

I've been there, and let me tell you, that's the moment you start wondering if pet insurance is really worth it. *Spoiler alert:* It might be. But before you sign on the dotted line, let's break it down in a way that doesn't feel like you're reading a legal contract.

1. What Does Pet Insurance Even Cover?
You'd think it would cover everything under the sun, but nope. There are some quirks. Let's start with the basics.

Accident and Illness Coverage: This is the bread and butter of most pet insurance plans. It covers the serious stuff—think broken bones, surgeries, and illnesses like your dog's bout with kennel cough that seemed to last forever.
Wellness Plans: Ever heard of an insurance plan that covers your pet's spa day? Okay, not quite. But some plans offer wellness coverage, which can help with routine care like vaccines, annual check-ups, and even flea and tick prevention. (Yes, those little critters seem to multiply overnight, don't they?)
Preventive Care: Think of this as insurance with a side of dental cleaning. Some policies throw in extras like routine teeth cleaning or preventive care, which can save you from your dog's bad breath of doom.

2. How Do They Pay You Back?
Ah, the million-dollar question: how do you actually get reimbursed for that surprise surgery your cat needed after discovering the mysterious allure of string?

Percentage of Vet Bills: They'll reimburse you for a percentage of what you paid. It's like cash back but for pet emergencies. So, if your plan covers 80%, and you drop $1,000 at the vet, you'll get $800 back. Not bad, right?
Coverage Limits: Heads up—there are limits! Some plans cap how much they'll cover annually, per incident, or over your pet's lifetime. Be sure to check this, because your adventurous dog might max out your plan in no time.

3. Deductibles and Co-pays: The Not-So-Fun Part
Okay, here's where it gets a bit like that fine print no one reads. But I'll make it simple.

Annual Deductibles: This is the amount you've got to shell out before your insurance kicks in. It's like a cover charge at a club but for pet emergencies.
Co-pays: Once you've hit the deductible, you're still on the hook for part of the bill. Usually, this is a percentage, like 10% or 20%. So, even after the deductible, you're sharing the cost a little bit.

4. What's Not Covered (And Trust Me, There Are Exclusions)
Pet insurance is great, but it's not magic. There are some things most policies won't touch with a ten-foot pole:

Pre-existing Conditions: If your dog already has a condition when you sign up—like arthritis or diabetes—most plans won't cover it. It's kind of like trying to buy fire insurance after your house is already on fire.
Waiting Periods: There's usually a waiting period before coverage kicks in. So, don't think you can sign up for insurance the day after your dog eats a sock. You'll likely have to wait a week or two for accidents and up to 14 days for illnesses to be covered.

5. Customer Service: Because No One Wants to Deal with a Hassle When They're Already Stressed
When your furball is sick, the last thing you want is to be stuck on hold with customer service. Seriously. That's why it's crucial to pick a company with good reviews for claim processing and support.

Ease of Claims: Some insurers make this process easy-peasy with apps where you can snap a pic of the vet bill and submit it within minutes. Others? Not so much. Do your research.
Responsive Customer Support: Nothing's worse than being in a panic over your sick pet and not being able to get help on the phone. Look for companies with solid reviews for fast, helpful service. Trust me, it'll save you a ton of frustration.

6. The Big Question: How Much Does It Cost?
Alright, let's get real. Pet insurance isn't free, but for what it offers, it might not be as expensive as you think.

Premiums: The monthly cost depends on a few things—your pet's breed, age, and even your location. My friend's Frenchie? She's paying a small fortune because apparently, Frenchies are high-maintenance (who knew?). Meanwhile, my mixed-breed pup's insurance is more like streaming tv subscription money.
Discounts: Some companies give you discounts for insuring multiple pets or if you pay annually instead of monthly. It's like a little bonus for being a responsible pet parent.

So, Is Pet Insurance Worth It?
Honestly, it depends. If your pet's a couch potato who never gets into trouble, you might feel like you're throwing money down the drain. But if your dog has a habit of trying to eat socks or your cat thinks it's invincible, that insurance might save your wallet a lot of heartache.

And trust me, there's nothing worse than facing a massive vet bill while you're already stressing over your pet's health. So, if peace of mind is what you're after, pet insurance could be just the safety net you need. In the end, it's about balancing the cost of the plan with the potential savings. And if you're like me and your dog's basically your child (and, let's be honest, accident-prone), it's worth every penny.

PET INSURANCE COMPANIES
Here are some well-known companies that offer pet insurance, each with its own set of features and coverage options:

1. Healthy Paws
Coverage: Comprehensive accident and illness coverage, optional wellness plans.
Reimbursement: 70%-90% of eligible vet bills.
Deductibles: Flexible annual deductibles.
Notable: No upper age limit; fast claims processing.

2. Trupanion
Coverage: Accident and illness coverage; optional add-ons for additional coverage.
Reimbursement: 90% of eligible vet bills.
Deductibles: Lifetime deductible.
Notable: High reimbursement rate, straightforward policy.

3. Pets Best
Coverage: Accident and illness coverage; optional wellness plans.
Reimbursement: 70%-90% of eligible vet bills.
Deductibles: Annual deductibles, customizable.
Notable: Wide range of plans, good customer support.

4. Nationwide
Coverage: Comprehensive accident and illness coverage; wellness plans available.
Reimbursement: 50%-90% of eligible vet bills.
Deductibles: Annual deductibles.
Notable: Broad range of plans, but premiums may be higher.

5. Figo
Coverage: Accident and illness coverage; wellness plans available.
Reimbursement: 70%-100% of eligible vet bills.

Deductibles: Flexible annual deductibles.
Notable: User-friendly app, extensive coverage options.

6. Lemonade
Coverage: Accident and illness coverage; wellness plans available.
Reimbursement: 70%-90% of eligible vet bills.
Deductibles: Annual deductibles.
Notable: Transparent pricing, easy-to-use app.

7. Embrace
Coverage: Accident and illness coverage; optional wellness plans.
Reimbursement: 65%-90% of eligible vet bills.
Deductibles: Annual deductibles.
Notable: Comprehensive coverage options, good customer service.

8. ASPCA Pet Health Insurance
Coverage: Accident and illness coverage; optional wellness plans.
Reimbursement: 70%-90% of eligible vet bills.
Deductibles: Annual deductibles.
Notable: Supports animal welfare initiatives, broad coverage options.

9. Petplan
Coverage: Accident and illness coverage; optional add-ons for additional coverage.
Reimbursement: 70%-90% of eligible vet bills.
Deductibles: Annual deductibles.
Notable: Customizable plans, good for chronic conditions.

10. Hartville Pet Insurance
Coverage: Accident and illness coverage; wellness plans available.
Reimbursement: 50%-70% of eligible vet bills.
Deductibles: Annual deductibles.
Notable: Affordable premiums, straightforward coverage.

When picking a pet insurance provider, it's a good idea to think about things like what's covered, how much you'll get reimbursed, the deductibles, and what other pet owners have to say. This will help you find the perfect match for both your pet's needs and your budget.

CHAPTER 7:
Exercise and Enrichment

Let's face it—our dogs are basically furry little fitness enthusiasts, each with their own workout style. Some are marathon runners, while others? Well, they're more of the "Netflix and snooze" type. But no matter their speed, one thing's for sure: exercise and enrichment are absolute musts for keeping our four-legged friends happy, healthy, and out of trouble. Yup, just like us, they need both a little physical sweat and some mental gymnastics to really thrive.

Now, here's the thing. Not all dogs are created equal in the energy department. So, let's break it down by breed, shall we? This way, you'll have a clearer idea of how to keep your pup's tail wagging and those zoomies under control.

EXERCISE NEEDS FOR DIFFERENT BREEDS

High-Energy Breeds - Ever met a dog that looks like it just drank six cups of coffee? Yeah, that's your high-energy breeds like Border Collies, Australian Shepherds, and Siberian Huskies. These pups don't just want exercise—they NEED it, like daily. I'm talking at least 1-2 hours of hardcore play. If you've ever tried keeping up with a Border Collie at the dog park, you'll know they treat fetch like an Olympic sport. Got a hiking trail nearby? Even better! These pups were practically born to run, leap, and chase. And let's not forget agility training, which for them is like recess for hyperactive kids.

Fun fact: I once tried to tire out a friend's Aussie Shepherd by playing fetch in the yard. After about 45 minutes of sprinting, I was the one huffing and puffing...and she? She was still staring at me like, "That's it?"

Moderate-Energy Breeds - Now, not all dogs have the endless energy of a Husky (thank goodness). Breeds like Labrador Retrievers, Golden Retrievers, and Boxers are a bit more balanced in their exercise needs. These guys are all about that steady, consistent workout—think an hour of brisk walking, some fetch, and maybe a little obedience training sprinkled in for mental stimulation. They're the type that enjoys a good romp at the park but doesn't mind a Netflix binge afterward (with you, of course). My Lab, for example, loves a good game of "who can catch the tennis ball faster" and somehow always manages to beat me. Go figure.

Low-Energy Breeds - For all you couch potato owners out there, meet the Bulldogs, Basset Hounds, and Shih Tzus of the world. These little cuties are more into a laid-back lifestyle, and that's okay! They only need about 30 minutes of leisurely exercise, like a stroll around the block or a chill play session. I mean, if you've ever tried to get a Bulldog to do a full sprint, you probably just got a side-eye in return. But even though they're low-energy, it's still super important to keep them moving to avoid that dreaded doggy weight gain.

My neighbor's Bulldog, Winston, enjoys what I like to call "the world's slowest game of fetch." You throw the ball, and he takes his sweet time waddling over, sniffing around a bit, and then (maybe) bringing it back. It's adorable...and very much on his terms.

Special Considerations

Puppies - Ah, puppies—those little bundles of energy and joy. They may seem like they can go non-stop, but you have to be careful not to overdo it. With their growing bones and developing joints, shorter, more frequent play sessions are the way to go. Trust me, your puppy will appreciate a quick nap in between rounds of tug-of-war.

Senior Dogs - As your dog gets older, you'll probably notice them slowing down a bit. They might not want to chase after that frisbee like they used to (or, let's be honest, they might give you the "I'm too old for this" look). For senior dogs, it's all about gentle exercise that keeps them moving without stressing their joints. Short walks and maybe a relaxed game of hide-and-seek with treats are great options. Always keep an eye on their comfort levels and adjust accordingly.

MENTAL STIMULATION AND ENRICHMENT ACTIVITIES

Now, here's where things get interesting: it's not just their bodies that need a workout. Their brains? Oh, they need some TLC too. Ever noticed your dog staring at you like, "Okay, what's next?" That's their way of saying, "Keep me entertained, human!"

Interactive toys are like the dog equivalent of a crossword puzzle (with way more slobber, of course). A Kong stuffed with peanut butter or a puzzle feeder can keep them busy for ages, and honestly, it's fun to watch them figure it out. If you've got a dog who's a bit of a smarty-pants, hiding treats under cups or playing a good old-fashioned game of tug-of-war is always a hit. My friend's Jack Russell is a total genius when it comes to these games—I swear, she could be the next Sherlock Holmes.

Ever seen your dog sniffing around like they're trying to solve a mystery? That's because their noses are like supercomputers—seriously, dogs have a sense of smell way beyond our imagination. So, why not let them use it? Hide some treats around the house or yard and watch them go on a treasure hunt. And don't be afraid to mix things up! Take them on new walking routes, visit different parks, or even a pet-friendly store. It's like giving their senses a little vacation.

Once, I hid treats all over my apartment and watched my dog go into full detective mode. By the time he found the last one, I half-expected him to pull out a tiny magnifying glass.

Social Interaction

Let's not forget that dogs are social creatures! Setting up playdates with other dogs is a great way for them to burn off energy and get some mental stimulation at the same time. Just make sure their playmates are a good match in size and energy levels, or you might end up with a wild game of tag that's a little too intense.

BALANCING PHYSICAL AND MENTAL HEALTH

So, what's the magic formula for a happy, healthy dog? It's all about balance. You've got to blend physical workouts with mental challenges—basically, a workout for the body and the brain.
Start with a routine, but don't be afraid to shake things up every now and then. Your dog will love the predictability of daily walks or playtime, but throwing in a new game or puzzle will keep them on their toes (paws?). And remember, rest is just as important as play. After all that running and brain-teasing, your pup will need some downtime to recharge.

And here's a pro tip: always keep an eye on their energy levels. If they're panting like crazy or limping, it's time to call it a day. Don't forget, treats, praise, and belly rubs go a long way in keeping your dog motivated to try new things!

In the end, keeping your dog happy and healthy is all about finding that sweet spot between physical exercise and mental enrichment. Every dog's different, so it's important to tailor activities to their unique needs and personalities. And hey, the time you spend together? That's the best part for both of you.
So go ahead—grab that leash, dust off the treat bag, and get ready for some fun. Your dog's next adventure is just around the corner!

CHAPTER 8:
Training and Socialization

If you're anything like me when I first brought my furry friend home, you're probably juggling between "Oh my gosh, you're so cute!" and "Oh no, what have I gotten myself into?" Don't worry, you're not alone. Every dog owner has been there, and trust me, with a little patience (and a lot of treats), you'll be well on your way to raising a happy, well-behaved dog. Let's dive into some of the basics of training and socialization—and I'll sprinkle in a few lessons I learned along the way.

TRAINING SUPPLIES: THE BASICS
Before we start teaching your puppy how to be a superstar, let's talk gear. You wouldn't show up to a tennis match without a racket, right? Same thing goes for training your pup—you need the right tools.
Here's what you'll need:
- **Leash and Collar/Harness:** You might feel like you're shopping for the perfect outfit when picking out a leash and collar (and honestly, I totally did), but really, it's about comfort and control. A sturdy leash and a comfy, adjustable collar or harness are non-negotiable. A friend of mine swears by a harness that has a front clip, which prevents her over-excited Golden Retriever from turning walks into a sled-pulling contest.
- **Training Treats:** Find something your dog *loves*—and I mean, like would-do-anything-for-it loves. My dog goes bananas for tiny pieces of boiled chicken (store-bought treats? Who's she?). Keep them small; you don't want your dog gaining ten pounds just from learning "sit."
- **Clicker (Optional):** If you're feeling fancy, a clicker can help you mark good behavior quickly. It's like the VIP pass to your dog's attention. I was skeptical at first, but after a few tries, my pup acted like the sound of the clicker was a direct line to all the chicken she could dream of.

HOUSE TRAINING: EXPECT PEE—A LOT OF IT
Okay, house training. The struggle is real. The first week I brought my dog home, I was a bit of a zombie from waking up every couple of hours for those 3 AM potty breaks. *Pro tip:* It helps to set up a routine early. Take your dog to the designated potty area frequently—like every two hours, or after meals, naps, and any time they look like they're about to squat. I once spent an entire afternoon trailing my dog with a treat in hand, ready to pounce with praise the second she did her business in the right spot.
When she got it right, you'd think I was throwing her a parade. Lots of praise and a little treat go a long way. And if accidents happen (because they will), don't stress. Just clean it up and move on—patience, my friend!

Here's the thing about dog training: It's not just about getting your dog to do tricks, it's about building a relationship. My dog isn't just my pet; she's like my tiny, furry shadow, and training helped us build that bond. One of the most important lessons I learned? **Consistency is king**. I used to say "come here" one day and "come" the next—no wonder my dog was confused! Pick your commands and stick with them. If it's "sit," always say "sit." Otherwise, you'll end up with a dog looking at you like, "I speak dog, not human gibberish." And don't just rely on words. Dogs are all about body language—sometimes, I think my dog can read my mind (or maybe it's just my facial expressions). Use hand signals along with your commands. A raised hand for "sit" or a palm out for "stay" helps reinforce what you're asking for.

One more thing: keep it positive! Imagine if your boss yelled at you every time you messed up a task—no way would you be motivated to keep trying. Dogs are the same. Positive reinforcement (treats, praise, belly rubs—you name it) will get you much further than frustration.

Socialization: Your Puppy's First World Tour
I'll never forget my dog's first trip to the park. She was a curious little thing—ears perked, tail wagging, trying to figure out why these giant four-legged creatures (horses, as we call them) weren't dogs. Getting your dog out and about is crucial, especially when they're young. Between 3 and 14 weeks old, puppies are like little sponges, soaking up all the experiences they can.
If you've got a shy pup, start slow. I once read a tip to carry treats with you to make new experiences feel positive, and it worked wonders for us. My dog was wary of meeting bigger dogs at first, but by tossing her a treat every time a friendly dog approached, she quickly learned that new dogs = good things.
Now, don't forget: each breed has its quirks. My friend's Corgi? Super friendly with people but not so fond of other dogs. Meanwhile, my Labrador wants to be best buds with every living creature. Pay attention to your dog's personality and adjust your socialization approach to what makes them feel comfortable.

Common Behavioral Issues: We've All Been There
No matter how much you train or socialize your pup, there will be bumps along the way. And that's okay! Here are some of the more common issues, along with a few tricks that worked for me (and yes, they might work for you too).
1. **Separation Anxiety:** If your dog freaks out every time you leave, you're not alone. My pup would cry the second I grabbed my keys. What helped? Gradually increasing alone time. I started with just five minutes, then stretched it longer. Also, leaving her with a puzzle toy full of treats was a game-changer.
2. **Leash Pulling:** Ah, the dreaded leash tug-of-war. I remember feeling like I was being dragged down the street the first time I took my pup for a walk. If your dog's a puller, try a front-clip harness or practice the "stop and go" method: every time your dog pulls, you stop walking. It's like pressing pause on their fun until they calm down.
3. **Jumping on People:** My dog still gets excited when guests come over—she'll bounce up like she's got springs in her paws. Teaching her to sit when she greets people was a lifesaver. It took some time (and consistency), but now she knows: paws on the ground = attention and treats.
4. **Destructive Chewing:** I lost a few shoes to the teething phase. Chew toys, my friend—*lots* of chew toys. Rotate them to keep things interesting. And if your dog's still chewing on furniture after teething, it could be boredom. More exercise and mental stimulation can help keep them out of trouble.

Dog training is a journey. Some days, you'll feel like a superhero when your dog finally nails "stay" after 10 tries. Other days, you'll wonder if your pup even hears a word you're saying. But every small victory is worth celebrating—whether it's the first time they go potty in the right spot or the moment they sit perfectly on command.
At the end of the day, training and socialization are about more than just teaching tricks—they're about building a bond with your dog. It's a process, sure, but it's also an incredibly rewarding one. And the best part? You get a loyal, loving companion who's by your side every step of the way.

Now, go grab those treats and get started! You've got this.

PART 3:
Special Considerations

CHAPTER 9:
Dogs for Special Needs

Choosing a dog for yourself or someone with special needs isn't just about picking out a cute face or a loyal friend—it's about finding a true partner in life. If you or someone you love faces physical, emotional, or psychological challenges, the right dog can be a game-changer, offering more than just support and security. They bring a sense of purpose, emotional comfort, and a kind of companionship that runs deep. Trust me, if you've ever watched the bond between a person and their assistance dog, you know it's nothing short of life-changing. In this chapter, we'll dive into how to choose the perfect dog, the different types of assistance animals, and the profound ways they enhance the quality of life. Ready to meet your new best friend?

SERVICE DOGS, THERAPY DOGS, AND EMOTIONAL SUPPORT ANIMALS—WHAT'S THE DIFFERENCE?
Let's break this down because, honestly, it can get a little confusing! Each type of assistance dog plays a unique role, and understanding the differences can help you find the right fit.

Service Dogs: Superheroes in Fur Coats
Ever been out and noticed a guide dog helping someone navigate a crazy busy street? Or maybe you've heard about dogs that can literally sense when their owner's about to have a medical emergency? Yeah, those are service dogs, and they're honestly little superheroes with paws. These pups are trained to help people with disabilities by doing all sorts of incredible stuff, like leading people who are visually impaired or even giving a heads-up when someone's blood sugar is dropping. It's wild what they can do! Thanks to the **Americans with Disabilities Act (ADA)**, these dogs can pretty much go wherever their humans go—from grocery stores to airplanes, no questions asked. I mean, they're not just tagging along like regular pets; sometimes they're actual lifesavers. And yeah, okay, they definitely score a treat or two along the way. Total bribery pros.

Speaking of lifesavers, I have a friend, Laura, who has epilepsy, and her service dog Bailey is basically her guardian angel in fur. I'll never forget the time they were out hiking—just the two of them, enjoying the outdoors. Suddenly, Bailey started acting all weird, pawing at Laura and whining. Turns out, he was alerting her to a seizure that was about to hit. Laura was able to sit down in a safe spot before it happened, avoiding what could've been a seriously dangerous fall. I'm not kidding—if that doesn't qualify for a medal or some kind of doggy badge of honor, I don't know what does.

Now, when you think of a service dog, I bet the first thing that comes to mind is all the practical, task-based stuff they do: guiding, fetching, alerting, that kind of thing. And yeah, sure, that's a big part of it. But honestly, the emotional connection they form with their handlers is just as important. Maybe even more, depending on who you ask. It's not just about the tasks—it's about love, loyalty, and that unbreakable bond. Like, they become this constant, steady presence in their owner's life, you know? And okay, side note—have you ever seen the way these dogs look at their humans? It's like they know they've got the most important job in the world, and they're all in.

I remember watching this documentary about a veteran with PTSD and his service dog, and it seriously hit me right in the feels. The veteran said something like, "Some days I wake up and don't even want to get out of bed, but then I see those big brown eyes looking up at me, and I know—I'm not alone." I mean, if that doesn't tug at your heartstrings, what will? This guy wasn't just talking about his dog as some helper or tool; this dog was his lifeline. There was a whole different level of connection there, one that goes way beyond training or tasks. Honestly, sometimes I wonder if the dogs know how much they mean to their humans. It's almost like they were born knowing their purpose.

So, you're thinking about getting a service dog, but where do you start? These incredible dogs specialize in different areas, each trained for unique tasks. Here's a look at a few:
- *Guide Dogs:* Guide dogs are specially trained to help people who are blind or visually impaired navigate their surroundings safely. These dogs are like GPS with a heartbeat! They steer their handlers away from obstacles, help them cross streets, and provide that sense of freedom and independence that's hard to imagine without them.
- *Hearing Dogs:* These loyal companions alert their owners to important sounds like doorbells, fire alarms, or even someone approaching from behind. Imagine the reassurance of knowing your hearing dog is there to have your back—or your ears!
- *Mobility Assistance Dogs:* If you have a physical disability, these dogs are like your personal assistants with paws. Need your phone from across the room? They'll fetch it. Need a steady companion to lean on? They've got that covered too. These dogs help their handlers move around and even open doors or hit elevator buttons—seriously, they're like furry little superheroes.
- *Medical Alert Dogs:* For people with conditions like diabetes or epilepsy, medical alert dogs can detect changes in blood sugar or sense when a seizure is coming. It's almost like they've got a sixth sense. These dogs can literally save lives by alerting their handlers before something serious happens. Bailey, Laura's dog I mentioned earlier? She's one of these miracle workers.
- *Psychiatric Service Dogs:* These pups help people dealing with mental health issues like PTSD, anxiety, or depression. They can sense when their handler is getting anxious, remind them to take medication, or even provide grounding techniques during panic attacks. Honestly, they're like emotional anchors in a storm.
- *Autism Assistance Dogs:* These dogs can make a world of difference for individuals with autism. They help manage sensory overload and provide a comforting, calming presence in overwhelming environments. They're more than just pets—they're bridges to the world.

LET'S DIVE INTO THE WORLD OF EMOTIONAL SUPPORT ANIMALS (ESAS)

Okay, so let's get real for a second—have you ever had a moment where the world felt like it was just too much? Maybe your mind's racing, your heart's doing that weird thing where it beats too fast, and all you want is for something—or someone—to pull you back down to earth? That's where Emotional Support Animals, or ESAs, come into play. These aren't just pets who hang around waiting for dinner time. Nope. They are like emotional anchors for those navigating some serious mental health waves.

I remember a time when my cousin Sarah was going through a really tough patch. Life was hitting her from all sides—work stress, family drama, you name it. She told me about her dog, Max, a scruffy little terrier with a heart way bigger than his body. Max wasn't trained to perform tricks or fetch things for her (unless we're talking about pizza crusts), but Sarah said that whenever she felt overwhelmed, Max had this almost mystical ability to just "be there." It was like he knew when to plop his furry body next to her, gently nudging her hand, as if saying, "Hey, I'm here. You're safe." Sarah swears he was the one thing keeping her sane during the craziest days.

Let me tell you, ESAs aren't just "nice to have" when things go south. For a lot of people, they're the reason to get out of bed in the morning—literally. Whether it's a loyal dog curled up beside someone in the throes of an anxiety attack or a cat that magically appears just when you're on the verge of tears, these animals somehow sense when their human needs them the most. And let's be real: anyone who's ever been greeted by a dog's wagging tail or felt the calming purr of a cat knows that kind of support hits different.

Take my neighbor Rick, for example. Ricks had a tough go of it, battling depression for years. If you didn't know him, you'd never guess it—he's always got a joke, always quick with a smile. But behind that smile, there are some really dark days. The only one who truly sees through all of it is his cat, Olive. She's a sleek black cat with this deep, almost hypnotic purr. Rick always says, "Olive's purr is like my 'safe place' sound, like white noise for my soul." Every time Rick feels like he's sinking into that black hole, Olive just *knows* and somehow appears—no fanfare, no meows—just softly jumps into his lap, nuzzles his hand, and purrs. Rick jokes that she's his unofficial therapist. But honestly? I think she's saved his life in more ways than one.

Now, let's break it down. ESAs don't need fancy training or certifications. They're not like service dogs that help guide you across busy streets or alert you if your blood sugar drops. What they do is a bit more... well, intangible. It's the emotional stuff. The kind of things that no pill or self-help book can fully fix. The comfort they provide is hard to put into words, but if you've ever felt completely lost and then suddenly found solace in the presence of an animal, you know exactly what I mean.

Have you ever had that feeling where your mind is going a thousand miles an hour, and no amount of breathing exercises or calming apps seems to work? Imagine, in that chaos, a soft head gently nudging your hand, or a pair of calm eyes meeting yours, as if to say, "I've got you." It's grounding. It's like the emotional equivalent of someone throwing you a life jacket when you're drowning in a sea of your own thoughts. That's what ESAs do—except its way more powerful than any metaphor can really capture.

I've seen it firsthand in my own family. My uncle, who suffers from PTSD after serving in the military, was pretty closed off emotionally. He'd spend days without leaving the house, barely speaking to anyone. Then came Sadie—a big, goofy golden retriever with a heart as golden as her fur. I remember the first time I saw them together; Sadie was sprawled out across my uncle's feet, and for the first time in what felt like years, he smiled. It wasn't a huge, flashy grin. Just a quiet, peaceful smile. When I asked him about it later, he said, "Sadie doesn't ask anything of me. She doesn't need me to explain why I'm sad or why today's harder than yesterday. She's just... there. And that's enough."

That's the magic of ESAs. They don't demand explanations, and they don't offer advice. They simply exist in the moment with you, and in doing so, they can lift you out of whatever dark cloud you might be stuck under. If you're reading this and wondering if an ESA could help someone you know—or maybe even yourself—just remember this: they're not a cure-all, but they sure can be part of the healing. Mental health is tricky and layered. There's no one-size-fits-all solution. But sometimes, the solution comes with four paws, a wet nose, and an unspoken understanding that says, "I'm here, and that's all that matters right now."

Maybe you've never considered an ESA before, or perhaps you're already lucky enough to have one in your life. Either way, it's hard to deny the incredible, life-changing impact these animals can have. I mean, who wouldn't want an unconditional love machine by their side, especially on those days when the world feels too heavy to carry on your own?

In a world where everything feels like it's moving too fast, where everyone is expected to be "on" all the time, ESAs give us permission to slow down, to just breathe. So if you know someone who's struggling, maybe suggest they consider the comfort of an ESA. And if you're struggling yourself, don't be afraid to seek out that kind of connection. Sometimes, the quiet, gentle presence of a furry friend can make all the difference in the world.

At the end of the day, we all need a little support. And for many, that support comes wrapped in fur with a wagging tail or a content purr. So, next time you see someone with an ESA, know that they aren't just pets—they're lifelines. They're reminders that none of us are truly alone, even when it feels like we are. And hey, maybe that's the most human thing of all.

Therapy Dogs: Spreading Love, One Wag at a Time

Have you ever had one of those days where everything just feels... off? Maybe the coffee machine broke, you missed your train, or a deadline snuck up on you out of nowhere. Then, out of the blue, a dog waltzes into your space, tail wagging like it's the happiest creature on the planet, and suddenly, things don't seem so bad. That's the magic of therapy dogs—they have this uncanny ability to turn the most ordinary day into something extraordinary, one wag at a time.

Now, if you've ever been in a hospital or school where a dog ambles through the halls, you might have come face-to-face with a therapy dog. These furry bundles of joy aren't there to fetch things or lead someone across the street like service dogs. No, their superpower is simpler but equally important: they spread pure love. Therapy dogs visit hospitals, nursing homes, and schools, spreading warmth like the sun on a cold day. And trust me, when you're going through a rough patch, that kind of light is priceless.

Let me take you back to one of the most heartwarming experiences of my life. I was volunteering at a children's hospital. It was a bright Tuesday afternoon, and Daisy, a golden retriever with the fluffiest ears you could imagine, trotted beside me. There was this one patient, a little girl with a bright scarf wrapped around her head, mid-way through a tough round of chemo. Each time Daisy and I visited, this little girl's face would light up, her eyes sparkling in a way that could rival Christmas morning. But one visit in particular still stands out in my mind.

Daisy walked up to the girl, nudging her hand softly, as if she somehow knew this was a day when a little extra love was needed. The girl reached out and wrapped her tiny fingers in Daisy's golden fur, her grip tight at first—like she was holding on to more than just fur but a moment of peace, a break from the pain. And then, as if Daisy had flipped a magical switch, the girl's face melted into the most radiant smile, tears turning into giggles. It was one of those rare, soul-lifting moments that make you stop and realize the depth of what these animals do. They don't just visit—they heal, in the way only a creature full of unconditional love can.

Therapy dogs are not about tasks—they're about connection. They're pros at knowing just when someone needs a nudge, a paw on their lap, or a head rested softly against their leg. It's almost as if they have this sixth sense for human emotions. And trust me, when you're in a hospital bed, unsure about what the next day will bring, that simple act of companionship is more powerful than words. The presence of a therapy dog can turn fear into comfort, isolation into companionship, and sadness into something that, at least for a moment, feels manageable.

In nursing homes, where days can blend into one another, therapy dogs become the highlight of the week. Imagine being 87 years old, living through long, quiet afternoons, and then, BAM! In trots a goofy Labradoodle, its eyes full of mischief, tongue lolling out like it's ready for a party. You bet that's going to turn your day around! These dogs give the elderly something to look forward to—something to smile about, laugh with, and remember. The kind of joy that lasts long after the dog has left the building.

There's something magical about the way therapy dogs work. They don't need to "do" anything—they just are. Their mere presence has a way of softening the edges of a rough day. I've seen it firsthand with Daisy, and it never ceases to amaze me. There was this one time when Daisy visited a man who'd just undergone surgery. He was anxious, tapping his fingers on the bed frame, clearly restless. Daisy didn't perform any tricks or jump around; she simply laid her head on his lap, letting out a soft huff, as if to say, "I'm here. It's okay." That simple gesture was enough. The man's tapping stopped, and for the first time that day, he relaxed.

The thing is, these dogs aren't just pets—they're emotional lifelines. They show up in places where people feel most vulnerable and offer exactly what's needed: comfort, distraction, a reminder that not everything in life is hard. Sometimes, just knowing that something—or someone—is there for you, without expecting anything in return, is the most healing gift of all.

It's funny how animals, especially dogs, have this unspoken language with us humans. They don't need words to understand when we're stressed, sad, or just plain tired. Therapy dogs, like Daisy, seem to have perfected that art of communication. And it's not just the people they visit who benefit. Volunteering with Daisy has been one of the most grounding, fulfilling experiences of my life. I've learned to appreciate the small things: a wagging tail, a joyful bark, a little girl's laughter. There's something about being in the presence of a dog who only knows how to give love that makes you realize how simple happiness can be.

Honestly, we could all use a little "Daisy" in our lives. Whether you're feeling down or just need a reason to smile, there's something about the way a dog looks at you with those big, soulful eyes that says, "Hey, I've got you." It's a kind of connection that's hard to explain, but once you've felt it, you know. And it's not just therapy dogs. Whether it's your own dog or one you pass by in the park, animals have this beautiful way of reminding us what's important.

So, next time you're having a tough day—whether it's the little things piling up or something bigger weighing on you—imagine a golden retriever like Daisy wandering into the room, tail wagging, eyes full of love. That's the kind of healing energy therapy dogs bring. They don't solve problems or take away the pain, but for a moment, they make life a little lighter. And sometimes, that's exactly what we need.
Therapy dogs might not wear capes, but they are heroes in their own right—spreading joy, one paw at a time. And honestly, that's a superpower worth celebrating.

Training: What Goes Into Making an Assistance Dog?
Training a service or assistance dog is no walk in the park—it's a serious commitment that takes time, patience, and a whole lot of love. Every assistance dog starts with the basics: sit, stay, heel, and come. Once they've

mastered those, the specialized training begins. A guide dog, for instance, learns how to navigate busy streets and keep their human safe from traffic. Medical alert dogs, on the other hand, are trained to pick up on subtle changes in their handler's body chemistry. It's fascinating stuff!

But it's not all about tasks. These dogs need to be comfortable in every environment, whether that's a noisy shopping mall, a crowded restaurant, or a quiet library. One of my friends who trains service dogs says that the hardest part is teaching the dogs to stay calm, cool, and collected no matter what's going on around them. But once they do, they're ready for anything!

Legal Protections for Service Dogs and ESAs: What You Need to Know (with Some Real Talk!)

Let me guess—you're either a proud owner of a service dog or you've got an emotional support animal (ESA) that's your little lifesaver. First of all, hats off to you for making that important choice. But here's the thing: knowing your rights when it comes to these amazing animals can be a bit confusing, especially with all the legal stuff floating around. Whether you're out and about with your service dog or trying to find a new place to live with your ESA, you've got protections. And trust me, understanding those protections is key to avoiding headaches later on.

Let's break it all down, one paw at a time.

Service Dogs: The VIPs of the Dog World

Service dogs are like the VIPs of the dog world. They have a special status thanks to the Americans with Disabilities Act (ADA). What does that mean for you? It means your service dog can go almost anywhere you go—whether it's a restaurant, a grocery store, or hopping on a bus. No one can legally tell you that your service dog isn't allowed (unless they want a hefty lawsuit on their hands, but let's not go there).

Here's a little story: A friend of mine, Laura, has a service dog named Max. Max is the calmest, most professional dog you'll ever meet. He helps Laura with her anxiety, and she once told me that having Max with her at all times feels like she has her own personal bodyguard. There was one time when she walked into a restaurant, and the host looked uneasy. But before he could even ask, Laura flashed her ADA card. No fuss, no problems. Max stayed right by her side through the entire dinner, like the true professional he is.

Moral of the story? If you have a service dog, don't stress. You're legally protected in public spaces. Your dog is a working dog, and people just need to understand that.

ESAs: Special Roommates with Perks (Mostly for Housing)

Now, ESAs (that's Emotional Support Animals, if you're new here) don't get quite the same level of access as service dogs, but they still have some important protections—especially when it comes to housing. Ever dealt with a landlord who says, "Sorry, no pets allowed"? Yeah, they can be tricky, but that's where the **Fair Housing Act (FHA)** steps in.

The FHA is like your secret weapon. It ensures that ESAs can live with their humans, even in housing with strict "no pets" policies. You just need to have the proper documentation from a licensed mental health professional. That's your golden ticket.

Let me tell you about Sarah. She's got an ESA—a fluffy cat named Oliver, who helps her manage her depression. When Sarah was moving into a new apartment, she was hit with a classic, "Sorry, no pets allowed" email from the landlord. But Sarah was prepared. She had her documentation ready, and after a quick conversation with the landlord, guess who was unpacking boxes with Oliver curled up on the couch? Yep, Sarah. The FHA had her back, and Oliver kept his place as the ultimate furry roommate.

Quick Tip: Keep That ESA Paperwork Handy

Here's the deal: if you've got an ESA, always—and I mean always—keep your paperwork handy. You never know when you might need to prove that your animal is more than just a pet. It's always better to be safe than sorry, right?

I know what you're thinking: "Can I take my ESA into a restaurant or store?" The short answer? No, not really. ESAs don't have the same access rights as service dogs when it comes to public spaces like restaurants, stores, or public transportation. It can feel unfair, but them's the rules. If you're going out with your ESA, you'll probably have to leave them at home.

But don't lose hope! Some places are ESA-friendly, and it never hurts to call ahead and ask. You'd be surprised how many places are willing to accommodate if you just explain your situation. Just don't expect it to be a guarantee like it is with service dogs.

Okay, let's dive a little deeper into housing. If you're applying for a new apartment with your ESA, you might feel a little anxious about how your landlord will react. The key? Be prepared. Here's what usually happens:
1. First, make sure your ESA documentation is legit. It should be from a licensed mental health professional. No, your cousin's handwritten note doesn't count.
2. Expect questions. Landlords might ask about the paperwork or what accommodations they need to make. Be polite but firm. You have rights.
3. Offer solutions. Sometimes, landlords are just worried about damage or noise. You can ease their concerns by mentioning that your ESA is well-trained or quiet.
4. Know your rights. Under the FHA, landlords *must* make reasonable accommodations for your ESA. If they try to give you a hard time, remind them (gently) that the law's on your side.

Whether you've got a service dog by your side or an ESA keeping you company at home, it's essential to know your rights. Service dogs have wide-reaching legal protections, but ESAs are still protected in critical ways—especially when it comes to housing.

Just remember: Be prepared, keep your paperwork handy, and never be afraid to assert your rights. Whether you're walking into a new apartment or sitting down at a restaurant, your furry companion is an essential part of your life, and the law recognizes that.

Whether you're considering a service dog, therapy dog, or ESA, it's important to find the right companion for your needs. These animals offer more than just practical help—they bring unconditional love, emotional support, and a bond that can truly enhance your life.

So, when you find that perfect dog—whether they're fetching your keys, guiding you through a crowd, or just curling up beside you on a hard day—you'll know you've found more than just a pet. You've found a friend for life.

CHAPTER 10:
Traveling with Your Dog

Traveling with your dog can be one of the most rewarding experiences. There's something about hitting the open road, your best furry friend by your side, ears flapping in the wind, that just screams adventure, right? Whether it's a quick weekend trip to the mountains or a cross-country trek, traveling with your dog gives you both a chance to create unforgettable memories. But, like any good road trip, a little prep goes a long way in ensuring things run smoothly for both you and your pup.

I've had my fair share of road trips with my dog, Luna—a scrappy rescue mix with a love for car rides and an aversion to cats (long story). From navigating tight city streets to finding the perfect dog-friendly beach, I've learned a thing or two about making sure your dog stays safe, happy, and comfortable on the road. Let's dive into some tips and tricks to make your next doggy adventure a breeze!

Planning Your Trip
Before you throw a leash in the car and start the engine, it's smart to have a game plan. Trust me, nothing kills the road trip vibes faster than realizing mid-trip that your destination doesn't allow pets, or worse, that you forgot your dog's favorite chew toy (cue sad puppy eyes).

First things first—**schedule a vet visit**. It's like that pre-flight checklist, but for your pup. Not only will your vet make sure your dog is in tip-top shape, but they'll also give you the lowdown on any vaccines or health certificates you might need. I made the mistake once of skipping this step and almost got turned away at a campsite because Luna wasn't up-to-date on her rabies shot. Lesson learned.

Also, depending on where you're headed, there might be some specific rules, like breed restrictions (yeah, some places still do that), leash laws, or even pet-friendly parks. You don't want to show up at your dream destination only to find out your dog can't join you on the hiking trails.

Preparing Your Dog for the Journey
Okay, so let's talk about your dog's comfort during the trip. Here's where things can get fun—or completely chaotic. Luna is a ball of energy, and on her first car ride, she spent the entire time trying to crawl into the front seat. Lesson learned: **crate training** is a game-changer. Not only does it keep your dog safe, but it gives them a cozy space to relax. Think of it as their little road-trip fortress.

Now, if your dog isn't used to the car yet, don't throw them into a four-hour drive on day one. Start with baby steps. Take them on shorter rides—maybe a quick trip to grab coffee or a run to the park. Turn these little adventures into positive experiences by giving treats and lots of praise. After a few trial runs, Luna started hopping into her crate like it was her personal chariot, ready for the next adventure.

And let's not forget the **power of familiar smells**. Pack your dog's favorite blanket or toy to make the ride more comforting. I've found that Luna travels best when her trusty chew toy, "Mr. Squeaks," is in tow. It's like her security blanket, except noisier (apologies to my fellow passengers).

If your dog gets a little anxious during travel (or if you're dealing with a dog that's more high-strung than chill), consider using calming aids. There are calming collars, pheromone sprays, or even vet-approved supplements. Just check with your vet to see what works best for your pup.

Hydration, Snacks, and Potty Breaks
Pack enough water. Seriously, it's easy to forget, but nothing's worse than a thirsty dog in the middle of nowhere. Luna once gave me the ultimate side-eye after I had to ration our water during a particularly hot day trip. Since then, I always bring extra and offer it regularly, especially in warmer weather.
Feed your dog a light meal a few hours before the trip. Trust me, you don't want your pup throwing up in the backseat. And, yes, that's from personal experience (rest in peace, car upholstery).
And, of course, **schedule potty breaks**. No one likes a grumpy, restless dog, and stopping every couple of hours for a quick walk or bathroom break will make the journey easier on both of you. Plus, it gives you a chance to stretch your legs and snag a snack (don't pretend like you don't want to stop for road-trip snacks).

Packing Essentials for Your Pup
Picture this: You've hit the road, your playlist is on point, and everything is going smoothly. Then, you realize you forgot your dog's leash. Or worse, their food. Been there, done that, never again. Here's a list of **must-haves** for traveling with your dog:
- *Crate or carrier:* A well-ventilated, sturdy crate is key. It should be roomy enough for your dog to stand, turn around, and lie down comfortably.
- *ID tags and microchip:* Make sure your dog's collar has a current ID tag with your contact info. I went the extra mile and got Luna microchipped, just in case.
- *Leash and harness:* Pack a strong leash and harness for bathroom breaks and walks.
- *Food and water:* Bring enough food to last the trip, plus some bowls. And don't forget those treats—road trips are better with snacks!
- *First aid kit:* Hopefully, you won't need it, but better safe than sorry.
- *Familiar items:* Blanket, toys, and anything else that will make your dog feel at home.

Finding Pet-Friendly Accommodations
Not all places roll out the red carpet for pets, so do your homework before you hit the road. Websites like **BringFido** and **PetsWelcome** are goldmines for finding pet-friendly spots. One time, I showed up at a hotel with Luna, only to find out they had a strict no-dogs policy (despite the paw print on their website). We ended up camping instead—Luna wasn't mad about it, but I could've used a proper bed.
Check the pet policies carefully—some places charge extra fees, have breed or size restrictions, or expect your dog to be a model citizen (spoiler alert: Luna is not). Find somewhere that's not only dog-friendly but **dog-welcoming**. You'll both have a much better time if the place has ample space for your dog to roam or even a nearby park for early morning walks.

Hitting the Road: Traveling by Car
There's something so classic about a road trip with your dog, windows down, music up, and the scent of adventure in the air. But safety first! Consider using a **dog seatbelt**, crate, or barrier to keep your pup secure. Not only does this prevent distractions, but it keeps your dog safe in case of any sudden stops.
Breaks are key. Every two or three hours, pull over for a quick stretch, bathroom break, and maybe even a little playtime. Luna loves these pit stops—they're her chance to sniff out new smells and burn off some energy.
Oh, and whatever you do, **don't leave your dog in the car**. Even with the windows cracked, temperatures can soar faster than you'd think. Trust me, you don't want to risk it.

Traveling by Air or Train? Do Your Homework
Not all adventures happen on the road. If you're taking your dog on a plane, make sure you're well-versed in the airline's pet policies. Some airlines allow small dogs to travel in the cabin with you (lucky little guys), while larger dogs usually need to fly in the cargo hold.

Pro tip: **Book a direct flight** if possible. Layovers can be stressful for both you and your pup. And if your dog is anything like Luna, a little pre-flight exercise will go a long way in helping them settle down.
Trains and buses? Same rules apply—check ahead for their pet policies, and make sure you've got a plan for bathroom breaks along the way.

Traveling with your dog can be an incredible adventure, filled with belly laughs, epic photo ops, and a whole lot of wagging tails. With a bit of planning, you'll not only have a smoother trip but also make memories you and your pup will treasure forever. And if things don't go exactly as planned? Well, those make for the best stories later, don't they?
So, what are you waiting for? Grab that leash, pack the treats, and hit the road with your four-legged travel buddy. Adventure awaits!

PART 4:

Dog Breeds A-Z

CHAPTER 11:
Dog Breed Profiles

Thanks for staying with us! You're now entering the chapter we've all been eagerly awaiting—the one where we dive into the wonderful world of our beloved dogs. Here, we'll explore the unique traits, quirks, and endearing charms of each breed. Whether you're a lifelong dog lover or considering adopting your first furry friend, this chapter is your guide to the rich diversity of dog breeds. We'll cover their origins, physical characteristics, personalities, exercise needs, grooming tips, and any potential health concerns, giving you all the info you need to find your perfect new companion.

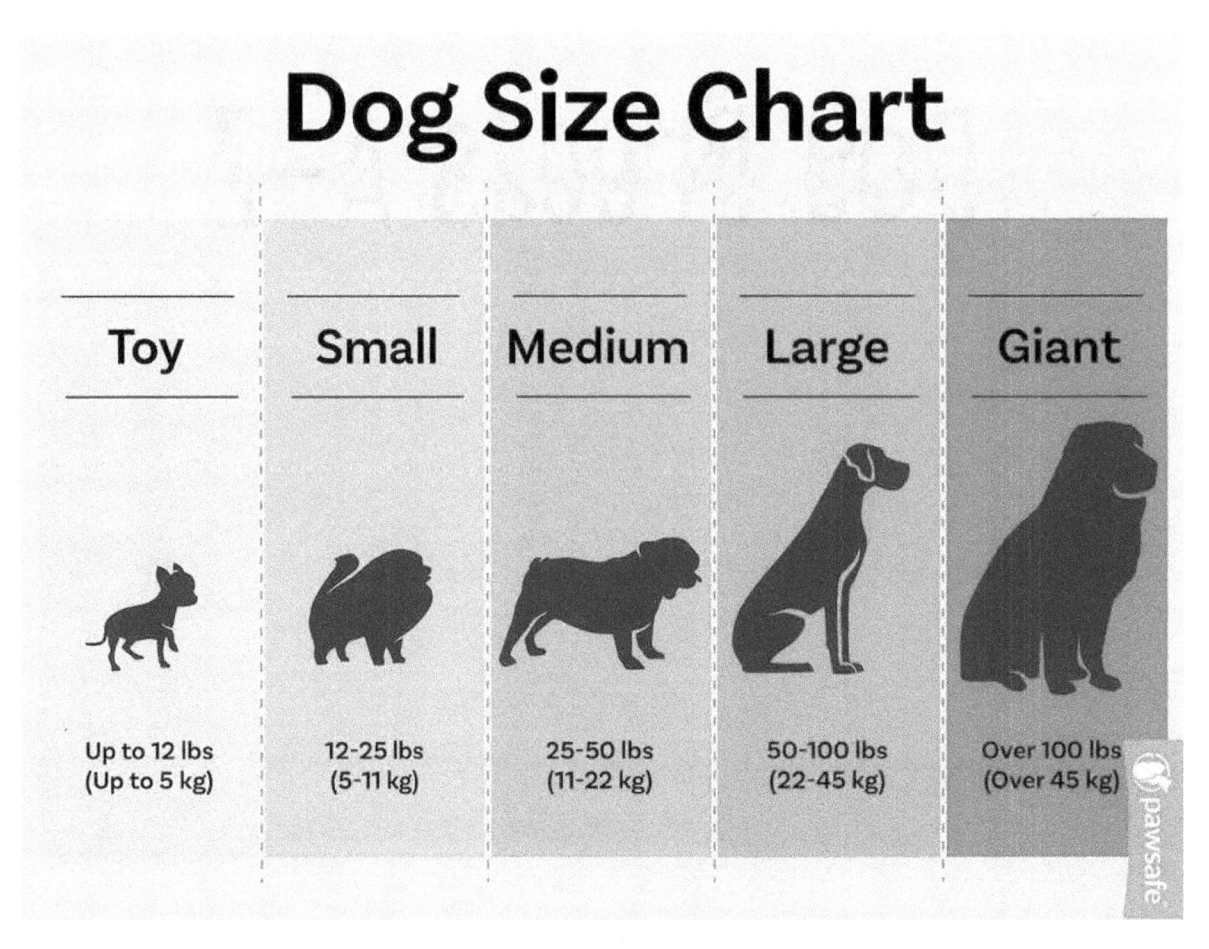

Dog Size Chart

Toy	Small	Medium	Large	Giant
Up to 12 lbs (Up to 5 kg)	12-25 lbs (5-11 kg)	25-50 lbs (11-22 kg)	50-100 lbs (22-45 kg)	Over 100 lbs (Over 45 kg)

© Pawsafe CC-BY-4.0

Affenpinscher

Other Names: Monkey Terrier, Affen, Affie
Color variations: Black, gray, silver, red, black and tan, belge
Average Lifespan: 12-14 years
Origins: Germany - 17th century - initially developed to catch rats, helping to keep homes, stables, and shops free of rodents.
Body Size: Males: 9.5-11.5 in, 7-10 lbs Females: 9.5-11.5 in, 7-10 lbs
Personality/Disposition/Compatibility: These dogs are curious, playful, and affectionate. Despite their small size, they have big personalities and often act like larger dogs. They are loyal, protective, and sometimes stubborn. With early socialization, they usually get along well with older kids and other pets. However, they might not be ideal for families with very young children, as they can nip or chase due to their instincts.
Grooming Needs: To keep their coat looking great, you'll need to brush them regularly to prevent mats and tangles. Occasional trims will help maintain the shape of their coat. Pay special attention to their facial hair, making sure it stays clean and tidy.
Training & Exercise Needs: They need regular exercise to stay healthy and happy. Daily walks, playtime, and engaging activities like agility training or interactive games are perfect for this breed.
Possible Health Issues: These pups can be prone to hip dysplasia, patellar luxation, and Legg-Calvé-Perthes disease. Watch for heart issues like mitral valve disease and eye conditions such as cataracts and progressive retinal atrophy (PRA). Due to their short snouts, Affenpinschers might have breathing difficulties, especially in hot or humid weather. Dental problems are common, so regular teeth cleaning is essential to keep their smiles bright.

Afghan Hound

Other Names: Tāžę, Balkh, Baluchi or Barakzai Hound
Color variations: Black, cream, red, blue, brindle, domino, white
Average Lifespan: 12-14 years
Origins: Afghanistan - Ancient times - Originally bred by nomadic tribes of Afghanistan, Pakistan, and northern India for hunting large game in harsh mountain terrains.
Body Size: Males: 27 in, 60 lbs. Females: 25 in, 50 lbs
Personality/Disposition/Compatibility: They have a proud and independent personality. While they might come across as aloof at first, they are truly loving and loyal to their families. Training them can be a bit tricky because of their independent streak. They tend to be shy around strangers but are playful with those they trust. Due to their strong hunting instinct, they might not be the best fit for homes with smaller pets. With the right training, they can get along well with children, but they generally don't enjoy rough play.
Grooming Needs: Their long, silky hair needs to be brushed several times a week to prevent tangles and mats. Regular baths are also necessary to keep their coat clean and shiny. Additionally, professional grooming every few months can help manage their coat and keep them looking their best.
Training & Exercise Needs: They're lively and energetic dogs that need plenty of exercise to keep them happy and healthy. They love their daily walks and really shine when they get the chance to run around in a secure, fenced area. These graceful hounds also have a blast with activities like agility training or lure coursing, which help keep both their minds and bodies engaged. If they don't get enough exercise, they might get bored and start finding their own ways to entertain themselves, which could lead to some mischief!
Possible Health Issues: They're generally healthy but can be prone to certain conditions such as hip dysplasia, cataracts, and hypothyroidism.

Airedale Terrier

Other Names: King of Terriers
Color variations: tan coat with a black or grizzled saddle
Average Lifespan: 10 to 13 years
Origins: England - mid-19th century - to catch otters and rats in the region between the Aire and Wharfe Rivers.
Body Size: Males: 23 in, 50 to 65 lbs. Females: 22 in, 40 to 55 lbs
Personality/Disposition/Compatibility: These dogs are intelligent, alert, and confident, which makes them easy to train and great at dog sports. They're friendly and playful, making them excellent companions for active families. While they can be a bit stubborn and independent, they generally get along well with children and other animals if properly socialized. However, due to their terrier instincts, they may have a high prey drive, so it's important to be cautious around smaller pets.
Grooming Needs: They have a straight, dense, and wiry outer coat with a softer undercoat. To keep their coat in good condition, you'll need to brush them several times a week and take them for professional grooming every few months.
Training & Exercise Needs: need a substantial amount of exercise to keep them mentally and physically stimulated. They enjoy activities such as running, hiking, agility training, and playing fetch.
Possible Health Issues: They can be prone to certain health issues, including hip dysplasia, allergies, hypothyroidism, and some skin conditions.

Akita (American)

Other Names: Akita Inu
Color variations: white, brindle, and various shades of red, with a distinct mask or blaze.
Average Lifespan: 10 to 15 years.
Origins: Japan - 1600s - bred for hunting boar, elk, and bear.
Body Size: Males: 26-28 in, 100-130 lbs. Females: 24-26 in, 70-100 lbs.
Personality/Disposition/Compatibility: They're known for loyalty, bravery, and a dignified nature. They're intelligent but can be a bit shy around strangers. Protective and territorial, they usually remain calm and quiet. They have a strong will and a streak of independence. With early training and socialization, they can get along well with children, though they might not tolerate other animals, especially those of the same sex.
Grooming Needs: Their dense, double coat needs some regular TLC to stay in tip-top shape. Brushing them weekly helps keep shedding under control and prevents those pesky mats from forming in their thick fur. An occasional bath will keep their coat looking and feeling fresh. Don't forget to check and clean their ears now and then to ward off infections. And, of course, regular nail trims will keep their paws comfy and in good shape.
Training & Exercise Needs: They are a bundle of energy that thrives on activity! To keep them happy and healthy, they need plenty of exercise. Daily walks and energetic playtime are a must to keep them mentally and physically stimulated. Whether it's a run, a game of fetch, or agility training, these activities will help burn off their abundant energy and keep them in top shape. Plus, regular exercise helps manage their strong, muscular build and can prevent any potential behavioral issues.
Possible Health Issues: hip dysplasia, hypothyroidism, progressive retinal atrophy (PRA), and autoimmune disorders.

Alaskan Husky

Other Names: None
Color variations: black, gray, white, brown, and red, often with various markings and patterns.
Average Lifespan: 10 to 15 years
Origins: Alaska - 20th century - bred for use as a sled dog in racing and working in cold climates. They were bred for performance and function rather than appearance.
Body Size: Males: 21-24 in, 40-60 lbs. Females: 20-23 in, 35-55 lbs.
Personality/Disposition/Compatibility: These dogs are energetic, intelligent, and friendly. They're affectionate with a great temperament and love being around people. Known for their strong work ethic and determination, they usually get along well with children and other dogs, making them excellent family pets. However, be aware that they might have a high prey drive when it comes to smaller animals.
Grooming Needs: To keep their dense double coat in good shape, especially when they're shedding, regular grooming is a must. It's best to brush them several times a week to maintain a healthy coat and cut down on shedding.
Training & Exercise Needs: They're an active breed that needs daily exercise to stay happy and healthy. Regular walks and energetic play are crucial for meeting their physical and mental needs. Activities like running, fetch, or agility training help burn off their excess energy and keep them balanced. Consistent exercise also helps manage their strong build and prevent behavioral issues.
Possible Health Issues: They're usually a hearty breed. You might see issues like hip dysplasia or eye conditions such as cataracts and progressive retinal atrophy (PRA).

Alaskan Klee Kai

Other Names: Miniature Husky
Color variations: black and white, gray and white, and red and white. Solid white also exists but its rare.
Average Lifespan: 12 to 16 years
Origins: United States - 1970s - bred by Linda Spurlin to create a smaller version of the Alaskan Husky suitable as a companion dog.
Body Size: Males: 15-17 in, 16-22 lbs. Females: 13-15 in, 10-18 lbs.
Personality/Disposition/Compatibility: These dogs are intelligent, energetic, and curious. They pick up new things quickly and love both mental and physical activities. Typically friendly, they can be a bit cautious around strangers. They form strong bonds with their families and can be quite protective. If socialized early, they get along well with children and other animals. However, they might have a tendency to chase smaller pets, so supervision is recommended.
Grooming Needs: They need regular grooming, including weekly brushing to keep their double coat in good shape and manage shedding. They shed more during certain times of the year, so you'll need to brush them more often during those periods.
Training & Exercise Needs: They love activities like walking, running, playing fetch, and doing agility training. Regular exercise is key to keeping them both physically fit and mentally sharp.
Possible Health Issues: patellar luxation, heart conditions, thyroid problems, and eye disorders such as cataracts and progressive retinal atrophy.

Alaskan Malamute
Other Names: Mal or Mally
Color variations: light gray through intermediate shadings to black, sable, and shades of sable to red. They often have white markings on the underbody, parts of the legs, feet, and part of the face.
Average Lifespan: 10 to 14 years.
Origins: Alaska - 2000 to 3000 years ago - developed by the native Mahlemut tribe. They were bred for strength and endurance to haul heavy freight as sled dogs and hunt seals and polar bears.
Body Size: Males: 25 in, 85 lbs. Females: 23 in, 75 lbs.
Personality/Disposition/Compatibility: They're known for their friendly and outgoing nature. They adore their families and are always up for playtime, showing lots of energy and liveliness. Generally loyal and gentle, they can also exhibit a bit of stubbornness and independence, making firm and consistent training essential. They do well with children and can get along with other dogs if properly socialized. However, due to their strong prey drive, they might not be the best fit for homes with smaller pets like cats or rabbits.
Grooming Needs: They require regular grooming to manage their thick double coat. They shed heavily twice a year, during which more frequent brushing is needed to remove dead hair and prevent matting.
Training & Exercise Needs: They thrive in activities like hiking, pulling carts or sleds, and agility training. Regular exercise is crucial to prevent boredom and destructive behavior.
Possible Health Issues: hip dysplasia, elbow dysplasia, hypothyroidism, and inherited polyneuropathy.

American Bulldog
Other Names: Old Country Bulldog.
Color variations: white, brindle, fawn, red, and brown, often with combinations of these colors.
Average Lifespan: 10 and 15 years
Origins: United States - 1121 BC - primarily for hunting, guarding, and farm work.
Body Size: Males: 22-27 in, 75-125 lbs. Females: 20-25 in, 60-100 lbs
Personality/Disposition/Compatibility: They're friendly and loving, making them great family pets. Confident and loyal, they have a calm and easy-going nature. While they bravely protect their loved ones, they're gentle with familiar faces. Early socialization helps them get along well with children and other animals. Their protective instincts also make them excellent watchdogs.
Grooming Needs: They're pretty low-maintenance when it comes to grooming. Their short coat just needs a good brushing now and then to keep it free of loose hair and in tip-top shape. A bath every once in a while will help keep them fresh, and don't forget about their teeth—regular brushing is key for a healthy smile. Also, check their nails periodically and trim them if needed to keep them comfortable.
Training & Exercise Needs: They thrive on regular exercise to keep both their bodies and minds in top shape. They need daily walks and playtime to stay happy and healthy. Whether it's jogging alongside you, playing fetch, or working on obedience training, these activities help burn off their energy and maintain their muscular build. Without enough exercise, they might get bored and develop some behavioral issues, so keeping them active is key to their well-being.
Possible Health Issues: hip dysplasia, elbow dysplasia, cherry eye, and skin allergies.

American English Coonhound
Other Names: English Coonhound or Redtick Coonhound.
Color variations: red and white ticked, blue and white ticked, tri-colored with ticking, and red and white.
Average Lifespan: 11 and 12 years
Origins: United States - 17th century - bred for hunting raccoons and other small game.
Body Size: Males: 24-26 in, 45-65 lbs. Females: 23-25 in, 40-60 lbs.
Personality/Disposition/Compatibility: These dogs are a bundle of joy—friendly, smart, and full of energy. They're incredibly loyal and make fantastic pets. Their enthusiasm for hunting and boundless stamina mean they're always up for an adventure. They love being around people and other dogs, and they're great with kids. Just keep in mind, they might need a bit of training to ensure they're safe around smaller pets.
Grooming Needs: They have relatively low grooming needs. Their short, smooth coat only requires occasional brushing to remove loose hairs and keep it looking shiny. Regular check-ups for ear cleaning and nail trimming are also essential. Bathing is typically only necessary when they get particularly dirty.
Training & Exercise Needs: They're full of energy and stamina, so they need plenty of exercise to stay happy and healthy. These lively pups love going on long walks, enjoying a good run, and playing in a safe, open space. Keeping them active is key to their well-being—it not only keeps them physically fit but also mentally stimulated, which helps prevent boredom and keeps any behavioral problems at bay.
Possible Health Issues: hip dysplasia, ear infections, and progressive retinal atrophy (PRA).

American Eskimo Dog
Other Names: Eskie
Color variations: white or white with biscuit cream
Average Lifespan: 12 to 15 years
Origins: Germany - early 20th century - bred to be a companion dog
Body Size: They come in 3 sizes:
Toy: 9-12 in, 6-10 lbs. Miniature: 12-15 in, 10-20 lbs.
Standard: 15-19 in, 25-35 lbs.
Personality/Disposition/Compatibility: They are not only smart but also incredibly friendly, thriving in the company of people. They're a great fit for families, eagerly picking up new tricks and shining in obedience and agility. While they're protective of their loved ones, they might be a tad shy around new faces initially. With early socialization, they warm up quickly to kids and other pets, making them a delightful addition to any home.
Grooming Needs: They're absolutely gorgeous with their thick double coats, but they do need a bit of attention to keep them looking their best. To keep their fur free from mats and tangles, you'll want to brush them a few times a week. Regular baths are essential to maintain their coat's cleanliness and health. Plus, don't overlook the little things—keeping their nails, ears, and teeth in check is crucial for their overall well-being. These small grooming habits will help keep your Eskie happy and healthy!
Training & Exercise Needs: They're lively and playful, and they need a good amount of exercise to keep them happy. They thrive on daily walks, interactive play sessions, and some mental challenges. If you have a fenced yard or a safe outdoor area, they'll love the chance to run around and explore. Regular activity not only keeps them entertained but also contributes to their overall health and happiness.
Possible Health Issues: hip dysplasia, progressive retinal atrophy, cataracts, and allergies.

American Foxhound
Other Names: None
Color variations: black, white, tan, and various combinations of these colors.
Average Lifespan: 11 to 13 years
Origins: United States - 1700s - bred primarily for the purpose of hunting foxes.
Body Size: Males: 22-25 in, 65-70 lbs. Females: 21-24 in, 60-65 lbs.
Personality/Disposition/Compatibility: They're a sweet and friendly breed with a dash of independence and a sharp hunting instinct. They thrive on family time and get along great with kids and other pets. Just keep in mind that their playful side might have them chasing after smaller animals.
Grooming Needs: They are pretty low-maintenance when it comes to grooming. Their short, dense coat just needs a quick brush now and then to stay clean and free of loose hair. Unless they get especially muddy, you won't need to bathe them too often. Regular ear and nail checks will keep them feeling their best and help ensure they stay healthy and comfortable.
Training & Exercise Needs: They're lively and full of energy, so they need plenty of exercise to stay content and in top shape. They love long walks, spirited playtime, and having space to run around safely. Getting regular exercise not only taps into their natural hunting instincts but also keeps them both physically and mentally engaged.
Possible Health Issues: hip dysplasia, ear infections, and thrombocytopathy.

American Hairless Terrier
Other Names: AHT
Color variations: black, blue, brown, red, and white, often with different combinations of markings and patterns.
Average Lifespan: 14 to 16 years
Origins: United States - 1970 - bred from the Rat Terrier to create a hairless breed suitable for allergy sufferers and as a companion.
Body Size: Males: 12-16 in, 12-16 lbs. Females: 12-16 in, 12-16 lbs.
Personality/Disposition/Compatibility: These dogs are pure sunshine in your life! Their endless energy and loving nature will win you over almost instantly. They're quick learners, so training them is more of an enjoyable journey than a chore. They love being social, forming close bonds with their families, and are always up for a game or a snuggle. With their friendly and warm demeanor, they also have a natural talent for keeping an eye on things, making them excellent watchdogs. They usually get along well with kids and, with some early socialization, can be great companions for other pets too.
Grooming Needs: These dogs are a breeze when it comes to grooming since they don't have a coat. However, keeping their skin in top shape is still important. Regular baths help keep their skin clean and hydrated, and don't forget to slather on some sunscreen to shield their sensitive skin from sunburn. Regular ear checks and cleanings are also a good idea to keep them feeling their best.
Training & Exercise Needs: They're a lively and spirited breed that thrives on activity. To keep this energetic pup healthy and content, daily walks and playtime are a must. They love to stay engaged with interactive games and activities that test their agility and smarts. Regular exercise not only keeps them from getting bored but also supports their overall well-being.
Possible Health Issues: skin problems, allergies, and dental issues.

American Leopard Hound

Other Names: Leopard Cur
Color variations: yellow, black, brindle, blue, and red, often with leopard-like spots.
Average Lifespan: 12 to 15 years
Origins: United States - 18th century - bred for hunting and herding.
Body Size: Males: 22-27 in, 45-70 lbs. Females: 20-25 in, 35-60 lbs.
Personality/Disposition/Compatibility: This breed is a delightful mix of smarts and loyalty, making training a breeze. Always alert and ready to work, they excel as working dogs. Friendly and eager to please, they also have an independent streak and can be a bit reserved around strangers. They're fantastic with children and, with early socialization, get along well with other animals.
Grooming Needs: They're pretty low-maintenance when it comes to grooming, thanks to its short, dense coat. A regular brushing session will keep their fur looking great by removing loose hair and dirt. They don't need too many baths—just an occasional one will do. Plus, keeping an eye on their ears and trimming their nails will help them stay in tip-top shape.
Training & Exercise Needs: They're a bundle of energy that truly comes alive with regular exercise. To keep them happy and healthy, they need lots of physical activity—think long walks, brisk runs, or playful romps in the yard. They also love activities that stimulate both their mind and body, like agility training or scent games. Without enough exercise, they might get bored and a bit restless, so keeping them active is key to their well-being.**Possible Health Issues:** hip dysplasia, ear infections, and certain eye conditions.

American Pitbull Terrier

Other Names: Pit Bull, Pitty, and APBT
Color variations: red, blue, brown, grey, black, white, and brindle.
Average Lifespan: 12 to 14 years
Origins: United States - early 19th century - bred for bull-baiting and later for farm work and companionship.
Body Size: Males: 18-21 in. 35-60 lbs. Females: 17-20 in. 30-50 lbs.
Personality/Disposition/Compatibility: These dogs are the epitome of loyalty and love, always eager to be the best companion they can be. They find joy in making their families happy and are great with kids. While they're generally friendly, a little socialization might help them feel more at ease with other animals.
Grooming Needs: They're pretty low-maintenance when it comes to grooming, thanks to their short, smooth coats. A quick brush now and then keeps their skin healthy and reduces shedding. They don't need frequent baths—just an occasional wash to keep them smelling fresh. Don't forget about the little things, like regular dental care, nail trimming, and ear cleaning, to keep them in tip-top shape.
Training & Exercise Needs: They're pretty easy to care for when it comes to grooming. Their short, dense coat doesn't need much fuss—just a regular brush to keep things tidy and remove any loose hair or dirt. They don't need frequent baths; an occasional wash will do the trick. A quick check of their ears and a trim of their nails now and then will keep them looking and feeling great.
Possible Health Issues: hip dysplasia, allergies, hypothyroidism, heart disease, and skin conditions.

American Staffordshire Terrier

Other Names: AmStaff or Staffy.
Color variations: blue, brindle, fawn, red, and black, often with white markings.
Average Lifespan: 12 to 16 years
Origins: United States - early 19th century - bred for farm work, guarding, and companionship.
Body Size: Males: 18-19 in, 55-70 lbs. Females: 17-18 in, 40-55 lbs.
Personality/Disposition/Compatibility: These dogs are the perfect companions – affectionate, loyal, and always friendly. They're confident and smart, and they absolutely love spending time with their humans. While they're protective of their families, they remain gentle and are typically great with kids. If they're socialized early, they can even become buddies with other pets. Just a heads-up, though: they might be a bit territorial when meeting new dogs.
Grooming Needs: They are pretty low-maintenance when it comes to grooming thanks to its short, smooth coat. A regular brushing session will help manage shedding and keep their fur looking shiny and healthy. They only need the occasional bath to stay fresh, and it's also a good idea to check their ears for infections and trim their nails regularly to keep them in tip-top shape.
Training & Exercise Needs: The American Staffordshire Terrier is a high-energy breed that thrives on regular exercise. Daily walks, playtime, and engaging activities like agility or obedience training are essential to keep them happy and healthy. Without enough physical and mental stimulation, they can become bored and potentially destructive. Consistent exercise helps maintain their muscular build and ensures they remain well-balanced and content.
Possible Health Issues: hip dysplasia, skin allergies, heart disease, and certain types of cancer.

American Water Spaniel

Other Names: AWS
Color variations: liver, brown, or chocolate colors
Average Lifespan: 10 to 14 years
Origins: United States - mid-1800s - bred for hunting and retrieving in water and marshland environments.
Body Size: Males: 15-18 in, 30-45 lbs. Females: 15-18 in, 25-40 lbs.
Personality/Disposition/Compatibility: These dogs are full of life, incredibly smart, and always ready to make you happy. They easily adjust to different activities and environments, making them great companions no matter your lifestyle. With their friendly and affectionate nature, they quickly become beloved members of the family. While they might be a bit shy around new people, they're almost never aggressive. They're great with kids and can get along well with other pets, especially if they're socialized from a young age.
Grooming Needs: This breed is full of life and energy, always ready for a good time. They love to stay active, so they need at least an hour of exercise each day. Whether it's jogging, hiking, or a good game of fetch, they're up for it. Their love for water means swimming is also a fantastic option for them. Keeping them active is key to their happiness and health—it keeps both their minds and bodies in top shape.
Training & Exercise Needs: They're a lively and spirited breed that loves to stay on the move. They're at their happiest with plenty of exercise, so make sure to include daily walks, playtime, and chances to swim in their routine. They thrive on activities that test their agility and stamina, so mixing things up keeps them engaged and content. Without enough to do, they might get bored and a bit fidgety,!
Possible Health Issues: hip dysplasia, progressive retinal atrophy, and ear infections.

Anatolian Shepherd Dog
Other Names: Anatolian Karabash and Kangal.
Color variations: white, brindle, pinto, and fawn, often with a black mask
Average Lifespan: 11 to 13 years
Origins: Turkey - ancient times - bred primarily for guarding livestock.
Body Size: Males: 29-32 in, 110-150 lbs. Females: 27-31 in, 80-120 lbs.
Personality/Disposition/Compatibility: These dogs are the whole package: loyal, smart, and fiercely independent with a natural instinct to protect their loved ones. They might seem a bit reserved or calm around new faces, but with their family, they're all about affection and gentleness. Great with kids and, if introduced early on, they can happily coexist with other pets too.
Grooming Needs: Grooming them is pretty straightforward. Their thick, double coat is built to handle all sorts of weather, so it doesn't need a lot of fuss. A regular brushing session will help control shedding and keep their fur tangle-free. An occasional bath will keep them fresh, and don't forget to check their ears and trim their nails regularly to keep them in tip-top shape.
Training & Exercise Needs: This is a breed that loves to stay active and engaged. They need lots of exercise to keep them healthy and content, so daily walks or runs are a must. They particularly enjoy being in a securely fenced area where they can wander and explore freely. Their natural guarding instincts mean they also thrive on mental challenges, so incorporating obedience training or interactive play into their routine is a great idea. Keeping them physically and mentally stimulated helps prevent boredom and supports a well-rounded, happy lifestyle.
Possible Health Issues: hip dysplasia, elbow dysplasia, hypothyroidism, and bloat

Appenzeller Sennenhund
Other Names: Appenzell Cattle Dog
Color variations: black or brown with white and rust markings
Average Lifespan: 12 to 14 years
Origins: Switzerland - 19th century - bred for herding and guarding livestock.
Body Size: Males: 20-23 in, 55-70 lbs. Females: 19-22 in, 50-65 lbs.
Personality/Disposition/Compatibility: These dogs are a lively bunch, brimming with intelligence and confidence. They're always on the lookout, fiercely loyal, and naturally protective, making them fantastic watchdogs. When socialized well, they typically get along great with kids and other pets.
Grooming Needs: They have a coat that's both beautiful and a bit of work. To keep it looking its best, you'll want to brush it regularly to handle shedding and avoid any tangles. A bath now and then will keep them fresh, and don't forget to check their ears and trim their nails to keep them comfy and happy.
Training & Exercise Needs: They are a lively and energetic breed that really loves to stay active. They need at least an hour of vigorous exercise every day—whether it's jogging, hiking, or playing interactive games. Without enough physical activity, they might get bored and develop some behavioral problems. So, giving them plenty of chances to burn off their energy keeps them happy, healthy, and well-balanced.
Possible Health Issues: hip dysplasia, elbow dysplasia, and certain eye conditions like cataracts.

Australian Cattle Dog

Other Names: Blue Heeler or Queensland Heeler
Color variations: blue or red speckle, with or without black, blue, or tan markings.
Average Lifespan: 12 to 16 years
Origins: Australia - early 19th century - bred to herd cattle over long distances and rough terrain.
Body Size: Males: 18-20 in, 35-50 lbs. Females: 17-19 in, 30-45 lbs.
Personality/Disposition/Compatibility: They are intelligent, alert, and courageous, known for their loyalty and protective nature. Energetic and hardworking, they have a strong work ethic and are eager to please despite their independence. They get along well with children and other pets, especially if raised together, but may try to herd them due to their instincts.
Grooming Needs: They're pretty low-maintenance when it comes to grooming, thanks to their short, dense coat. A weekly brushing is usually all it takes to keep their fur looking great and manage shedding. They don't need baths very often—just when they get especially muddy or start to smell. Regular nail trimming and occasional ear checks will also keep them in top shape.
Training & Exercise Needs: They are an energetic bundle that needs plenty of exercise to stay happy and healthy. They absolutely love spending 1 to 2 hours a day in action—whether it's running, tackling agility courses, or chasing a ball. If they don't get enough activity, they can get a bit restless and might even develop some behavioral quirks. To keep them content and well-behaved, regular exercise is a must!
Possible Health Issues: hip dysplasia, progressive retinal atrophy, and deafness.

Australian Kelpie

Other Names: Australian Sheepdog, Barb, Working Kelpie
Color variations: black, black and tan, red, red and tan, chocolate, fawn, and blue.
Average Lifespan: 10 to 14 years
Origins: Australia - 19th century - bred to work in the harsh environment and vast landscapes of Australian farms, primarily for herding.
Body Size: Males: 18-20 in, 31-45 lbs. Females: 17-19 in, 26-35 lbs..
Personality/Disposition/Compatibility: These dogs are smart, energetic, and hardworking. Their dedication and loyalty make them excellent workers. They are eager to please, which makes them easy to train. However, they can be shy around strangers and need proper socialization. They usually get along well with children and other animals, especially if they are raised together. Their herding instincts might lead them to try and herd smaller animals or children, so supervision and training are important.
Grooming Needs: They're pretty low-maintenance when it comes to grooming, thanks to their short, dense coats. A weekly brush is usually all they need to keep their fur looking great and to reduce shedding. They don't require frequent baths—just the occasional one to keep them fresh. Don't forget to check their ears and trim their nails regularly; it helps keep them healthy and comfortable.
Training & Exercise Needs: They are an energetic breed that really needs plenty of exercise to stay happy. Aim for at least two hours of vigorous activity each day—whether that's running, herding, or playing some exciting games. Without enough physical and mental stimulation, they can get restless and may start acting out. Keeping your Kelpie active not only keeps them content but also helps them be their best-behaved selves!
Possible Health Issues: hip dysplasia, progressive retinal atrophy (PRA), and cryptorchidism

Australian Shepherd
Other Names: Aussie
Color variations: blue merle, red merle, and tri-color
Average Lifespan: 12 to 15 years
Origins: United States - 19th century - was created to work as a versatile stock dog, particularly for herding sheep.
Body Size: Males: 20-23 in, 50-65 lbs. Females: 18-21 in, 40-55 lbs.
Personality/Disposition/Compatibility: They're smart, energetic, and eager to please. They are loyal and affectionate with their families, and are known for being good-natured, alert, and adaptable. With a strong work ethic, they excel in various tasks. They are generally good with children and can get along well with other animals if socialized.
Grooming Needs: They have quite the glamorous coat, which means they need a bit more grooming love. To keep their thick, double coat looking its best, aim to brush them 2-3 times a week. This helps prevent pesky matting and keeps shedding under control. A bath every now and then will keep them fresh, too! Don't forget to check their ears and trim their nails regularly.
Training & Exercise Needs: They're lively and energetic, so they need at least an hour of vigorous exercise each day—think running, hiking, or playing fetch. Mental stimulation is just as crucial, so agility training or interactive games are ideal. Regular exercise helps keep them happy and prevents behavioral problems. With the right mix of physical and mental activity, your Aussie will be a happy and well-behaved companion!
Possible Health Issues: hip dysplasia, elbow dysplasia, epilepsy, cataracts, and Collie eye anomaly.

Australian Stumpy Tail Cattle Dog
Other Names: Stumpy Tail Cattle Dog or Stumpy.
Color variations: blue or red speckled with distinct mottling and no solid patches or markings.
Average Lifespan: 12 to 15 years
Origins: Australia - early 19th century - for the purpose of herding cattle, using a mix of the Australian Cattle Dog and native Australian Dingoes to create a resilient and efficient working dog.
Body Size: Males: 18-20 in, 35-50 lbs. Females: 17-19 in, 32-45 lbs.
Personality/Disposition/Compatibility: These dogs are smart, independent, and energetic. They're loyal and confident, though they may be reserved around strangers. They're loving and protective with their family and usually good with kids if socialized early. They get along with other dogs but might chase smaller pets due to their herding instincts.
Grooming Needs: They're pretty low-maintenance when it comes to grooming. Their short, dense coat doesn't need much fuss—just a weekly brush to handle shedding and keep their fur looking great. They'll also benefit from an occasional bath and regular checks on their ears and nails to keep everything clean and healthy.
Training & Exercise Needs: They're active and energetic by nature, so they need a lot of exercise to keep them healthy and content. They love activities like running, agility drills, and playtime that engages their minds and bodies. Daily exercise is a must to keep them from getting bored and to ensure they stay in top shape. Without enough physical activity, they can become restless and might even start acting out.
Possible Health Issues: deafness, progressive retinal atrophy (PRA), hip dysplasia, and spinal problems.

Australian Terrier

Other Names: Aussie Terrier or Aussie
Color variations: blue and tan, solid sandy, or solid red.
Average Lifespan: 11 to 15 years
Origins: Australia - early 19th century - bred for hunting and as a companion.
Body Size: Males: 10-11 in, 14-16 lbs. Females: 9-10 in, 12-14 lbs.
Personality/Disposition/Compatibility: These dogs are a bundle of energy and smarts. They thrive on being involved in family activities and have a natural curiosity about everything around them. Confident and spirited, they have a touch of independence that makes them unique. They generally do well with kids and, with the right socialization, can live harmoniously with other pets too.
Grooming Needs: Australian Terriers have a wiry, weather-resistant coat that needs regular care. Brush them several times a week to prevent tangles and keep their coat smooth. They also benefit from occasional baths and trims to manage coat length and prevent mats. Regular ear checks and nail trims are important too, keeping them happy and healthy.
Training & Exercise Needs: Australian Terriers are energetic dogs that need regular exercise to stay happy and healthy. They enjoy brisk walks, playing in the yard, and mentally stimulating games. Daily activity helps prevent boredom and keeps them fit and content.
Possible Health Issues: diabetes, allergies, patellar luxation, and Legg-Calvé-Perthes disease.

Azawakh

Other Names: Tuareg Sloughi or Idi
Color variations: sand, fawn, red, brindle, blue, black, brown, and particolored.
Average Lifespan: 12 to 15 years
Origins: Mali - early 20th century - bred by the Tuareg nomads for hunting and as a guard dog.
Body Size: Males: 25-29 in, 44-55 lbs. Females: 23-27 in, 33-44 lbs.
Personality/Disposition/Compatibility: These dogs are incredibly loving and loyal to their families, though they might be a bit reserved with newcomers. They're gentle and calm by nature, yet they have a strong sense of independence and a protective streak. Generally, they get along well with kids and other dogs, especially if they've grown up together. However, their strong prey drive could make them a less ideal choice for homes with small pets.
Grooming Needs: Azawakhs are easy to groom with their short, smooth coat. Regular brushing keeps their skin healthy and removes loose hair. They don't need frequent baths—just enough to maintain their natural oils. Also, make sure to check their ears and teeth regularly for overall health.
Training & Exercise Needs: They're energetic dogs that require regular exercise to stay healthy and happy. Daily walks or playtime in a secure yard are ideal for them to burn off energy. They also enjoy mental challenges, so incorporating interactive games and training can keep them engaged. Balancing physical activity with mental stimulation is key to keeping them content.
Possible Health Issues: They're generally a healthy breed but can be prone to certain health issues such as hip dysplasia, autoimmune diseases, and heart conditions.

Barbado da Terceira

Other Names: Terceira Cattle Dog
Color variations: black, fawn, and yellow, often with white markings
Average Lifespan: 12 to 15 years
Origins: Terceira, Portugal - early 20th century - bred for herding.
Body Size: Males: 19-22 in, 55-66 lbs. Females: 18-21 in, 44-55 lbs.
Personality/Disposition/Compatibility: This breed is smart, loyal, and affectionate. Training is easy because they're eager to please. They're energetic and hardworking, with natural herding and guarding instincts that make them good watchdogs. They usually get along well with kids and other pets if introduced early, though they might try to herd smaller animals and children.
Grooming Needs: They have a thick double coat that needs regular care. Weekly brushing helps prevent tangles and keeps their fur looking great. They don't need frequent baths—every few months or after a particularly messy outing is usually enough. Regular ear checks and nail trims are also important for their overall health.
Training & Exercise Needs: They're full of energy and needs regular exercise to stay healthy and happy. Daily long walks, playtime, and mental challenges are essential. They thrive with interactive activities that engage both their body and mind, so keeping them active and stimulated is crucial for their well-being.
Possible Health Issues: hip dysplasia, progressive retinal atrophy (PRA), and other genetic conditions common to herding breeds.

Barbet

Other Names: French Water Dog
Color variations: black, brown, fawn, gray, and pied (white with patches of another color).
Average Lifespan: 12 to 14 years
Origins: France - 16th century - bred primarily for retrieving waterfowl.
Body Size: Males: 21-24.5 in, 40-60 lbs. Females: 19-22.5 in, 35-50 lbs.
Personality/Disposition/Compatibility: These dogs are cheerful, intelligent, and eager to please. They're quick learners and enjoy mastering new tricks. Friendly and affectionate, they make excellent companions. Their adaptable nature and calm temperament make them suitable for various living situations. They're good with kids and get along well with other pets, including dogs and cats, making them ideal for family life.
Grooming Needs: They're known for their unique curly coats, which need a bit of extra care to stay in top shape. To keep their fur from turning into a tangled mess, you'll want to brush them several times a week. Every 6-8 weeks, a good grooming session will help trim their coat and keep it looking neat. Regular baths will keep their coat clean and free of debris. Don't forget to also clean their ears and trim their nails to keep them happy and healthy.
Training & Exercise Needs: They're pretty easygoing when it comes to exercise but still need a good dose of activity to stay their happy, healthy selves. A daily walk paired with some playtime, like a game of fetch, does wonders for keeping them engaged and stimulated. They love interactive games and are up for a bit more if they're in good shape. Keeping them active not only keeps boredom at bay but also ensures they stay in tip-top condition.
Possible Health Issues: hip dysplasia, ear infections, and progressive retinal atrophy (PRA)

Basenji
Other Names: African Barkless Dog
Color variations: red, black, tricolor (black and tan with white), and brindle, all with white markings on the feet, chest, and tail tip.
Average Lifespan: 12 to 16 years
Origins: Central Africa - 19th century - bred to hunt and control village rodent populations.
Body Size: Males: 17 in, 24 lbs. Females: 16 in, 22 lbs.
Personality/Disposition/Compatibility: They're independent, intelligent, curious, playful and can be mischievous. While they may be reserved around strangers, they form strong bonds with their families and often have a cat-like demeanor. With proper socialization, they can get along well with children and other dogs. However, their strong prey drive might make them unsuitable for homes with smaller pets.
Grooming Needs: Their short coat requires occasional brushing to remove loose hair, and they are known for their fastidious grooming habits.
Training & Exercise Needs: need moderate exercise, including daily walks and playtime. They enjoy activities that challenge them mentally and physically, such as agility training and puzzle toys.
Possible Health Issues: Fanconi syndrome, hip dysplasia, progressive retinal atrophy (PRA), and hypothyroidism

Basset Bleu de Gascogne (Grand)
Other Names: GBBDG
Color variations: white with striking black patches and a sprinkle of ticking, creating a unique mottled or roan effect. The ticking can range from sparse to more dense, but the overall look often has a beautiful blue-gray hue thanks to the mix of black and white.
Average Lifespan: 12 to 14 years
Origins: France - 19th century - bred for tracking and hunting small game such as rabbits and hares.
Body Size: Males: 15.5-17 in. 40-44 lbs Females: 14-15.5 in. 36-40 lbs.
Personality/Disposition/Compatibility: a charming, laid-back companion with a personality that's as endearing as it is gentle. Known for its friendly and affectionate nature, this breed thrives on human interaction and loves being part of the family. It has a calm demeanor that makes it an excellent choice for a relaxed home environment. While it's not overly energetic, it enjoys a good romp and is always up for a leisurely stroll. They get along well with children and other pets, making it a great fit for families and households with multiple animals. Its easygoing temperament means it adapts well to different living situations, from city apartments to country homes, as long as it gets its fair share of attention and affection.
Grooming Needs: Regular brushing is necessary to keep its short coat clean and free of loose hair. Occasional baths, ear cleaning, and nail trimming are also important to maintain overall health and hygiene.
Training & Exercise Needs: an active breed that requires regular exercise to stay healthy and happy. Daily walks, playtime in a secure area, and activities like tracking or scent work suit this breed well. They enjoy using their noses and have a strong hunting instinct.
Possible Health Issues: hip dysplasia, ear infections, and bloat (gastric torsion)

Basset Bleu de Gascogne (Petit)
Other Names: Petit Bleu
Color variations: typically has a blue mottled coat with black patches
Average Lifespan: 12 to 14 years
Origins: France - 16th century - bred in the for hunting small game, particularly rabbits.
Body Size: Males & Females: 13-15 in. 25-40 lbs.
Personality/Disposition/Compatibility: a delightful blend of charm and character. Known for its affectionate nature, this breed is a true people-pleaser, making it a fantastic companion for families and individuals alike. Its friendly disposition means it gets along well with children and other pets, though its hunting instincts might occasionally make it a bit stubborn. Despite its laid-back appearance, this breed is quite alert and can be surprisingly lively. It's also known for its gentle and loving demeanor, making it an excellent choice for a loyal and loving family pet. With a bit of patience and understanding, they will reward you with a faithful and affectionate friendship.
Grooming Needs: Brush their short, dense coat once a week to control shedding and keep their skin healthy. They don't need frequent baths—just as needed to stay clean. Regularly check and clean their ears to prevent infections, as their floppy ears can trap moisture.
Training & Exercise Needs: has moderate exercise needs and enjoys activities such as long walks, playtime in a secure yard, and scent-tracking games, which engage their natural hunting instincts.
Possible Health Issues: hip dysplasia, ear infections, and occasionally, intervertebral disc disease

Basset Fauve de Bretagne
Other Names: Fawn Brittany Basset
Color variations: fawn, ranging from golden-wheaten to red-wheaten
Average Lifespan: 12 to 14 years
Origins: France - 16th century - bred for hunting small game due to its excellent scent-tracking abilities and stamina.
Body Size: Males: 12.5-15.5 in, 36-40 lbs.
Females: 12.5-15.5 in, 32-36 lbs.
Personality/Disposition/Compatibility: a delightful and spirited companion with a personality that's both charming and endearing. This breed is known for its friendly and playful nature, making them a joy to have around. They're affectionate and eager to please, often forming strong bonds with their families. Their curious and intelligent demeanor makes them great problem-solvers, but it also means they need mental stimulation to stay happy. They're generally good with children and can get along well with other pets, especially if they've been socialized from a young age. With their lively and adventurous spirit, they're always up for a game or a romp in the yard, but they also know how to chill out and enjoy some downtime with their loved ones.
Grooming Needs: They require regular brushing to maintain its rough coat and minimize shedding. Occasional baths, ear cleaning, and nail trimming are also part of their grooming routine.
Training & Exercise Needs: They have moderate exercise needs and enjoys daily walks, playtime, and mental stimulation. They are well-suited for activities like tracking, scent work, and agility, which cater to their natural hunting instincts.
Possible Health Issues: hip dysplasia, ear infections, and certain eye conditions.

K9 Chatter

Basset Griffon Vendeen (Grand)

Other Names: GBGV
Color variations: white and lemon, white and orange, white and black, white and sable, and tricolor.
Average Lifespan: 12 to 14 years
Origins: France - late 19th century - bred for hunting small game, particularly rabbits and hare, due to its keen scenting ability and endurance.
Body Size: Males 15.5-18 in. 40-45 lbs. Females: 15-17 in. 35-40 lbs.
Personality/Disposition/Compatibility: a breed known for its friendly and affectionate nature. They're playful and energetic, making them a lively companion for family activities. Despite their spirited personality, they're also quite adaptable and enjoy spending time with both people and other animals. They tend to get along well with children and can fit comfortably in various living situations. Their independent streak means they'll sometimes do their own thing, but they're always ready to join in on family fun. Overall, they're a well-rounded breed that brings warmth and enthusiasm to any home.
Grooming Needs: requires regular grooming to maintain its coat. Brushing a few times a week is necessary to prevent matting and tangling. Occasional trimming and bathing are also recommended to keep the coat clean and healthy
Training & Exercise Needs: an active and energetic breed that requires plenty of exercise. Daily walks, playtime in a secure yard, and activities like tracking and scent work are ideal to keep this breed physically and mentally stimulated.
Possible Health Issues: hip dysplasia, ear infections, and eye problems such as glaucoma

Basset Griffon Vendeen (Petit)

Other Names: PBGV
Color variations: white with any combination of lemon, orange, black, sable, tricolor, or grizzle markings.
Average Lifespan: 12 to 14 years
Origins: France - 16th century - bred to hunt small game, particularly rabbits, in the rugged terrain of the Vendee region.
Body Size: Males & Females: 13-15 in. 25-40 lbs.
Personality/Disposition/Compatibility: a lively and affectionate breed with a friendly disposition. They're playful and enjoy active playtime, but they also appreciate relaxing with their family. This breed gets along well with other dogs and pets, making them a good fit for multi-pet households. They're generally great with children, though they do best with gentle handling. Overall, their energetic and loving nature makes them a charming companion.
Grooming Needs: They need regular brushing to prevent matting and occasional hand-stripping to maintain the coat's texture. Their ears should be checked regularly to prevent infections.
Training & Exercise Needs: They enjoy activities such as walking, hiking, and playing games that allow them to use their keen sense of smell, like scent work or tracking.
Possible Health Issues: hip dysplasia, patellar luxation, epilepsy, and hypothyroidism

Basset Hound

Other Names: "Hush Puppy" due to its association with the popular shoe brand.
Color variations: black, white, tan, red, brown, lemon, and combinations of these colors in bicolor or tricolor patterns.
Average Lifespan: 10 to 12 years
Origins: France - 16th century - bred for hunting small game, particularly rabbits.
Body Size: Males: 12-15 in, 50-65 lbs. Females: 11-14 in, 45-60 lbs.
Personality/Disposition/Compatibility: Think of them as the canine version of a charming couch potato with an adventurous spirit. With their easygoing and friendly nature, they're perfect companions for both families and individuals. They're affectionate and loving, always ready for a cuddle. Their curiosity and determination are especially noticeable when they pick up an intriguing scent—this natural tracking talent can make them a bit stubborn at times, especially on walks. They usually get along wonderfully with kids and other pets, thanks to their gentle and patient demeanor. Of course, their occasional stubbornness might lead to some funny moments along the way.
Grooming Needs: require regular grooming to maintain their coat and prevent skin issues. Their ears need frequent cleaning to avoid infections, and their nails should be trimmed regularly. They also shed moderately, so brushing a few times a week is beneficial.
Training & Exercise Needs: Daily walks and playtime are essential, but they do not require intense physical activity. They enjoy activities that engage their sense of smell, such as scent tracking games.
Possible Health Issues: hip dysplasia, elbow dysplasia, bloat (gastric torsion), ear infections, and intervertebral disc disease due to their long back and short legs

Bavarian Mountain Scent Hound

Other Names: Bayerischer Gebirgsschweißhund
Color variations: various shades of red, from deep reddish-brown to a lighter deer-red, with possible small patches of white on the chest and toes.
Average Lifespan: 10 to 14 years.
Origins: Germany - 19th century - bred for its exceptional ability to track wounded game in mountainous regions.
Body Size: Males: 18.5-20.5 in, 44-66 lbs. Females: 17-19 in, 37-55 lbs.
Personality/Disposition/Compatibility: a delightful mix of smarts and enthusiasm. Known for their gentle and steady nature, they're dependable whether you're out in the field or relaxing at home. They're incredibly loyal and protective, yet their calm and friendly demeanor makes them a hit with families and individuals alike. They're not the type to jump at every little thing; instead, they handle new situations with a thoughtful approach. This laid-back but engaging personality makes them perfect for those who value a dog that's both composed and personable. They generally get along well with other dogs and enjoy socializing. While their hunting background means they might be tempted to chase smaller animals, with the right training and socialization, they can smoothly adapt to life with other pets.v
Grooming Needs: Regular brushing to remove dead hair and occasional baths to keep the coat clean are sufficient.
Training & Exercise Needs: They require regular exercise to stay healthy and happy. They thrive on activities that engage their tracking and scenting abilities, such as long walks, hikes, and scent work.
Possible Health Issues: hip dysplasia, ear infections, and certain skin conditions

K9 Chatter

Beagle
Other Names: None
Color variations: tri-color (black, white, and tan), red and white, lemon (light tan and white), and orange and white.
Average Lifespan: 12 to 15 years
Origins: England - the 1500s - bred primarily for hunting hare.
Body Size: Males: 14-16 in, 22-24 lbs. Females: 13-15 in, 20-22 lbs.
Personality/Disposition/Compatibility: The ultimate bundle of joy, guaranteed to light up any space with their friendly and inquisitive personalities. They're always eager to meet new people and make friends, and their affectionate nature means they'll often trail behind you with a wagging tail. Beagles are fantastic with kids and thrive in lively, social environments. But don't be fooled by their sweet demeanor—these dogs have a cheeky side too. Their impressive sense of smell can lead to some entertaining adventures around the house. They may have a bit of an independent streak and can be stubborn at times, but their lovable nature usually wins out. They get along well with other pets, including cats, especially if they've been socialized early on. Their playful energy makes them perfect for active families or anyone ready to give them plenty of exercise and mental stimulation.
Grooming Needs: They have a short coat that is easy to groom. Regular brushing to remove loose hair and occasional baths are usually sufficient to keep their coat healthy.
Training & Exercise Needs: Daily walks and play sessions are important, and they enjoy activities such as running, hiking, and scent-tracking games.
Possible Health Issues: including hip dysplasia, epilepsy, hypothyroidism, glaucoma and progressive retinal atrophy (PRA)

Bearded Collie
Other Names: Beardie
Color variations: black, blue, brown, and fawn. These colors may also appear in various shades, often with white markings.
Average Lifespan: 12 to 14 years
Origins: Scotland - early 16th century - bred primarily for herding sheep and cattle in the rugged Scottish Highlands.
Body Size: Males: 21-22 in, 45-55 lbs. Females: 20-21 in, 40-50 lbs.
Personality/Disposition/Compatibility: a delightful mix of lively energy and sweet affection. With their playful antics and wagging tails, they're like a burst of joy on four legs. Their enthusiasm for life is truly contagious, whether they're racing through a field or playing fetch in the backyard. They're quick learners and can pick up tricks easily, but their free-spirited nature means they need a bit of patience and positive reinforcement during training. They thrive on companionship and are known for being affectionate, making them wonderful family pets. They get along well with children and other animals, blending playfulness with gentleness. They adapt well to various living situations as long as they get plenty of exercise and mental stimulation. Their friendly attitude makes them great socializers, but they also value a strong bond with their family.
Grooming Needs: require regular grooming to maintain their coat. This includes brushing several times a week to prevent matting and occasional bathing to keep them clean.
Training & Exercise Needs: They have high energy levels and need regular exercise. They enjoy activities such as running, hiking, and playing fetch, and they excel in agility training and other dog sports.
Possible Health Issues: hip dysplasia, hypothyroidism, and allergies

Beauceron
Other Names: Berger de Beauce, Bas Rouge
Color variations: Black and tan, harlequin
Average Lifespan: 10-12 years
Origins: France - late 16th century - bred primarily for herding sheep and cattle.
Body Size: Males: 25.5-27.5 in, 70-110 lbs. Females: 24-26.5 in, 65-85 lbs.
Personality/Disposition/Compatibility: They have a personality that's both captivating and complex. They're known for their impressive loyalty and smarts, striking a perfect balance between being hardworking and affectionate. They're natural protectors, always ready to guard their family, but their loyalty goes far beyond just keeping watch. They do best in lively environments where they can stay mentally and physically active. Ideal for active families or individuals who can match their energetic spirit, these dogs also get along well with kids, showing a patience that makes them great family companions.
Grooming Needs: They require regular brushing to remove dead hair and maintain a healthy shine. They shed moderately throughout the year and more heavily during shedding seasons.
Training & Exercise Needs: Highly trainable and eager for mental challenges, they excel in dog sports and various activities. Daily walks, runs, and play sessions are essential to meet their exercise needs.
Possible Health Issues: hip dysplasia, bloat (gastric torsion), and progressive retinal atrophy (PRA)

Bedlington Terrier
Other Names: Rothbury Terrier
Color variations: blue, liver, and sandy colors, with possible combinations of these shades with tan markings.
Average Lifespan: 12 to 14 years
Origins: England - early 19th century - bred for hunting vermin and participating in dog racing.
Body Size: Males: 16-17.5 in, 17-23 lbs. Females: 15-16.5 in, 17-23 lbs.
Personality/Disposition/Compatibility: Naturally affectionate and quickly become cherished members of the family. They thrive on human interaction and generally get along well with children, making them a great choice for families. Their playful and energetic spirit shines through, whether they're chasing a ball or enjoying a run in the park. Yet, they're just as content to wind down and relax with their loved ones. While they might show a bit of stubbornness now and then, their smarts and desire to please make training relatively easy. They also tend to get along with other dogs and pets thanks to their friendly and adaptable nature. They're not inclined to start trouble, but they do enjoy a good play session with their furry friends.
Grooming Needs: requires regular grooming, including brushing a few times a week and professional clipping every few months to maintain their unique coat texture and appearance.
Training & Exercise Needs: need moderate exercise, such as daily walks and playtime in a secure area. They enjoy activities like agility training, fetch, and other games that challenge their agility and intelligence.
Possible Health Issues: copper toxicosis, retinal dysplasia, and renal cortical hypoplasia

Belgian Laekenois
Other Names: Laeken
Color variations: fawn, red, and gray, often with a mix of black shading.
Average Lifespan: 10 to 12 years
Origins: Belgium - 1800s - bred for herding and guarding livestock, particularly at the Royal Castle of Laeken.
Body Size: Males: 24-26 in, 55-65 lbs. Females: 22-24 in, 45-55 lbs.
Personality/Disposition/Compatibility: Imagine having a loyal, enthusiastic friend who's always ready for an adventure. With a personality that's both spirited and sharp, this breed loves interaction and thrives on mental stimulation. They're not just great watchdogs, known for their alertness and protective instincts, but they're also incredibly loving with their families. These dogs are adaptable and form strong connections with children, making them fantastic family pets. They generally get along well with other animals, especially if they're socialized early, though their boundless energy and playful spirit might be a bit much for more reserved pets.
Grooming Needs: requires regular grooming to maintain their wiry coat, including weekly brushing and occasional trimming to prevent matting. They also need routine bathing and ear cleaning.
Training & Exercise Needs: active dogs that need plenty of exercises, such as daily walks, runs, or play sessions. They excel in activities like obedience training, agility, and herding trials.
Possible Health Issues: hip dysplasia, elbow dysplasia, progressive retinal atrophy (PRA), and certain heart conditions

Belgian Malinois
Other Names: Belgian Shepherd Malinois, Malinois
Color variations: Fawn, mahogany, red, with a black mask and ears
Average Lifespan: 12 to 14 years
Origins: Belgium - late 19th century - bred primarily for herding and guarding livestock.
Body Size: Males: 24-26 in, 60-80 lbs. Females: 22-24 in, 40-60 lbs.
Personality/Disposition/Compatibility: They are a powerhouse of energy and intelligence. With a personality that's both vibrant and focused, this breed thrives on action and challenges. Always on the go, they're incredibly alert and eager to tackle new tasks. Their loyalty is steadfast, making them not just pets but devoted family members. They need plenty of mental and physical stimulation, so they're ideal for active households that can match their enthusiasm. They generally get along well with children and other pets, especially when properly socialized. While they're protective and make excellent watchdogs, their high energy means they do best with owners who can offer lots of exercise and engagement.
Grooming Needs: requiring regular brushing to manage shedding and keep the coat healthy. Bathing is needed only occasionally.
Training & Exercise Needs: have very high exercise needs and require plenty of physical and mental stimulation. They excel in activities such as obedience training, agility, herding, and protection work.
Possible Health Issues: hip and elbow dysplasia, progressive retinal atrophy, and sensitivity to anesthesia

Belgian Sheepdog

Other Names: Groenendael
Color variations: black, occasionally with small white markings on the chest and toes.
Average Lifespan: 12 to 14 years
Origins: Belgium - late 19th century - bred primarily for herding sheep and other livestock.
Body Size: Males: 24-26 in, 65-75 lbs. Females: 22-24 in, 60-70 lbs.
Personality/Disposition/Compatibility: These dogs are incredibly smart and always eager to please. Their work ethic is top notch, and they absolutely thrive on both mental challenges and physical activity. They're affectionate and loyal, forming strong bonds with their families and often taking on a protective role, which makes them fantastic watchdogs. They approach new experiences and people with curiosity and confidence, never shying away. With the right socialization, they get along wonderfully with other pets and children. Their high energy and playful nature make them eager participants in family activities, so be prepared to give them plenty of exercise and mental stimulation to keep them happy and healthy. If you're an active family or someone who loves staying busy, these dogs will be a perfect match.
Grooming Needs: To keep its dense coat looking great and free from tangles, this breed needs regular brushing. And when it's shedding season, you'll want to step up your grooming game to keep those loose hairs in check.
Training & Exercise Needs: They really enjoy activities like herding, obedience training, agility courses, and long walks. Keeping them mentally and physically stimulated is key to their well-being.
Possible Health Issues: hip dysplasia, elbow dysplasia, progressive retinal atrophy (PRA), epilepsy, and thyroid disorders.

Belgian Tervuren

Other Names: Tervuren or Terv
Color variations: shades of fawn to mahogany with a black overlay, and some have a black mask.
Average Lifespan: 12 to 14 years
Origins: Belgium - late 19th century - developed for herding and guarding livestock.
Body Size: Males: 24-26 in, 55-75 lbs. Females: 22-24 in, 45-60 lbs.
Personality/Disposition/Compatibility: These dogs are like the brains and brawn of the canine world—they're always eager for an adventure or a challenge. They form tight-knit bonds with their families and are especially great with kids, making them wonderful family pets. They usually get along well with other animals, too, as long as they've had some early socialization. Just keep an eye on them around smaller pets, since they have a strong prey drive. In new social situations, they might be a bit reserved at first, but once they feel comfortable, their playful and affectionate side really comes to life.
Grooming Needs: To keep their long coat looking its best, they need regular grooming. Brush them weekly to avoid tangles and get rid of loose hair, and be prepared for extra brushing during shedding seasons. Occasional baths, along with regular checks for clean ears and trimmed nails.
Training & Exercise Needs: Daily walks, runs, and playtime are essential for your dog's well-being. They thrive on activities that keep them both physically and mentally engaged, like obedience training, agility courses, herding, and various dog sports. These challenges not only keep them fit but also stimulate their minds and help maintain a happy, balanced life.
Possible Health Issues: hip dysplasia, elbow dysplasia, progressive retinal atrophy (PRA), epilepsy, and certain skin allergies

Bergamasco
Other Names: None
Color variations: shades of gray, ranging from light gray to black, including merle.
Average Lifespan: 13 to 15 years
Origins: Italy - 2000 years ago - bred primarily for herding and guarding sheep.
Body Size: Males: 23.5-24.5 in, 70-84 lbs.
Females: 21.5-23.5 in, 57-71 lbs.
Personality/Disposition/Compatibility: They're known for their laid-back and patient nature, making it a wonderful companion for both families and individuals. They're remarkably smart and in tune with your feelings, often sensing what you need before you even say a word. Naturally protective, they're a loyal guardian of its home and loved ones. They're gentle with kids and have a playful streak that can turn any mundane moment into an exciting adventure. Despite their rugged look, they're quite adaptable and can thrive in various living situations, whether it's a busy household or a serene rural setting. They usually get along well with others due to their easygoing personality, but they might show a bit of a territorial side, so early socialization is a good idea.
Grooming Needs: Grooming involves separating its unique mats and flocks of hair to ensure they do not become too dense, which can take a few hours initially but then requires minimal maintenance.
Training & Exercise Needs: enjoy activities such as herding, hiking, and long walks. They thrive in environments where they can perform tasks and have a purpose.
Possible Health Issues: hip & elbow dysplasia, and some eye conditions

Berger Picard
Other Names: Picardy Shepherd
Color variations: shades of fawn or brindle, with variations ranging from light to dark hues.
Average Lifespan: 12 to 14 years
Origins: France - the 9th century - bred for herding and guarding livestock.
Body Size: Males: 23.5-25.5 in, 60-70 lbs.
Females: 21.5-23.5 in, 50-60 lbs.
Personality/Disposition/Compatibility: The Berger Picard is a delightful and charismatic dog with a personality that's both engaging and unique. Known for their intelligence and playful spirit, these dogs are full of energy but also have a calm side that makes them great companions. They're always ready for an adventure, whether it's a hike through the woods or a game of fetch in the backyard. They form strong bonds with their families, showing loyalty and protectiveness without being overly possessive. They love spending time with their human friends and can be quite social, getting along well with kids and other pets if introduced properly. Their mix of enthusiasm and steadiness makes them adaptable to various living environments, from lively households to quieter homes, as long as they receive plenty of mental and physical stimulation.
Grooming Needs: requiring regular brushing to remove dead hair and prevent matting. Their coats should be kept natural and not overly trimmed.
Training & Exercise Needs: need regular exercise, including daily walks and playtime. They excel in activities like agility, herding, and obedience training, which help keep them mentally and physically stimulated.
Possible Health Issues: hip dysplasia, progressive retinal atrophy (PRA), and certain heart conditions

Bernese Mountain Dog
Other Names: Berner Sennenhund or Berner
Color variations: tri-color coat consisting of black, white, and rust.
Average Lifespan: 7 to 10 years
Origins: Switzerland - the 19th century - bred to work as a farm dog, specifically for herding cattle, pulling carts, and serving as a loyal watchdog.
Body Size: Males: 25-27.5 in, 85-115 lbs. Females: 23-26 in, 70-95 lbs.
Personality/Disposition/Compatibility: Affectionately called a "Bernie," this gentle giant truly lives up to its name. With a heart as big as its size, they're known for their friendly demeanor. Their calm and loving nature makes them perfect companions, adding warmth and joy to any home. They are incredibly patient, making them wonderful with children, and they're also smart and eager to please. Although they might be a bit shy around new faces, they warm up quickly once they feel comfortable. They also get along great with other pets, happily sharing their space.
Grooming Needs: Their thick, double coat needs regular brushing to keep it from getting tangled and matted. They shed a lot, especially during seasonal changes, so extra grooming during these times will keep things under control and make both you and your pup more comfortable.
Training & Exercise Needs: Daily walks, playtime in a secure yard, and activities like hiking or pulling carts are great ways to keep this breed happy and healthy. They'll love the chance to stretch their legs and have some fun!
Possible Health Issues: Hip and elbow dysplasia, bloat, different kinds of cancer, progressive retinal atrophy (PRA), and von Willebrand's disease

Bichon Frise
Other Names: Bichon Tenerife or Bichon
Color variations: white, though some may have cream, apricot, or gray markings.
Average Lifespan: 14 to 15 years
Origins: Spain - 14th century - bred for companionship
Body Size: Males: 9.5-11.5 in, 11-16 lbs.
Females: 9.5-11.5 in, 10-15 lbs.
Personality/Disposition/Compatibility: These dogs are like little bundles of sunshine, always ready to brighten up any room with their cheerful and playful energy. They absolutely love being the center of attention and thrive on spending time with their families. If you're someone who enjoys playtime and has a lively spirit, these dogs will be your perfect match. They're incredibly adaptable, so whether you live in a cozy apartment or a house with a big yard, they'll fit right in. Plus, their sociable nature means they get along great with everyone—people and other pets alike.
Grooming Needs: Grooming is a big part of keeping them happy and healthy. You'll want to brush their fluffy coat several times a week and take them for a professional grooming session every four to six weeks. This helps keep their fur looking fantastic and free from tangles and mats.
Training & Exercise Needs: They need some good, regular exercise—think daily walks and playtime. They love activities like fetching, agility courses, and obedience training.
Possible Health Issues: Some common issues to watch for include allergies, dental troubles, patellar luxation, hip dysplasia, and bladder problems.

Biewer Terrier

Other Names: Biewer à la Pom Pon
Color variations: tri-color coat featuring white, black, and tan, with specific color patterns unique to each dog.
Average Lifespan: 12 to 15 years
Origins: Germany - 1980s - when a pair of Yorkshire Terriers produced a uniquely colored offspring. It was bred for its distinctive tri-colored coat and as a companion dog.
Body Size: Males and females: 7-11 in, 4-8 lbs.
Personality/Disposition/Compatibility: Their playful antics can light up any space, making them the heart of family fun. They love to be involved in everything going on around them, so they thrive on constant companionship. If left alone for too long, they might experience separation anxiety, so they're best suited for homes where someone is around most of the time. Their friendly and outgoing nature makes them great with other pets and fantastic with kids. Whether you have a cozy apartment or a spacious house, their small size and energetic personality make them a great fit. Just remember to give them plenty of daily exercise and mental stimulation to keep them happy and healthy.
Grooming Needs: To keep their silky coat looking its best, regular grooming is a must. Daily brushing will help prevent matting and keep things smooth. A bath now and then will also help, and a visit to a professional groomer every few weeks can ensure their coat stays in top shape.
Training & Exercise Needs: This breed thrives on daily walks, playtime in a safe space, and interactive games. They love activities that keep both their minds and bodies engaged.
Possible Health Issues: patellar luxation, portosystemic shunt, dental problems, and tracheal collapse

Black and Tan Coonhound

Other Names: Coonhound
Color variations: primarily black with rich tan markings above the eyes, on the sides of the muzzle, chest, legs, and underside of the tail.
Average Lifespan: 10 to 12 years
Origins: United States - 18th century - to track and hunt raccoons and other game.
Body Size: Males: 25-27 in, 65-75 lbs. Females: 22-25 in, 55-65 lbs.
Personality/Disposition/Compatibility: Their friendly and outgoing personality makes them the life of the party. Their adventurous spirit and boundless curiosity are perfect for those who love the great outdoors. Their patience and tolerance make them particularly good with children, ensuring they fit comfortably into a variety of households. Training them might come with a few challenges due to their stubborn streak, but their intelligence and eagerness to please usually make it manageable. They get along well with families, singles, and other pets, as long as they receive ample exercise and mental stimulation.
Grooming Needs: Its short, dense coat requires regular brushing to remove dead hair and keep it looking healthy. The breed also needs routine ear cleaning due to its long, floppy ears that can trap moisture and debris.
Training & Exercise Needs: an active and energetic breed that requires regular exercise to stay healthy and happy. Daily walks, runs, and play sessions are essential. The breed excels in activities such as tracking, hunting, and field trials.
Possible Health Issues: hip dysplasia, ear infections, and obesity

Black Russian Terrier
Other Names: Chornyi Terrier and BRT
Color variations: predominantly black, though it may have a few gray hairs.
Average Lifespan: 10 to 14 years
Origins: Russia - late 1940s to early 1950s - bred for military and working purposes, particularly for guarding and protection.
Body Size: Males: 27-30 in, 80-130 lbs. Females: 26-29 in, 80-110 lbs.
Personality/Disposition/Compatibility: These dogs are known for their calm and confident nature, radiating a quiet strength that's both reassuring and impressive. They're smart and in tune with their family's needs and feelings, showing a remarkable loyalty and protectiveness. While they're excellent watchdogs, they also have a playful and loving side that shines through. They're fantastic with kids and enjoy being involved in family activities, making them a versatile companion. They generally get along well with other pets, though early socialization is important. They thrive when they're included in family life and get plenty of exercise and mental stimulation. With their mix of seriousness and playfulness, they make a truly unique and rewarding addition to any home.
Grooming Needs: You'll want to brush it a few times a week to keep those mats and tangles at bay, and a professional grooming every few months will help keep it looking its best.
Training & Exercise Needs: Daily walks, play sessions, and activities that stimulate its mind and body are essential. This breed enjoys activities such as obedience training, agility, and protection work.
Possible Health Issues: hip and elbow dysplasia, progressive retinal atrophy, and certain heart conditions.

Bloodhound
Other Names: St. Hubert hounds
Color variations: black and tan, liver and tan, or red
Average Lifespan: 10 to 12 years
Origins: Belgium - 1000 AD - bred for their exceptional tracking abilities, primarily used for hunting deer and boar.
Body Size: Males: 25-27 in, 90-110 lbs. Females: 23-25 in, 80-100 lbs.
Personality/Disposition/Compatibility: They bring a delightful mix of playfulness and intelligence to any home. Their good-natured demeanor is complemented by their sharp minds and unyielding determination, especially when they're on a scent trail. Their remarkable sense of smell is matched only by their curiosity. They're adaptable and generally get along well with kids and other pets, thanks to their easygoing nature. However, their large size and endless energy mean they do best in homes with plenty of s pace and a family ready to join them in their adventurous escapades.
Grooming Needs: They need regular grooming to keep their coat in top shape and to control shedding. Don't forget to give their ears and facial wrinkles some extra care to help prevent infections.
Training & Exercise Needs: They thrive on regular exercise to stay both physically and mentally engaged. Activities like tracking and scent games really tap into their natural instincts and keep them happily occupied.
Possible Health Issues: hip dysplasia, bloat, ear infections, and skin conditions due to their loose, wrinkled skin

Bluetick Coonhound
Other Names: Bluetick
Color variations: mottled black and blue. There may also be tan markings on the face and legs.
Average Lifespan: 11 to 12 years
Origins: United States - 18th century - bred primarily for hunting raccoons and other small game.
Body Size: Males: 22-27 in. 55-80 lbs. Females: 21-25 in. 45-65 lbs.
Personality/Disposition/Compatibility: They're the ultimate tail waggers, always ready to greet you with a big smile and boundless enthusiasm. These dogs have a heart full of adventure and a playful spirit that makes them perfect for active families or outdoor enthusiasts. They're at their happiest when they're on the move, whether it's tracking scents on a hike or chasing after a ball in the backyard. Their easy-going attitude makes them great with kids. They usually get along well with other dogs and can live harmoniously with other pets if introduced properly. Just be mindful of their strong hunting instinct, their excitement might be a bit much for smaller pets or critters.
Grooming Needs: Their short coat only needs a quick brush now and then to keep it smooth and healthy. Don't forget to check and clean their long, droopy ears regularly—they're prone to collecting dirt and moisture.
Training & Exercise Needs: These dogs are full of energy and thrive on lots of daily exercise. They're great at activities like hiking, running, and tracking scents. If you keep them busy with hunting or scent-based tasks, they'll be in their element and truly satisfied.
Possible Health Issues: They're generally healthy but can be prone to certain health issues such as hip dysplasia, ear infections, and bloat

Boerboel
Other Names: South African Mastiff
Color variations: fawn, red, brown, brindle, and black
Average Lifespan: 10 to 12 years.
Origins: South Africa - mid-1600s - bred primarily for guarding farms and homes against predators and intruders.
Body Size: Males: 24-27 in. 150-200 lbs. Females: 22- 25 in. 120-160 lbs.
Personality/Disposition/Compatibility: They're smart and alert, which makes them fantastic watchdogs. They pick up on new commands quickly and are usually easy to train as long as you're consistent and patient. That said, they do have a strong-willed side, so it's important to start socializing them early and set clear boundaries. They generally get along well with other dogs they've grown up with or those that match their energy level. They might be a bit reserved around new animals, so it's best to introduce them slowly. With their impressive size and commanding presence, they are natural protectors of their home and family. Despite their imposing look, they're incredibly affectionate and loyal. They form deep bonds with their humans and are especially gentle and caring with children, revealing a softer side that endears them to everyone.
Grooming Needs: They've got short, dense coats that are pretty low-maintenance. Just a regular brushing to catch any loose hair and an occasional bath will keep their fur looking great and healthy.
Training & Exercise Needs: They love daily walks, playtime in a safe yard, and activities like obedience training or agility exercises.
Possible Health Issues: hip and elbow dysplasia, heart disease, and bloat

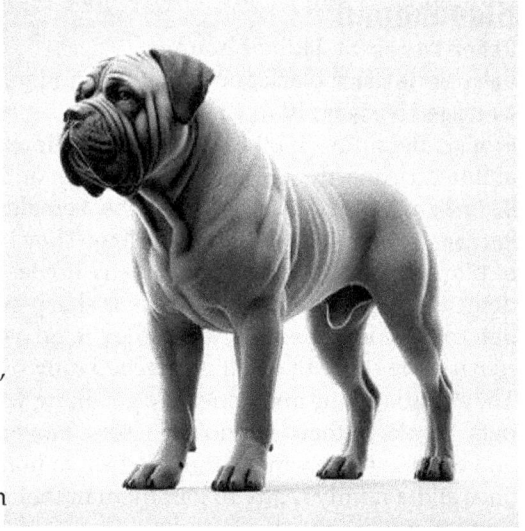

Bohemian Shepherd

Other Names: Chodský pes or Chodenhund.
Color variations: black coat with rich tan markings
Average Lifespan: 12 to 15 years
Origins: Czech Republic - the 1300s - originally bred for guarding and herding purposes.
Body Size: Males: 21.5-22.5 in. 53-60 lbs.
Females: 19.5-21 in. 44-53 lbs.
Personality/Disposition/Compatibility: They're the life of the party with their energetic and friendly nature, making every moment with them a delight. They bring a contagious zest for life wherever they go. They love being around people and can turn into the most affectionate cuddle-buddies once they've had their fun. Their sociable personality means they usually get along great with other pets and children, making them a perfect fit for a lively household. But don't forget—they have tons of energy and smarts, so they need plenty of mental and physical stimulation. If they don't get enough activities to keep them busy, they might get bored and come up with their own mischievous ways to entertain themselves.
Grooming Needs: They require regular brushing to maintain their coat and reduce shedding. Occasional baths and routine care for their nails, ears, and teeth are also necessary.
Training & Exercise Needs: These dogs are full of energy and need regular exercise to stay happy. They thrive on activities like hiking, running, and playing fetch, which keep them both physically fit and mentally sharp.
Possible Health Issues: is generally a healthy breed, but they can be prone to certain health issues such as hip dysplasia, elbow dysplasia, and progressive retinal atrophy (PRA).

Bolognese

Other Names: Bichon Bolognese or Bolo
Color variations: pure white
Average Lifespan: 12 to 14 years
Origins: Italy - 11th century - primarily bred to be a companion dog for the nobility.
Body Size: Males and females: 10-12 in. 5.5-9 lbs.
Personality/Disposition/Compatibility: They're the kind of dogs that just make you smile. Their affectionate nature means they're always up for a cuddle or a game, and they form tight bonds with their owners. They're playful and energetic but also have a mellow side that's perfect for those quiet evenings on the couch. They love being the center of attention and are known for their charming antics that can make anyone laugh. They get along well with kids and other pets, making them great additions to any family. They're adaptable to different living situations, whether you're in an apartment or a bigger home, as long as they get plenty of attention and playtime.
Grooming Needs: To keep their fluffy coat in top shape, regular grooming is a must. This means brushing a few times a week to keep things from getting tangled and giving them the occasional bath. Luckily, their coat doesn't shed much, so they're a great choice for those with allergies.
Training & Exercise Needs: They thrive on daily walks, playtime, and activities that keep both their minds and bodies active.
Possible Health Issues: patellar luxation, dental problems, and hip dysplasia

K9 Chatter

Border Collie
Other Names: Scotch Sheep Dog
Color variations: black and white, red and white, tricolor, blue merle, and sable
Average Lifespan: 12 to 15 years
Origins: border regions of Scotland and England - 19th century - bred specifically for herding sheep and other livestock.
Body Size: Males: 19-22 in. 30-45 lbs. Females: 18-21 in. 27-42 lbs.
Personality/Disposition/Compatibility: These dogs are like a splash of sunshine wrapped in fur. They're smart, enthusiastic, and make for some of the most engaging companions you'll ever meet. If you're someone who thrives on staying active, these dogs will be your perfect match. Their energy is boundless, and they're always up for anything—from a game of fetch to agility training or just a good romp in the yard. Loyal and quick learners, they flourish in environments where they can stay both mentally and physically stimulated. They build strong bonds with their families and are eager to please. If you can keep up with their energy and keep them entertained, they'll bring endless joy and excitement into your life.
Grooming Needs: They enjoy a good brushing session and will appreciate an occasional bath. Don't forget about their nails, ears, and teeth.
Training & Exercise Needs: They love activities that really get them moving and thinking, like agility training, herding, obedience drills, and a good game of fetch. Keeping them active every day is key to avoiding boredom and any potential mischief.
Possible Health Issues: are generally healthy, but they can be prone to certain health issues such as hip dysplasia, progressive retinal atrophy, epilepsy, and Collie eye anomaly

Border Terrier
Other Names: None
Color variations: red, grizzle and tan, blue and tan, and wheaten.
Average Lifespan: 12 to 15 years
Origins: border region between England and Scotland - 18th century - bred for their ability to assist in hunting foxes and other small game.
Body Size: Males: 10-11 in. 13-15.5 lbs. Females: 9-10 in. 11.5-14 lbs.
Personality/Disposition/Compatibility: These dogs are full of life and affection, always brimming with energy and curiosity. Their sharp minds love a good challenge, so they can get a little stubborn if they're not mentally engaged. But with the right mix of exercise and attention, they turn into loving, well-behaved companions who light up any room. Their loyalty is unmatched, and they quickly form strong bonds with their families. They're great with kids and other pets, making them perfect for all kinds of home settings. With their bold and lively personalities, they're ideal for those who lead an active lifestyle and appreciate a spirited, fun-loving friend.
Grooming Needs: To keep their wiry coats looking great, they need to be brushed weekly and occasionally hand-stripped. Keeping up with their dental care, cleaning their ears, and trimming their nails are all part of the routine.
Training & Exercise Needs: These dogs are lively and full of energy, and they thrive on daily exercise. They love to stay active with activities like walking, running, and playing fetch. Plus, they're enthusiastic participants in dog sports like agility and obedience training.
Possible Health Issues: hip dysplasia, heart defects, epilepsy, allergies, and progressive retinal atrophy (PRA)

Borzoi
Other Names: Russian Wolfhound
Color variations: white, golden, tan, gray, and black, often with combinations of these colors in their coat.
Average Lifespan: 10 to 12 years
Origins: Russia - 17th century - bred to hunt wolves and other game across vast estates.
Body Size: Males: 28-32 in. 75-105 lbs. Females: 26-30 in. 60-85 lbs.
Personality/Disposition/Compatibility: They exude an air of elegance with a hint of mystery. With their long, silky coats and graceful movements, they seem like living pieces of art. These dogs are known for their calm and gentle nature, making them perfect companions for those who enjoy a touch of regal charm in their pets. While they're not the type to demand constant attention, they truly value the company of their families and build strong, loving bonds. They're often seen lounging around, soaking up the sun, and their sweet, affectionate side emerges in those quiet moments. Generally easygoing with other dogs, they might chase after smaller animals due to their strong prey drive, so keeping an eye on them is a good idea. With children, they're usually patient and gentle, making them a great choice for families willing to give them the space and affection they thrive on.
Grooming Needs: To keep your dog's coat looking its best, make sure to brush it a few times a week to avoid mats and tangles. Every now and then, give them a bath and trim their nails to keep everything neat and tidy.
Training & Exercise Needs: Daily walks and a chance to run around safely are musts for them. They thrive on activities like lure coursing, which really lets their natural hunting instincts shine.
Possible Health Issues: hip dysplasia, heart problems, and bloat

Boston Terrier
Other Names: "American Gentleman" due to its tuxedo-like markings and gentle demeanor.
Color variations: black, brindle, or seal with white markings.
Average Lifespan: 11 to 13 years
Origins: United States - late 19th century - initially bred for pit fighting and ratting, but over time, it became a companion dog.
Body Size: Males: 17 in. 15-25 lbs. Females: 16 in. 10-20 lbs.
Personality/Disposition/Compatibility: Often dubbed the "American Gentleman" because of their polished looks and charming personality, these little dogs are as endearing on the inside as they are on the outside. They're known for their friendly, affectionate nature and an energy that seems boundless. Whether you're an active family or someone who enjoys a quieter life, they quickly adapt to any environment. Despite their small size, they carry themselves with a dignified confidence that's hard to miss. They get along well with kids, other pets, and pretty much anyone willing to share some attention and playtime. Their social nature means they thrive on human interaction, making them a fantastic choice for families looking for a devoted and engaging companion.
Grooming Needs: Regular brushing, occasional baths, and routine care of ears, teeth, and nails are sufficient to keep them in good condition.
Training & Exercise Needs: To keep them happy and healthy, these dogs need a bit of exercise every day. A good routine includes daily walks, playtime, and fun activities like fetch or agility training. These activities help keep both their bodies and minds active and engaged.
Possible Health Issues: brachycephalic syndrome, cataracts, and patellar luxation.

Bouvier des Flandres

Other Names: Flanders Cattle Dog and Vlaamse Koehond.
Color variations: fawn, black, brindle, and salt and pepper (grey) colors.
Average Lifespan: 10 to 12 years
Origins: Belgium and France (Flanders region) - early 20th century - bred primarily for herding cattle and other livestock.
Body Size: Males: 24.5-27.5 in. 80-120 lbs.
Females: 23.5-26.5 in. 60-80 lbs.
Personality/Disposition/Compatibility: these dogs are as charming in personality as they are in appearance. They're fiercely loyal and protective, naturally keeping a watchful eye over their family, which makes them fantastic guard dogs. But their loyalty goes beyond just their humans—they're also wonderful with children and generally get along well with other pets, especially when introduced properly from a young age. If you're looking for a low maintenance, laid-back companion, this might not be the breed for you.
Grooming Needs: This breed has a double coat that needs some regular attention to keep it looking its best. Make sure to brush it a few times a week to prevent tangles and mats. Also, a trim every few months will help maintain its shape and keep it looking sharp.
Training & Exercise Needs: They're lively and thrive when they have a task to tackle—whether that's taking part in agility trials, herding, or just joining you on your outdoor escapades. They're quick learners thanks to their sharp minds, but that also means they need plenty of mental stimulation to stay happy. Without enough to do, they might find their own ways to entertain themselves, which can lead to a bit of mischief.
Possible Health Issues: hip dysplasia, elbow dysplasia, and bloat

Boxer

Other Names: None
Color variations: fawn, brindle, and white. They may also have white markings.
Average Lifespan: 10 to 12 years
Origins: Germany - late 19th century - bred for working purposes, such as hunting and guarding, and later became popular as family pets and show dogs.
Body Size: Males: 23-25 in. 65-80 lbs. Females: 21.5-23.5 in. 50-65 lbs.
Personality/Disposition/Compatibility: They're incredibly loving and quickly bond with their families, always ready to jump into whatever's going on. Their playful nature makes them fantastic with kids, often seen bouncing around and joining in the games. They also have a strong protective instinct, so they're loyal and dependable guardians. They usually get along well with other dogs if they've been properly socialized from a young age. Just remember, their high energy and enthusiastic play might be a bit overwhelming for more laid-back pets.
Grooming Needs: Just give them a good brush now and then to keep loose hair at bay and treat them to an occasional bath to keep their coat looking sharp. Don't forget to trim their nails regularly and check their ears to make sure they're clean and healthy.
Training & Exercise Needs: These dogs are full of energy and need regular exercise to stay healthy and happy. Daily walks, playtime, and engaging activities like agility training or obedience exercises are perfect for keeping them both physically and mentally stimulated.
Possible Health Issues: hip dysplasia, aortic stenosis and cardiomyopathy, and certain cancers

Boykin Spaniel
Other Names: None
Color variations: solid liver, brown, or dark chocolate colors
Average Lifespan: 10 to 15 years
Origins: South Carolina, United States - early 1900s - bred for its hunting abilities, particularly for waterfowl and turkey hunting.
Body Size: Males: 15.5-18 in. 30-40 lbs. Females: 14-16.5 in. 25-35 lbs.
Personality/Disposition/Compatibility: They're incredibly loving and friendly dogs that form deep connections with their families. They're not just loyal companions; they're also fantastic with kids and get along well with other pets, making them a perfect fit for lively households. These energetic dogs thrive on plenty of physical and mental activity, so they're best suited for active families who can offer them the exercise and attention they need. Their trainability and eagerness to please make them a joy to train, and their gentle nature means they blend seamlessly with other animals, including cats and dogs.
Grooming Needs: To keep their coat looking its best, regular grooming is a must. Brush them several times a week to avoid matting and tangling, and don't forget that an occasional visit to a professional groomer can make a big difference. Also, be sure to clean their ears and trim their nails regularly to keep them healthy and happy.
Training & Exercise Needs: They love running, hiking, swimming, and retrieving—basically, any activity that keeps them moving and engaged. To keep them happy and healthy, regular physical activity is a must.
Possible Health Issues: hip dysplasia, eye problems like cataracts, and ear infections due to their floppy ears

Bracco Italiano
Other Names: Italian Pointer or Italian Setter
Color variations: white with orange or chestnut markings, white with brown or roan markings, and sometimes solid colors of brown or orange.
Average Lifespan: 10 to 14 years
Origins: Italy - 4th or 5th century BC - primarily bred for hunting and retrieving game, utilizing its keen sense of smell and excellent tracking abilities.
Body Size: Males: 23-27 in. 55-88 lbs. Females: 21-25 in. 44-77 lbs.
Personality/Disposition/Compatibility: This breed has a heart warming personality that's both friendly and approachable. They strike a delightful balance between enthusiasm and relaxation, making them a joy to live with and hard to resist. They're especially great with kids and usually get along well with other pets, provided they're introduced properly. They love being part of the family, whether it's playing fetch or snuggling up on the couch. Though they have a strong hunting instinct, they're adaptable and do well in various living situations as long as they get enough exercise and social interaction.
Grooming Needs: The breed has short, dense hair that's pretty low-maintenance. A quick brush to get rid of loose hair and an occasional bath should keep their coat looking great. Just remember to check and clean their ears regularly to keep them infection-free.
Training & Exercise Needs: To keep them healthy and happy, they need regular exercise. Daily walks, playtime, and activities like tracking, hunting, and agility are perfect for them. They really enjoy having a job to do and flourish when they can tap into their natural hunting instincts.
Possible Health Issues: hip dysplasia, ear infections, and bloat (gastric torsion)

K9 Chatter

Braque de Bourbonnais
Other Names: Bourbonnais Pointing Dog
Color variations: liver and white or fawn and white, often with ticking or roan patterns
Average Lifespan: 12 to 15 years
Origins: France - early 16th century - bred to be a versatile hunting dog capable of pointing and retrieving game.
Body Size: Males: 19-22 in. 35-53 lbs. Females: 18-21 in. 32-49 lbs.
Personality/Disposition/Compatibility: These dogs are truly gems when it comes to companionship. Their gentle and loving nature makes them great friends for both families and individuals. With their sharp minds and eagerness to make you happy, they're easy to train and respond well to positive reinforcement. They have a playful spirit, so they'll love running around in the park or playing fetch. But they're just as happy snuggling up with you on the couch. Their friendly and sociable temperament helps them get along well with other dogs and pets. They thrive in environments where they're included in family activities and can adapt to different living situations—whether it's a spacious countryside home or a cozy city apartment—as long as they get their daily dose of exercise and mental stimulation.
Grooming Needs: To keep their short coat looking its best, just give them a regular brush and an occasional bath. It's a simple routine that will keep them clean and happy!
Training & Exercise Needs: To keep this breed healthy and happy, they need regular exercise. They thrive on activities like hunting, hiking, and agility training, as these provide the physical and mental stimulation they love.
Possible Health Issues: hip & elbow dysplasia, and certain heart conditions

Braque Francais Pyrenean
Other Names: Pyrenean Pointing Dog, French Pointer
Color variations: white with brown or chestnut markings.
Average Lifespan: 12 to 14 years
Origins: France - 15th century - bred primarily for hunting and retrieving game birds.
Body Size: Males: 19-23 in. 40-55 lbs. Females: 18-22 in. 35-50 lbs.
Personality/Disposition/Compatibility: This breed perfectly combines enthusiasm and gentleness, making it a great choice for anyone who loves both energy and affection in their dogs. They thrive on human interaction, naturally sociable and always eager to be involved in family activities. Their affectionate nature means they're always looking for attention and are incredibly loyal, with a real desire to please their owners. They're typically great with kids, making them a fantastic addition to families. Their playful, gentle demeanor also means they get along well with other dogs, and with the right socialization, they can adapt smoothly to life with other pets.
Grooming Needs: Regular brushing to remove loose hair and occasional baths to keep the coat clean are sufficient. Routine ear cleaning and nail trimming should also be part of the grooming regimen.
Training & Exercise Needs: This breed is full of energy and needs regular exercise to stay both healthy and happy. Daily walks, playtime, and chances to run around in a safe space are musts. They thrive in activities like hunting, agility, and obedience training, making them a great companion for active adventures.
Possible Health Issues: generally a healthy breed, but it can be prone to hip dysplasia, ear infections, and certain eye conditions

Braque Saint-Germain
Other Names: Saint-Germain Pointer
Color variations: white with orange markings
Average Lifespan: 12 to 15 years
Origins: France - early 19th century - bred primarily for hunting, particularly as a pointer and retriever, to combine the best qualities of the French pointer and English pointer.
Body Size: Males: 22-24 in. 48-62 lbs. Females: 21-23 in. 44-60 lbs.
Personality/Disposition/Compatibility: These dogs are known for their warm and engaging personalities, making them fantastic companions. They're full of energy and love nothing more than an active play session or an outdoor adventure. Smart and eager to learn, they respond well to positive reinforcement, which makes training a breeze. Their loyalty is remarkable—they form strong bonds with their families and generally get along well with kids and other pets if they're properly socialized. They're pretty adaptable and tolerant, but they do best in homes where they can get plenty of exercise and mental stimulation.
Grooming Needs: Its short coat requires regular brushing to keep it clean and free from dead hair. Occasional baths and routine checks for ear cleanliness, dental hygiene, and nail trimming are also recommended.
Training & Exercise Needs: They're full of energy and love to stay active. Whether it's hunting, field trials, or simply enjoying a good hike or run, this breed truly shines. To keep your Braque happy and healthy, make sure they get plenty of vigorous exercise each day.
Possible Health Issues: hip dysplasia, ear infections, and certain skin conditions

Brazilian Terrier
Other Names: Fox Paulistinha
Color variations: tricolor variations, including white with black, tan, or blue markings.
Average Lifespan: 12 to 14 years
Origins: Brazil - the 19th century - bred primarily for hunting and controlling vermin.
Body Size: Males: 14-16 in. 15-20 lbs. Females: 13-15 in. 14-18 lbs.
Personality/Disposition/Compatibility: These dogs are bursting with energy and enthusiasm, and their zest for life is absolutely contagious. They're always up for fun and adventure, making them perfect companions for active families or anyone who loves to stay on the move. Their smarts and eagerness to learn mean that training them is not just effective, but a blast. They quickly pick up new tricks with a twinkle of mischief in their eye. They're great with kids and other pets, especially if they've been socialized early on. Their playful spirit makes them wonderful playmates for children, and they usually get along well with other dogs too.
Grooming Needs: Regular brushing to remove loose hair and occasional baths are sufficient to keep their coat in good condition.
Training & Exercise Needs: To keep this lively breed happy and healthy, they need regular exercise. Daily walks, playtime in a safe yard, and fun activities like agility training or a good game of fetch are perfect for keeping them energized and content.
Possible Health Issues: Overall, they're pretty healthy, but they can have a few health quirks, like patellar luxation, hip dysplasia, and allergies.

Briard

Other Names: Berger de Brie
Color variations: shades of black, gray, or tawny
Average Lifespan: 10 to 12 years
Origins: France - 8th century - primarily bred for herding and guarding sheep.
Body Size: Males: 23-27 in. 70-100 lbs. Females: 22-25.5 in. 55-75 lbs.
Personality/Disposition/Compatibility: Briards are a blend of brains and heart, known for their intelligence and unwavering loyalty. They're spirited and affectionate, making them both a joy and a bit of a challenge for first-time dog owners. Their independent streak can be a handful, but their dedication and eagerness to please make them incredibly rewarding companions. Always alert and protective, Briards keep a watchful eye on their loved ones, but they're not just serious watchdogs. Their playful antics and sense of humor bring plenty of fun into the home. Whether they're sprinting around the yard or snuggling on the couch, Briards know how to make life more vibrant. They're social dogs who love the company of other pets, and with early socialization, they grow into well-rounded adults. These energetic pups thrive in active households, so they're ready to join you on hikes, runs, or agility courses.
Grooming Needs: To keep their long hair from tangling, these dogs need regular grooming. Make sure to brush them several times a week and give them an occasional bath to keep their coat in top shape.
Training & Exercise Needs: This breed thrives on daily exercise and loves to stay active. They're happiest with long walks, energetic runs, and playtime in a safe, enclosed yard. Plus, they're stars in dog sports like agility, obedience, and herding trials.
Possible Health Issues: hip dysplasia, progressive retinal atrophy, and gastric torsion (bloat)

Brittany

Other Names: Brittany Spaniel
Color variations: orange and white, liver and white, black and white, and tricolored (black, liver, and white).
Average Lifespan: 12 and 14 years
Origins: France - 17th century - bred primarily for hunting birds.
Body Size: Males: 17.5-20.5 in. 30-40 lbs.
Females: 17.5-20 in. 30-40 lbs.
Personality/Disposition/Compatibility: These dogs are full of energy and smarts, picking up new tricks quickly and always eager to make you happy. Their friendly and outgoing personalities help them make friends everywhere they go. Brittanys thrive on both mental and physical activity, so they're ideal for active families or anyone who loves the great outdoors. They generally get along well with kids and other pets, making them a fantastic addition to many households. With their love for family and their quick ability to win hearts, Brittanys often become cherished members of the family in no time.n and can get along well with other animals if properly socialized.
Grooming Needs: To keep their coat looking great, just brush them regularly—it's usually all they need. An occasional bath will keep them fresh, and don't forget to clean their ears regularly to avoid any infections.
Training & Exercise Needs: To keep them healthy and happy, they need plenty of exercise. They really come alive with activities like running, hiking, and engaging in dog sports such as agility and obedience trials. Regular, energetic play is crucial to keep them from getting bored and to keep them feeling their best.
Possible Health Issues: Overall, they're a healthy breed, but they can sometimes face a few health challenges like hip dysplasia, epilepsy, and ear infections.

Broholmer

Other Names: Danish Mastiff
Color variations: yellow with a black mask, golden-red, and black.
Average Lifespan: 8 to 10 years
Origins: Denmark - Middle Ages - bred for guarding homes and estates.
Body Size: Males: 27.5-29.5 in. 110-150 lbs.
Females: 25.5-27.5 in. 90-130 lbs.
Personality/Disposition/Compatibility: These dogs are known for their calm, patient, and easygoing nature, making them wonderful companions for both families and individuals. Their loyalty and protective instincts mean they're always looking out for their loved ones, ensuring they feel safe and cherished. They're typically very good-natured and patient, especially with kids, and they love being close to their family. Whether it's a cozy cuddle or a gentle play session, they're always up for some quality time. They generally get along well with other dogs and pets, though their size and playful energy might be a bit much for smaller animals. These social dogs thrive on interaction and will be happiest in a home where they're an active part of family life.
Grooming Needs: With their short coats they need regular brushing to keep its coat looking great and to keep shedding under control.
Training & Exercise Needs: They need a good amount of exercise, so daily walks and playtime are essential. They love staying active with activities that challenge both their mind and body, like obedience training and interactive games.
Possible Health Issues: hip and elbow dysplasia, heart problems, and gastric torsion (bloat)

Brussels Griffon

Other Names: Griffon Bruxellois
Color variations: red, black and tan, and solid black.
Average Lifespan: 12 to 15 years
Origins: Belgium - early 1800s - bred primarily to hunt and kill rats in stables.
Body Size: Males & Females: 7-10 inches tall, 8-12 pounds.
Personality/Disposition/Compatibility: These little dogs are known for their adorable, expressive faces and their almost human-like gaze. They're as lively as they are lovable, with a personality that blends intelligence, curiosity, and a hint of mischief—always keeping things interesting. Fiercely loyal, they thrive on close, affectionate bonds with their families. They seem to have a knack for sensing their owner's moods, offering comfort when needed or joining in on your excitement. They're great with people of all ages, although their high energy might be a bit much for very young kids. They generally get along well with other pets, especially when introduced properly from an early age. Their sociable and adaptable nature means they can easily fit into any living situation, whether you have a spacious home or a snug apartment.
Grooming Needs: For the rough-coated variety, you'll need to brush them regularly and schedule an occasional visit to the groomer. The smooth-coated variety, on the other hand, is a bit easier to manage and only needs brushing now and then.
Training & Exercise Needs: Daily walks and playtime usually do the trick, and they really thrive on fun activities like agility and obedience training.
Possible Health Issues: hip dysplasia, patellar luxation, eye problems, and respiratory issues

Bull Terrier

Other Names: English Bull Terrier
Color variations: white, black, brindle, fawn, red, and tri-color.
Average Lifespan: 10 to 14 years
Origins: England - early 19th century - initially bred for bull-baiting and later became a fashionable companion for gentlemen.
Body Size: Males: 18-22 in. 50-70 lbs. Females: 17-21 in. 45-65 lbs.
Personality/Disposition/Compatibility: These dogs are as lively and unique as they look, charmingly stubborn with an infectious zest for life. They're the kind of pets who turn everyday moments into exciting adventures with their playful and mischievous antics. Their loyalty to their families is unshakeable, and they form deep bonds with their human companions. They have a talent for getting into funny situations, keeping you entertained for hours. They're best suited for active families or individuals who can match their high energy, they generally get along well with children, though their exuberance might accidentally knock over a toddler during playtime. Socializing them is important for helping them get along with other pets; they can be a bit picky about their doggy friends but usually warm up with the right introductions.
Grooming Needs: Regular brushing to remove loose hair and occasional baths are sufficient to keep them clean and healthy.
Training & Exercise Needs: Though they're known for their independent streak and occasional stubbornness, these dogs really shine with consistent training and a positive approach. They love going for brisk walks, playing, and diving into interactive games. With their boundless energy, they thrive best in active environments where they can keep busy and stay engaged.
Possible Health Issues: deafness, heart disease, kidney problems, and skin allergies

Bulldog

Other Names: British Bulldogs or English Bulldogs
Color variations: brindle, white, fawn, red, and piebald.
Average Lifespan: 8 to 10 years
Origins: England - 13th century - bred primarily for bull-baiting, a popular sport at the time.
Body Size: Males: 14-15 in. 50-55 lbs. Females: 12-14 in. 40-50 lbs.
Personality/Disposition/Compatibility: Even though Bulldogs might look tough on the outside, they're actually big softies at heart. They're known for their friendly and laid-back vibe, making them fantastic companions in a family setting. Bulldogs love to take it easy and can often be found lounging around the house rather than running wild. But don't let their relaxed demeanor fool you—they have a playful side too and enjoy a good romp in the yard or a game of fetch. They're especially good with kids, displaying patience and a gentle approach to playtime. They also get along well with other pets and, while they might be a bit stubborn now and then, they're generally tolerant and friendly. Their loyalty and affectionate nature make them eager to snuggle up on the couch with their families, always ready for some quality bonding time.
Grooming Needs: To keep their coat looking its best, these dogs need regular brushing to manage loose hair and maintain a healthy shine. Don't forget to clean their facial wrinkles regularly to prevent any potential infections.
Training & Exercise Needs: To keep a healthy weight, this breed needs a bit of exercise, but not too much. Short walks and play sessions are perfect for them. They can easily overheat and aren't up for intense workouts, so keeping things light and fun is the way to go.
Possible Health Issues: respiratory problems, hip dysplasia, skin infections, and heart conditions

Bullmastiff

Other Names: "Gamekeeper's Night Dog" due to their historical use in protecting estates from poachers.
Color variations: fawn, red, and brindle, often with a black mask
Average Lifespan: 7 to 10 years
Origins: England - mid 19th century - bred specifically for the purpose of guarding estates and protecting gamekeepers from poachers
Body Size: Males: 25-27 in. 110-130 lbs.
Females: 24-26 in. 100-120 lbs.
Personality/Disposition/Compatibility: They're known for their calm and gentle nature, making them incredibly loyal companions who take their guarding duties to heart. Even though they might look intimidating, they're surprisingly affectionate and develop strong bonds with their families. These gentle giants are usually patient and easygoing, which makes them great with kids and other pets especially if they're socialized from a young age. While they do have a natural protective instinct, they're more likely to be a loving presence than a fierce guard dog. They'll keep a watchful eye on their home and loved ones without being overly aggressive. One thing to note is that They can be a bit stubborn, so training might require a bit of patience and consistency. But once they learn the ropes, they're incredibly obedient and respectful.
Grooming Needs: Regular brushing to remove loose hair and occasional baths are sufficient to keep them clean.
Training & Exercise Needs: Daily walks and some playtime are usually enough. They enjoy activities that involve obedience training, tracking, and agility exercises.
Possible Health Issues: hip and elbow dysplasia, bloat, hypothyroidism, and certain types of cancer.

Cairn Terrier

Other Names: None
Color variations: cream, wheaten, red, gray, and nearly black. Brindle-colored coats are also common.
Average Lifespan: 13 to 15 years.
Origins: Scotland - early 20th century - bred primarily for hunting and burrowing prey among the cairns in the Scottish Highlands.
Body Size: Males: 10 in. 14-18 lbs. Females: 9.5 in. 13-17 lbs.
Personality/Disposition/Compatibility: These little dogs are full of life, courage, and smarts. They're always up for an adventure and have a nose for finding excitement. They bring a lot of fun to their families and are incredibly affectionate. They form tight bonds with their humans and love to be involved in everything. They usually get along well with other pets and kids, though their boundless energy might be a bit much for more relaxed animals. Kids who can keep up with their playful spirit will find a great buddy in them.
Grooming Needs: To keep their wiry coat looking its best, these dogs need regular grooming. Aim to brush them a few times a week and give them a hand-stripping now and then to get rid of dead hair. It's a bit of work, but they'll look and feel great!
Training & Exercise Needs: To keep them healthy and happy, they need regular exercise. Their curious nature means they might test your patience during training, but with a firm yet kind approach, they'll soon show you just how clever they are. Daily walks and play sessions in a secure area are perfect for them. They love engaging in activities that tap into their natural instincts, like digging and chasing.
Possible Health Issues: hip dysplasia, Legg-Calvé-Perthes disease, cataracts, and hypothyroidism

Canaan Dog

Other Names: Kelev K'naani
Color variations: sand, red, white, and black. They can also have various patterns such as patches, masks, and shading.
Average Lifespan: 12 to 15 years
Origins: Israel - 20th century - primarily for guarding and herding purposes.
Body Size: Males: 20-24 in. 45-55 lbs. Females: 19-23 in. 35-45 lbs.
Personality/Disposition/Compatibility: These dogs are a delightful mix of smarts and independence, which makes training them both intriguing and fulfilling. With a demeanor that's both calm and confident, they charm with their playful side while keeping their cool. They're great with families, singles, and even other pets, as long as they get the right socialization. Their high energy makes them perfect companions for those who love outdoor adventures. They're protective of their loved ones without being aggressive, so you get a loyal friend who's also approachable. Their sharp observation skills make them excellent watchdogs, always alert to their surroundings. Despite their independent nature, they form strong, loving bonds with their families and thrive in environments where they feel appreciated and involved.
Grooming Needs: Their thick double coat needs regular brushing to keep shedding under control and avoid tangles. Luckily, they're generally pretty clean dogs and don't have much of an odor.
Training & Exercise Needs: This breed really comes alive with daily walks, playtime, and activities that engage both their mind and body. Things like obedience training, agility exercises, and herding are especially great for keeping them happy and healthy.
Possible Health Issues: hip dysplasia, elbow dysplasia, and hypothyroidism

Cane Corso

Other Names: Italian Mastiff
Color variations: black, gray, fawn, red, and brindle
Average Lifespan: 9 to 12 years
Origins: Italy - the 1980s - bred for guarding property and hunting large game.
Body Size: Males: 25-27.5 in. 99-110 lbs. Females: 23.5-26 in. 88-99 lbs.
Personality/Disposition/Compatibility: They're a wonderful blend of strength and affection, making it a fantastic companion for anyone who values both a reliable protector and a loving friend. This breed has a confident yet calm nature and shows incredible loyalty to its family. They love being an integral part of the household and thrive in an environment where they can be actively involved. While they're naturally protective, they respond best to consistent training and early socialization. They're excellent with families, including kids, and they have a unique way of forming deep connections with their people. Just remember, they need careful introductions to other pets, especially smaller ones, due to their strong prey drive.
Grooming Needs: To keep their short coat looking its best, make sure to brush them regularly to get rid of any dead hair and keep that healthy shine. Don't forget to check and clean their ears regularly, and trim their nails as needed to keep them comfortable.
Training & Exercise Needs: These dogs are full of energy and love to stay active! They need daily exercise to keep them happy and healthy, so they thrive on long walks, runs, and playtime in a secure yard. They also have a blast with canine sports like obedience training, tracking, and protection work.
Possible Health Issues: hip dysplasia, elbow dysplasia, idiopathic epilepsy, demodectic mange, and gastric torsion (bloat)

Carolina Dog

Other Names: American Dingo, Dixie Dingo
Color variations: deep red, orange, yellow, and tan to cream and buff. Some may have white markings or a black overlay on the back and shoulders.
Average Lifespan: 12 to 15 years
Origins: United States - pre-Columbian times - originally bred for survival and adaptation in the wild, functioning as free-ranging, feral dogs.
Body Size: Males: 18-20 in. 30-44 lbs. Females: 17-19 in. 25-35 lbs.
Personality/Disposition/Compatibility: These dogs are a delightful mix of curiosity and alertness. They're always up for new experiences and thrive on activities that engage their sharp minds and boundless energy. Friendly and intelligent, they might not be ready to cuddle right away. They tend to be a bit reserved around strangers, making them excellent watchdogs. But once they warm up to you, they're incredibly affectionate and loyal. They're a great fit for active families or individuals who can keep up with their enthusiasm. They usually get along well with other pets, especially if introductions are done carefully. Just keep an eye on their natural hunting instincts around smaller animals. They love spaces where they can roam and explore.
Grooming Needs: Their coat is pretty low-maintenance—just a regular brushing to get rid of loose hair and keep that healthy shine. Plus, they're generally clean dogs with barely any odor.
Training & Exercise Needs: They're full of energy and need plenty of exercise to keep them happy and healthy. They love daily walks, runs, and playtime, and they really shine in places where they have room to explore and roam. They're especially enthusiastic about activities like hiking, agility training, and interactive play.
Possible Health Issues: hip dysplasia and certain eye conditions

Catahoula Leopard Dog

Other Names: Catahoula Cur, Catahoula Hound, and Louisiana Catahoula Leopard Dog
Color variations: blue merle, red merle, brindle, black, red, yellow, and they often have unique leopard-like spots.
Average Lifespan: 10 to 14 years
Origins: Louisiana, United States - early 1800s - bred for their versatility in hunting, herding, and tracking.
Body Size: Males: 22-26 in. 65-90 lbs. Females: 20-24 in. 50-65 lbs.
Personality/Disposition/Compatibility: These dogs are bursting with energy and love for adventure, making them perfect companions for active families and individuals. They're incredibly smart and thrive when they have a job to do, thanks to their strong work ethic. Affectionate and loyal, they form deep bonds with their families. While they might be a bit reserved around strangers at first, they warm up quickly with the right introduction. Their playful and occasionally goofy nature can fill any home with joy and laughter. They generally get along well with other dogs, especially if introductions are handled smoothly. However, their high energy and natural herding instincts might not be the best fit for households with very small pets.
Grooming Needs: Regular brushing and occasional baths are sufficient to keep their coat healthy. They also require routine ear cleaning, nail trimming, and dental care.
Training & Exercise Needs: These dogs are full of energy and enthusiasm, whether they're herding, zooming through agility courses, or playing a spirited game of fetch. To keep them happy and well-behaved, they need plenty of exercise and mental challenges. They thrive on activities like hiking, running, and agility training—anything that keeps their minds sharp and their bodies active.
Possible Health Issues: hip dysplasia, deafness, and progressive retinal atrophy (PRA)

Caucasian Shepherd Dog
Other Names: Caucasian Ovcharka or Caucasian Mountain Dog
Color variations: white, fawn, tan, pied, and brindle.
Average Lifespan: 10 and 12 years
Origins: Caucasus region - ancient times - bred primarily for guarding livestock against predators and for protecting property.
Body Size: Males: 27-30 in. 110-220 lbs. Females: 25-28 in. 99-180 lbs.
Personality/Disposition/Compatibility: Picture a gentle giant with a heart as expansive as its impressive frame. They radiate a natural confidence and have a protective instinct that makes them a steadfast guardian of family and home. While not one to demand constant attention, they stand ready to watch over their loved ones with a vigilant eye. They have a sense of independence and might be reserved around strangers, so it might not be the best fit for a bustling urban environment. They thrive in spaces with room to roam and a purpose to fulfill. With proper socialization from an early age, it can get along well with other pets and children, although its size might be a bit daunting to those unfamiliar with the breed.
Grooming Needs: Their thick double coat means grooming can be a bit of a commitment. Regular brushing is key to keeping their fur from tangling and to manage shedding. When they're shedding heavily, which happens during certain times of the year, you'll need to brush them more often to keep things under control.
Training & Exercise Needs: To keep them happy and healthy, regular exercise is key. Daily walks, fun playtime, and activities that keep their minds engaged—like obedience training and interactive games—are great for their well-being.
Possible Health Issues: hip dysplasia, elbow dysplasia, heart problems, and obesity.

Cavalier King Charles Spaniel
Other Names: CKCS, Cavalier, Cav
Color variations: Blenheim (chestnut and white), Tricolor (black, white, and tan), Ruby (solid red), and Black and Tan.
Average Lifespan: 9 to 14 years
Origins: United Kingdom - 1600s - bred to be a companion dog for royalty and aristocrats.
Body Size: Males: 12-13 in. 13-18 lbs. Females: 12-13 in. 12-17 lbs.
Personality/Disposition/Compatibility: With a personality that could warm even the coldest of hearts, these dogs are known for their gentle and friendly nature. They thrive on human interaction and always aim to please, making them exceptional family pets and delightful companions. They have a special talent for sensing their owners' moods and offering comfort with their sweet, affectionate demeanor. Their adaptability allows them to fit into various living situations, whether you have a bustling household or a quieter home. They get along famously with other pets and children, bringing joy and a touch of grace wherever they go. They're not fond of being left alone for long stretches; they flourish with daily playtime and plenty of snuggles.
Grooming Needs: regular grooming is a must. Brush their fur a few times a week to keep it from getting tangled or matted. Don't forget to clean their ears, trim their nails, and take care of their teeth to keep them happy and healthy!
Training & Exercise Needs: They enjoy a nice balance of activity and relaxation. Daily walks and playtime keep them happy, and they love getting involved in fetch, agility training, or a gentle jog. But don't let their active side fool you—they also relish cozying up and relaxing indoors.
Possible Health Issues: mitral valve disease, hip dysplasia, syringomyelia, cataracts and retinal problems

Central Asian Shepherd Dog
Other Names: Alabai, Central Asian Ovcharka, and Aziat.
Color Variations: white, black, brindle, fawn, and shades of gray. Some dogs may also have patches or spots.
Average Lifespan: 12 to 15 years
Origins: Central Asia - 4,000 years ago - primarily bred as livestock guardian dogs to protect flocks from predators and intruders.
Body Size: Males: 28-30 in. 110-170 lbs. Females: 26-28 in. 88-140 lbs.
Personality/Disposition/Compatibility: They have a natural instinct to protect their home and family, blending authority with a touch of elegance. While they might be a bit reserved with strangers, they shower their loved ones with genuine affection. With their independent spirit, they don't need endless interaction but truly value quality time with those they care about. They do best in a spacious environment where they can roam and have a sense of purpose. Perfect for families or individuals who appreciate their strong-willed nature and are ready to offer the right training and exercise, they usually get along well with other pets if they're socialized from a young age. Just keep in mind they might need a little patience to adjust, thanks to their protective instincts.
Grooming Needs: They need a bit of grooming to stay looking their best. Regular brushing helps manage shedding and keeps their coat clean. You might find yourself brushing a bit more often during those seasonal shedding times.
Training & Exercise Needs: They thrive on daily walks and love having plenty of room to explore and patrol safely. Activities like walking, hiking, and tasks that let them tap into their natural guarding instincts are perfect for keeping them happy and fulfilled.
Possible Health Issues: hip and elbow dysplasia, heart problems, and certain eye conditions

Cesky Terrier
Other Names: Czech Terrier or Bohemian Terrier
Color Variations: gray, ranging from charcoal to platinum
Average Lifespan: 12 to 15 years
Origins: Czechoslovakia - 1949 - bred by crossing a Scottish Terrier and a Sealyham Terrier, with the aim of creating a hunting dog with a narrower chest that could go to ground for burrowing prey such as foxes and badgers.
Body Size: Males: 10-13 in. 16-22 lbs. Females: 9-12 in. 14-20 lbs.
Personality/Disposition/Compatibility: Their friendly and affectionate nature makes them wonderful companions, always eager to join in family activities, whether it's a game or a cozy cuddle session. Smart and eager to please, they're usually a breeze to train—though they do have a hint of stubbornness. This means they thrive on consistent, positive reinforcement and a bit of patience. They adapt well to various living situations, from apartments to larger homes, as long as they get their daily exercise and mental stimulation. Generally good with kids and other pets, especially if they're well-socialized from a young age.
Grooming Needs: Regular grooming is a must. Brush their coat several times a week to avoid mats and tangles, and plan on trimming their fur every few months to keep that signature look. Don't forget to give their ears a clean and keep up with dental care too—these steps are key to maintaining their overall health and style.
Training & Exercise Needs: They have moderate exercise needs and thrive on activities like walks, playtime in a fenced yard, and interactive games. Their versatility shines through as they eagerly join in various dog sports, from agility courses to obedience challenges.
Possible Health Issues: hip dysplasia, patellar luxation, and certain eye conditions such as cataracts

Chesapeake Bay Retriever

Other Names: Chessie
Color variations: brown, sedge, and deadgrass
Average Lifespan: 10 to 13 years
Origins: United States - early 19th century - bred was to retrieve waterfowl for hunters in the Chesapeake Bay area.
Body Size: Males: 23-26 in. 65-80 lbs. Females: 21-24 in. 55-70 lbs.
Personality/Disposition/Compatibility: These dogs have a warm, down-to-earth nature that makes them both reliable and charming. They're incredibly loyal to their families and form deep bonds with their loved ones. While they're protective, they're not over-the-top aggressive, making them fantastic watchdogs and affectionate family pets. Their love for retrieving means they dive right into games and activities, especially those involving water. Whether it's a spirited game of fetch or a splash in the lake, their enthusiasm is truly contagious. They thrive on physical exercise and mental stimulation, so they're perfect for active families or anyone who loves the great outdoors. They generally get along well with kids and can be very tolerant of other pets, especially if they're socialized early on.
Grooming Needs: To keep your dog's coat in top shape, regular brushing is essential to remove dead hair and keep their fur healthy. During shedding seasons, you might need to brush a bit more often. Bathing should be done only occasionally to help maintain those natural oils in their coat.
Training & Exercise Needs: To keep their bodies and minds in top shape, this energetic breed needs regular exercise. They thrive on activities like swimming, playing fetch, and running around.
Possible Health Issues: hip dysplasia, progressive retinal atrophy (PRA), and hypothyroidism

Chihuahua

Other Names: None
Color variations: fawn, black, white, chocolate, cream, and gold, with various patterns and markings.
Average Lifespan: 12 and 20 years
Origins: Mexico - ancient times - bred for companionship.
Body Size: Males & Females: 6-9 in. 2-6 lbs.
Personality/Disposition/Compatibility: These tiny dogs might be small in size, but they have hearts that are as big as their personalities! Their loyalty is off the charts, often forming a close bond with one special person in their family. Despite their little stature, they're always on the go, eager to join in on whatever's happening with their curious and lively nature. Don't underestimate them—these little guys can be incredibly brave and have a surprisingly loud bark, especially when it comes to protecting their home. They're great for apartment living or smaller spaces, where their size is a plus. Usually, they get along well with other pets, especially if they've been socialized early on. Just be aware of their feisty streak—they might try to boss around bigger dogs if they can. While they're generally more comfortable around familiar faces, they might be a bit shy with newcomers.
Grooming Needs: Short-haired Chihuahuas are pretty low-maintenance when it comes to grooming, but if you have a long-haired Chihuahua, you'll need to brush them regularly to keep their coat free from tangles and mats. No matter which type you have, they'll both need their nails trimmed regularly, ears cleaned, and teeth cared for to stay healthy and happy.
Training & Exercise Needs: They enjoy short walks, indoor play, and activities that engage their minds, such as puzzle toys. They are also well-suited for agility and obedience training.
Possible Health Issues: patellar luxation, heart problems, dental issues, hypoglycemia, and tracheal collapse

Chinese Crested
Other Names: Crested and Chinese Edible Dog
Color variations: pink, black, white, and mahogany, with spots
Average Lifespan: 13 to 18 years
Origins: China - 13th century - bred for companionship and as vermin hunters.
Body Size: Males and Females: 11-13 in 8-12 lbs.
Personality/Disposition/Compatibility: These little dogs bring a lot of personality despite their small stature. They're known for being confident and outgoing, always ready to soak up attention and be the star of the show. Whether you're a family, a single person, or someone enjoying their golden years, they can be a fantastic companion. They get along well with kids and other pets, making them a great fit for various households. While they do love being with their humans, they can also show a touch of independence and stubbornness. With some patience and positive reinforcement, though, they pick things up quickly. They adapt well to different living spaces, whether it's a cozy apartment or a house with a yard, as long as they get their daily exercise and playtime.
Grooming Needs: Hairless Chinese Cresteds need a bit of extra love when it comes to their skin—regular care helps keep them moisturized and protected from the sun. On the other hand, Powderpuffs need frequent brushing to keep their fluffy coats from getting tangled and matted.
Training & Exercise Needs: They need a good bit of exercise, so daily walks and fun playtime are perfect. They thrive on agility training and love games that keep their minds active and engaged.
Possible Health Issues: dental problems, patellar luxation, Legg-Calvé-Perthes disease, and skin conditions like acne and sunburn

Chinese Shar-Pei
Other Names: Shar-Pei or Chinese Fighting Dog.
Color variations: black, cream, fawn, red, sable, and blue.
Average Lifespan: 8 to 12 years
Origins: China - 200 BC - bred for guarding, hunting, and fighting due to its strength and protective nature.
Body Size: Males: 18-20 in. 50-60 lbs. Females: 18-20 in. 45-55 lbs.
Personality/Disposition/Compatibility: These dogs often come across as reserved and independent, taking their time to observe their surroundings rather than jumping straight into the action. Their calm and composed demeanor might make them seem a bit aloof at first, but once they form a bond, they become incredibly loyal and affectionate. They have a strong protective instinct and will watch over their loved ones with quiet confidence. They generally get along well with other pets if introduced properly and early, although their strong-willed nature can sometimes lead to conflicts with more dominant animals. With children, they're usually gentle and patient, but they do best in a home where they're respected and not overwhelmed.
Grooming Needs: Brushing your dog regularly and giving them an occasional bath will keep their coat looking great. Just make sure to give extra care to the folds of their skin, cleaning and drying them thoroughly to avoid any infections.
Training & Exercise Needs: Daily walks and playtime in a safe area are perfect for them. They love getting out for a walk, a jog, or an interactive play session where they can really engage and have fun.
Possible Health Issues: hip dysplasia, entropion (a condition where the eyelids roll inward), skin infections, hypothyroidism, and amyloidosis

Chinook
Other Names: None
Color variations: tawny gold to a reddish-gold, often with darker shading on the ears and muzzle.
Average Lifespan: 12 and 15 years
Origins: United States - early 20th century - Arthur Treadwell Walden bred them to be the ultimate sled dogs, combining strength, endurance, and a friendly, gentle nature.
Body Size: Males: 23-27 in. 70-90 lbs. Females: 21-25 in. 50-70 lbs.
Personality/Disposition/Compatibility: These dogs are renowned for their gentle temperament and steadfast loyalty, making them perfect partners for families and individuals alike. They adapt seamlessly to both lively households and more tranquil settings. Highly intelligent, they quickly grasp training commands and enjoy having a task to focus on. Their eagerness to please, combined with their smarts, makes them a delight to train. They typically get along well with other pets, including both dogs and cats, and their easygoing nature means they're more likely to go with the flow than cause any fuss.
Grooming Needs: To keep their thick, double coat looking its best, these dogs need regular grooming. A weekly brush usually does the job, but when they're shedding, you might find yourself brushing more often to keep all that loose hair in check.
Training & Exercise Needs: These spirited, energetic pups really come alive with regular exercise. Whether it's hitting the trails for a hike, going for a run, or jumping into dog sports like agility and obedience, they thrive on staying active. Keeping them moving every day isn't just great for their physical health; it also keeps their minds sharp and happy.
Possible Health Issues: hip dysplasia, epilepsy, and cataracts

Chow Chow
Other Names: Chow, Chowdren
Color variations: red, black, blue, cinnamon, and cream.
Average Lifespan: 8 to 12 years
Origins: China - 2000 years ago - bred for all sorts of important tasks, from hunting and herding to pulling carts and protecting homes.
Body Size: Males: 18-22 in. 55-70 lbs. Females: 17-20 in. 45-60 lbs.
Personality/Disposition/Compatibility: Picture a dog that combines aloof elegance with unwavering loyalty, all wrapped up in a fluffy coat. This breed has a distinct independent streak and won't be shadowing you every step you take. But don't let their cool exterior fool you—these dogs form deep bonds with their families and express their affection in their own unique, reserved way. They might come off as a bit of a lone wolf, and while they can be standoffish with strangers, this trait makes them excellent watchdogs. With a bit of socialization from an early age, they can become more at ease around new faces and other pets. They generally do well with families, but they may be a bit assertive with other dogs, so introducing them carefully is important.
Grooming Needs: To keep their thick, double coat looking fabulous, make sure to brush their fur a few times a week to prevent any annoying mats from forming. Treat them to a bath every now and then to keep them feeling fresh. And don't overlook their eyes and ears.
Training & Exercise Needs: They really enjoy their daily walks and playtime. They're happiest when they're out on brisk strolls, light jogs, or engaged in fun, interactive games.
Possible Health Issues: hip dysplasia, elbow dysplasia, entropion (a condition where the eyelid rolls inward), and allergies

Cirneco Dell'Etna

Other Names: Sicilian Greyhound or Sicilian Hound
Color variations: tan, ranging from light to dark, and sometimes have white markings on the chest, toes, or face.
Average Lifespan: 12 to 14 years
Origins: Sicily, Italy - around 1000 BCE - bred for hunting small game, particularly rabbits, in the rugged terrain of Mount Etna.
Body Size: Males: 18-20.5 in. 22-26 lbs. Females: 16-18 in. 17-22 lbs.
Personality/Disposition/Compatibility: These dogs are a bundle of joy with their lively and affectionate personalities. Not only are they skilled hunters, but they also make wonderful, devoted companions. Always full of energy and ready for the next adventure, they're perfect for active families or anyone who loves the great outdoors. Their playful nature wins over both adults and kids, though they also have a touch of independence that adds to their charm. They generally get along well with other dogs and pets, especially if they're properly socialized.
Grooming Needs: Brushing your dog's coat regularly to get rid of dead hair and giving them an occasional bath is all it takes to keep their fur looking and feeling great.
Training & Exercise Needs: To keep them at their best, both physically and mentally, regular exercise is key. Make sure they get daily walks, runs, and playtime in a secure area. Their strong hunting instincts mean they love activities that involve tracking and chasing. With their boundless curiosity and high energy, they really shine in environments where they can get plenty of exercise and mental stimulation.
Possible Health Issues: Overall, this breed tends to be quite healthy, but there are a few health issues to keep an eye on. These can include hip dysplasia, patellar luxation, and dental problems.

Clumber Spaniel

Other Names: None
Color variations: white with lemon or orange markings
Average Lifespan: 10 to 12 years
Origins: France - late 18th century - bred for hunting, for their ability to work through dense underbrush and retrieve game.
Body Size: Males: 17-20 in. 70-85 lbs. Females: 16-19 in. 55-70 lbs.
Personality/Disposition/Compatibility: They're the ultimate easy going and affectionate companions. They don't just enjoy being around people—they absolutely thrive on it. If you're after a loving, laid-back friend, look no further than a Clumber Spaniel. These charming dogs are naturally friendly, making them fantastic family pets. They get along famously with kids, other dogs, and even cats, effortlessly fitting into all sorts of social settings. Their calm and steady nature means they stay cool under pressure and handle new experiences with ease. While they have a playful side, they're not overly energetic; they're just as happy enjoying a relaxed walk, or snuggling up for a cozy nap.
Grooming Needs: To keep their thick coats in top shape, regular grooming is a must. That means brushing a few times a week to prevent mats and manage shedding. And don't forget the ears and nails
Training & Exercise Needs: To keep them in top shape, they need a good mix of exercise, so daily walks and some playtime are a must. They really enjoy activities like retrieving and swimming, which let them indulge their natural instincts as hunting dogs.
Possible Health Issues: hip dysplasia, elbow dysplasia, entropion, ectropion, ear infections, disc/back issues.

Cocker Spaniel (American)
Other Names: Cocker
Color variations: black, black and tan, merle, red, buff, silver, brown, and parti-colors.
Average Lifespan: 10 and 14 years
Origins: United States - late 1800s - bred primarily for hunting and retrieving game birds.
Body Size: Males: 15 in. 25-30 lbs. Females: 14 in. 20-25 lbs.
Personality/Disposition/Compatibility: These dogs are the definition of warmth and charm. They're friendly and affectionate, always ready to bring a smile with their playful spirit and eagerness to please. Perfect for families, they get along wonderfully with kids and truly thrive in a home where they're part of the action. Their sociable nature means they're not just happy to be around—they genuinely enjoy it. Whether they're meeting new people or playing with the family, their loving and lively personality makes them fantastic companions. They flourish in environments where they get plenty of attention and interaction, and they'll repay that with endless loyalty and a wagging tail.
Grooming Needs: Regular brushing is essential to keep your dog's coat free from mats and tangles. Be sure to trim their coat, ears, and feet regularly to keep them looking and feeling great. Don't forget that bathing and cleaning their ears are also crucial for their overall health and well-being.
Training & Exercise Needs: Daily walks and playtime are essential for keeping them healthy and happy. They thrive on activities like fetching, agility training, and swimming, which keep them both engaged and entertained.
Possible Health Issues: hip dysplasia, progressive retinal atrophy (PRA), cataracts, ear infections, and autoimmune diseases.

Cocker Spaniel (English)
Other Names: Cocker
Color variations: black, liver, red, golden, and shades of these colors. They may also have markings like tan points or roaning.
Average Lifespan: 12 to 14 years
Origins: England - 1800s - bred for flushing and retrieving game birds.
Body Size: Males: 16-17 in. 28-34 lbs. Females: 15-16 in. 26-32 lbs.
Personality/Disposition/Compatibility: These dogs are incredibly affectionate and love nothing more than spending time with their families. Their enthusiasm for life is truly heartwarming, and their cheerful, easygoing nature makes them a joy to have around. They're great with kids and get along well with other pets, making them a wonderful addition to any household. These social dogs thrive on attention and enjoy being involved in family activities, so they might not be the best choice if you're away from home a lot. They also need regular exercise and mental stimulation to keep them happy and healthy, which suits their energetic and smart personalities perfectly.
Grooming Needs: To keep their medium-length coat in top shape, give it a good brush a few times a week to prevent mats and tangles. Regular trims, especially around the ears and feet, will keep their fur looking fresh and tidy.
Training & Exercise Needs: They love to stay active, whether it's going for walks, running around, or playing fetch. Plus, they shine in dog sports like agility, obedience, and hunting trials.
Possible Health Issues: hip dysplasia, progressive retinal atrophy (PRA), cataracts, and ear infections

Collie

Other Names: Scotch Collies or Scottish Collies
Color variations: sable and white, tricolor (black, white, and tan), blue merle, and white with colored markings.
Coat Type: Rough and Smooth
Average Lifespan: 10 to 14 years
Origins: Scotland - 1800s - bred for herding sheep and cattle.
Body Size: Males: 24-26 in. 60-75 lbs, Females: 22-24 in. 50-65 lbs.
Personality/Disposition/Compatibility: With its gentle and affectionate nature, this breed quickly becomes a cherished member of the family. They're known for their loyalty, intelligence, and eagerness to please, which makes training a breeze. They're fantastic with kids, showing both patience and a protective streak that makes them ideal family dogs. Their friendly attitude also extends to other pets, though their herding instinct might lead to some playful nipping at the heels of other animals. These dogs flourish in homes where they receive lots of attention and mental stimulation.
Grooming Needs: Rough Collies benefit from a few brushing sessions each week to keep mats at bay and manage shedding. Smooth Collies, on the other hand, need a bit less frequent brushing. Regular grooming for both types helps keep their coats healthy and shiny.
Training & Exercise Needs: They really come alive with a mix of daily walks, playtime, and mental stimulation. They're always up for staying active, whether it's herding, agility, or obedience training. A brisk walk or a playful game keeps them engaged and ensures they stay happy and healthy.
Possible Health Issues: Collie Eye Anomaly (CEA), progressive retinal atrophy (PRA), hip dysplasia, and drug sensitivities, particularly to medications containing ivermectin.

Coton De Tulear

Other Names: Cotie or Coton
Color variations: white, but they can also have shades of light gray or light tan on their ears.
Average Lifespan: 14 to 16 years
Origins: Madagascar - 16th century - as a companion dog for the Merina royalty.
Body Size: Males: 10-12 in. 9-15 lbs. Females: 9-11 in. 8-13 lbs.
Personality/Disposition/Compatibility: They're all about spreading joy and love. With their playful antics and warm, affectionate nature, they have a talent for brightening everyone's day. They're the kind of pets who thrive on human company and are especially great with kids, making them perfect for families. They get along well with other dogs and pets, so they fit seamlessly into many households. Whether they're enjoying a lively play session or cozying up on the couch with their favorite person, they're always happy. Just keep in mind, they're not fans of being alone for too long, so they do best in a home where they can be an active, cherished part of family life.
Grooming Needs: To keep that soft, fluffy coat looking its best, regular grooming is essential. Aim to brush it a few times a week and give it the occasional bath to keep it clean and free of tangles.
Training & Exercise Needs: They need a moderate amount of exercise, which you can easily provide with daily walks and some fun playtime. Games like fetch and interactive activities are perfect for keeping them engaged and mentally stimulated.
Possible Health Issues: hip dysplasia, progressive retinal atrophy, and allergies.

K9 Chatter

Croatian Sheepdog
Other Names: Hrvatski Ovčar
Color variations: black, although some may have small white markings on the chest and toes.
Average Lifespan: 12 to 14 years
Origins: Croatia - 1969 - bred for herding and guarding livestock.
Body Size: Males: 17-21 in. 29-43 lbs. Females: 16-20 in. 29-43 lbs.
Personality/Disposition/Compatibility: The Croatian Sheepdog is a true family favorite, forming strong, loving bonds with everyone in the household. Their boundless energy and eagerness to please make them a joy for those who love an active lifestyle. With a natural flair for herding, they're hardworking and smart, though their intelligence sometimes shows up as a bit of mischief. Despite their playful side, they're deeply responsible and protective. They shine in environments where they can stay active and mentally engaged. They're fantastic with kids and get along well with other pets, especially if they've been well-socialized from a young age. Their friendly and adaptable nature makes them a fantastic addition to any home.
Grooming Needs: Their thick coat needs regular brushing to keep it tangle-free and to get rid of loose hair. Luckily, they don't need baths often since their fur naturally repels dirt.
Training & Exercise Needs: These dogs have a lot of energy and love activities that keep both their bodies and minds engaged. They really shine in herding, agility training, and obedience exercises. To keep them happy and healthy, make sure they get daily walks and lots of playtime.
Possible Health Issues: hip dysplasia, progressive retinal atrophy (PRA), and epilepsy

Curly-coated Retriever
Other Names: None
Color variations: black or liver (a deep reddish-brown) colors
Average Lifespan: 10 to 12 years
Origins: England - late 18th century - bred for retrieving game from water and land, making it popular among hunters.
Body Size: Males: 25-27 in. 65-80 lbs. Females: 23-25 in. 60-70 lbs.
Personality/Disposition/Compatibility: With their boundless energy and playful nature, these dogs are the perfect match for active families and outdoor enthusiasts. They're friendly and sociable, getting along well with kids and other pets, making them a great fit for any household. Not only are they quick learners, but they also thrive on engaging and varied training sessions. Just keep in mind that their high energy levels need plenty of physical and mental stimulation. If they don't get it, they might come up with their own creative ways to stay entertained, which can sometimes lead to a bit of mischievous fun!
Grooming Needs: To keep your furry friend's coat looking its best and to avoid those pesky mats, regular grooming is a must. A weekly brushing usually does the trick, but during shedding seasons, you might find that a bit more frequent grooming is needed to keep things under control.
Training & Exercise Needs: These energetic dogs thrive on regular exercise and love staying busy. Whether it's splashing around in the pool, playing fetch, or tackling agility courses, these activities keep them both physically fit and mentally sharp.
Possible Health Issues: hip dysplasia, elbow dysplasia, eye problems such as cataracts and progressive retinal atrophy (PRA), and bloat

Czechoslovakian Vlack

Other Names: Czechoslovakian Wolfdog, Ceskoslovenský Vlciak
Color variations: shades of gray, ranging from silver-gray to darker gray, with a characteristic light mask.
Average Lifespan: 12 to 16 years
Origins: Czechoslovakia - 1950s - came about when German Shepherds were crossed with Carpathian wolves. The goal was to combine the wolves' incredible strength and endurance with the dogs' trainability and friendly temperament.
Body Size: Males: 26-28 in. 55-79 lbs. Females: 24-26 in. 48-64 lbs.
Personality/Disposition/Compatibility: These dogs are full of life and energy! They're quick learners who love to please, so training them is a breeze. However, they thrive on mental challenges, so keep them busy with puzzles or tasks to keep boredom at bay. Their loyalty and protective nature make them incredibly devoted family members, forming strong bonds with their humans. They usually get along well with other pets if introductions are handled properly, but their high prey drive means they might be a bit of a challenge around smaller animals. They're typically fantastic with kids, especially if the kids can match their playful, high-energy vibe.
Grooming Needs: They require occasional brushing to remove dead hair.
Training & Exercise Needs: These energetic pups thrive on action and need plenty of it every day! They love long walks, runs, and exciting activities like agility training and tracking. If your home is active and you can keep them busy with hikes, runs, or agility courses, they'll be in doggy heaven.
Possible Health Issues: hip dysplasia, elbow dysplasia, and degenerative myelopathy

Dachshund

Other Names: Doxies, Sausage Dogs, Wiener Dogs, and Teckels
Color variations: red, black and tan, chocolate, cream, blue, and fawn. They can also have patterns such as dapple, brindle, sable, and piebald.
Coat type: Smooth, long-haired or wire-haired
Average Lifespan: 12 to 16 years
Origins: Germany - 15th century - bred for hunting badgers and other burrowing animals.
Body Size: Males & Females: 8-9 in. 16-32 lbs.
Miniature Dachshunds: 5 to 6 in. 11 lbs or less.
Personality/Disposition/Compatibility: These lively little dogs are known for their spirited and sometimes stubborn personalities, making them a bundle of energy in any home. They've got a brave streak that can border on fearless, and their mix of independence and affection makes them both entertaining and endearing. They might be a bit shy around new faces, but once they're comfortable, they're all warmth and love. They adapt well to different living situations, but they do need consistent training and socialization to manage their sometimes strong-willed tendencies. They generally get along with kids and can adjust to other pets, especially if introduced in the right way.
Grooming Needs: Smooth-coated Dachshunds require minimal grooming, while long-haired Dachshunds need regular brushing to prevent tangles and mats. Wire-haired Dachshunds need regular brushing and occasional trimming.
Training & Exercise Needs: enjoy activities such as walking, playing fetch, and digging. They benefit from daily walks and playtime to keep them physically and mentally stimulated.
Possible Health Issues: intervertebral disc disease (IVDD) due to their long spine, obesity, dental problems, and hip dysplasia

Dalmatian
Other Names: Dal
Color variations: white coat with black or liver spots
Average Lifespan: 11 and 13 years
Origins: Croatia - 18th century - bred for guarding carriages and as coach dogs.
Body Size: Males: 22-24 in. 55-70 lbs. Females: 20-22 in. 45-60 lbs.
Personality/Disposition/Compatibility: Dalmatians are truly social butterflies, and they absolutely thrive on human interaction. They're known for their affectionate and playful nature, which makes them fantastic companions for both families and individuals. Their zest for life is contagious, and they're always up for a game of fetch or just hanging out with their favorite humans. With proper introduction and socialization, they generally get along well with other dogs and pets. They love being part of a pack, so having the company of other dogs or their human family is something they really appreciate.
Grooming Needs: To keep their coat looking great and manage shedding, regular brushing is a must. Bathing can be done as needed to keep them fresh and clean.
Training & Exercise Needs: If your family loves running, hiking, or playing fetch, you'll find these dogs to be the perfect fit. They need lots of exercise to stay happy and healthy, so regular playtime and walks are essential to keep them content and engaged.
Possible Health Issues: deafness, urinary stones, and skin allergies

Dandie Dinmont Terrier
Other Names: Dandie
Color variations: "pepper," which ranges from dark bluish-black to light silvery gray, and "mustard," which ranges from reddish-brown to pale fawn.
Average Lifespan: 12 and 15 years
Origins: border region between England and Scotland - 1600s - bred for hunting otters and badgers.
Body Size: Males & Females: 8-11 in. 18-24 lbs.
Personality/Disposition/Compatibility: These terriers are a delightful mix of lively energy and sweet charm. They're confident and spirited, yet their playful and loving nature makes them fantastic family companions. Their curiosity leads them on many little adventures, so you can always expect some entertaining antics. Even though they're small, their hearts are enormous and overflowing with affection. They generally get along well with kids and can tolerate other pets, though their strong terrier instincts might prompt them to assert themselves if needed. They thrive in a home where they receive plenty of attention and where their playful spirit is celebrated.
Grooming Needs: To keep their coat looking its best and prevent tangles, regular brushing is a must. They also need an occasional trim to maintain their unique, eye-catching look.
Training & Exercise Needs: To keep them healthy and happy, they need regular exercise. Daily walks and play sessions are perfect, and they especially enjoy activities that tap into their natural hunting instincts, like tracking games.
Possible Health Issues: intervertebral disc disease, glaucoma, and hypothyroidism

Danish-Swedish Farmdog

Other Names: Dansk-Svensk Gårdshund
Color variations: white coat with various markings, which can include black, tan, or shades of brown.
Average Lifespan: 12 to 15 years
Origins: Denmark and Sweden - the 1700s - bred as a versatile farm dog for tasks such as hunting, herding, and guarding.
Body Size: Males: 13-15.5 in. 15-25 lbs.
Females: 12.5-14.5 in. 13-20 lbs.
Personality/Disposition/Compatibility: These dogs are incredibly friendly and outgoing, making them perfect companions for both active families and lively individuals. Their intelligence and curiosity keep them engaged and eager to learn, so training them is usually smooth sailing, especially with a bit of patience and positive reinforcement. They're also excellent watchdogs—alert and quick to notice anything unusual, though they're not typically aggressive. With proper introductions, they get along well with other pets, including dogs and cats. They thrive on human interaction and are particularly great with kids, making them an ideal choice for family life.
Grooming Needs: Regular brushing is essential to keep their coat looking its best and to manage loose hairs. They also benefit from occasional baths and routine care, like nail trimming and teeth cleaning, to stay in top shape.
Training & Exercise Needs: This breed is full of energy and thrives on regular exercise to stay in top shape and keep their spirits high. They love their daily walks and playtime, and activities like agility training and obedience exercises are perfect for them. They're playful and affectionate, always eager to jump into a game or snuggle up after a day full of adventures.
Possible Health Issues: hip dysplasia, patellar luxation, and dental problems

Deutscher Wachtelhund

Other Names: German Spaniel or German Quail Dog.
Color variations: solid brown or brown roan, sometimes with white markings.
Average Lifespan: 12 and 14 years
Origins: Germany - around 1903 - bred for hunting, tracking and retrieving game.
Body Size: Males: 18-21 in. 40-55 lbs. Females: 17-20 in. 35-50 lbs.
Personality/Disposition/Compatibility: These dogs are the epitome of friendly and charming. They're not just loyal; they form deep bonds and want to be involved in all your activities. They get along wonderfully with just about everyone, making them perfect family companions. They're great with kids and can get along with other pets, including dogs and cats, as long as they're introduced properly. Their intelligence and eagerness to please make them easy to train, though their playful nature might keep you on your toes!
Grooming Needs: To keep your dog's coat smooth and free from mats and tangles, regular brushing is a must, especially since their coat is so dense and wavy. Don't forget the occasional bath and routine ear cleaning to help prevent any infections.
Training & Exercise Needs: They thrive on lots of physical and mental activity. They need daily exercise, whether it's a long walk, a run, or a playful game, and they shine in hunting, tracking, and retrieving. Whether you're out for a vigorous hike, playing fetch in the yard, or just relaxing on the couch, this breed will match your energy and shower you with their affectionate, enthusiastic spirit.
Possible Health Issues: hip dysplasia, ear infections, and eye problems

Doberman Pinscher
Other Names: Dobie
Color variations: black and rust, blue and rust, red and rust, and fawn and rust
Average Lifespan: 10 to 12 years
Origins: Germany - late 19th century - bred by Karl Friedrich Louis Dobermann, a tax collector who wanted a loyal and protective companion.
Body Size: Males: 26-28 in. 75-100 lbs. Females: 24-26 in. 60-90 lbs.
Personality/Disposition/Compatibility: Dobies truly embody a blend of power and grace. Their impressive looks are just the surface of their fascinating personalities. At heart, they're incredibly loyal and fiercely protective of their families. This strong instinct to guard makes them top-notch watchdogs and guardians. But don't let their serious side fool you—these dogs are also incredibly affectionate and thrive on being close to their loved ones. They might be a bit reserved with strangers at first, but with a little time and the right introductions, they warm up and can even become friendly with new people and other pets.
Grooming Needs: Regular brushing to remove loose hair and the occasional bath are usually sufficient to keep them clean and healthy.
Training & Exercise Needs: These dogs are smart and eager to please, making training straightforward with positive reinforcement. They enjoy having a job, whether it's obedience, agility, or playing fetch. To stay healthy and happy, they need regular exercise, including daily walks and playtime.
Possible Health Issues: dilated cardiomyopathy, hip dysplasia, von Willebrand's disease, and hypothyroidism

Dogo Argentino
Other Names: Argentine Mastiff or Dogo
Color variations: predominantly white, with occasional dark patches around the eye.
Average Lifespan: 10 to 15 years
Origins: Argentina - 1920s - Dr. Antonio Nores Martínez set out to create a versatile hunting dog that could tackle Argentina's rugged terrain and double as a loyal family guardian.
Body Size: Males: 24-27 in. 88-100 lbs. Females: 23-26 in. 88-95 lbs.
Personality/Disposition/Compatibility: These dogs are as striking in personality as it is in appearance. They exude loyalty and a protective nature, making them fantastic guardians for families and homes. Despite their robust build, they have a surprisingly gentle and playful side with those they love. They thrive with experienced owners who can offer consistent training and socialization. While they generally get along well with other dogs, especially if introduced early, their strong prey drive might make them less suited for homes with smaller pets. With their natural protective instincts, they are both brave and affectionate, often forming deep, lasting bonds with their human companions.
Grooming Needs: Regular brushing and occasional baths will help maintain its coat and skin health. It is also important to check its ears, teeth, and nails regularly.
Training & Exercise Needs: To keep this breed happy and healthy, they need to stay active and mentally engaged. They absolutely flourish with plenty of exercise and playtime, so long walks, runs, and fun activities are right up their alley. They also enjoy mental challenges, so obedience training and agility drills are great ways to keep their minds sharp and their spirits high.
Possible Health Issues: hip dysplasia, deafness (due to their white coat), hypothyroidism, and skin allergies

Dogue de Bordeaux

Other Names: French Mastiff or Bordeaux Mastiff
Color variations: comes in shades of fawn, from a light fawn to a dark red fawn. Some may have a small white patch on the chest and feet.
Average Lifespan: 5 to 8 years
Origins: France -14th century - bred for guarding, hunting large game, and working as a farm dog.
Body Size: Males: 23.5-27 in. 110-150 lbs.
Females: 23-26 in. 99-130 lbs.
Personality/Disposition/Compatibility: Known for their fierce loyalty and protective instincts, these dogs form deep, loving bonds with their families. While their devotion might sometimes seem a bit overprotective, it's all about keeping their loved ones safe. Beneath their tough exterior, they're surprisingly sensitive and mellow at home. Their calm and patient demeanor makes them wonderful companions for families, especially those with kids.
They generally get along well with other animals, especially when socialized early. They might take a little time to warm up to new pets, but their steady, patient nature usually helps them build lasting friendships.
Grooming Needs: To keep their short coat looking its best, you'll need to brush them regularly to get rid of any dead hair. Don't forget to clean the skin folds on their face often, too.
Training & Exercise Needs: They love getting outside for daily walks and playtime in a safe area. They thrive on activities that keep both their minds and bodies active, so obedience training and interactive games are right up their alley.
Possible Health Issues: hip dysplasia, elbow dysplasia, heart problems, and bloat

Drentsche Patrijshond

Other Names: Dutch Partridge Dog or Drent.
Color variations: white coat with brown or orange markings, and it may also have some ticking.
Average Lifespan: 12 to 15 years
Origins: Netherlands - 16th century - bred for hunting game birds.
Body Size: Males: 23-25 in. 55-73 lbs. Females: 21-23 in. 45-60 lbs.
Personality/Disposition/Compatibility: These dogs truly exude natural grace and intelligence in everything they do. Their engaging and laid-back personality makes them a joy to be around, effortlessly making everyone feel at home. With their friendly attitude and endless energy, they quickly become favorites among families and singles alike. They get along great with other pets and kids, making them a perfect fit for a lively household. Their playful spirit means they're always ready to jump into a game of fetch or snuggle up on the couch for a cozy evening.
Grooming Needs: To keep their coat looking great and free from tangles, regular brushing is a must. They also benefit from the occasional bath, along with routine checks to make sure their ears and teeth are in good shape.
Training & Exercise Needs: They need plenty of exercise to stay happy and healthy. Not only are they good-natured, but they're also highly trainable, thriving on positive reinforcement and eager to pick up new tricks or commands. They enjoy activities like running, hiking, and participating in dog sports like agility or obedience training. Keeping them active ensures they're not just physically fit but mentally stimulated and content.
Possible Health Issues: hip dysplasia, elbow dysplasia, and progressive retinal atrophy (PRA)

K9 Chatter

Drever
Other Names: Swedish Dachsbracke
Color variations: fawn, black, and tricolor, often with white markings.
Average Lifespan: 12 to 15 years
Origins: Sweden - early 20th century - bred for tracking deer.
Body Size: Males: 12-15 in. 32-34 lbs. Females: 11-14 in. 30-32 lbs.
Personality/Disposition/Compatibility: These dogs are full of energy and personality, making them wonderful friends for both families and individuals alike. Their joyful attitude lights up any family gathering, and they usually get along great with kids and other pets. Adaptable and always eager to make you happy, they fit effortlessly into different living situations. Whether they're in the thick of the action or just relaxing with their human family, they're perfectly happy as long as they're surrounded by their loved ones. Their laid-back nature helps them adjust to new places and changes with impressive ease.
Grooming Needs: Their short, dense coat benefits from a regular brushing to keep loose hair in check, and an occasional bath is all they need to stay clean and healthy.
Training & Exercise Needs: They love getting out for long walks, hitting the trails for a good hike, or taking part in tracking and hunting activities that really let their natural instincts shine.
Possible Health Issues: hip dysplasia, ear infections, and intervertebral disc disease due to their long backs and short legs

Dutch Shepherd
Other Names: Dutch Herder
Color variations: various shades of brindle, including gold brindle and silver brindle.
Coat Type: Smooth, Rough-coated and Long-haired
Average Lifespan: 11 to 14 years
Origins: Netherlands - 19th century - bred for herding sheep and other livestock.
Body Size: Males: 22.5-24.5 in. 50-70lbs.
Females: 21.5-23.5 in. 40-60 lbs.
Personality/Disposition/Compatibility: This breed is known for its loyalty and affection. With its sharp mind and a playful spirit, they're always up for an adventure. Their versatility shines through, whether they're a family pet or a working dog. They are naturally protective and alert and make excellent watchdogs, yet they're incredibly friendly and social with their loved ones. They generally get along well with children and other pets due to their balanced and social nature. They thrive in environments that offer plenty of activities and mental stimulation, so a home that keeps them engaged is perfect for them.
Grooming Needs: Short-haired dogs just need a regular brushing to keep loose hair in check. Long-haired and rough-coated breeds, on the other hand, need a bit more attention to avoid matting and tangles, so more frequent grooming is a must. Regardless of their coat type, all dogs will appreciate a good bath and a nail trim now and then.
Training & Exercise Needs: They absolutely love going for long walks, jogging, hiking, or even engaging in agility training and other dog sports. Plus, they really shine when they have a job to do—whether it's herding, obedience training, or even helping out in search and rescue missions.
Possible Health Issues: hip dysplasia, elbow dysplasia, and thyroid problems

English Foxhound
Other Names: None
Color Variations: black, white, tan, and any combination of these colors.
Average Lifespan: 10 to 13 years
Origins: England - 16th century - bred primarily for hunting foxes.
Body Size: Males: 22-25 in. 65-75 lbs. Females: 21-24 in. 60-70 lbs.
Personality/Disposition/Compatibility: They're known for their friendly and easygoing nature, making them great companions for both families and individuals. These sociable dogs thrive on interaction with people and other animals, and they naturally want to be part of the family pack. They get along well with kids and other pets, and their calm demeanor helps them adapt to different living situations. Regular exercise is important to keep their energy levels in check, but overall, they're quite adaptable. While they might not be the most excitable or outgoing breed, their steady, affectionate personality makes them reliable and loving companions. Plus, their intelligence and eagerness to please make training them a breeze.
Grooming Needs: Its short coat requires regular brushing to remove loose hair and maintain its condition. Baths should be given as needed, depending on the dog's activity level and environment.
Training & Exercise Needs: These dogs are full of energy and love staying active. To keep them happy and healthy, they need plenty of exercise—think long walks, runs, or playtime every day. They really shine in activities like tracking, agility, and obedience training, so if you're up for some action-packed fun, they'll be right there with you!
Possible Health Issues: hip dysplasia, ear infections, and kidney disease

English Setter
Other Names: Laverack Setter or Setter
Color Variations: white with black (blue belton), white with orange (orange belton), white with lemon (lemon belton), white with liver (liver belton), and tricolor, which includes blue belton with tan points.
Average Lifespan: 10 to 12 years
Origins: England - 14th century - bred hunting and retrieving game birds.
Body Size: Males: 25-27 in. 65-80 lbs. Females: 23-25 in. 45 to 55 lbs.
Personality/Disposition/Compatibility: They're a delightful blend of energy and tranquility. They're always up for a game or a romp in the yard, but they also know how to kick back and enjoy a cozy nap with their favorite humans. This balance makes them adaptable to just about any living situation, whether you're in a busy household or a quieter setting. Their affectionate nature means they're always ready to shower their family with love and companionship. They thrive on interaction and make fantastic family pets, getting along beautifully with kids and other animals.
Grooming Needs: To keep their silky coat looking its best, regular grooming is a must. Brush your dog several times a week to avoid mats and tangles, and don't forget to trim around their ears and feet every now and then.
Training & Exercise Needs: To keep their spirits up and avoid boredom, these dogs need regular exercise. They're energetic and thrive on activities like long walks, running, and playing fetch. With their hunting background, they also love activities that let them use their natural scenting and retrieving skills.
Possible Health Issues: hip dysplasia, elbow dysplasia, deafness, hypothyroidism, and certain eye conditions such as progressive retinal atrophy

English Springer Spaniel
Other Names: Springer Spaniel
Color variations: liver and white, black and white, and tricolor (black, white, and tan).
Average Lifespan: 12 and 14 years.
Origins: England - early 19th century - bred for flushing and retrieving game during hunting.
Body Size: Males: 19-21 in. 45-55 lbs. Females: 18-20 in. 40-50 lbs.
Personality/Disposition/Compatibility: These dogs are a bundle of joy, brimming with friendliness and an infectious zest for life. Springers are incredibly loyal and always eager to please, making training them a breeze—just be sure to provide consistent guidance and lots of positive reinforcement. They're great with other pets and kids, thanks to their gentle and patient nature. If you have a family or enjoy socializing with other dogs, a Springer might just be the perfect companion for you.
Grooming Needs: To keep your dog's coat looking its best, you'll want to brush it several times a week to avoid tangles and mats, and give it an occasional trim to keep it neat. Don't forget to check their ears regularly for any signs of infection and keep those nails trimmed to keep them comfortable.
Training & Exercise Needs: They thrive on long walks, running, and playing fetch, and they're enthusiastic participants in dog sports like agility and obedience. Their high-energy nature means they're always up for an adventure, whether it's a vigorous game in the yard or a brisk walk around the neighborhood. If you love the outdoors and staying active, this breed will match your pace and bring an extra dose of joy to your routine.
Possible Health Issues: hip dysplasia, elbow dysplasia, progressive retinal atrophy (PRA), ear infections, and autoimmune conditions

English Toy Spaniel
Other Names: King Charles Spaniel
Color variations: Blenheim (chestnut and white), Prince Charles (tricolor), King Charles (black and tan), and Ruby (solid red).
Average Lifespan: 10 to 12 years
Origins: England - 1600s - bred to serve as companions for royalty and nobility.
Body Size: Males and Females: 9-10 in. 8-14 lbs.
Personality/Disposition/Compatibility: This breed is a true sweetheart, known for its friendly and gentle nature. Even though they're small, their loyalty and playful spirit make them feel like a big part of the family. They're not just looking for a place to live—they want a cozy spot right next to you on the couch. These spaniels thrive when they're close to their human family and generally get along wonderfully with kids and other pets. They're surprisingly adaptable, too. Whether you live in a snug apartment or a house with a yard, they're perfectly happy as long as they get plenty of attention and playtime.
Grooming Needs: To keep them looking their best and feeling comfy, regular brushing is a must to avoid tangles and mats, especially around their ears and chest. Make sure to check and clean their ears regularly to keep infections at bay, and trim their nails as needed to keep them happy and healthy.
Training & Exercise Needs: They love their daily walks and a bit of playtime, though they're not bursting with energy. Gentle games of fetch and some indoor fun can keep them happy and engaged both physically and mentally.
Possible Health Issues: mitral valve disease, patellar luxation, syringomyelia, ear infections, and respiratory problems due to their short noses

Entlebucher Mountain Dog

Other Names: Entlebucher Sennenhund or Entlebucher Cattle Dog
Color variations: a tricolor coat consisting of black, white, and tan.
Average Lifespan: 11 to 13 years
Origins: Switzerland - early 20th century - bred for herding cattle and guarding livestock.
Body Size: Males: 17-21 in. 45-65 lbs. Females: 16-20 in. 40-55 lbs.
Personality/Disposition/Compatibility: These dogs are a fantastic mix of energy, smarts, and affection. With their playful and lively personalities, they really shine when they're active and have something to do. Their loyalty and devotion make them wonderful family members, especially with kids—they're great companions for children. They usually get along well with other pets, especially if they've been socialized early on. They do have strong herding instincts, which might lead them to try and herd other animals or even people during play. But don't worry, this behavior is usually harmless and can be managed with the right training and plenty of exercise.
Grooming Needs: To keep their coat looking great and free of loose hair, they need regular brushing. They also appreciate the occasional bath, along with routine nail trimming, ear cleaning, and dental care.
Training & Exercise Needs: These dogs are incredibly intelligent and quick learners, but their independent and strong-willed nature means they benefit from a firm and consistent approach to training. They're full of energy and thrive on both physical exercise and mental challenges. Daily walks, playtime, and activities like herding, agility training, and obedience exercises are perfect for keeping them happy and healthy.
Possible Health Issues: hip dysplasia, progressive retinal atrophy, and certain hereditary eye conditions

Estrela Mountain Dog

Other Names: Cão da Serra da Estrela and Estrela Mountain Mastiff.
Color variations: fawn, brindle, and wolf gray.
Coat Type: long or short haired.
Average Lifespan: 10 to 12 years
Origins: Portugal - 12th century - bred to guard livestock and protect flocks from predators.
Body Size: Males: 25.5-28.5 in. 88-110 lbs.
Females: 24-27 in. 66-88 lbs.
Personality/Disposition/Compatibility: These dogs are the epitome of calm and steady, making them fantastic companions for all kinds of households. They strike a perfect balance between loyalty and independence, offering affection without being overly clingy. Their protective nature means they'll always have an eye on their family, providing a comforting sense of security. With a strong sense of duty, they're ready to spring into action when needed but are just as content curling up for a cozy evening with their loved ones.
They thrive in homes with plenty of space to explore and families who can provide consistent training and socialization. Generally, they get along well with children and other pets, though early socialization helps ensure they're well-adjusted and happy.
Grooming Needs: Regular brushing is required to maintain the coat, especially for the long-haired variety, to prevent matting and remove loose fur.
Training & Exercise Needs: Daily walks and regular playtime are essential to keep this breed healthy and happy. Activities such as hiking, running, and playing fetch suit this breed well.
Possible Health Issues: hip dysplasia, elbow dysplasia, and gastric torsion (bloat)

Eurasier
Other Names: Eurasian
Color variations: red, fawn, wolf-gray, black, black and tan, and sable.
Average Lifespan: 12 to 14 years
Origins: Germany - 1960 - Julius Wipfel started with a Chow Chow and a Keeshond and then mixed in some Samoyed to craft a well-rounded, family-friendly dog.
Body Size: Males: 20.5-23.5 in. 50-70 lbs.
Females: 19.5-22 in. 40-60 lbs.
Personality/Disposition/Compatibility: The Eurasier is a fantastic choice if you're looking for a friendly and laid-back dog. With a calm and affectionate personality, the Eurasier enjoys playtime and social activities but isn't overly energetic. They're adaptable and get along well with children, other pets, and even new people when introduced properly. Their gentle demeanor and loyalty make them a loving companion, and their polite and well-mannered behavior is a plus. They tend to be pretty low-key, so they won't add to the noise of a busy household. Whether you live in an apartment or a house, they will thrive as long as they receive daily attention and moderate exercise.
Grooming Needs: To keep their thick double coat in top shape, regular grooming is a must. You'll want to brush them weekly to avoid tangles and reduce shedding. During those times when they shed more than usual, you might need to groom them a bit more often.
Training & Exercise Needs: They need a good amount of exercise, so daily walks and playtime are a must. They thrive on activities that challenge both their body and mind, like agility training and interactive games.
Possible Health Issues: hip dysplasia, patellar luxation, hypothyroidism, and various eye problems

Field Spaniel
Other Names: None
Color variations: black, liver, golden liver, or roan. They can also have tan markings or be solid colored.
Average Lifespan: 12 to 14 years
Origins: England - late 19th century - bred primarily for hunting and retrieving game in the field.
Body Size: Males: 18 in. 35-50 lbs. Females: 17 in. 35-45 lbs.
Personality/Disposition/Compatibility: They have a wonderful mix of enthusiasm and gentleness that makes them an absolute delight to be around. Naturally social, they thrive on spending time with their human family and often become a beloved member of the household. One minute they're full of energy and playfulness, and the next, they're curling up as a loving, peaceful companion. This adaptability makes them a great fit for various families and living situations. They're typically great with kids and other pets because of their easygoing nature. Their gentle demeanor usually means they get along well with other dogs and animals, though starting socialization early is always a plus.
Grooming Needs: Regular grooming is necessary due to their dense, silky coat. This includes weekly brushing to prevent matting and occasional trimming to maintain a tidy appearance. Their ears should be checked regularly for signs of infection.
Training & Exercise Needs: These dogs are wonderfully friendly and eager to please, making training a truly enjoyable experience. They're quite energetic and thrive on regular exercise to stay in top shape and keep their spirits high. Daily walks, playtime in a secure area, and fun activities like fetch or agility training are perfect for keeping them happy and healthy.
Possible Health Issues: hip dysplasia, ear infections, hypothyroidism, and progressive retinal atrophy (PRA)

Finnish Lapphund
Other Names: Suomenlapinkoira and Lapinkoira.
Color variations: black, brown, tan, cream, and white, often with distinct markings.
Average Lifespan: 12 to 15 years
Origins: Finland - 1940s - bred to help the indigenous Sami people herd reindeer.
Body Size: Males: 18-21 in. 33-53 lbs. Females: 16-19 in. 28-47 lbs.
Personality/Disposition/Compatibility: These dogs are known for their gentle, affectionate nature. They form strong, loving bonds with their families and make fantastic companions. But they're not all cuddles—they also have a playful streak that can turn any ordinary day into an adventure. They love being part of family activities and get along great with kids, making them an ideal choice for homes with little ones. As for other pets, they usually get along just fine. Their easygoing attitude and friendly disposition help them adapt to different living situations, whether you're in a lively household with other animals or a more peaceful environment.
Grooming Needs: Their thick double coat means they need regular grooming to stay in top shape. Brushing them a few times a week helps prevent mats and keeps shedding under control. During shedding seasons, daily brushing is a good idea to manage all that extra fur.
Training & Exercise Needs: They love staying active with activities like herding, agility, and obedience training, and they're always up for a long walk. They really thrive on both mental and physical challenges and have a blast spending time outdoors.
Possible Health Issues: hip dysplasia, progressive retinal atrophy (PRA), and cataracts

Finnish Spitz
Other Names: Suomenpystykorva and the Finsk Spets
Color variations: shades of red, ranging from honey to auburn, often with lighter shades on the undercoat, tail, and legs.
Average Lifespan: 12 to 15 years
Origins: Finland - 19th century - bred for hunting game birds and small mammals.
Body Size: Males: 17.5 to 20 in. 25-33 lbs.
Females: 15.5-18 in 20-28 lbs.
Personality/Disposition/Compatibility: They're full of life and playfulness, making them the perfect partner for active families or individuals. They approach life with an infectious enthusiasm, often expressing their joy through a happy bark and a wagging tail. They love being a part of the family and build strong, affectionate bonds with their people, yet they also have a delightful streak of independence. Generally, they get along well with kids and other dogs, especially if they've been socialized early on. Their friendly nature helps them adjust to different living situations, but they thrive in homes where they receive plenty of attention and interaction.
Grooming Needs: They require regular brushing to manage shedding and keep their double coat healthy. Bathing should be done as needed.
Training & Exercise Needs: They really come alive in places where they can get lots of exercise and mental stimulation. Whether it's running around, playing fetch, or tackling fun activities, they're always up for action. To keep them healthy and happy, regular exercise is a must. They thrive on brisk walks, playtime in a safe space, and interactive games that challenge their minds and bodies.
Possible Health Issues: hip dysplasia, patellar luxation, and progressive retinal atrophy

Flat-Coated Retriever

Other Names: Flattie
Color variations: solid black or liver
Average Lifespan: 8 to 10 years
Origins: United Kingdom - mid-19th century - bred for retrieving game both on land and in water.
Body Size: Males: 23-24.5 in. 60-80 lbs. Females: 22-23.5 in. 55-70 lbs.
Personality/Disposition/Compatibility: Their cheerful and friendly nature makes them an ideal companion for an active family. With their endless energy and playful spirit, these dogs bring a burst of joy wherever they go. They're always up for an adventure and ready to dive into the next fun activity. These retrievers are more than just pets—they're cherished family members who form deep, loving bonds with everyone in the household. They're fantastic with kids and get along well with other pets, making them a great fit for a variety of homes.
Grooming Needs: To keep its sleek coat looking its best, they need regular grooming. Weekly brushing will help prevent matting and cut down on shedding. Don't forget the occasional bath and routine ear cleaning to keep everything in top shape!
Training & Exercise Needs: Training them is often a joyful experience because these dogs are smart and eager to make their owners happy. They respond well to positive reinforcement and love picking up new tricks. Whether it's fetching, swimming, or tackling agility courses, they dive in with enthusiasm. Their boundless curiosity and zest for life mean they're always ready for a new adventure.
Possible Health Issues: hip dysplasia, cancer (particularly hemangiosarcoma), progressive retinal atrophy (PRA), and bloat

Fox Terrier (Toy)

Other Names: American Toy Terrier and Amertoy
Color variations: white with black, tan, or chocolate markings
Average Lifespan: 13 to 15 years
Origins: United States - 1930s - by breeding small Smooth Fox Terriers with various toy breeds like the Chihuahua and Manchester Terrier, primarily to create a small, agile, and versatile companion and hunting dog.
Body Size: Males and Females: 8.5-11.5 in. 3.5-7 lbs.
Personality/Disposition/Compatibility: Toy Fox Terriers are like little bundles of joy packed with personality. Even though they're small, they have a big, bold spirit. They aren't shy about making their presence felt and often have a playful, mischievous side that keeps things lively. With their affectionate and loyal nature, they make wonderful companions whether you're on your own or part of a family. They love being in the spotlight and will shower you with their endless devotion in return. They generally get along well with other pets, though their energetic enthusiasm might be a bit much for more laid-back companions. They adapt well to various living situations, from cozy apartments to spacious homes, as long as they get their daily exercise and mental stimulation.
Grooming Needs: Regular brushing and occasional baths are sufficient to keep their coat in good condition.
Training & Training & Exercise Needs: Their intelligence really stands out with how quickly they pick up new tricks and solve problems, making training a truly enjoyable experience—as long as you keep it fun and engaging. They thrive on regular exercise to stay healthy and happy, so daily walks, playtime, and activities like agility or obedience training are perfect for keeping them energized and content.
Possible Health Issues: patellar luxation, Legg-Calvé-Perthes disease, hypothyroidism, and allergies

Fox Terrier
Other Names: None
Color variations: white, white with black or tan markings, or tri color.
Coat Type: Smooth or Wire-haired
Average Lifespan: 12 to 15 years
Origins: England - 18th century - bred primarily for fox hunting.
Body Size: Males: 15.5 in. 17-19 lbs. Females: 14-15 in. 15-17 lbs.
Personality/Disposition/Compatibility: Their curiosity is truly limitless, making them both enthusiastic explorers and delightful companions. Brimming with zest for life, these dogs are incredibly energetic and playful. They usually get along well with other dogs and pets, especially if they've had early socialization. While their enthusiasm might be a bit much for more reserved animals, their friendly nature tends to win hearts. Known for their strong bonds with their human families, they make fantastic companions for active individuals and families with children alike. Just be ready for their endless energy and playful antics—living with a Fox Terrier is always an adventure!
Grooming Needs: They require regular brushing to maintain their smooth coat and occasional baths.
Training & Exercise Needs: These dogs are a blast to be around, thanks to their smarts and quick sense of humor. Training them is a breeze when you use positive reinforcement and a few treats. Just keep in mind that their intelligence can make them a bit stubborn, so patience and consistency are key. They're full of energy, so they need plenty of exercise. They love brisk walks, playtime, and agility training to keep them happy and healthy.
Possible Health Issues: hip dysplasia, cataracts, Legg-Calvé-Perthes disease, and various eye disorders

French Bulldog
Other Names: Frenchie
Color variations: brindle, fawn, white, cream, and various patterns such as piebald
Average Lifespan: 10 to 12 years
Origins: England - 1800s - bred as companions for lace workers.
Body Size: Males: 11-12 in. 20-28 lbs. Females: 10-11 in. 16-24 lbs.
Personality/Disposition/Compatibility: They're a wonderful blend of playful and calm, making them fantastic companions for all kinds of living situations. Their affectionate nature and ability to bring a smile to anyone's face are truly endearing. Whether they're lounging on the couch or chasing after a toy, they have an easy-going charm that's hard to resist. They adapt well to both city and country life, fitting seamlessly into family settings. They're especially great with kids, preferring gentle play over rough-housing. When it comes to other pets, they generally get along well, especially if introductions are made thoughtfully. They're friendly with other dogs and can coexist peacefully with cats, though their playful spirit might lead them to engage in some fun interactions with their feline housemates.
Grooming Needs: Regular brushing to remove loose hair and occasional baths are usually sufficient. It's also important to clean their facial folds to prevent infections.
Training & Exercise Needs: Their charming personalities come with a hint of stubbornness, which might make training a bit tricky at times. However, their desire to please often helps them overcome these challenges. They're not incredibly high-energy and can easily overheat, so keeping an eye on their activity levels, especially in warm weather, is important.
Possible Health Issues: brachycephalic syndrome, hip dysplasia, allergies, and skin infections

French Spaniel
Other Names: Epagneul Français
Color variations: white with brown markings that can range from cinnamon to dark liver.
Average Lifespan: 10 to 12 years
Origins: France - 14th century - bred primarily for bird hunting.
Body Size: Males: 22-24 in. 55-65 lbs. Females: 21-23 in. 45-55 lbs.
Personality/Disposition/Compatibility: This breed is a true delight, brimming with warmth and friendliness. They're always up for making new friends and playing fetch with anyone who has a ball or a kind word. Their natural charm wins hearts wherever they go, making them fantastic family pets and a great fit for any home. Whether they're the only pet or part of a multi-pet household, they get along wonderfully with children and adapt easily to other animals, including cats and dogs. They thrive on companionship and are always ready for a game or a cozy cuddle on the couch, bringing joy and affection to every corner of your home.
Grooming Needs: Regular brushing is required to maintain the coat and prevent matting. Occasional baths and routine checks for ear infections are also necessary.
Training & Exercise Needs: They're renowned for their intelligence and eagerness to please, making training both effective and enjoyable. They quickly pick up commands and thrive on engaging in a range of activities, from obedience drills to entertaining tricks. This breed has high exercise needs and flourishes with ample physical activity. They excel in pursuits like hunting, field trials, obedience training, and agility courses, where their energy and enthusiasm truly shine.
Possible Health Issues: hip dysplasia, ear infections, and certain genetic eye disorders

German Pinscher
Other Names: Deutscher Pinscher
Color variations: black and tan, red, fawn, and blue.
Average Lifespan: 12 to 14 years
Origins: Germany - early 19th century - bred as a farm dog for hunting vermin and guarding property.
Body Size: Males: 17-20 in. 25-45 lbs. Females: 17-19 in. 25-40 lbs.
Personality/Disposition/Compatibility: They're a bundle of energy and brains. With a strong sense of loyalty, they're incredibly devoted to their families and never shy away from showing it. Whether they're up for a game of fetch or just snuggling on the couch, they're always right by your side. Their keen alertness makes them fantastic watchdogs, always ready to sound the alarm if anything seems off. They generally get along well with other dogs and are friendly overall, though they might need a bit of help when it comes to interacting with smaller pets or new animals. They thrive in an active household where they can join in on family activities and stay mentally and physically stimulated.
Grooming Needs: Their short coat requires regular brushing to remove loose hair and occasional baths to keep it clean. Regular ear cleaning, nail trimming, and dental care are also essential.
Training & Exercise Needs: To keep them healthy and happy, they need plenty of physical and mental stimulation. Regular walks, playful sessions, and engaging activities like obedience training or agility courses are perfect for this high-energy breed.
Possible Health Issues: hip dysplasia, eye disorders such as cataracts, and von Willebrand's disease

German Long-haired Pointer

Other Names: Deutsch Langhaar and German Longhaired Pointing Dog
Color variations: liver and white, often with roaning or ticking
Average Lifespan: 12 to 14 years
Origins: Germany - 19th century - bred for hunting and retrieving game in various terrains.
Body Size: Males: 24-28 in. 66-80 lbs. Females: 22-26 in. 55-70 lbs.
Personality/Disposition/Compatibility: They're a bundle of joy, radiating a spirited and friendly vibe. This breed is known for its outgoing and affectionate personality, making it a loyal and loving member of the family. They get along well with both kids and other animals, thanks to their gentle temperament and high energy. These dogs thrive in a lively environment where they can interact with people and pets regularly. Their playful nature and eagerness for fun make them a perfect fit for a busy, active household.
Grooming Needs: To keep their beautiful long coat looking its best, they need regular brushing to prevent tangles and mats. They also benefit from occasional baths and routine ear cleaning to stay healthy and happy.
Training & Exercise Needs: These dogs are incredibly smart and adaptable, which means they're a breeze to train and always ready for a new challenge. They have a natural love for hunting and outdoor adventures, so they thrive on being active. With their high energy levels, they need plenty of exercise to stay happy and healthy. Whether it's hunting, field trials, agility courses, or just a good long walk or run, keeping them physically and mentally engaged is key to their well-being.
Possible Health Issues: hip dysplasia, ear infections, and eye problems

German Short-haired Pointer

Other Names: GSP
Color variations: solid liver, liver and white, liver roan, or liver and ticked color variations.
Average Lifespan: 10 to 14 years
Origins: Germany - 19th century - bred for versatility in hunting both game and waterfowl.
Body Size: Males: 23-25 in. 55-70 lbs. Females: 21-23 in. 45-60 lbs.
Personality/Disposition/Compatibility: Imagine a dog bursting with energy, always up for a game or a cozy cuddle on the couch. They are friendly and outgoing personality makes them a favorite at any gathering. They love being around people and are fiercely loyal to their families. Picture having a versatile buddy who gets along with everyone—kids, other pets, and even new faces—thanks to their laid-back and playful nature. If you're an active person who enjoys outdoor fun, this breed is the ideal partner for your adventures.
Grooming Needs: They require only regular brushing to remove loose hair and occasional baths to keep their coat clean.
Training & Exercise Needs: These dogs are bundles of energy who thrive on lots of exercise! They need daily walks, runs, and playtime to stay happy. They're also up for a good hike, a splash in the pool, or even a run through agility courses or hunting trials. If you're looking for a companion who loves staying active, this breed is a great match.
Possible Health Issues: hip dysplasia, bloat, entropion, and certain heart conditions

German Wire-haired Pointer
Other Names: Deutscher Drahthaariger Vorstehhund.
Color variations: liver and white, sometimes with patches of solid liver or roaning, and occasionally black and white.
Average Lifespan: 12 to 14 years
Origins: Germany - late 19th century - bred to create an all-purpose hunting dog that could work in various terrains and conditions.
Body Size: Males: 24-26 in. 60-70 lbs. Females: 22-24 in. 50-60 lbs.
Personality/Disposition/Compatibility: This breed is known for its friendly and outgoing personality, making it a beloved choice for families and individuals alike. They're incredibly affectionate and always eager to please, so they'll happily join in a game of fetch or a run in the park. They get along great with other pets and kids, though their high energy and playful nature might be a bit overwhelming for very small animals or those who enjoy a quieter setting.
Grooming Needs: They require regular grooming to maintain its wiry coat. Weekly brushing is recommended, along with occasional hand-stripping to remove dead hair. Regular ear cleaning and nail trimming are also necessary.
Training & Exercise Needs: These dogs catch on quickly and really shine when you use positive reinforcement. They love upbeat training sessions filled with praise and rewards. Starting with early socialization and obedience training is crucial to help them grow into well-rounded, disciplined companions. They've got lots of energy and need plenty of exercise, so they'll thrive with activities like running, hiking, swimming, and even hunting. They're a perfect match for active families who can keep them physically and mentally engaged.
Possible Health Issues: hip dysplasia, elbow dysplasia, eye conditions like cataracts, and some heart conditions

German Shepherd
Other Names: GSD or Alsatian
Color variations: black and tan, black and red, black and silver, solid black, and sable.
Average Lifespan: 9 to 13 years
Origins: Germany - 1899 - bred for their intelligence, strength, and trainability to herd and guard sheep.
Body Size: Males: 24-26 in. 65-90 lbs. Females: 22-24 in. 50-70 lbs.
Personality/Disposition/Compatibility: These dogs are a wonderful mix of smarts, loyalty, and adaptability. They're excellent guard dogs thanks to their strong protective instincts, but they're equally loving and devoted to their families. They get along well with kids and other pets, especially if they're socialized from a young age. They form tight bonds with their family members and are known for their protective nature. Just remember, their high energy and intelligence mean they thrive in a home where they can get lots of exercise and mental stimulation.
Grooming Needs: They require regular grooming due to their double coat, which sheds year-round and more heavily during shedding seasons. Weekly brushing helps to manage their shedding and keep their coat healthy.
Training & Exercise Needs: These dogs are full of energy and purpose, really coming alive when they have a task to tackle. They learn commands and tricks quickly, making them stars in both basic and advanced training. To keep them happy, they need a mix of mental stimulation and physical activity. Their intelligence and energy mean they respond best to consistent, positive reinforcement.
Possible Health Issues: hip and elbow dysplasia, degenerative myelopathy, and various heart and skin conditions

German Spitz
Other Names: Spitz, Deutscher Spitz, and Spitz Mittel.
Color variations: white, black, brown, orange, and wolf sable.
Average Lifespan: 13 to 15 years
Origins: Germany - late 19th century - bred for companionship and as a watchdog.
Body Size: Toy 8-12 in. 10-11 lbs. Medium: 12-16 in. 15-25 lbs. Large: 16-20 in. 30-50 lbs.
Personality/Disposition/Compatibility: These dogs are renowned for their warm, loving personalities and deep connections with their families, making them truly fantastic companions. With their energetic spirit and those sparkling, expressive eyes, they have a knack for bringing joy and fun into every situation. While they enjoy their independence, they also love being the center of attention and soaking up affection. They usually get along great with other pets and children, though their lively energy might be a bit overwhelming for very young kids. They're also excellent watchdogs, always looking out for their home and loved ones, but their friendly demeanor keeps them from being overly aggressive.
Grooming Needs: Their thick double coat requires regular brushing to prevent matting and tangling. They also need routine ear cleaning and nail trimming.
Training & Exercise Needs: They're incredibly smart and pick up new things quickly, always eager to make you happy. Just be prepared for a touch of stubbornness—it's part of their charm! Consistent training is essential to keep them on track. They thrive on daily walks, enjoy running around in a safe yard, and love activities that challenge their minds, like obedience drills and agility courses.
Possible Health Issues: patellar luxation, hip dysplasia, epilepsy, and progressive retinal atrophy (PRA)

Glen of Imaal Terrier
Other Names: the Glen
Color variations: wheaten, blue, and brindle
Average Lifespan: 12 to 15 years
Origins: Ireland - 16th century - bred to hunt vermin and work as a general farm dog.
Body Size: Males: 12.5-14 in. 32-40 lbs. Females: 12.5-14 in. 32-37 lbs.
Personality/Disposition/Compatibility: These terriers might look tough on the outside, but they're incredibly gentle and affectionate at heart. It's a lovely surprise considering their rugged appearance! They also have a streak of independence, so they handle being alone better than some breeds. Loyal to their families, Glens are not only loving companions but also vigilant watchdogs. They adapt well to various situations and generally get along with both kids and other pets. However, their strong prey drive means you might need to keep an eye on them around smaller animals. With their playful energy, they're a hit with active kids, but they're just as happy to relax and cuddle up with their people after a good play session.
Grooming Needs: requires regular brushing to keep its coat free from mats and tangles. Occasional hand-stripping is also needed to maintain the coat's texture. Bathing should be done as needed.
Training & Exercise Needs: Training these terriers is usually a breeze compared to some of their more headstrong relatives. Their smarts and desire to please make them quick learners, though they do have a bit of an independent streak that can sometimes make them seem stubborn. To get the best results, stick with consistent, positive reinforcement. They thrive on moderate exercise, so daily walks and playtime are a must. They also love activities like agility, obedience, and earthdog trials, which tap into their natural instincts and high energy.
Possible Health Issues: hip dysplasia, progressive retinal atrophy (PRA), and hypothyroidism

Golden Retriever
Other Names: Golden
Color Variations: various shades of gold, ranging from light cream to dark golden.
Average Lifespan: 10 to 12 years
Origins: Scotland - mid-19th century - bred for retrieving game during hunting, these dogs were designed to excel in fetching from both water and challenging terrain.
Body Size: Males: 23-24 in. 65-75 lbs. Females: 21.5-22.5 in. 55-65 lbs.
Personality/Disposition/Compatibility: They're incredibly social and absolutely love spending time with their people. Whether it's a game of fetch or a romp in the park, they're always up for fun. With their friendly and affectionate nature, these dogs are the perfect family companion, bringing joy and laughter wherever they go. They fit in wonderfully with families, singles, and seniors alike. They thrive in environments where they're involved in family activities and get plenty of exercise. Just keep in mind, their love for people and playful energy means they're not fans of being left alone for too long.
Grooming Needs: Regular grooming is necessary to manage their thick coats. This includes brushing several times a week to prevent matting and reduce shedding, as well as occasional baths.
Training & Exercise Needs: These dogs are incredibly smart and eager to please, which makes training them a real joy. Whether they're working as therapy dogs or helping with search and rescue missions, they excel in a variety of roles. To keep them happy and healthy, they need plenty of exercise. Daily walks, playtime, and activities like swimming, fetch, and agility training are perfect for this energetic breed.
Possible Health Issues: hip dysplasia, elbow dysplasia, cataracts, progressive retinal atrophy, and certain heart conditions

Gordon Setter
Other Names: Gordon Castle Setter
Color Variations: black with tan markings
Average Lifespan: 10 to 12 years
Origins: Scotland - early 17th century - bred primarily for hunting and retrieving game birds.
Body Size: Males: 24-27 in. 55-80 lbs. Females: 23-26 in. 45-70 lbs.
Personality/Disposition/Compatibility: These dogs are a perfect blend of grace and charm, with their expressive eyes and dignified looks that make them truly unforgettable. Their loving nature means they're fiercely loyal and form deep bonds with their families. Whether you're a family, a single person, or someone who can give them plenty of exercise and attention, they'll thrive with you. Their friendly and patient demeanor makes them great with children, and they usually get along well with other animals, particularly if they're socialized from a young age.
Grooming Needs: To keep their beautiful long, wavy coat looking its best, these dogs need regular grooming. Make sure to brush them a few times a week to prevent those pesky mats and tangles. Don't forget about their ears—cleaning them regularly and giving their fur a trim every now and then will help keep them clean and sharp-looking.
Training & Exercise Needs: These dogs are bright and eager to please, so training usually goes pretty smoothly. That said, their boundless energy and independent nature can occasionally challenge a trainer's patience. They thrive on positive reinforcement, so treats and praise work wonders. Consistency and clear, firm commands are crucial since they might lose focus if things aren't engaging enough. To keep their interest up, mix in play and exercise with training sessions. They love activities like long walks, running, and playing fetch.
Possible Health Issues: hip dysplasia, elbow dysplasia, progressive retinal atrophy, and bloat

Great Dane
Other Names: German Mastiff and Deutsche Dogge
Color variations: fawn, brindle, blue, black, harlequin, and mantle
Average Lifespan: 7 to 10 years
Origins: Germany - 16th century - bred for hunting boar and protecting estates.
Body Size: Males: 30-34 in. 140-175 lbs.
Females: 28-32 in. 110-140 lbs.
Personality/Disposition/Compatibility: Even though they're impressively large, they're anything but intimidating. These majestic dogs are naturally friendly and sociable, making them fantastic family pets. They usually get along great with kids and are known for their patience, though their size means it's a good idea to keep an eye on them around smaller children to avoid any accidental bumps. When it comes to other pets, they generally do well, but their size and energetic nature can sometimes be a bit much for smaller animals.
Grooming Needs: Regular brushing to remove loose hair and occasional baths to keep their coat clean are sufficient. Their nails should be trimmed regularly, and their ears should be checked for cleanliness.
Training & Exercise Needs: They really thrive on positive reinforcement. Consistency is crucial in their training. To keep them engaged, keep training sessions short and lively—long sessions might bore them. They need daily walks and playtime to stay happy, but it's important not to overdo it, especially when they're puppies. Their growing joints are sensitive, so stick to activities like walking, light jogging, and supervised play in a safe, fenced area.
Possible Health Issues: hip dysplasia, heart disease, bloat (gastric dilatation-volvulus), and certain types of cancer

Great Pyrenees
Other Names: Pyrenean Mountain Dog
Color variations: white, but may also have markings in gray, badger, reddish-brown, or tan.
Average Lifespan: 10 to 12 years
Origins: France and Spain - 3000 B.C. - bred to guard livestock in the Pyrenees Mountains.
Body Size: Males: 27-32 in. 100-160 lbs. Females: 25-29 in. 85-115 lbs.
Personality/Disposition/Compatibility: They have a fascinating blend of independence and affection, thanks to their history as livestock guardians. With their calm, patient demeanor, they make wonderful companions and are naturally protective. They flourish in homes where they have room to roam and a comfy spot to unwind. They're especially good with kids because of their gentle nature. Although they might be a bit reserved with new people at first, they warm up quickly once they sense there's no danger.
Grooming Needs: requires regular grooming due to their thick double coat. Weekly brushing is necessary to prevent mats and tangles, and more frequent brushing is needed during shedding seasons.
Training & Exercise Needs: Training them can be a bit of a challenge because of their independent and sometimes stubborn streak. They were originally bred to think on their own while guarding livestock, so they're used to making their own choices. But don't let that discourage you—they're also smart and eager to please once they see the rewards of training. The secret is to use positive reinforcement, be consistent, and have plenty of patience. Starting their socialization and training early is crucial to help them understand their place in the family and manage their protective instincts. They thrive with daily walks and playtime in a secure yard, which helps keep them happy and healthy.
Possible Health Issues: hip dysplasia, elbow dysplasia, patellar luxation, bloat, and certain heart conditions

Greater Swiss Mountain Dog
Other Names: Swissy
Color variations: tricolor coat, consisting of black, rust, and white.
Average Lifespan: 8 to 11 years
Origins: Switzerland - 1908 - bred for herding and as a draft dog.
Body Size: Males: 25.5-28.5 in. 105-140 lbs.
Females: 23.5-27 in. 85-110 lbs.
Personality/Disposition/Compatibility: Affectionately known as the "Swissy," this gentle giant is as big-hearted as it is large. With a calm and laid-back nature, they are a serene presence in any home. Friendly and sociable, they get along well with kids and other pets, making them a great addition to family life. While they enjoy being part of the family action, they also know how to appreciate their downtime. Their loyalty and protective instincts make them excellent watchdogs, though they're more attentive than aggressive. Eager to please and quick to bond, Swissies are both reliable and loving companions.
Grooming Needs: Regular brushing is necessary to keep the coat healthy and to manage shedding.
Training & Exercise Needs: Swissys are usually pretty eager to learn, making training a rewarding experience. The trick is to be consistent, use positive reinforcement, and have a good dose of patience. Starting early with socialization and basic obedience helps them grow into well-mannered adults. Since they're a larger breed, beginning training early helps manage their size and energy. Regular exercise is crucial for their health and happiness, so make sure they get daily walks, playtime in a secure yard, and fun activities like hiking or cart-pulling.
Possible Health Issues: hip dysplasia, elbow dysplasia, bloat, and splenic torsion

Greyhound
Other Names: English Greyhound
Color variations: black, white, brindle, fawn, blue, red, and a combination of these colors
Average Lifespan: 10 to 14 years
Origins: Egypt - 4,000 BC - bred for hunting game due to their speed and keen eyesight.
Body Size: Males: 28-30 in. 65-70 lbs. Females: 27-28 in. 60-65 lbs.
Personality/Disposition/Compatibility: Greyhounds are famous for their sweet and affectionate nature, and they're incredibly loyal to their families. Although they have a reputation as race dogs, they're surprisingly laid-back and enjoy nothing more than lounging around the house, earning them the endearing nickname of "couch potatoes." They generally get along well with other animals, though they might need a bit of time to warm up to smaller pets because of their prey drive. Friendly with other dogs and great with kids, Greyhounds make wonderful companions for families.
Grooming Needs: Regular brushing and occasional baths are sufficient to keep their coat healthy.
Training & Exercise Needs: Greyhounds are generally a breeze to train compared to some other breeds. Their intelligence and eagerness to please mean they quickly learn commands and routines. However, if they're coming from a racing background, a bit of patience might be needed. Consistent, positive reinforcement is key, and keeping training sessions short and fun can make the process smoother. These sleek athletes need regular exercise to stay healthy, so daily walks and chances to sprint in a secure area are perfect. They love activities like sprinting and playing fetch.
Possible Health Issues: bloat, hip dysplasia, and heart conditions

Greyhound (Italian)
Other Names: Italian Sighthound
Color variations: black, blue, fawn, red, white, cream, and sable, with or without white markings.
Average Lifespan: 12 to 15 years
Origins: Italy - ancient times - bred for companionship and as a status symbol among the noble class.
Body Size: Males and Females: 13-15 in. 13-15 lbs.
Personality/Disposition/Compatibility: These dogs have a special charm that combines elegance with a warm, affectionate nature, making them truly stand out among dogs. These little guys love being close to their families and are known for their gentle and sweet personalities, which makes them fantastic companions. They usually get along well with other pets and children, but because of their delicate build, they do best with gentle handling. Their calm demeanor means they fit in nicely with other animals, as long as those animals aren't too rowdy.
Grooming Needs: Regular brushing to remove loose hairs and occasional baths are sufficient to keep their coat in good condition. Their teeth should be brushed regularly, and nails trimmed as needed.
Training & Exercise Needs: They're generally eager to please and respond well to training, though they do have a few quirks. Their sensitive nature means they can get stressed or overwhelmed easily, so positive reinforcement is key. A bit of patience and consistency goes a long way, and with the right approach, they can pick up commands and behaviors pretty well. Daily walks and safe, enclosed areas to run are ideal. Activities like agility and lure coursing are perfect for tapping into their sighthound instincts and keeping them engaged.
Possible Health Issues: dental problems, patellar luxation, hip dysplasia, hypothyroidism, and progressive retinal atrophy (PRA). They are also prone to fractures due to their delicate bone structure.

Hamiltonstovare
Other Names: Swedish Foxhound or Hamilton Hound
Color variations: tricolor pattern, with a black saddle, and tan and white markings on the head, legs, and underbelly.
Average Lifespan: 12 to 14 years
Origins: Sweden - late 19th century - bred by Count Adolf Hamilton for tracking and hunting foxes and hares.
Body Size: Males: 19.5-24 in. 50-60 lbs. Females: 18-22 in. 45-55 lbs.
Personality/Disposition/Compatibility: These dogs are true social butterflies, radiating cheerfulness wherever they go. Always ready to have a blast, they love everything from running around at the park to snuggling up on the couch. Their friendly and outgoing nature makes them wonderful with families and kids. They're not just playful; they're also incredibly sensitive and intuitive, always in tune with their family's emotions. When it comes to other pets, they generally get along well, though their boundless energy might be a bit much for smaller animals. They thrive in active households where they can be part of outdoor adventures and fun activities. An owner who can keep up with their enthusiasm and provide plenty of exercise and mental stimulation will find a perfect companion in them.
Grooming Needs: Their short coat requires regular brushing to remove loose hair and occasional baths to keep them clean.
Training & Exercise Needs: These dogs are incredibly eager to please and pick up new things quickly, so training them is usually a breeze. They thrive on positive reinforcement and love interactive training sessions. To get the best results, stick with consistent, reward-based methods. With their high energy levels, they need plenty of activity each day—aim for at least an hour. This can include walks, playtime, and activities that challenge their minds.
Possible Health Issues: hip dysplasia, ear infections, and allergies.

Hanoverian Scenthound

Other Names: Hanoverian Hound
Color variations: shades of red, ranging from light to dark, and may have a brindle pattern or black overlay.
Average Lifespan: 10 to 14 years
Origins: Germany - 19th century - bred by combining bloodhounds with other breeds to create a dog with excellent tracking abilities.
Body Size: Males: 19-21 in. 79-99 lbs. Females: 18-20 in. 66-77 lbs.
Personality/Disposition/Compatibility: These dogs are like the wise, yet playful uncle of the canine world. Known for their calm and focused nature, they're perfect for those who enjoy a blend of serenity and enthusiasm. They're typically easygoing and patient, but don't be fooled by their relaxed demeanor—these dogs have a remarkable work ethic and a keen nose that makes them outstanding at tracking. Their loyalty is steadfast, and they form deep connections with their families. Great with kids and other pets, they're friendly and sociable without being in the limelight. They're the type to quietly stand by your side, offering comfort and companionship whenever you need it.
Grooming Needs: Their short coat requires regular brushing to remove loose hair and occasional baths to keep them clean.
Training & Exercise Needs: They're smart and always ready to make you happy, so they pick up training quickly. Positive reinforcement and consistency are key, and you'll likely see them shine in obedience and dog sports. They love activities like tracking, hiking, and running—things that let them tap into their natural hunting instincts.
Possible Health Issues: hip dysplasia, ear infections due to their long ears, and bloat.

Harrier

Other Names: Harehound
Color variations: lemon, red, white, and black, often in combination as tri-color.
Average Lifespan: 10 to 12 years
Origins: England - 13th century - bred for hunting hares by scent.
Body Size: Males and Females: 19-21 in. 45-60 lbs.
Personality/Disposition/Compatibility: These hounds are bursting with enthusiasm and loyalty. They're a joy to have around, always up for family fun and ready to offer their warm companionship. Their easygoing nature makes them great with kids and other pets. Whether it's a game of fetch or a run in the park, their playful spirit shines through, making them an excellent choice for active families. Friendly and sociable, they get along with everyone they meet, from people to other dogs. They thrive in spaces where they can move around and explore but can adapt to various living situations as long as they get their daily exercise and mental stimulation.
Grooming Needs: Their short coat requires regular brushing to remove loose hair and maintain a healthy shine. Bathing is needed only occasionally.
Training & Exercise Needs: These dogs are usually eager to please, but their strong hunting instincts can make training a bit of a challenge. They're smart and can pick up commands, though they might get sidetracked by interesting smells or their surroundings. To get the best results, stick with consistent, positive reinforcement techniques. They're quite active and need plenty of exercise to stay healthy and happy. Long walks, energetic play sessions, and off-leash runs are all things they love. Keeping them engaged with a job or activity, like games or agility training, is also a great way to meet their exercise needs.
Possible Health Issues: hip dysplasia, ear infections, and certain eye conditions

Havanese

Other Names: Havana Silk Dog and Bichon Havanais
Color Variations: white, black, chocolate, cream, gold, silver, blue, and parti-color
Average Lifespan: 14 to 16 years
Origins: Cuba - 1500s - bred from the Bichon Tenerife brought by Spanish settlers to be companion dogs for the Cuban aristocracy.
Body Size: Males and Females: 8.5-11.5 in. 7-13 lbs.
Personality/Disposition/Compatibility: These dogs are like little bundles of joy, always ready to brighten your day with their cheerful and loving nature. These social butterflies absolutely thrive on human interaction and are always up for a game or a cuddle. Their playful energy and affectionate demeanor make them wonderful companions, whether you're a family or an individual who can shower them with love. They get along famously with kids, other pets, and even new faces, so they're a great fit for all kinds of living situations.
Grooming Needs: require regular grooming due to their long, silky coats. This includes frequent brushing to prevent tangles and matting, as well as occasional baths to keep their coat clean and healthy.
Training & Exercise Needs: These dogs are usually very eager to please and do well with training, though they can occasionally show a bit of stubbornness. The best way to guide them is through positive reinforcement—lots of praise and treats work wonders. Being consistent and patient will help them learn commands and tricks quickly. They have moderate activity needs, so daily walks and some playtime will keep them content. They're not overly demanding, so a good romp in the yard or a few short walks each day will keep them happy and healthy.
Possible Health Issues: patellar luxation, hip dysplasia, cataracts, deafness, and heart disease

Hokkaido

Other Names: Ainu-ken, Seta, and Ainu dog
Color Variations: Ainu-ken, Seta, and Ainu dog
Average Lifespan: 11 to 13 years
Origins: Japan - 1140 AD - bred for hunting large game such as bears and boars.
Body Size: Males: 18-20 in. 45-65 lbs. Females: 16-18 in. 40-55 lbs.
Personality/Disposition/Compatibility: These dogs are full of spirit and courage, always ready to take on the world with a sense of independence that's truly remarkable. They're friendly and affectionate, making them wonderful companions for kids. Their keen alertness and natural protective instincts make them excellent watchdogs. While they do enjoy their space and might be a bit reserved around newcomers, they're not unfriendly—just a little cautious. They usually get along well with other pets, especially if they've had the chance to socialize from a young age. With their strong-willed nature, they thrive best with an owner who provides consistent training and understands their need for a bit of freedom.
Grooming Needs: has a double coat that requires regular brushing to manage shedding and keep the coat healthy. They shed more heavily twice a year.
Training & Exercise Needs: Training these dogs can be a bit of a challenge because they have a strong sense of independence. While they're smart and pick things up quickly, they also like to do things their own way, so patience and consistency are essential. They thrive on physical activity, so make sure they get plenty of exercise to stay both happy and healthy. Daily walks, playtime, and engaging activities like fetch or agility training are perfect for burning off their energy and keeping their minds active.
Possible Health Issues: generally, a healthy breed but can be prone to hip dysplasia, patellar luxation, and certain eye conditions

Hovawart

Other Names: Hovie
Color variations: black, black and gold, and blond
Average Lifespan: 10 to 14 years
Origins: Germany - early 13th century - bred for their guarding and protection abilities on farms and estates.
Body Size: Males: 25-29 in. 66-110 lbs. Females: 23-26 in. 55-88 lbs.
Personality/Disposition/Compatibility: These dogs have a natural knack for being protective and take their role as guardians to heart, making them fantastic watchdogs and family protectors. While they may come off as serious about keeping their home safe, they've got a playful side that shines through with their family, especially with kids. They're friendly with other pets and people once they've had a proper introduction. They thrive best in homes where their protective nature is appreciated and where they can get lots of exercise and mental stimulation.
Grooming Needs: regular brushing to keep their coat free of tangles and mats. They shed moderately, so routine grooming helps manage loose hair. Occasional baths and regular ear cleaning, nail trimming, and dental care are also recommended.
Training & Exercise Needs: Training these dogs can be a bit of a challenge because of their strong-willed personalities. But with patience, consistency, and a lot of positive reinforcement, they pick up new skills quickly. They thrive on having plenty to do, so make sure they get at least an hour of energetic activity each day. This can include walks, playtime, and fun, engaging games to keep them happy and healthy.
Possible Health Issues: hip dysplasia, hypothyroidism, and certain heart conditions.

Ibizan Hound

Other Names: Podenco Ibicenco
Color variations: white, red, or a combination of white and red.
Coat Type: Smooth or Wire haired
Average Lifespan: 12 to 14 years
Origins: Balearic Islands, Spain - 3400 BCE - bred for hunting small game, such as rabbits and hares.
Body Size: Males: 23.5-27.5 in. 50-65 lbs.
Females: 22.5-26 in. 45-60 lbs.
Personality/Disposition/Compatibility: With their graceful looks and those captivating, expressive eyes, these dogs are both playful and sophisticated. They generally mesh well with kids and other pets, though they might be a bit reserved around new faces initially. Their gentle nature and independent spirit make them confident without being too pushy. They thrive on regular exercise and mental challenges, making them a great match for an active family or individual.
Grooming Needs: The smooth-coated variety only needs a bit of regular brushing to keep loose hair in check. However, the wire-haired variety demands a bit more attention, as it needs frequent grooming to avoid matting.
Training & Exercise Needs: These dogs have a strong independent streak, which can make them a bit stubborn. To keep them engaged during training, it's important to be consistent, positive, and make the sessions enjoyable. They're also pretty high-energy, so they need lots of exercise to stay in tip-top shape and keep their spirits up. They love sprinting in a secure space, tackling agility courses, and playing interactive games. If they don't get enough activity, they might get bored and could start showing some mischievous behaviors.
Possible Health Issues: hip dysplasia, deafness, hypothyroidism, and eye problems.

Icelandic Sheepdog

Other Names: Icelandic Spitz, Iceland Dog
Color variations: Tan, black, gray, and chocolate, often with white markings.
Average Lifespan: 12 to 14 years
Origins: Iceland - 9th century - Bred by Vikings for herding livestock and guarding farms.
Body Size: Males: 18 in. 30 lbs. Females: 16.5 in. 25 lbs.
Personality/Disposition/Compatibility: These dogs are like bundles of joy wrapped in fur. They're always brimming with cheerfulness and have an infectious, outgoing personality. Playful and affectionate, they're constantly eager to make new friends and dive into family activities. Their friendly nature makes them a hit with both kids and adults, making them perfect family companions. They have a natural herding instinct, so don't be surprised if they try to gather up family members or even your other pets. They flourish in environments where they get lots of attention and exercise, and they're at their happiest when they're part of your everyday adventures.
Grooming Needs: Regular brushing is required to manage their thick double coat and reduce shedding. They do not need frequent baths, but occasional grooming is necessary to keep their coat healthy.
Training & Exercise Needs: These dogs are usually a breeze to train because they're smart and really eager to please. Consistency and patience go a long way. With their high energy levels, they need plenty of exercise to stay in top shape and content. Daily walks, playtime, and a good game of fetch are musts. Plus, agility training or fun interactive toys can keep them engaged and smiling.
Possible Health Issues: hip dysplasia, cataracts, and patellar luxation.

Irish Red and White Setter

Other Names: None
Color variations: red and white color pattern, with clearly defined red patches on a white background.
Average Lifespan: 11 to 15 years
Origins: Ireland - 17th century - bred for hunting and retrieving game birds.
Body Size: Males: 24-26 in. 65-75 lbs. Females: 22-24 in. 55-65 lbs.
Personality/Disposition/Compatibility: These dogs are beloved for their warm and loving personalities, making them fantastic companions for families and individuals. They thrive in social settings, getting along wonderfully with both other pets and kids, and they fit right in with a lively household. Their friendly nature makes them easy to bond with, though they do need regular training to channel their boundless energy and keep their behavior in check.
Grooming Needs: Regular grooming is required to maintain the breed's silky coat, including brushing several times a week to prevent matting and occasional baths to keep the coat clean and healthy.
Training & Exercise Needs: Training these dogs is pretty straightforward with a little dedication. They're enthusiastic and pick things up quickly, so positive reinforcement and consistent practice really make a difference. Daily walks, playtime, and mental challenges are key to keeping them happy and healthy. Regular activity not only helps to direct their energy in a positive way but also keeps boredom at bay.
Possible Health Issues: hip dysplasia, progressive retinal atrophy (PRA), and autoimmune disorders

Irish Setter
Other Names: Red Setter
Color variations: shades of mahogany or rich chestnut red.
Average Lifespan: 12 to 15 years
Origins: Ireland - 18th century - bred for hunting and retrieving game birds.
Body Size: Males: 27-29 in. 70 lbs. Females: 25-27 in. 60 lbs.
Personality/Disposition/Compatibility: These dogs are the life of the party, known for their friendly and outgoing personalities. They absolutely love being around people and other pets, and their playful nature is simply irresistible. Imagine coming home to a wagging tail and a mischievous sparkle in their eyes—that's the kind of greeting you'll get every day. With their boundless energy and enthusiasm for outdoor adventures, they're perfect for active families or anyone who can keep up with their vibrant zest for life.
Grooming Needs: Regular grooming is necessary for the Irish Setter, including brushing their coat a few times a week to prevent matting and tangles. They may also require occasional trimming, especially around the ears and feet.
Training & Exercise Needs: Training these dogs can be a blast! They're usually enthusiastic learners who love to please, making training with consistent, positive reinforcement a smooth process. With their high energy and zest for life, they need plenty of activity to stay happy and healthy. Think daily walks, fun play sessions in the yard, or even more engaging activities like running or agility training. They thrive when they have a job to do, so keeping them both physically and mentally active is key.
Possible Health Issues: hip dysplasia, progressive retinal atrophy, epilepsy, hypothyroidism, and bloat

Irish Terrier
Other Names: Daredevil
Color variations: red, golden red, red wheaten, or wheaten.
Average Lifespan: 12 to 15 years
Origins: Ireland - 1700s - bred for hunting, guarding, and companionship.
Body Size: Males: 18-20 in. 27-29 lbs. Females: 17-19 in. 25-27 lbs.
Personality/Disposition/Compatibility: These terriers are full of boldness and confidence that can instantly brighten up any home. Their energy and enthusiasm are infectious, and their loyalty to their family is truly heartwarming. Always up for joining in on family fun, they get along well with kids and adjust nicely to various living situations. Just keep in mind that their strong prey drive means they might need some careful introductions if there are small animals or cats around. Their sociable nature makes them fantastic companions for active families or anyone who can give them plenty of exercise and mental stimulation.
Grooming Needs: regular brushing to maintain the coat's texture and prevent matting. They require occasional hand-stripping to remove dead hair and maintain coat quality.
Training & Exercise Needs: Training them can be a bit of a challenge due to their strong-willed and independent nature. While they're smart and eager to learn, they benefit greatly from consistent, firm guidance and lots of positive reinforcement. Patience and persistence will go a long way in helping them master commands and develop good behavior. They need regular activity to stay happy and healthy, so daily walks, playtime, and mental stimulation through games or puzzles are crucial. They really thrive in environments where they can burn off their energy and engage in activities that challenge their minds.
Possible Health Issues: hip dysplasia, hypothyroidism, and skin allergies

Irish Water Spaniel
Other Names: Shannon Spaniel and the Rat-Tail Spaniel
Color variations: liver-colored
Average Lifespan: 10 to 12 years
Origins: Ireland - 1830s - bred for water retrieving and hunting waterfowl.
Body Size: Males: 22-24 in. 55-68 lbs. Females: 21-23 in. 45-58 lbs.
Personality/Disposition/Compatibility: This breed is a real bundle of joy—spirited, smart, and always up for some fun. Their natural curiosity and endless energy make them perfect for active families who love games and exercise. They're friendly and affectionate, forming deep bonds with their families and showing a lot of loyalty. They get along well with kids and other pets, so they fit right in with a bustling household. Plus, they absolutely adore water-related activities and love being included in all kinds of family adventures.
Grooming Needs: requires regular grooming to prevent matting and to keep its curly coat in good condition. This includes brushing several times a week and periodic trimming.
Training & Exercise Needs: They're a delight to train because they're naturally eager to please. They thrive on positive reinforcement and benefit from a steady, patient approach to training. These energetic pups need lots of activity to stay happy and healthy. Aim for at least an hour of exercise each day, mixing in some vigorous activities like running, playing fetch, or swimming, along with mental stimulation from interactive toys or training exercises.
Possible Health Issues: hip dysplasia, hypothyroidism, and ear infections

Irish Wolfhound
Other Names: None
Color variations: gray, brindle, red, black, white, and fawn.
Average Lifespan: 6 to 8 years
Origins: Ireland - 5th century - bred for the purpose of hunting large game, such as wolves and elk.
Body Size: Males: 32-34 in. 140-180 lbs. Females: 30-32 in. 115-140 lbs.
Personality/Disposition/Compatibility: This breed is all about calm and friendly vibes, bringing a touch of regal charm wherever they go. Their relaxed attitude makes them great with kids and other pets, including the tiny ones, though their size can sometimes lead to a bit of accidental clumsiness. They're known for their quiet, easy-going nature and aren't likely to show aggression. Instead, they face new experiences with a gentle curiosity. They thrive in homes with plenty of space to stretch out and a loving family who cherishes their sweet demeanor. While they generally get along well with other dogs, introducing them to smaller pets should be done thoughtfully.
Grooming Needs: requires regular brushing to prevent matting and tangling. Occasional bathing and trimming are also necessary to maintain a clean and healthy coat.
Training & Exercise Needs: They're smart and always keen to make you happy, which means they pick up commands in no time. Consistent, positive reinforcement is the way to go, and they really thrive on gentle guidance and encouragement. They don't need a ton of exercise—regular walks and a bit of playtime usually do the trick to keep them content and in good shape. They love having room to move around, so having access to a yard or a space where they can stretch their legs is perfect for them.
Possible Health Issues: hip dysplasia, heart disease, bone cancer, bloat (gastric torsion), and progressive retinal atrophy

Jagdterrier

Other Names: German Hunt Terrier
Color variations: black, dark brown, or greyish-black, often with tan or rust markings on the eyebrows, chest, legs, and tail.
Average Lifespan: 10 to 14 years
Origins: Germany - early 20th century - bred for hunting a variety of game.
Body Size: Males: 13-16 in. 20-22 lbs. Females: 12-15 in. 17-19 lbs.
Personality/Disposition/Compatibility: Their intelligence and determination give them a bold, spirited charm that can be absolutely captivating. Despite their size, these dogs are fearless and approach life with a delightful mix of confidence and tenacity. They're adaptable, but they do best with owners who are ready for consistent training and exercise. They generally get along well with other pets. With kids, they're playful and affectionate, though they're probably a better fit for families with older children who can handle their boundless energy.
Grooming Needs: Their dense, harsh coat requires regular brushing to remove loose hair and occasional bathing to keep it clean.
Training & Exercise Needs: Training them can be a bit of a challenge due to their strong-willed and independent personalities. The key to success with them is consistent, positive reinforcement. They thrive on plenty of physical activity, so daily vigorous exercise is a must—think running, hiking, or engaging in fun, interactive play. Jagdterriers also love tasks that keep their minds busy, so mixing in some mental challenges will keep them happy and healthy.
Possible Health Issues: hip dysplasia, eye problems, and allergies

Japanese Akitainu

Other Names: Akita Inu or Akita
Color variations: red fawn, brindle, and white. Every color of this breed includes the Urajiro pattern, with white markings on the muzzle, cheeks, undersides of the jaw, neck, body, tail, and inside of the legs.
Average Lifespan: 10 to 15 years
Origins: Japan - 1600s - bred for hunting bears, boars, and deer.
Body Size: Males: 25-28.5 in. 100-130 lbs. Females: 22.5-25 in. 70-100 lbs.
Personality/Disposition/Compatibility: With their strong, independent spirit, they move with a natural grace that's impossible to overlook. Loyal and protective, they're always there for their family, showing their love through playful antics and affectionate gestures. Whether it's a gentle nudge or simply lying quietly by your side, their devotion is clear. They make wonderful companions for those who appreciate a strong-willed dog and are ready to put in the effort for training and socialization. While they're usually friendly with other dogs, especially if they've grown up together, they might be a bit reserved with newcomers.
Grooming Needs: requires regular grooming, including brushing several times a week to manage shedding and maintain their thick double coat. During shedding seasons, daily brushing is recommended.
Training & Exercise Needs: Training them can be a bit of a challenge because of their strong-willed nature, but don't worry—patience and consistency will get you there. Regular training sessions are key to keeping them engaged and well-behaved. They love their daily walks, playtime, and mental stimulation. Activities like fetch, agility training, or puzzle toys can keep them both physically and mentally satisfied.
Possible Health Issues: hip dysplasia, progressive retinal atrophy (PRA), hypothyroidism, and autoimmune disorders

Japanese Chin

Other Names: Japanese Spaniel
Color variations: black and white, red and white, and occasionally in a tricolor pattern.
Average Lifespan: 10 to 14 years
Origins: Japan - ancient times - bred as a companion dog.
Body Size: Males and Females: 8-11 in. 7-11 lbs
Personality/Disposition/Compatibility: This breed carries an air of royalty, but don't be deceived—underneath that majestic exterior, they're playful and loving. With a gentle and friendly nature, they make for a truly delightful companion. They adapt effortlessly to different living situations, whether it's a snug apartment or a spacious house. They generally get along well with both other pets and kids, making them a fantastic choice for a range of households. While they're not overly demanding, they enjoy family time and also value their quiet moments.
Grooming Needs: requires regular grooming, including brushing several times a week to maintain its silky coat and prevent tangles and mats. Occasional bathing and trimming around the eyes and feet are also recommended.
Training & Exercise Needs: Their sharp minds and eagerness to please make them quick learners, especially with positive reinforcement. They pick up commands and tricks in no time. Regular walks and playtime usually keep them in top shape and spirits. They thrive on interactive games and mental challenges, so mixing in a few training sessions with their daily routine can be a great way to keep them engaged and happy.
Possible Health Issues: heart problems, patellar luxation, cataracts, and respiratory issues due to their brachycephalic (short-nosed) structure.

Japanese Spitz

Other Names: Nihon Supittsu
Color variations: pure white
Average Lifespan: 10 to 16 years
Origins: Japan - 1920s and 1930s - bred for being a companion dog.
Body Size: Males: 12-15 in. 10-15 lbs. Females: 12-14 in. 10-15 lbs.
Personality/Disposition/Compatibility: With their friendly, affectionate nature, this breed loves being the center of attention and is always ready to flash a big, bright smile. They thrive on human interaction and make wonderful companions for both families and individuals. They get along great with kids, other pets, and even strangers, though they might let out a bark or two to let everyone know they're on the lookout. Their adaptable nature means they're comfortable in a range of living situations, whether you're in an apartment or have a house with a yard.
Grooming Needs: To keep their thick coat in top shape, these dogs need regular grooming. Brush them a few times a week to avoid pesky mats and tangles. They shed seasonally, so when that time comes around, you'll want to brush them more often to keep up with the extra fur.
Training & Exercise Needs: They're usually very eager to make you happy and respond well to positive reinforcement training. With a little patience and encouragement, they pick up commands and good habits quickly. Consistency really helps, so keeping a steady routine will make them feel secure and involved. They love staying active, so try to give them 30 to 60 minutes of exercise each day, whether that's through walks, playtime, or engaging activities.
Possible Health Issues: patellar luxation, allergies, and runny eyes

K9 Chatter

Japanese Terrier
Other Names: Nippon Terrier or Nihon Terrier
Color variations: white with black and tan markings
Average Lifespan: 12 to 15 years
Origins: Japan -17th century - bred for companionship and as rat hunters.
Body Size: Males: 12-13 in. 5-9 lbs. Females: 11-12 in. 5-8 lbs.
Personality/Disposition/Compatibility: These dogs are all about love and fun. They're the perfect mix of playful energy and devotion, always ready to join in on a game of fetch or curl up beside you on the couch. While they have a lively side, they're also pretty mellow indoors, so they fit into different living situations with ease. Their friendly, sociable vibe means they get along great with other pets and kids. They really thrive in homes where they can get lots of attention and mental stimulation.
Grooming Needs: Their short coat requires occasional brushing to remove loose hair and maintain a healthy shine. Regular dental care, nail trimming, and ear cleaning are also essential.
Training & Exercise Needs: These dogs are naturally eager to please, so training them is usually a breeze. They thrive on positive reinforcement, so showering them with praise and rewards is the way to go. Getting them socialized and starting obedience training early will set them up to be well-rounded, happy companions. They're quite active and need their daily dose of exercise to stay in top shape—think daily walks, playtime, and engaging activities to keep them both physically and mentally stimulated. They love playing fetch, trying their paws at agility training, or just having a blast running around the yard.
Possible Health Issues: patellar luxation, deafness, and some dental problems

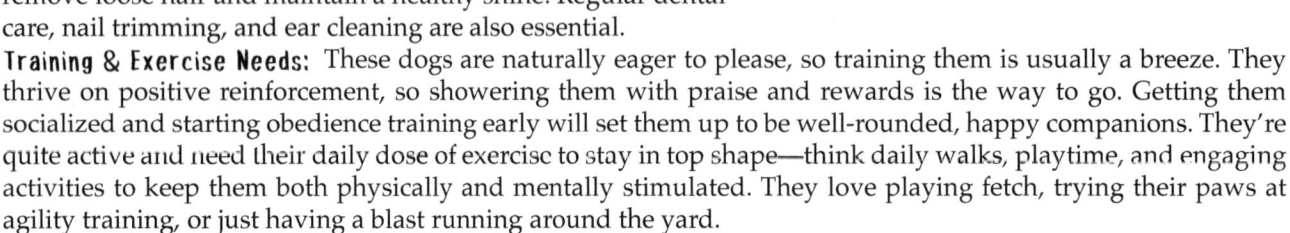

Kai Ken
Other Names: Tora Inu or Tiger Dog
Color variations: brindle patterns, which can be black brindle, red brindle, or a mix of the two.
Average Lifespan: 12 to 15 years
Origins: Japan - early 20th century - bred for tracking and hunting game in mountainous regions.
Body Size: Males: 18-22 in. 30-50 lbs. Females: 17-20 in. 25-45 lbs.
Personality/Disposition/Compatibility: These dogs are lively and perceptive, making them fantastic watchdogs. Despite their medium size, they have the personality of a much larger dog—full of intelligence and sharp instincts. While they might be a bit reserved with newcomers, they're great with both families and individuals thanks to their adaptable nature. They're wonderful with kids, especially when they're well-socialized. They're happiest in an active environment where they can stay physically and mentally engaged, making them ideal for an energetic household or anyone who loves outdoor adventures.
Grooming Needs: Regular brushing is required to manage shedding, especially during seasonal changes. Bathing should be done as needed.
Training & Exercise Needs: Kai Kens are smart and eager to please, making them pretty responsive to training. However, they also have an independent streak and might need a firm but gentle approach to keep them on track. These active pups thrive on plenty of physical activity to stay happy and healthy, so they'll appreciate daily walks, playtime in a secure area, and engaging mental exercises to keep them stimulated.
Possible Health Issues: hip dysplasia, patellar luxation, and allergies

Karelian Bear Dog

Other Names: Karjalankarhukoira
Color variations: black with distinctive white markings on the head, neck, chest, abdomen, and legs.
Average Lifespan: 10 to 12 years
Origins: Finland - 19th century - bred for hunting bears, moose, and wild boar.
Body Size: Males: 21-24 in. 45-50 lbs. Females: 19-22 in. 40-45 lbs.
Personality/Disposition/Compatibility: These dogs are as vibrant in personality as they are striking in appearance. Brave and independent, they're fiercely loyal and protective of their families, making them top-notch watchdogs. While they might be a bit reserved with strangers, they're usually warm and affectionate with their loved ones. If you have smaller pets, keep in mind that their strong prey drive could be a factor, so they might not be the best match for a household with tiny animals. However, they're never ones to shy away from a challenge and are always up for an adventure.
Grooming Needs: Its dense double coat requires regular brushing to minimize shedding and prevent matting, especially during the shedding seasons.
Training & Exercise Needs: Training can be a bit of a challenge because of their strong-willed and independent nature. While they're smart and quick to pick things up, they can also be quite stubborn, so a firm but consistent approach works best. These dogs are full of energy and need plenty of physical activity. They thrive on vigorous exercise and mental stimulation, so daily long walks, runs, or activities like hiking and tracking are perfect for meeting their needs.
Possible Health Issues: hip dysplasia, elbow dysplasia, and eye conditions such as cataracts

Keeshond

Other Names: Dutch Barge Dog
Color variations: gray, black, and cream colors. Their coats often have a distinctive "spectacles" pattern around their eyes, formed by markings and shading.
Average Lifespan: 12 to 15 years
Origins: Netherlands - 18th century - bred as a watchdog and companion on river barges.
Body Size: Males: 18-19 in. 45-55 lbs. Females: 17-18 in. 35-45 lbs.
Personality/Disposition/Compatibility: Often called the "Smiling Dutchman," this breed lives up to its name with a personality that's as warm and inviting as its fluffy, wolf-like coat. They're spirited and affectionate, making them fantastic companions for both individuals and families. Their playful energy and loving nature make them great with kids, and they get along well with other pets, including dogs and even cats. Plus, their keen alertness and protective instincts make them excellent watchdogs. They fit in well in any living situation, whether it's a snug apartment or a spacious home with a big yard.
Grooming Needs: require regular grooming due to their thick double coat. Weekly brushing is necessary to prevent matting and reduce shedding, and more frequent grooming may be needed during their shedding seasons.
Training & Exercise Needs: These dogs are smart and always ready to make you happy, so they're usually quick learners when it comes to training. They love their daily walks and play sessions, which keep them both physically and mentally engaged. Mixing in some fun activities like fetch or agility training keeps them joyful and in great shape.
Possible Health Issues: hip dysplasia, patellar luxation, and certain heart conditions

Kerry Blue Terrier

Other Names: Kerry, Irish Blue Terrier
Color variations: black coat that gradually changes to a shade of blue-gray as the dog matures.
Average Lifespan: 12 to 15 years
Origins: Ireland - 1700s - bred for hunting and retrieving, as well as for herding sheep and cattle.
Body Size: Males: 18-19.5 in. 33-40 lbs. Females: 17.5-19 in. 30-35 lbs.
Personality/Disposition/Compatibility: These dogs are a bundle of energy and personality, making any home more lively and fun. Their playful antics and endless enthusiasm bring a joyful spark to daily life. They're incredibly affectionate, forming strong bonds with their families and thriving on close companionship. Great with kids, they're an ideal choice for families who want a loving, spirited pet. While they generally enjoy socializing, their terrier instincts might make them a bit cautious around other animals, so early socialization is important.
Grooming Needs: requires regular grooming, including brushing several times a week to prevent matting and professional trimming every six to eight weeks to maintain its distinctive appearance.
Training & Exercise Needs: Training these dogs might be a bit of a challenge because they can sometimes be a bit stubborn. They're smart and really want to make you happy, so with a bit of patience and lots of positive reinforcement, they'll catch on to commands and good behavior. They absolutely love activities that keep both their bodies and minds busy, so daily walks, playtime, and mental stimulation are key to keeping their high energy in check.
Possible Health Issues: hip dysplasia, eye conditions like cataracts and entropion, and a genetic condition known as cerebellar abiotrophy, which affects coordination

Kishu Ken

Other Names: Kishu
Color variations: white, red, and sesame (a mix of red, black, and white hairs).
Average Lifespan: 11 to 13 years
Origins: Japan - ancient times - bred for hunting large game like deer and boar.
Body Size: Males: 20.5-22 in. 30-45 lbs. Females: 17-19 in. 30-45 lbs.
Personality/Disposition/Compatibility: Kishu Kens are known for their independent and spirited nature. They may not be the most affectionate dogs, but they show their love through their steadfast presence and loyalty. These alert and energetic dogs are always up for an adventure, and their keen senses and strong prey drive make them fantastic watchdogs and hunting companions. While they might seem reserved around strangers, their devotion to their families is unwavering. With proper socialization from a young age, they get along well with other dogs, though their strong prey drive means they might be inclined to chase smaller animals.
Grooming Needs: Regular brushing is necessary to manage shedding, especially during seasonal changes. Bathing should be done as needed.
Training & Exercise Needs: Training them can be a bit of a challenge because of their independent and strong-willed nature. They respond best to a mix of consistency, positivity, and a firm yet respectful approach to their need for space. They're active and need plenty of exercise. Aim for at least an hour of vigorous activity each day to keep them happy and healthy.
Possible Health Issues: hip dysplasia, luxating patella, and various eye conditions

Komondor

Other Names: Hungarian Komondor or the Hungarian Sheepdog.
Color variations: white
Average Lifespan: 10 to 12 years
Origins: Hungary - 9th century - bred to guard livestock.
Body Size: Males: 27.5 in. 100-130 lbs. Females: 25.5 in. 80-100 lbs.
Personality/Disposition/Compatibility: They're a breed that stands out with its impressive corded coat and a personality that's both dignified and gentle. These dogs are incredibly loyal and form tight bonds with their families, making them fantastic protectors. Beneath their calm and steady exterior, they have a playful and affectionate side, especially with children. While they might be reserved around new people, their curiosity and smarts shine through. With proper introductions, they can get along well with other pets. Their natural protective instincts make them exceptional watchdogs, and they truly thrive when they have a job to do, whether that's guarding the home or participating in dog sports.
Grooming Needs: requires significant effort, especially in maintaining their unique corded coat, which needs regular cleaning and separation to prevent matting and ensure hygiene.
Training & Exercise Needs: Training can definitely have its tough moments, but with a bit of patience, consistency, and lots of positive reinforcement, your dog will pick up commands and good behaviors in no time. Starting early with socialization and training sets the stage for them to grow into confident, well-rounded adults. Dogs love having a job to do, so incorporating activities that stimulate their minds and bodies, like obedience training or agility exercises, is perfect. Regular walks and playtime are key, but don't worry—your pup doesn't need an endless amount of exercise.
Possible Health Issues: hip dysplasia, bloat, and skin problems due to their heavy coat

Korean Jindo Dog

Other Names: Jindo, Chindo, and Jindo Gae
Color variations: white, fawn, red, black, black and tan, and brindle.
Average Lifespan: 14 to 15 years
Origins: Jindo Island, South Korea - 13th century - bred for hunting and guarding.
Body Size: Males: 19.5-21 in. 40-50 lbs. Females: 18.5-20 in. 33-42 lbs.
Personality/Disposition/Compatibility: Jindos are known for their fiercely loyal and protective nature, making them fantastic companions for those who value a dog with a strong sense of self. They're often described as smart and alert, blending dignity with a playful streak. With a natural instinct to keep their loved ones safe, they make great watchdogs. While they might not be the most snuggly breed, their affection is heartfelt and evident in quiet moments spent together. They can be a bit reserved with strangers at first, but they warm up once they get to know you. They thrive in a structured environment and benefit from early socialization and training.
Grooming Needs: They require regular brushing to manage shedding, especially during seasonal changes when they shed heavily. Bathing should be done as needed.
Training & Exercise Needs: Training can be a bit of a challenge because of their independent and occasionally stubborn streak. They pick up commands quickly, but if they're not motivated, they might just choose to ignore you. They're also quite energetic, they thrive on activities that engage both their minds and bodies, like long walks, playtime, and agility training. Aim for at least an hour of exercise each day.
Possible Health Issues: hypothyroidism, hip dysplasia, and autoimmune disorders

K9 Chatter

Kromfohrlander
Other Names: Kromi
Color variations: white with tan, red, or brown markings.
Average Lifespan: 12 to 14 years
Origins: Germany - 1945 - developed primarily as a companion dog
Body Size: Males: 15-18 in. 22-35 lbs. Females: 14-17 in. 18-30 lbs.
Personality/Disposition/Compatibility: These dogs are incredibly friendly and adaptable, making them a fantastic fit for families of all kinds, whether you have kids, other pets, or a lively household. They're social butterflies, thriving in environments where they can mingle with people and animals alike. Easygoing and good natured, they get along well with other animals, so they're a great choice if you have a multi-pet home. While they're not demanding, they do appreciate attention and enjoy spending time with their human friends.
Grooming Needs: They require regular brushing to keep their coat free of tangles and mats. Occasional baths are necessary to maintain cleanliness, and their ears should be checked regularly to prevent infections.
Training & Exercise Needs: Training them is usually a real joy. They're smart and eager to please, so they're quick to pick up new tricks and commands. To keep their enthusiasm high, make sure training sessions are fun and engaging. When it comes to exercise, they love a good play session or a brisk walk, but they're not too demanding. A bit of daily exercise is perfect for keeping them both physically and mentally stimulated, but they're adaptable enough to fit into your routine.
Possible Health Issues: hip dysplasia, patellar luxation, and certain genetic eye conditions

Kuvasz
Other Names: None
Color variations: white, with some slight cream variations allowed according to breed standards.
Average Lifespan: 10 to 12 years
Origins: Hungary - 15th century - bred for guarding livestock and property.
Body Size: Males: 28 to 30 in. 100-115 lbs.
Females: 26-28 in. 70-90 lbs.
Personality/Disposition/Compatibility: They're the kind of loyal companion who will win your heart with their big, loving personality. These dogs are known for their strong and independent nature, always ready to protect their families. While they might seem a bit reserved around strangers, they're incredibly affectionate once you've earned their trust. Even though they have a commanding presence, they're gentle and loving with kids, and love being part of family activities. Their relationship with other pets can take some time to develop, especially with smaller animals, but with the right socialization, they can get along just fine.
Grooming Needs: requires regular grooming due to its thick double coat, including weekly brushing and occasional baths. During shedding season, more frequent brushing is necessary to manage the heavy shedding.
Training & Exercise Needs: Training them can be a bit of a challenge because they're both smart and stubborn. They do best with clear commands and lots of positive reinforcement. When it comes to exercise, they need plenty of it to stay happy and healthy. Regular walks, playtime, and mental stimulation are key. These dogs are full of energy and love activities that engage both their bodies and minds, so mixing in games and training sessions each day can be really rewarding for them.
Possible Health Issues: hip dysplasia, elbow dysplasia, and progressive retinal atrophy

Labrador Retriever

Other Names: Labrador, Lab
Color variations: Black, Yellow, Chocolate
Average Lifespan: 10-12 years
Origins: Newfoundland, Canada - early 19th century - bred for retrieving fishing nets and assisting fishermen.
Body Size: Males: 22.5-24.5 in. 65-80 lbs.
Females: 21.5-23.5 in. 55-70 lbs.
Personality/Disposition/Compatibility: Labs are a delight to have around! Their friendly, outgoing, and gentle nature makes them a joy to be with. They're known for their incredible patience and loyalty, which makes them wonderful companions for kids and other pets alike. Labs seem to have a special talent for getting along with everyone they meet, making them a perfect fit for families of all kinds. Their loving and easygoing attitude means they're likely to go with the flow and stay happy, no matter what's going on.
Grooming Needs: requiring regular brushing to manage their shedding and maintain their coat's condition. Occasional baths and routine ear cleaning are also necessary.
Training & Exercise Needs: Labs are known for their eager-to-please nature, making them generally easy to train. They're sharp and quick learners, though they thrive on consistent, positive reinforcement to stay motivated. Starting their training and socialization early can help them grow into well-behaved adults. Labs are full of energy and need plenty of physical activity to stay happy and healthy. Aim for at least an hour of exercise a day, whether that's walking, running, swimming, or a game of fetch. Without enough activity, they might get bored and restless.
Possible Health Issues: hip and elbow dysplasia, progressive retinal atrophy, and obesity

Lagotto Romagnolo

Other Names: Water Dog of Romagna
Color variations: off-white, white with brown or orange patches, solid brown, and brown roan.
Average Lifespan: 14 to 16 years
Origins: Romagna region, Italy - 16th century - bred for hunting waterfowl in the marshlands and later for truffle-hunting.
Body Size: Males: 17-19 in. 28-35 lbs. Females: 16-18 in. 24-32 lbs.
Personality/Disposition/Compatibility: These dogs are a bundle of joy, known for their warmth and affectionate nature. They're incredibly sociable, making them great for families and individuals. Their sensitivity means they're in tune with their owners' feelings, making them especially attentive companions. They typically get along well with kids and other pets, though starting socialization early helps them become well-adjusted adults. Their approachable and loving demeanor makes them a wonderful fit for any home, whether you're an active person, a busy family, or simply in need of a loyal, affectionate friend.
Grooming Needs: Regular grooming is required including brushing to prevent matting and professional grooming every few months to maintain their curly coat. Their ears should also be checked regularly to prevent infections.
Training & Exercise Needs: These dogs are eager to please and catch on quickly, especially when you use positive reinforcement. They're full of energy, so they need plenty of physical activity to stay happy and healthy. Regular walks, playtime, and some energetic games in the yard are a must to keep them in shape. They thrive on daily activity, so keeping them busy with a mix of exercise and mental challenges will keep them fit and satisfied.
Possible Health Issues: hip dysplasia, progressive retinal atrophy, and juvenile epilepsy

Lakeland Terrier
Other Names: Lakies
Color variations: black, blue, liver, red, wheaten, grizzle, and black & tan.
Average Lifespan: 12 to 15 years
Origins: Lake District of England - 18th century - bred for hunting foxes and protecting sheep from predators.
Body Size: Males: 14.5-15 in. 17 lbs. Females: 13.5-14.5 in. 15 lbs.
Personality/Disposition/Compatibility: Lakies are known for their playful spirit and zest for life, always ready to keep you entertained with their antics. These dogs have a natural confidence and a touch of courage that makes them stand out. Their sharp minds and mischievous streak mean they need plenty of mental stimulation to keep them happy. They're perfect for active families or individuals who can keep up with their lively energy. They get along well with kids and can be quite friendly with other pets, making them a wonderful addition to any home.
Grooming Needs: require regular grooming to maintain their wiry coat. This includes brushing several times a week and professional hand-stripping or clipping every few months to keep their coat in good condition.
Training & Exercise Needs: Training them can be a bit of a puzzle because of their sharp intelligence and strong independence. Without enough exercise and stimulation, they might get bored and find their own ways to entertain themselves, which isn't always a good thing. They absolutely thrive on regular, energetic activities like daily walks, playtime in a secure yard, or interactive games.
Possible Health Issues: Legg-Calve-Perthes disease, lens luxation, hypothyroidism, and von Willebrand's disease

Lancashire Heeler
Other Names: Ormskirk Heeler
Color variations: black and tan or liver and tan
Average Lifespan: 12 to 15 years
Origins: England - 17th century - bred for herding cattle and for ratting on farms.
Body Size: Males and Females: 10-12 in. 6-13 lbs.
Personality/Disposition/Compatibility: These dogs are full of life and curiosity, and their enthusiasm is truly contagious. Even though they're small, they're big on affection and love snuggling up with their families, often becoming the ultimate lapdog. Their smarts and boundless energy make them perfect for active individuals or families. They're usually good with kids and other pets, though their natural herding instincts might lead them to try and keep everyone in check, just like they would with a herd.
Grooming Needs: requiring only occasional brushing to remove loose hair and maintain coat health.
Training & Exercise Needs: Training these dogs can be a blast and really fulfilling. They're smart and eager to please, so with a little patience and positive reinforcement, they pick up on commands quickly. Their curious nature means they might get sidetracked easily, so keeping training sessions short and fun is key. These dogs are full of energy and need plenty of physical activity. They thrive on having a purpose, so mixing in some training exercises or agility games is a great way to keep them active and mentally stimulated.
Possible Health Issues: lens luxation, Collie eye anomaly, and patellar luxation

Lapponian Herder
Other Names: Lapinporokoira
Color variations: black, brown, gray, and tan, often with white markings.
Average Lifespan: 12 to 14 years
Origins: Finland - 1966 - bred for herding reindeer in the northern regions.
Body Size: Males: 19.5-21.5 in. 55-65 lbs.
Females: 17.5-19.5 in. 45-55 lbs.
Personality/Disposition/Compatibility: These dogs are all about love and companionship. Their natural attentiveness and eagerness to please make them perfect for anyone wanting a devoted and interactive pet. With their sweet and friendly personalities, they're always ready to be by your side and join in on whatever you're doing. They get along well with kids and other animals, so they're a great fit for families with multiple pets.
Grooming Needs: Regular brushing is required to keep its dense coat free of mats and tangles, especially during shedding seasons.
Training & Exercise Needs: Training them is usually a breeze, thanks to their smarts and willingness to please. With consistent, gentle training, they'll pick up new skills quickly and you'll build a strong connection with them. These energetic dogs thrive on activity, so make sure they get at least an hour of exercise each day. Without enough physical and mental stimulation, they might get bored and could develop some pesky behavior problems.
Possible Health Issues: hip dysplasia, progressive retinal atrophy (PRA), and other eye conditions

Leonberger
Other Names: Leos
Color variations: yellow, red, reddish-brown, and sand, often with a black mask.
Average Lifespan: 8 to 10 years
Origins: Germany - mid-19th century - developed by Heinrich Essig to resemble the lion on the town's crest.
Body Size: Males: 28-31.5 in. 110-170 lbs.
Females: 25.5-29.5 in. 90-140 lbs.
Personality/Disposition/Compatibility: This breed is known for its friendly and outgoing nature, making it a fantastic family companion. While they might initially be a bit reserved around new faces, they quickly warm up and become a beloved member of any household. Their easygoing temperament makes them a perfect fit whether you're living alone, as a couple, or with a lively family. They're incredibly patient and good-natured, getting along well with children and other pets alike. Their strong bonds with family members and protective instincts make them both loving and dependable guardians.
Grooming Needs: require regular grooming due to their thick, double coat. They need to be brushed several times a week to prevent matting and reduce shedding. Occasional baths and routine maintenance of ears, teeth, and nails are also important.
Training & Exercise Needs: Training them is usually a breeze, they love to please and respond really well to positive reinforcement. They thrive when they have a job to do, so a few lively training sessions each day will keep them happy. Their exercise needs are easily managed, but staying active is essential for their overall health and joy.
Possible Health Issues: hip and elbow dysplasia, heart problems, bloat and certain types of cancer.

Lhasa Apso

Other Names: Lhasa Terrier
Color variations: black, white, gold, red, and cream, often with different shadings and markings
Average Lifespan: 12 to 15 years
Origins: Tibet - 800 AD - bred as a sentinel dog for Buddhist monasteries and temples to alert monks to any intruders.
Body Size: Males: 10-11 in. 12-18 lbs. Females: 9-10 in. 11-17 lbs.
Personality/Disposition/Compatibility: These little dogs are confident and make excellent watchdogs. They bond closely with their families and can be unexpectedly playful and loving, perfect for those who enjoy their unique quirks. They adapt well to different living situations as long as they get enough exercise and mental stimulation. While they might seem a bit reserved with new people, their loyalty to their loved ones is strong and steadfast.
Grooming Needs: Their dense coat requires regular grooming to prevent matting and tangling. They need to be brushed several times a week, and occasional professional grooming is recommended.
Training & Exercise Needs: Training might be a bit tricky because they have a strong independent streak. They're definitely clever, but they like to do things their own way. They'll happily join you for daily walks and playtime, though they don't need strenuous exercise.
Possible Health Issues: hip dysplasia, patellar luxation, progressive retinal atrophy, and kidney disease

Lowchen

Other Names: Little Lion Dog
Color variations: black, white, chocolate, cream, red, and sable, often with different markings and patterns.
Average Lifespan: 13 and 15 years
Origins: Germany or France - 16th century - bred as companion dogs and were often depicted in art as lapdogs for nobility.
Body Size: Males: 12-14 in. 10-18 lbs. Females: 11-13 in. 9-15 lbs.
Personality/Disposition/Compatibility: The "Little Lion Dog" is a charming blend of lively and loving. This breed thrives as a family companion, always eager to be at the heart of the action. With their friendly, outgoing personality, they're fantastic with kids and get along well with other pets. Their sociable and gentle nature means they make friends wherever they go. Never shy about expressing their affection, they'll quickly become a cherished part of your family.
Grooming Needs: They require regular grooming to maintain their coat, including brushing several times a week and professional grooming every few months to keep their lion trim. Their ears should be checked regularly, and their nails should be trimmed as needed.
Training & Exercise Needs: Training is usually a breeze thanks to their smarts and eagerness to please. Short, consistent training sessions are the key to keeping them interested and engaged. They're lively and playful but don't need tons of exercise. A mix of mental challenges and physical activity will keep them satisfied and well-behaved.
Possible Health Issues: hip dysplasia, patellar luxation, progressive retinal atrophy (PRA), cataracts, and allergies

Maltese

Other Names: Maltese Lion Dog
Color variations: pure white, though some slight lemon or tan markings are permissible.
Average Lifespan: 12 to 15 years
Origins: Malta - 1500 BC - bred as companion dogs for royalty and nobility.
Body Size: Males and Females: 7-9 in. 4-7 lbs.
Personality/Disposition/Compatibility: This breed is famous for its warm and friendly personality. These dogs are full of life and have a knack for brightening your day with their playful antics. They're incredibly loyal and form deep bonds with their families. They thrive on human interaction, making them fantastic companions for kids and other pets alike.
Grooming Needs: They require daily brushing to prevent matting and tangling of their long, silky coats. Regular bathing and professional grooming are also necessary.
Training & Exercise Needs: Training can be a truly fulfilling experience, though it might require a bit of patience. Begin with basic commands and make sure your training sessions are brief and enjoyable to keep them engaged. For exercise, a few short walks each day combined with some playful moments will generally keep them happy and healthy. They thrive on quality time with their family rather than intense physical activity.**Possible Health Issues:** dental problems, patellar luxation, and respiratory issues due to their small size

Manchester Terrier (Standard)

Other Names: Black and Tan Terrier
Color variations: black and tan
Average Lifespan: 14 to 16 years
Origins: England - 19th century - bred for hunting vermin, such as rats.
Body Size: Males: 16-18 in. 12-22 lbs. Females: 15-17 in. 12-22 lbs.
Personality/Disposition/Compatibility: Friendly and outgoing, these dogs are true social butterflies who thrive on attention and interaction. They quickly form strong, loving bonds with their families and are known for their affectionate and loyal nature. Always alert and watchful, they make excellent watchdogs, ready to alert you if anything seems out of the ordinary. Their natural curiosity and zest for life make them engaging companions. They usually get along well with kids and can live harmoniously with other pets, though they may have a strong prey drive, so it's wise to keep an eye on them around smaller animals.
Grooming Needs: Their short, smooth coat requires regular brushing to remove loose hair and occasional baths to keep them clean.
Training & Exercise Needs: Training these dogs is pretty straightforward when you use consistent and positive reinforcement. They thrive on clear commands and really enjoy interactive training sessions, which makes the process fun and keeps them engaged. To keep them happy and healthy, regular exercise is key. Daily walks, playtime, and interactive activities will help burn off their energy and keep their minds sharp.
Possible Health Issues: patellar luxation, hip dysplasia, progressive retinal atrophy (PRA), and von Willebrand's disease

Manchester Terrier (Toy)
Other Names: English Toy Terrier
Color variations: black and tan
Average Lifespan: 14 to 16 years
Origins: England - early 19th century - bred for ratting and as a companion dog.
Body Size: Males and Females: 10-12 in. 6-8 lbs.
Personality/Disposition/Compatibility: These dogs are full of life and confidence, turning every day into an adventure. They're not just lapdogs, they're lively companions who love to be in the thick of family activities. Friendly and sociable, they usually get along well with kids and other pets, though their high energy might be a bit much for more laid-back animals. They thrive in active homes where they can play and engage with everyone. Despite their small size, their sharp alertness makes them surprisingly good watchdogs, always on the lookout for anything out of the ordinary.
Grooming Needs: Regular brushing will help maintain their sleek coat and keep shedding under control.
Training & Exercise Needs: Training these lively dogs can be both a fun and fulfilling experience. Their boundless energy and eagerness mean they might require a little extra patience and consistency from you. To keep their focus, opt for short, frequent training sessions. They'll do best in a busy household where they're actively involved, as this helps prevent boredom and excess energy from turning into behavioral problems. Make sure to include daily walks, playtime, and plenty of mental stimulation in their routine. Activities like fetch, agility drills, or puzzle toys are great ways to keep them happy and engaged.
Possible Health Issues: patellar luxation, heart problems, and eye conditions such as progressive retinal atrophy (PRA)

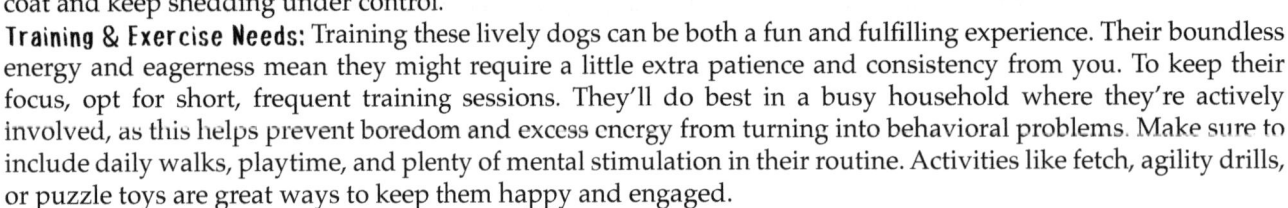

Mastiff (English)
Other Names: Old English Mastiff
Color variations: fawn, apricot, or brindle colors, often with a dark mask around the eyes and muzzle.
Average Lifespan: 6 to 10 years
Origins: England - 19th century - bred as a guard dog and for use in blood sports such as bull-baiting.
Body Size: Males: 30-34 in. 160-230 lbs.
Females: 27.5-30 in. 120-170 lbs.
Personality/Disposition/Compatibility: English Mastiffs are the gentle giants of the dog world, known for their warm and loving personalities. These dogs are incredibly loyal and forge strong bonds with their families, often following their favorite people around like devoted shadows. When it comes to kids, they're not just patient, they're downright protective, making them fantastic playmates and guardians. When it comes to other pets, including cats, they usually get along well, provided they're introduced properly and given a bit of time to adjust.
Grooming Needs: Their short coat requires minimal grooming, with regular brushing to remove loose hair and occasional baths to keep the coat clean. Their facial wrinkles should be cleaned regularly to prevent infections.
Training & Exercise Needs: Training them can be a bit of a rollercoaster. On one hand, they're smart and eager to make you happy, which makes training a lot easier. On the other hand, their size and occasional stubbornness can throw a wrench in the works. They love a good run around the yard or a friendly game of fetch, but they're just as content to chill out at home. Just keep in mind that their larger frame can lead to joint issues, so it's best to steer clear of overly strenuous activities.
Possible Health Issues: hip dysplasia, elbow dysplasia, heart conditions, bloat (gastric torsion), and certain types of cancer.

Mastiff (Pyrenean)
Other Names: Mastín del Pirineo
Color variations: White with patches of gray, brindle, fawn, black, or badger (gray with reddish or blackish shading).
Average Lifespan: 10-13 years
Origins: Pyrenees region, Spain - late Middle Ages - bred to guard livestock against predators like wolves and bears.
Body Size: Males: 30-32 in. 140-240 lbs.
Females: 28-30 in. 120-200 lbs.
Personality/Disposition/Compatibility: The Pyrenean Mastiff is truly a heart-stealer. With its calm and easygoing demeanor, this breed offers a quiet strength that's both comforting and impressive. They're naturally gentle and protective, making them fantastic playmates for kids. While their large size might be a bit overwhelming at times, their patience and nurturing spirit usually keep things in check. They're also known for getting along well with other pets, whether it's dogs or even cats, thanks to their relaxed attitude that promotes a harmonious home.
Grooming Needs: Regular brushing is required to maintain their thick double coat, with increased attention during shedding season. Occasional baths and routine care for ears, teeth, and nails are also necessary.
Training & Exercise Needs: Training them can be a bit of a challenge, thanks to their independent and sometimes stubborn streak. While they're sharp and can pick up commands, they might need a firm, consistent approach paired with plenty of patience. They're usually happy with moderate exercise. Since they're on the larger side, they can be prone to joint issues, so it's best to steer clear of excessive running or high-impact activities.
Possible Health Issues: Hip dysplasia, elbow dysplasia, bloat (gastric torsion), and eye conditions such as entropion or ectropion.

Mastiff (Neapolitan)
Other Names: Mastino Napoletano or Mastino
Color variations: black, blue, mahogany, and tawny. They may also have brindle patterns or white markings.
Average Lifespan: 7 to 9 years
Origins: Italy - 1949 - bred for guarding property and family.
Body Size: Males: 26-31 in. 150-200 lbs.
Females: 24-29 in. 120-175 lbs.
Personality/Disposition/Compatibility: This breed truly turns heads with its impressive size and unique charm. Known for their gentle and affectionate nature, especially towards their families, they are incredibly loyal and protective, making them excellent watchdogs. They thrive in homes where they have plenty of space to move around and generally get along well with children and other pets, especially if introduced properly. Their steady, easygoing nature makes them a perfect choice for families or individuals seeking a devoted companion who also doubles as a loving guardian.
Grooming Needs: They have minimal grooming needs due to its short coat. Regular brushing to remove loose hair and skin care to clean the folds and wrinkles are necessary to prevent infections.
Training & Exercise Needs: Training can be a bit of an adventure due to their independent and sometimes stubborn streak. They thrive on consistent, patient, and firm guidance, so starting training early is key. These gentle giants need a good mix of exercise, like daily walks and playtime, to keep them healthy and happy. Thankfully, they're not overly demanding and can adjust well to a more laid-back lifestyle.
Possible Health Issues: hip and elbow dysplasia, cardiac conditions, bloat (gastric torsion), and skin infections, particularly in the folds of their skin

Mastiff (Spanish)

Other Names: Mastín Español
Color variations: fawn, brindle, black, and red. Some may also have white markings.
Average Lifespan: 10 to 12 years
Origins: Spain - Middle Ages - bred for guarding livestock against predators such as wolves.
Body Size: Males: 28-35 in. 140-200 lbs.
Females: 26-33 in. 130-170 lbs.
Personality/Disposition/Compatibility: The Spanish Mastiff is a gentle giant with a heart as big as its impressive size. They exude a calm, composed vibe that's perfect for anyone who enjoys a relaxed companion. With a mix of dignified serenity and tender affection, they're often reserved around strangers but shower their families with deep loyalty and love. They stay cool and collected, even when things get hectic, making them great with kids and other pets. Socialize them early, and they'll get along just fine with other animals. While their protective instincts make them reliable guardians, their easygoing nature keeps them from being too aggressive or overbearing.
Grooming Needs: Their dense coat requires regular brushing to remove loose hair and prevent matting. Bathing should be done as needed.
Training & Exercise Needs: Training them might be a bit tricky because of their independent streak, but with a little patience and consistency, they'll come around. They're not the type that needs intense workouts. They're perfectly fine with moderate exercise, like a daily walk and some playtime.
Possible Health Issues: hip and elbow dysplasia, bloat (gastric torsion), and heart conditions

Mastiff (Tibetan)

Other Names: Do-Khyi and Tsang-Khyi
Color variations: black, brown, blue-gray, and gold, often with tan or white markings.
Average Lifespan: 10 to 12 years
Origins: Tibet - ancient times - bred to guard livestock and property, particularly in the harsh conditions of the Himalayas.
Body Size: Males: 26-30 in. 90-150 lbs. Females: 24-28 in. 70-120 lbs.
Personality/Disposition/Compatibility: With its impressive size and striking mane, they command attention with a calm and dignified presence. They might come off as aloof, but don't be deceived; they're incredibly loyal and loving with their families. Their natural protective instincts make them superb watchdogs. However, they're not the best choice for first-time owners, as they require firm and consistent training. This breed thrives with families who appreciate their strong, silent demeanor and can provide the right blend of structure and affection.
Grooming Needs: require regular grooming, particularly during their shedding seasons. Their dense double coat needs to be brushed several times a week to prevent matting and to remove loose hair.
Training & Exercise Needs: Training them can definitely be a bit of a challenge. While they're smart, they also have a strong will and an independent streak, so they might push the limits now and then. That's why starting consistent and firm training early on is key. They love a good walk and some playtime, but they don't need a ton of exercise to stay happy. A balanced routine of regular activity is usually all they need to stay healthy and content.
Possible Health Issues: hip and elbow dysplasia, hypothyroidism, and entropion

Miniature American Shepherd

Other Names: Mini American Shepherd or Mini Aussie
Color variations: black, blue merle, red, and red merle. They often have white and tan markings.
Average Lifespan: 12 to 15 years
Origins: United States - late 1960s - bred for their herding ability and to create a smaller, more manageable version of the Aussie.
Body Size: Males: 14-18 in. 20-40 lbs. Females: 13-17 in. 20-40 lbs.
Personality/Disposition/Compatibility: These dogs are the perfect mix of brains and charm. They're confident and assertive without Being pushy, they have a real talent for reading their owner's mood and adapting their behavior, making them truly empathetic companions. They get along well with kids and other pets, especially if introduced the right way. Their high energy means they're happiest with families who can keep them active and mentally stimulated.
Grooming Needs: Regular brushing is key to keeping their double coat in check and minimizing shedding. During shedding seasons, you might need to brush them more often. Don't forget that occasional baths, nail trims, and ear cleanings are also part of the grooming routine.
Training & Exercise Needs: Training these dogs is often a pleasure due to their sharp minds and enthusiasm for learning. They catch on to new commands and tricks swiftly, especially when you use positive reinforcement. They also need plenty of physical activity to stay happy and healthy. With their high energy levels, keeping them active is essential to avoid boredom and any potential behavioral issues.
Possible Health Issues: hip dysplasia, progressive retinal atrophy (PRA), epilepsy, and patellar luxation

Miniature Bull Terrier

Other Names: None
Color variations: white, black, brindle, red, fawn, and tri-color.
Average Lifespan: 11 to 14 years
Origins: England - 19th century - bred for hunting vermin and as a companion dog.
Body Size: Males & Females: 10-14 in. 20-35 lbs.
Personality/Disposition/Compatibility: These dogs are full of life and always ready to make you smile. With their playful antics and endless energy, they have a way of brightening up any room. They love being the center of attention, often playing the role of the class clown. Whether it's chasing a ball in the backyard or tagging along on family adventures, they thrive on being part of the action. They get along well with other pets, especially if they're introduced early and properly. Just remember, their strong personalities mean they do best with owners who can offer steady guidance and training.
Grooming Needs: To keep its short coat looking its best, just give it a regular brush to whisk away loose hairs and treat it to an occasional bath to keep it fresh and clean.
Training & Exercise Needs: Training these dogs can be a bit of a challenge, thanks to their lively and sometimes stubborn personalities. They're smart and eager to please, but their own excitement can sometimes get in the way. These dogs have boundless energy and need plenty of activity to stay happy and healthy. They do best in environments where they can stay active and interact with their families. If they don't get enough physical and mental stimulation, they might get bored and show some unwanted behaviors.
Possible Health Issues: deafness, heart problems, skin allergies, and kidney disease

K9 Chatter

Miniature Pinscher

Other Names: Min Pin
Color variations: red, black and rust, chocolate and rust, and stag red.
Average Lifespan: 12 to 16 years
Origins: Germany - 1800s - bred to hunt rats in homes and stables.
Body Size: Males and Females: 10-12.5 in. 8-12 lbs
Personality/Disposition/Compatibility: These lively little dogs are bursting with energy and charm. Their enthusiasm for life is both entertaining and, at times, a little overwhelming. They build strong bonds and crave attention but might be a bit reserved with newcomers. They're a perfect match for active individuals or families who can keep up with their spirited pace. They usually get along well with other dogs, especially if they're socialized early, but their high-energy nature might not be ideal for quieter, more relaxed homes.
Grooming Needs: They require minimal grooming due to its short coat. Regular brushing and occasional baths are sufficient to keep its coat clean and healthy.
Training & Exercise Needs: Training these lively little dogs is a mix of fun and challenge. They're clever and keen to make you happy, which is a big plus, but their boundless energy can sometimes lead to a bit of distraction. They thrive on regular activity to stay joyful and fit. Playing games like fetch or getting into agility training can help them use up that extra energy and stay in great shape.
Possible Health Issues: patellar luxation, hip dysplasia, Legg-Calvé-Perthes disease, hypothyroidism, and progressive retinal atrophy (PRA)

Mountain Cur

Other Names: Mountain Kerr or Cur Dog
Color variations: brindle, blue, yellow, brown, and black with white markings.
Average Lifespan: 12 to 16 years
Origins: Appalachian region, United States - early 19th century - bred for hunting and protecting homesteads.
Body Size: Males: 18-26 in. 40-60 lbs. Females: 16-24 in. 30-50 lbs.
Personality/Disposition/Compatibility: These dogs are full of life and energy, making them perfect for active families or anyone who can match their boundless enthusiasm. Despite their high energy, they're incredibly affectionate and form deep, loyal bonds with their families. They love to stay busy and engaged, so they're happiest in an environment that keeps them on the go. They're generally good with other pets and children, though their lively nature might be a bit much for very young kids.
Grooming Needs: Regular brushing once a week is usually sufficient to keep their coat healthy and reduce shedding. They also require regular dental care, nail trimming, and ear cleaning.
Training & Exercise Needs: Training them is truly a rewarding experience. They're smart and eager to please, which usually makes them quick learners. However, don't be surprised if they show a bit of stubbornness now and then! These dogs love having space to run and play, so regular exercise is crucial for their happiness and health. Make sure to include daily walks, playtime, and activities that challenge their minds to keep them active and content.
Possible Health Issues: hip dysplasia, ear infections, and skin allergies

Mudi
Other Names: Hungarian Mudi, Canis Ovilis Fenyesi
Color variations: black, white, fawn, blue, ash, brown, and marbled merle.
Average Lifespan: 12 to 14 years
Origins: Hungary - 19th century - bred for herding livestock, particularly sheep and cattle.
Body Size: Males: 15-18 in. 24-29 lbs. Females: 14-17 in. 18-24 lbs.
Personality/Disposition/Compatibility: These dogs are like a ray of sunshine breaking through a cloudy day. With their endless energy and playful nature, they make amazing companions for active families or anyone who loves outdoor adventures. They get along great with kids and other pets, especially if they've been socialized from an early age. Because they're so energetic, they'll need a lot of exercise and aren't ideal for homes where they'll be alone for too long.
Grooming Needs: Regular brushing is required to keep their coat free of tangles and mats. They shed seasonally and may need more frequent brushing during those times.
Training & Exercise Needs: Training these dogs might take a bit of effort, but with a little patience and consistency, you'll find it's totally doable. They're enthusiastic learners and love to make you happy, so with the right methods, they'll catch on to commands and skills pretty quickly. Just be prepared to give them at least an hour of energetic activities each day—whether that's running, hiking, or playing fetch. They do best in lively homes where they can burn off their endless energy and stay mentally engaged.
Possible Health Issues: hip dysplasia, elbow dysplasia, patellar luxation, and eye conditions such as progressive retinal atrophy (PRA)

Musterlander Pointer (Large)
Other Names: Großer Münsterländer.
Color variations: white and black, often with black patches and ticking.
Average Lifespan: 12 to 14 years.
Origins: Germany - 19th century - bred for its versatile hunting abilities, capable of pointing and retrieving game.
Body Size: Males: 23.5-26 in. 60-70 lbs. Females: 21.5-24 in. 50-60 lbs.
Personality/Disposition/Compatibility: These dogs are celebrated for their gentle nature and loving hearts. They're the kind of companions who bring a sense of calm and reliability wherever they go, making them a delight to be around. They're great with kids and get along well with other pets, even cats. Their friendly, easygoing attitude makes them an ideal addition to any home seeking a warm and adaptable friend.
Grooming Needs: regular brushing to maintain the coat's condition and prevent matting. Occasional baths, ear cleaning, and nail trimming are also necessary.
Training & Exercise Needs: Training these dogs is usually a breeze thanks to their eager-to-please nature. They pick up on things quickly and thrive on positive reinforcement. While they do need a fair bit of activity to stay happy and healthy, it's nothing overwhelming. They're quite adaptable, so whether your home is lively or more laid-back, they'll fit right into your routine.
Possible Health Issues: hip dysplasia, elbow dysplasia, and certain eye conditions such as cataracts

Musterlander Pointer (Small)
Other Names: Kleiner Münsterländer and Small Munsterlander.
Color variations: brown and white or brown roan with brown patches or spots.
Average Lifespan: 12 to 14 years
Origins: Germany - early 20th century - bred for versatile hunting purposes, including tracking, pointing, and retrieving game.
Body Size: Males: 20.5-22 in. 44-60 lbs. Females: 19.5-21 in. 40-55 lbs.
Personality/Disposition/Compatibility: This breed is a true sweetheart, known for its friendly and affectionate nature. Whether you're a family or a single person, it's a fantastic companion who'll quickly become a beloved part of your life. With a naturally outgoing and sociable personality, this dog forms strong bonds with its human family almost instantly. It's gentle with kids and gets along wonderfully with other pets, from dogs to cats. If you're looking for a furry friend who loves to be involved in family activities and thrives on interaction, this breed is perfect for you.
Grooming Needs: They require regular brushing to keep their coat free of tangles and mats, especially after outdoor activities. Occasional baths and routine ear cleaning, nail trimming, and dental care are also important.
Training & Exercise Needs: Training this breed is usually a breeze. They're smart and eager to please, so they respond really well to positive reinforcement. Keeping them happy and healthy is all about balancing physical activity with mental challenges. Regular playtime and some fun interactive toys will not only fulfill their exercise needs but also keep their minds sharp and engaged.
Possible Health Issues: hip dysplasia, elbow dysplasia, and eye conditions such as progressive retinal atrophy (PRA)

Nederlandse Kooikerhondje
(Nay-der-lahn-suh Koy-ker-hond-yuh)
Other Names: Kooiker or Dutch Decoy Dog.
Color variations: white coat with red or orange patches. The ears are often reddish with black tips, known as "earrings."
Average Lifespan: 12 to 15 years.
Origins: Netherlands- 16th century - bred to lure ducks into traps for hunters.
Body Size: Males: 15-17 in. 20-30 lbs. Females: 14-16 in. 18-28 lbs.
Personality/Disposition/Compatibility: They're a wonderful mix of energy and charm. This breed is full of playful spirit and affection, making them an excellent buddy for both families and individuals. They're quite in tune with their owners' emotions and have a natural talent for providing comfort when it's needed most. They usually get along well with kids and other pets, especially if they're introduced the right way. Their upbeat attitude and adaptability mean they thrive in an active home that can offer the engagement and love they adore.
Grooming Needs: requires regular grooming, including brushing a few times a week to maintain its coat and prevent matting. Regular ear cleaning and nail trimming are also necessary.
Training & Exercise Needs: Training your dog can be incredibly fulfilling. These dogs are usually quick learners and love to make you happy. But don't be surprised if they show a bit of independence now and then—patience and persistence will go a long way. Daily walks, playtime, and chances to run around and explore are essential. Interactive games and dog sports are fantastic for keeping them physically active and mentally engaged.**Possible Health Issues:** patellar luxation, epilepsy, and eye disorders such as cataracts and progressive retinal atrophy

Newfoundland
Other Names: Newfie
Color variations: black, brown, gray, and Landseer (white with black markings).
Average Lifespan: 8 to 10 years
Origins: Newfoundland, Canada - early 18th century - bred for hauling nets for fishermen and carrying wood from the forest.
Body Size: Males: 28 in. 130-150 lbs. Females: 26 in. 100-120 lbs.
Personality/Disposition/Compatibility: These dogs are incredibly affectionate, quickly forming deep bonds with their families and often providing a comforting presence. Their relaxed demeanor makes them fantastic with kids and other pets, and new people, greeting visitors with a wagging tail and a friendly nudge. While they're generally laid-back, they do appreciate having something to do, whether it's frolicking in the yard or joining you on family outings. Just keep in mind their size; they do need a bit more space than your average dog.
Grooming Needs: requires regular grooming due to its thick, double coat. Brushing several times a week is necessary to prevent matting and reduce shedding.
Training & Exercise Needs: Training these dogs is usually a breeze because they're so eager to please and quick-witted. They pick up new skills fast and thrive on positive reinforcement, so sticking with a consistent, patient approach will yield great results. They love to stay active but aren't high-maintenance, so a good balance of exercise and mental challenges keeps them happy and well-rounded. Keep them busy with engaging activities, and they'll be both content and balanced.
Possible Health Issues: hip dysplasia, elbow dysplasia, cystinuria, and heart problems such as subvalvular aortic stenosis

Norfolk Terrier
Other Names: Norfolks
Color variations: red, wheaten, black and tan, and grizzle.
Average Lifespan: 12 and 16 years
Origins: England - early 20th century - bred for hunting small vermin and as barnyard ratters
Body Size: Males: 10 in. 12-14 lbs. Females: 9-10 in. 11-12 lbs.
Personality/Disposition/Compatibility: This little terrier is bursting with personality and energy, making it a fantastic buddy for anyone who loves a lively spirit. With its quick wit and intelligence, this breed can definitely keep you on your toes, especially if it's not getting enough mental stimulation. They usually get along well with other pets, as long as introductions go smoothly. Their playful nature makes them a great match for kids, though their small size means they'll do best in families that can handle their vibrant, spirited ways with a bit of patience and understanding.
Grooming Needs: require regular grooming to maintain their wiry coat. This includes brushing several times a week and occasional hand-stripping to remove dead hair and keep the coat healthy.
Training & Exercise Needs: Training this spirited terrier can be quite the adventure thanks to its independent nature and endless energy. These smart pups are quick learners, but they also need plenty of mental stimulation to keep them out of trouble. They thrive on regular activity, so daily walks and playtime are a must. Whether it's a game of fetch or a playful romp in the yard, they're always ready for fun. Keep them engaged and active, and you'll find that a well-exercised terrier is a happy and well-behaved companion!
Possible Health Issues: hip dysplasia, patellar luxation, mitral valve disease, and eye conditions such as cataracts and lens luxation

K9 Chatter

Norrbottenspets
Other Names: Norrbotten Spitz or Nordic Spitz.
Color variations: white with distinct yellow or red patches.
Average Lifespan: 14 to 17 years
Origins: Sweden - early 1600s - bred for hunting small game and birds.
Body Size: Males: 17-18 in. 20-30 lbs. Females: 16-17 in. 17-26 lbs.
Personality/Disposition/Compatibility: These dogs are naturally curious and full of life, making them a delight to be around. Their keen intelligence and alertness come with a warm, affectionate side, which makes them fantastic family pets. They usually get along well with kids and other animals, including cats, thanks to their friendly and adaptable nature. Their boundless energy and eagerness to learn mean they really shine in active households where they can join in on family fun.
Grooming Needs: Its dense double coat requires regular brushing to remove loose hair and prevent matting, especially during shedding seasons. Routine baths, nail trimming, and ear cleaning are also recommended.
Training & Exercise Needs: Training them is usually a breeze because they pick up things quickly and love to make you happy. They thrive on positive reinforcement, so if you keep training sessions fun and rewarding, you'll see great results. They've got a lot of energy to burn! Regular physical activity is key to keeping them happy and healthy, so daily walks, playtime, and mental stimulation are a must. If you keep them engaged and active, they'll flourish both mentally and physically.
Possible Health Issues: generally a healthy breed but can be prone to certain genetic health issues such as hip dysplasia and patellar luxation.

Norwegian Buhund
Other Names: Norsk Buhund
Color variations: wheaten, ranging from pale cream to bright orange, and black.
Average Lifespan: 12 to 15 years
Origins: Norway - 900 AD - bred for herding and guarding livestock.
Body Size: Males: 17-18.5 in. 31-40 lbs. Females: 16-17.5 in. 26-35 lbs.
Personality/Disposition/Compatibility: With their sunny disposition and endless zest for life, they're like a little whirlwind of joy. They mesh well with just about everyone, from kids to other pets, thanks to their friendly and gentle nature. Their knack for getting along with both dogs and cats is truly remarkable; they adapt effortlessly to having furry friends in the house. Plus, their loyalty and protective instincts mean you can always rely on them to be a devoted and watchful family member.
Grooming Needs: requires regular brushing to maintain its coat and reduce shedding. They have a double coat that sheds seasonally, requiring more frequent grooming during these times.
Training & Exercise Needs: Training these pups is usually a breeze because they're so eager to make you happy and pick up new tricks quickly. They thrive on consistent, positive reinforcement, thanks to their enthusiastic and smart nature. When it comes to exercise, they're full of energy and need plenty of activity to stay content and healthy. Activities like fetch or agility courses are perfect for keeping them both physically active and mentally engaged.
Possible Health Issues: generally a healthy breed but can be prone to hip dysplasia, progressive retinal atrophy (PRA), and cataracts.

Norwegian Elkhound
Other Names: Norsk Elghund and the Elk Dog
Color variations: shades of gray with black-tipped guard hairs, giving it a distinctive wolf-like appearance.
Average Lifespan: 12 to 15 years
Origins: Norway - 5000 BC - bred to hunt large game, particularly elk and moose, as well as to serve as a guardian and herding dog.
Body Size: Males: 19.5-21.5 in. 50-60 lbs.
Females: 18.5-20.5 in. 40-55 lbs.
Personality/Disposition/Compatibility: They're not just friendly; they're loyal and form deep connections with their families, serving as devoted and protective watchdogs. Their curiosity and intelligence drive them to seek out mental challenges, so they might get a little mischievous if they're bored. Generally great with kids and friendly toward other pets, they do need careful introductions to ensure everyone gets along. Just keep in mind their strong prey drive, smaller animals might find themselves in for a chase!
Grooming Needs: Their dense double coat requires regular grooming. Weekly brushing is necessary to remove loose hairs and prevent matting, with more frequent brushing during shedding seasons. Bathing should be done occasionally, as needed.
Training & Exercise Needs: They're smart and eager which makes training them a rewarding experience. Just keep in mind, they have a bit of an independent side. These lively dogs have tons of energy and need plenty of exercise to stay content. They love activities that challenge both their mind and body, so think about incorporating agility training or interactive toys into their routine to keep them engaged and thriving.
Possible Health Issues: hip dysplasia, progressive retinal atrophy, hypothyroidism, and kidney problems

Norwegian Lundhund
Other Names: Norwegian Puffin Dog
Color variations: reddish-brown to tan, often with black-tipped hairs and white markings. Some may also be black or gray with white markings.
Average Lifespan: 12 to 15 years
Origins: Norway - 16th century - bred for hunting puffins and their eggs in the rocky cliffs and crevices of Norway's coastal regions.
Body Size: Males: 13-15 in. 20-30 lbs. Females: 12-14 in. 15-25 lbs.
Personality/Disposition/Compatibility: These lively dogs are brimming with energy and affection. They're always up for a new adventure, whether it's exploring the great outdoors or having a blast in the backyard. With their keen alertness, they're excellent watchdogs, but they're also gentle and get along well with kids, making them a fantastic family companion. They flourish when they get plenty of mental and physical stimulation. Their playful and social nature means they love being around people and other dogs. Just keep in mind, they do have a bit of an independent streak, so they'll appreciate some space and quiet time now and then.
Grooming Needs: requires regular brushing to manage its double coat and minimize shedding. Bathing should be done as needed, and attention should be given to ear cleaning and nail trimming.
Training & Exercise Needs: Training these energetic pups is a real delight. They're eager to please and catch on quickly, making them stars in both basic commands and more advanced tricks. With their boundless energy, they thrive on regular exercise to stay happy and healthy. Keeping them active not only ensures they're well-behaved but also helps them avoid the mischief that boredom can bring.
Possible Health Issues: gastrointestinal disorders, particularly Lundehund Syndrome, which can cause digestive issues and malabsorption

Norwich Terrier

Other Names: Cantab Terrier or Jones Terrier
Color variations: red, wheaten, black and tan, and grizzle.
Average Lifespan: 12 to 15 years
Origins: England - late 19th century - bred to hunt small vermin and act as loyal companions for farmers and hunters.
Body Size: Males and Females: 10 in. 11-12 lbs.
Personality/Disposition/Compatibility: The Norwich Terrier is a delightful little bundle of energy wrapped up in a tough, charming package. This spirited terrier is always ready for a new adventure and brings a lot of personality to the table. They're generally great with other pets, especially if they're introduced properly from the start. Kids will find a playful friend, as their lively energy matches well with little ones. However, their excitable nature means they thrive in homes where they receive plenty of attention and engagement.
Grooming Needs: Regular brushing is necessary to maintain their wiry coat, and occasional hand-stripping is recommended to remove dead hair and keep the coat looking its best.
Training & Exercise Needs: These dogs are smart and eager to please, making them fairly easy to train. However, they do have a bit of an independent streak, so a touch of patience and persistence goes a long way. These lively little dogs love interactive play and mental challenges, so puzzle toys and agility exercises can be great for keeping them engaged. They're energetic without being overwhelming, which makes them a perfect match for active families or anyone who can give them plenty of attention and activities.
Possible Health Issues: hip dysplasia, patellar luxation, mitral valve disease, and respiratory problems due to their small windpipes.

Nova Scotia Duck Tolling Retriever

Other Names: Toller, Nova Scotia Retriever
Color variations: various shades of red and orange, often with white markings on the face, feet, and chest.
Average Lifespan: 12 to 14 years
Origins: Canada - 19th century - bred to lure and retrieve waterfowl.
Body Size: Males: 18-21 in. 45-52 lbs. Females: 17-20 in. 35-42 lbs.
Personality/Disposition/Compatibility: Picture a dog that blends boundless energy with a loving heart, that's the Toller. They're known for their warm and friendly demeanor, thriving on social interaction and making great companions. They have a knack for sensing when someone needs a little extra comfort, often offering a gentle nuzzle just when you need it most. Generally, they get along well with other pets, especially if they're introduced early on. While their playful antics might be a bit much for smaller animals, with the right approach, they can build wonderful relationships with both other dogs and even cats.
Grooming Needs: require regular brushing to maintain their double coat and minimize shedding. Occasional baths and routine ear cleaning, nail trimming, and dental care are also necessary.
Training & Exercise Needs: Training a Toller is often a delightful journey. These dogs are sharp and eager to please, so they usually catch on to training quickly. However, their playful and energetic spirit means they need engaging and consistent sessions to keep them focused. They thrive on a good mix of exercise to stay happy and healthy. Daily activities should include brisk walks, some playtime, and a bit of mental stimulation. A well-exercised Toller is a content Toller, so keeping them active is essential for their overall well-being.
Possible Health Issues: hip dysplasia, progressive retinal atrophy, autoimmune diseases, and hypothyroidism

Old English Sheepdog
Other Names: Bobtail
Color variations: blue, blue merle, or gray, often with white markings.
Average Lifespan: 10 to 12 years
Origins: England - early 19th century - bred for herding sheep and cattle.
Body Size: Males: 22-24 in. 70-100 lbs. Females: 21-23 in. 60-85 lbs.
Personality/Disposition/Compatibility: These dogs are famous for their sweet and friendly nature, making them a fantastic fit for families big and small. Their playful antics and endless energy will keep you laughing and on your toes. They have a knack for getting along with everyone, from kids to other pets, thanks to their easy-going and patient attitude. Whether it's a new furry friend or a house full of guests, they handle it all with a calm and cheerful demeanor. They love being part of the family hustle and bustle and are at their happiest when they're getting plenty of attention and interaction.
Grooming Needs: requires regular grooming due to its thick, double coat, which can mat easily. Weekly brushing and occasional professional grooming are necessary to maintain the coat's condition.
Training & Exercise Needs: Training these dogs is usually a joy because they're so eager to please and quick-witted. They're full of energy and need regular activity to stay content and healthy. They love interactive games and are always ready for a game of fetch or a lively romp in the yard. In general, they do best in a setting where they get plenty of both physical and mental stimulation.
Possible Health Issues: hip dysplasia, cataracts, hypothyroidism, and progressive retinal atrophy

Otterhound
Other Names: Otter Dog
Color variations: black, tan, grizzle, and wheaten.
Average Lifespan: 10 to 13 years
Origins: England - early 19th century - bred specifically for hunting otters.
Body Size: Males: 27-29 in. 115 lbs. Females: 24-27 in. 80 lbs.
Personality/Disposition/Compatibility: They're a true joy to have around, bringing both fun and a bit of a challenge, especially for first-time dog owners. Their playful spirit is perfect for families, and they're always eager for a new adventure. With a knack for comedy, they'll keep you entertained with their delightful antics. They're fiercely loyal and can be quite protective of their loved ones, though they're generally friendly and easygoing with new people. They get along well with children and other pets, thanks to their sociable nature. Just remember that their hunting background means they have a strong prey drive, so early socialization and training are essential for a happy, well-adjusted pup.
Grooming Needs: They require regular grooming due to their dense, water-resistant double coats. This includes weekly brushing to prevent matting and occasional baths to keep their coat clean.
Training & Exercise Needs: Training this breed can be a bit of an adventure thanks to their independent and occasionally stubborn streak. They're full of energy and need plenty of activity to stay happy and healthy. Think long walks, runs, and playtime, these dogs thrive on vigorous exercise. Keeping them engaged with activities that challenge both their minds and bodies is key to their well-being and can keep boredom at bay.
Possible Health Issues: hip dysplasia, elbow dysplasia, bloat (gastric torsion), and ear infections due to their large, floppy ears.

Papillon

Other Names: Continental Toy Spaniel
Color variations: white with patches of black, red, sable, or lemon.
Average Lifespan: 12 to 16 years
Origins: France and Belgium - 16th century - bred as a companion for the nobility and royal families.
Body Size: Males: 8-11 in. 5-10 lbs. Females: 8-11 in. 4-9 lbs.
Personality/Disposition/Compatibility: Papillons are a burst of joy with their cheerful and lively personalities. They're known for being smart, playful, and incredibly affectionate. With their beautiful, butterfly-like ears and graceful movements, they love to be the center of attention and don't mind showing off a little. Their boundless energy makes them perfect for active families or anyone who enjoys a bit of fun. They usually get along well with other pets and can be surprisingly good with kids, though their small size means they should be handled with care.
Grooming Needs: require regular grooming to maintain their long, silky coat. Brushing a few times a week is necessary to prevent tangles and mats. They also need regular dental care and occasional nail trimming.
Training & Exercise Needs: Training Papillons can be a truly gratifying experience. These little furballs are sharp as a tack and always ready to make you proud, making training with positive reinforcement a breeze. They're like sponges for new tricks, soaking up commands quickly as long as the sessions stay fun and engaging. Though they're small, they've got plenty of energy and love their playtime, so daily walks and some interactive games are a must for keeping them both happy and healthy. While they don't need intense exercise, keeping their minds and bodies active is crucial to their overall well-being.
Possible Health Issues: patellar luxation, progressive retinal atrophy, and dental problems

Parson Russell Terrier

Other Names: Parson Jack Russell Terrier.
Color variations: white, white with black or tan markings, or a combination of these colors.
Average Lifespan: 13 to 15 years
Origins: England - 19th century - bred primarily for hunting foxes.
Body Size: Males: 14 in. 13-17 lbs. Females: 13 in. 10-15 lbs.
Personality/Disposition/Compatibility: These dogs are a bundle of joy and energy, turning every gathering into a lively celebration. With their endless curiosity they're always ready for the next adventure. Their sharp intelligence and quick wit make them not just charming but also a source of endless entertainment. They do have a playful side, which can sometimes tip into mischief. They thrive in a home with an active family or individual who can keep up with their spirited pace. While they generally get along well with other pets when introduced thoughtfully, their strong prey drive might lead them to view smaller animals as exciting playmates rather than buddies.
Grooming Needs: Regular brushing to remove loose hair and occasional baths are usually sufficient.
Training & Exercise Needs: Training these dogs might be a bit of a challenge, but it's definitely doable with the right approach. Their smarts mean they catch on to commands quickly, though their curiosity and playful nature can sometimes lead to distractions. They're pretty active and need plenty of exercise to stay happy and healthy. Daily vigorous activities like long walks, energetic play sessions, and engaging mental tasks keep them content. Giving them enough physical and mental stimulation helps burn off their boundless energy and keeps them from getting into trouble.
Possible Health Issues: patellar luxation, deafness, and eye disorders such as cataracts and lens luxation

Pekingese

Other Names: Peke
Color variations: gold, red, sable, black, cream, white, black and tan, and occasionally a combination of these colors.
Average Lifespan: 12 to 14 years
Origins: China - ancient times - bred to be a companion dog for Chinese royalty.
Body Size: Males and females: 6-9 in. 8-14 lbs.
Personality/Disposition/Compatibility: With their unique pushed-in faces these dogs exude a regal presence as if they've just stepped off a royal throne. They're deeply loyal to their families and love being the center of attention. But don't let their affectionate nature fool you, they have a strong will and a confident personality that sometimes shows as a bit of stubbornness. While they generally get along with other pets, their royal demeanor might make them prefer being the top dog in the household. They thrive in homes where they can be pampered and adored.
Grooming Needs: require regular grooming due to their long double coat. This includes daily brushing to prevent matting and tangling, as well as regular baths and trimming around the eyes and paws.
Training & Exercise Needs: Training these majestic dogs can be a bit of a challenge, but with some patience and consistency, they'll catch on. They love having a purpose, so adding mental activities to their routine can really help keep them engaged. While they do need regular walks and playtime, they don't require intense workouts. A few short walks and some fun play each day should do the trick.
Possible Health Issues: prone to several health issues, including brachycephalic syndrome, heart problems, eye conditions such as progressive retinal atrophy and cataracts, and joint issues like patellar luxation

Peruvian Inca Orchid

Other Names: Peruvian Hairless Dog or PIO.
Color variations: black, brown, grey, pink, and mottled.
Average Lifespan: 11 to 13 years
Origins: Peru - pre-Incan times - bred for companionship and as a hunting dog.
Body Size: The breed comes in three sizes.
Small Males & Females: 9.75-15.75 in. 8.5-17.5 lbs.
Medium Males & Females: 15.75-19.75 in. 17.5-26.5 lbs.
Large Males & Females: 19.75-25.75 in. 26.5-55 lbs.
Personality/Disposition/Compatibility: These dogs are known for their gentle and affectionate personalities, making friends wherever they go. While they might seem calm and reserved, don't let that fool you. They're not shy, just careful about who they let into their circle. Once you're in, they're playful and spirited, always up for a game or a cozy cuddle. They generally get along well with other pets, though they might need a bit of time to warm up to new furry friends. With a patient and gentle approach, they're fantastic with kids, making them a great choice for families who appreciate a balance of calm and fun.
Grooming Needs: Regular skin care, including moisturizing and sun protection, is important to maintain healthy skin.
Training & Exercise Needs: Training these dogs is usually a breeze because they're smart and eager to please. They love a good play session in the yard or a game of fetch, but they're also perfectly happy with a few leisurely walks each day. To keep them content and engaged, mix in some mental stimulation with puzzle toys or basic obedience training.
Possible Health Issues: skin conditions due to their hairless nature, dental problems, and a predisposition to sunburn.

Pharaoh Hound
Other Names: Kelb tal-Fenek
Color variations: tan or chestnut with white markings on the chest, toes, and tail tip.
Average Lifespan: 12 to 14 years
Origins: Malta - 1000 BC - bred for hunting rabbits.
Body Size: Males: 23-25 in. 45-55 lbs. Females: 21-24 in. 40-50 lbs.
Personality/Disposition/Compatibility: The Pharaoh Hound is the kind of dog that's impossible not to adore. With its sleek, graceful look and friendly, sunny personality, this breed radiates charm wherever it goes. Full of energy and always up for a good time, they thrive in homes where they're part of the action. They usually get along well with kids and other pets, though their hunting background might spark a bit of a chase instinct now and then. To keep this spirited pup happy, make sure they're included in family activities and get plenty of exercise.
Grooming Needs: Regular brushing to remove loose hair and occasional baths are sufficient to keep their coat healthy.
Training & Exercise Needs: These dogs are smart and always keen to make you happy, which helps them learn commands and tricks quickly. They do have a bit of an independent side, though, so they can be a little stubborn or easily distracted at times. That's why staying consistent and patient with them is important. They're pretty active and need regular exercise to stay happy and healthy. Daily activities that challenge both their bodies and minds are ideal. Without enough to do, they might get bored and show some destructive behaviors.
Possible Health Issues: hip dysplasia, patellar luxation, and sensitivity to anesthesia.

Plott Hound
Other Names: Plott
Color variations: variety of brindle patterns and may also be seen in black or with a black saddle.
Average Lifespan: 12 to 14 years
Origins: North Carolina, United States - 1750s - bred for hunting wild boar and other large game.
Body Size: Males: 20-25 in. 50-60 lbs. Females: 20-23 in. 40-55 lbs.
Personality/Disposition/Compatibility: This breed is all about fun and enthusiasm, with a playful spirit and an unshakeable determination. They're naturally curious and alert, which makes them fantastic watchdogs. Their strong family bond is heartwarming, and they get along well with kids and other pets. These social dogs love being involved in everything and truly shine when they're part of the action. If you're an active family or individual who can match their high energy, the Plott Hound is definitely the right companion for you.
Grooming Needs: short, smooth coat, which requires regular brushing to keep it clean and healthy. Occasional baths and routine ear cleaning are also recommended.
Training & Exercise Needs: Training a Plott Hound can be a truly gratifying adventure. These dogs are not only smart but also have a genuine desire to make you happy, which is a big plus. However, their strong-willed personalities mean they do best with consistent and clear guidance. Plott Hounds are high-energy and thrive on physical activity, so they'll love you even more if you take them for long runs, adventurous hikes, or play games that tap into their natural hunting instincts. Keeping them active is key to their well-being and happiness!
Possible Health Issues: hip dysplasia, bloat, and ear infections.

Pointer
Other Names: English Pointer
Color variations: liver, lemon, black, and orange, either in combination with white or solid.
Average Lifespan: 12 to 17 years
Origins: England - 17th century - bred to point and locate game birds for hunters.
Body Size: Males: 25-28 in. 55-75 lbs. Females: 23-26 in. 44-65 lbs.
Personality/Disposition/Compatibility: These dogs greet you with a wagging tail and a beaming smile, always eager to dive into whatever you have planned for the day. With their boundless energy, they're ideal for active families or anyone who loves spending time outdoors. They generally get along well with other dogs and pets, though their spirited nature might be overwhelming for more reserved animals. They're typically fantastic with kids, especially if they've grown up with them, and often take on the role of the family's playful guardian.
Grooming Needs: have low grooming needs due to their short coat. Regular brushing to remove dead hair and occasional baths are usually sufficient to keep their coat healthy and clean.
Training & Exercise Needs: Training these dogs can be a bit of a rollercoaster due to their spirited and independent nature. With their boundless energy, they need plenty of exercise to stay both happy and healthy. Keeping them engaged and mentally stimulated is crucial, so finding fun ways to keep them busy will keep them thriving.
Possible Health Issues: hip dysplasia, elbow dysplasia, and eye conditions like progressive retinal atrophy (PRA)

Polish Lowland Sheepdog
Other Names: Polski Owczarek Nizinny or PON.
Color variations: white, gray, and black, often with patches of other colors.
Average Lifespan: 12 to 14 years
Origins: Poland - 16th century - bred for herding and guarding livestock.
Body Size: Males: 18-20 in. 40-50 lbs. Females: 17-19 in. 35-45 lbs.
Personality/Disposition/Compatibility: The PON, for short, is a lively and lovable bundle of fur. With their shaggy coat and spirited personality, they bring a lot of fun and laughter into any home. These dogs are not just clever; they have a knack for mischief and a great sense of humor that keeps everyone entertained. Their playful nature makes them fantastic companions for families with kids, and they usually get along well with other pets, especially if they've been socialized early on. Though their herding instincts might make them try to corral smaller animals or even the kids, it's all done with a gentle and playful touch.
Grooming Needs: requires regular grooming to prevent matting and tangles. Their long, dense coat needs to be brushed several times a week, and occasional trimming may be necessary.
Training & Exercise Needs: Training can be a truly gratifying experience, though it does call for a dash of patience. Their intelligence and eagerness to please usually make them quite receptive to training. However, their independent spirit and boundless energy might require a bit more persistence and consistency to keep their attention. They're energetic and thrive on physical activity. Engaging them in activities that challenge both their minds and bodies like agility courses or interactive games—can help them burn off their energy and stay content.
Possible Health Issues: hip dysplasia, progressive retinal atrophy, and hypothyroidism

K9 Chatter

Pomeranian
Other Names: Poms
Color variations: orange, black, white, blue, chocolate, and cream.
Average Lifespan: 12 to 16 years
Origins: Germany and Poland - 18th century - bred for companionship and as smaller versions of larger sled dogs.
Body Size: Males and Females: 6-7 in. 3-7 lbs.
Personality/Disposition/Compatibility: These dogs are full of life and confidence, always making their presence known with a bit of flair. They're loving and devoted to their families but can be a touch dramatic when they want to make a point. They typically get along well with kids, especially if they've had good socialization from the start. With their energetic personality, they thrive on attention and affection, so they're happiest with families or individuals who can shower them with both.
Grooming Needs: require regular grooming due to their thick double coat. Brushing several times a week is necessary to prevent matting and reduce shedding.
Training & Exercise Needs: enjoy activities such as short walks, playtime, and mental stimulation through interactive toys.
Possible Health Issues: dental problems, luxating patella, tracheal collapse, and heart disease.

Pont-Audemer Spaniel
Other Names: Epagneul Pont-Audemer.
Color variations: brown, brown and white, or brown and grey color variations, often with roan or ticked patterns.
Average Lifespan: 12 to 14 years
Origins: France - 19th century - bred for its superior hunting skills, particularly in waterfowl retrieval.
Body Size: Males: 21-23 in. 40-60 lbs. Females: 20-22 in. 35-55 lbs.
Personality/Disposition/Compatibility: They love being around people and have a delightful curiosity that keeps them lively and engaged. With their gentle temperament, they're fantastic with kids and other pets, effortlessly getting along with everyone they meet. They're adaptable and thrive in environments where they get plenty of attention, exercise, and mental stimulation. Whether you're a busy family, a single person, or a senior, these spaniels' easy-going nature and friendly attitude make them a wonderful choice for any home.
Grooming Needs: requires regular grooming to maintain its curly coat. Brushing several times a week is necessary to prevent matting, and occasional trimming may be needed. The ears should be checked regularly for signs of infection, and the coat should be kept clean and free of debris.
Training & Exercise Needs: Their eagerness to please and responsiveness to positive reinforcement make them fairly easy to train, as long as you provide consistent and patient guidance. They love activities that engage both their bodies and minds, so adding interactive toys or puzzle games to their routine can be a real hit. Regular exercise is key to keeping them fit and preventing boredom, helping them stay the happy, well-mannered companions you cherish.
Possible Health Issues: generally healthy but may be prone to certain conditions such as hip dysplasia, ear infections, and skin issues.

Poodle
Other Names: Standard Poodle
Color variations: black, white, apricot, blue, brown, cream, gray, red, and silver.
Average Lifespan: 12 to 15 years
Origins: Germany and France - 15th century - bred for hunting and retrieving waterfowl.
Body Size: Males: 18-24 in. 45-70 lbs. Females: 18-22 in. 40-60 lbs.
Personality/Disposition/Compatibility: They're incredibly affectionate and loyal, forming deep bonds with their families. Whether it's a cozy evening at home or a lively family gathering, they're more than happy to be the center of attention. Friendly with other pets and generally warm towards strangers, they fit right in with households that have multiple animals or lots of visitors. Their gentle temperament and boundless energy make them a perfect match for families with kids, keeping up with the little ones' playful antics while offering a comforting presence.
Grooming Needs: Their curly coats require regular brushing to prevent matting and professional grooming every six to eight weeks to maintain the desired clip.
Training & Exercise Needs: These dogs are sharp and eager to make you happy, which means they pick up new tricks pretty quickly. They might show a bit of stubbornness now and then, but with a little patience and consistent practice, they'll get the hang of commands and good behavior. They thrive on regular walks, playtime, and activities that challenge their minds. Engaging them in things like agility training or interactive games not only burns off their energy but also keeps their minds sharp and their spirits high.
Possible Health Issues: hip dysplasia, progressive retinal atrophy (PRA), Addison's disease, bloat, and thyroid issues

Poodle (Miniature)
Other Names: Mini Poodle
Color variations: white, black, brown, apricot, and gray.
Average Lifespan: 10 to 18 years
Origins: Germany and France - 15th century - bred for water retrieving and hunting.
Body Size: Males and Females: 10-15 in. 10-15 lbs.
Personality/Disposition/Compatibility: With their bright, curious eyes and playful nature, these dogs are always ready for a new adventure or a cozy cuddle session. Their lively and spirited personality turns every day into a thrilling journey. These pint-sized pups are friendly with just about everyone, getting along wonderfully with kids and other pets. While they love company, they also enjoy having a little space to call their own.
Grooming Needs: require regular grooming due to their curly, non-shedding coat. This includes frequent brushing to prevent matting and regular professional grooming every 4 to 6 weeks.
Training & Exercise Needs: Keeping training sessions short and fun is key to keeping them engaged and motivated. Their sharp minds and willingness to please mean they pick up new tricks quickly. To keep them happy and balanced, regular exercise is a must—it wards off boredom and keeps them in good spirits. They thrive on interactive play like fetch or agility games, which not only channels their energy but also keeps their brains active and stimulated.
Possible Health Issues: hip dysplasia, progressive retinal atrophy, epilepsy, and Addison's disease

Poodle (Toy)
Other Names: None
Color Variations: white, black, apricot, gray, silver, blue, brown, and cream.
Average Lifespan: 12 to 15 years
Origins: France and Germany - 18th century - bred as a companion dog and also served as a truffle hunter.
Body Size: Males and females: 10 in. 4-6 lbs.
Personality/Disposition/Compatibility: With their sparkling eyes and lively demeanor, these little dogs have a special way of brightening up everyone's day. Their smarts and loving nature make them a joy to have around, and they're known for their friendliness. Whether you're a kid or an adult, you're sure to enjoy their cheerful company.
Grooming Needs: require regular grooming due to their curly, dense coat. They need to be brushed several times a week and professionally groomed every six to eight weeks to prevent matting and keep their coat healthy.
Training & Exercise Needs: Training these little dogs is often a breeze because they're not only smart but also eager to make you happy. They catch on to commands and tricks in no time, especially when training sessions are fun and interactive. Despite their small size, they have plenty of energy and need regular exercise to keep them joyful and healthy. They love a good romp and will really shine with a bit of playtime and exploration.
Possible Health Issues: patellar luxation, progressive retinal atrophy, epilepsy, and dental problems

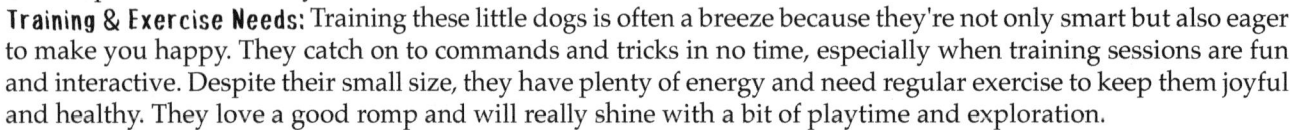

Porcelaine
Other Names: Chien de Franche-Comté
Color Variations: white coat with orange spots, though the spots are often faint or sparse.
Average Lifespan: 12 and 13 years
Origins: France - 18th century - bred for hunting hare and other small game.
Body Size: Males: 22-23 in. 55-62 lbs. Females: 21-22 in. 50-59 lbs.
Personality/Disposition/Compatibility: Their friendly and eager-to-please attitude makes them wonderful companions who love being part of family activities. They form deep bonds with their families and have a natural gentleness, especially around kids. They're not just attentive but also full of enthusiasm, which keeps things lively and fun. Their sociable and non-aggressive personality makes them a perfect match for both families and individuals. With their easy-going nature, they generally get along well with other pets and adapt effortlessly to any living situation..
Grooming Needs: Their short coat only requires occasional brushing to remove dead hair and keep it looking shiny.
Training & Exercise Needs: These dogs are smart and love to make you happy, so they respond really well to positive reinforcement. Just be consistent and patient, and they'll quickly pick up on commands and good habits. They're not overly demanding, but they do enjoy regular exercise to stay fit and keep their minds active. Interactive games and puzzle toys are perfect for keeping them engaged and entertained.
Possible Health Issues: These dogs are generally pretty healthy, but their long ears can sometimes lead to ear infections. Regular ear cleaning can help keep this at bay. They might also be prone to hip dysplasia and other common health issues, so keeping an eye on their overall well-being is a good idea.

Portuguese Podengo (Medio)
Other Names: Podengo Português
Color variations: yellow, fawn, black, or brown colors, often with white markings.
Average Lifespan: 12 to 15 years
Origins: Portugal - ancient times - bred for hunting purposes.
Body Size: Males and Females: 16-22 in. 35-44 lbs.
Personality/Disposition/Compatibility: With eyes that sparkle with warmth and a personality to match, this breed is a delightful blend of smarts, loyalty, and endless enthusiasm. They won't cling to you constantly but will surprise you with their affection and attention. Always alert and ready for a bit of fun, they're natural adventurers with a playful streak. They're perfect for families who love staying active, and they get along famously with kids and other pets. Their friendly and energetic nature means they're right at home in a lively household where they can play and interact, whether it's with other dogs or even cats, as long as there's space for everyone to enjoy each other's company.
Grooming Needs: The smooth-coated variety requires minimal grooming, while the wiry-coated variety needs regular brushing to prevent matting.
Training & Exercise Needs: These dogs are smart and eager to please, which makes training a breeze. Their playful and sometimes mischievous side means that being consistent and using positive reinforcement really pays off. They're full of energy and need plenty of exercise to keep them happy and healthy. They thrive on interactive games and activities that let them show off their natural curiosity and agility.
Possible Health Issues: generally healthy but can be prone to certain issues such as hip dysplasia, patellar luxation, and eye conditions.

Portuguese Podengo (Pequeno)
Other Names: Portuguese Warren Hound
Color variations: yellow, fawn, or black, often with white markings.
Average Lifespan: 12 to 15 years.
Origins: Portugal - ancient times - bred for hunting small game such as rabbits.
Body Size: Males and Females: 8-12 in. 9-13 lbs
Personality/Disposition/Compatibility: This breed is a delightful mix of energy and charm, packed into a small, compact frame. With their sharp intelligence and ever-alert nature, they're both adventurous explorers and loyal companions. Their affectionate nature makes them a hit with family members, and their playful spirit ensures there's never a dull moment. They're adaptable and can get along well with kids, other dogs, and even some cats, as long as introductions are handled with care.
Grooming Needs: the smooth coat variety, requiring regular brushing to maintain a healthy coat. The wire-haired variety needs more frequent brushing and occasional trimming.
Training & Exercise Needs: These dogs are incredibly smart and pick up commands in no time, but their playful side means they might push boundaries every now and then. To keep them on track, consistent and positive reinforcement is key. They're full of energy and need regular activity to stay both happy and healthy. They really thrive in settings where they can burn off their energy and stay mentally stimulated. Daily walks, playtime, and engaging activities like puzzle toys or training exercises are essential for their well-being.
Possible Health Issues: generally, a healthy breed, but it can be prone to some genetic conditions such as patellar luxation and hip dysplasia.

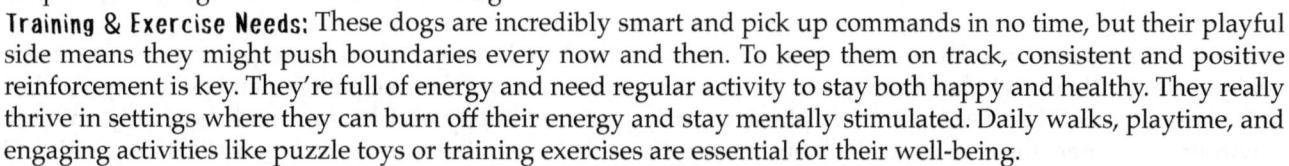

Portuguese Pointer
Other Names: Perdigueiro Português
Color variations: yellow and brown, often with white markings.
Average Lifespan: 12 to 14 years.
Origins: Portugal - 12th century - bred for hunting and retrieving game birds.
Body Size: Males: 22-24 in. 44-59 lbs. Females: 20-22 in. 35-48 lbs.
Personality/Disposition/Compatibility: This breed is a true joy to have around, thanks to its warm and loving nature. It thrives on human companionship and is always eager to be part of the family action. Whether it's playtime with the kids or lounging with other pets, this dog's friendly and cheerful attitude makes it a wonderful addition to any home. Its playful spirit will keep the whole family entertained and smiling!
Grooming Needs: their short, dense coat. Regular brushing is sufficient to keep their coat healthy and clean.
Training & Exercise Needs: These dogs are incredibly smart and always ready to make you happy, so training them is a breeze. They're not just good at following commands, they shine in everything from obedience drills to agility challenges. Their enthusiasm and sharp minds make them quite versatile. Just keep in mind that their energy and curiosity are off the charts, so they'll need plenty of exercise and mental stimulation to stay content and healthy.
Possible Health Issues: hip dysplasia, elbow dysplasia, and some eye conditions such as progressive retinal atrophy.

Portuguese Sheepdog
Other Names: Cão da Serra de Aires
Color variations: yellow, chestnut, gray, fawn, and black, often with white markings.
Average Lifespan: 12 to 14 years
Origins: Portugal - early 20th century - bred for herding livestock.
Body Size: Males: 19-22 in. 37-60 lbs. Females: 18-21 in. 37-60 lbs.
Personality/Disposition/Compatibility: This breed is known for its incredible energy and zest for life, making them perfect companions for active families or anyone who loves outdoor adventures. They've got a strong work ethic, thanks to their herding instincts, and are always eager to pitch in or join family fun. Friendly and social, they have a gentle touch, especially with kids and other pets. Their adaptability is a standout quality; they can thrive in different living situations as long as they get plenty of exercise and mental stimulation.
Grooming Needs: requires regular grooming to prevent matting and tangling of its long coat. Brushing several times a week and occasional trimming are necessary to keep its coat healthy.
Training & Exercise Needs: These pups are quick learners and love having a job to do, so positive reinforcement really pays off. They might have a bit of an independent streak now and then, so patience and persistence will be your best friends. They need plenty of physical activity to stay happy and healthy, and they truly shine in environments where they can expend all their energy. Be ready to keep them active and mentally stimulated, and you'll have a joyful, content companion on your hands!
Possible Health Issues: hip dysplasia, progressive retinal atrophy (PRA), and allergies.

Portuguese Water Dog
Other Names: Cão de Água
Color variations: black, white, and brown, or a combination of these colors, often with white markings.
Average Lifespan: 10 to 14 years
Origins: Portugal - 1500s - bred to help fishermen herd fish into nets, retrieving lost tackle, and delivering messages between boats and the shore.
Body Size: Males: 20-23 in. 42-60 lbs. Females: 17-21 in. 35-50 lbs.
Personality/Disposition/Compatibility: This breed is bursting with energy and enthusiasm, making them a fantastic companion for active families or anyone who loves an adventurous buddy. Friendly and affectionate, they're also keenly alert and protective, making them excellent watchdogs. Despite their protective instincts, their playful and warm-hearted nature shines through. They're great with kids and generally get along well with other dogs, though they might show a hint of competitiveness.
Grooming Needs: requires regular grooming to maintain its coat, which includes brushing several times a week and professional grooming every few months to prevent matting.
Training & Exercise Needs: With a little patience and lots of positive reinforcement, these dogs quickly learn commands and new skills. They really shine when they're mentally stimulated, so making training a regular part of their day keeps them both happy and engaged. They're full of energy and need plenty of exercise to stay in top shape. They love activities that challenge them, whether it's agility training or interactive games, which keeps them both physically and mentally stimulated.
Possible Health Issues: hip dysplasia, progressive retinal atrophy, and Addison's disease.

Presa Canario
Other Names: Canary Mastiff and Dogo Canario
Color variations: brindle, fawn, black, and sometimes has white markings.
Average Lifespan: 9 to 11 years
Origins: Canary Islands - 15th and 16th centuries - bred for working livestock and guarding property.
Body Size: Males: 23-26 in. 110-130 lbs. Females: 22-25 in. 85-110 lbs.
Personality/Disposition/Compatibility: These dogs are sharp and spirited, with a strong will that can be as delightful as it is challenging. They're fiercely loyal and protective, always ready to keep their loved ones safe. Even though their size might seem intimidating, they have a soft side, especially with those they trust. With a natural confidence and a healthy dose of skepticism towards strangers, they make fantastic watchdogs. They thrive in homes where they can be the star of the show and where their protective instincts are embraced. While they're usually great with older kids and can get along with other pets if introduced carefully, they do best with experienced dog owners who can appreciate their unique personality and give them the consistent training they need.
Grooming Needs: Regular brushing to remove loose hair and occasional baths will suffice.
Training & Exercise Needs: Training these dogs is definitely an adventure! Their strong-willed personalities mean they thrive under a firm but loving approach. They respond best to consistent, positive reinforcement and really enjoy having a job to do. Patience and persistence are your best friends, especially in the beginning. These energetic pups need regular exercise to stay happy and healthy, so activities like agility training or interactive games are perfect for keeping them both physically fit and mentally engaged. Balancing their exercise with training and socialization will help them blossom into a well-rounded and joyful companion.
Possible Health Issues: hip dysplasia, elbow dysplasia, demodectic mange, and gastric torsion (bloat).

Pudelpointer
Other Names: Poodle Pointer
Color variations: liver, black, and occasionally chestnut.
Average Lifespan: 12-14 years
Origins: Germany - late 19th century - bred as a versatile hunting dog that could excel in both water and field.
Body Size: Males: 24-26 in. 60-70 lbs. Females: 22-24 in. 45-65 lbs.
Personality/Disposition/Compatibility: This breed is a delightful mix of energy, smarts, and loyalty, making it a fantastic companion for a lively home. Imagine a Pointer's zest for life combined with a Poodle's sharp intelligence, and you've got a dog that's not only friendly and affectionate but also incredibly adaptable. Whether you're a bustling family, a single person, or an active individual, this breed will fit right in. They're natural social butterflies, always ready to greet guests with a wagging tail and a friendly attitude. Plus, they generally get along well with other pets. They're usually great with other dogs and, with the right introduction, can be pretty friendly with cats too.
Grooming Needs: Their wiry coat requires regular brushing to prevent matting and occasional hand-stripping to maintain its texture. Routine ear cleaning and nail trimming are also necessary.
Training & Exercise Needs: Training them is often a breeze thanks to their smarts and eagerness to please. They pick up commands quickly and enjoy the mental challenge that training brings. They need plenty of physical activity, so daily walks, playtime, and maybe some agility drills or fetch sessions are key. They thrive in lively households where they can channel their boundless energy into fun activities.
Possible Health Issues: hip dysplasia, eye conditions such as progressive retinal atrophy (PRA), and skin problems.

Pug
Other Names: Chinese Pugs and Dutch Mastiffs
Color variations: fawn, apricot fawn, silver fawn, and black
Average Lifespan: 12 to 15 years
Origins: China - 400 BC - bred as companions for royalty and later became popular in European courts.
Body Size: Males: 12-14 in. 14-18 lbs. Females: 10-12 in. 13-18 lbs.
Personality/Disposition/Compatibility: With a heart as big as their personality, these dogs have a natural knack for bringing smiles to everyone around them. Their playful and affectionate nature is hard to resist, and those big, round eyes and expressive faces seem to be in a constant state of curiosity and mischief. They're known for their easygoing attitude and delightful sense of humor, often indulging in silly antics that are sure to keep you entertained. While they're not high-maintenance, they'll certainly make their desires known with their characteristic snorts and grunts. Friendly and sociable, they get along well with just about everyone, from kids to other pets, making them a lovable addition to any home.
Grooming Needs: require regular grooming due to their short coat, which sheds moderately. Weekly brushing helps reduce shedding, and their facial wrinkles need to be cleaned regularly to prevent infection.
Training & Exercise Needs: Pugs are smart cookies with a playful side that can sometimes make them a little stubborn. The trick is to be consistent and use positive reinforcement. They're not as high-energy as some breeds, so they're happy with playtime and short walks. However, because of their short noses, they can tire out quickly, especially in the heat. Keep an eye out for signs they're getting too tired and adjust their activities to keep them happy and healthy.
Possible Health Issues: brachycephalic airway syndrome, hip dysplasia, patellar luxation, and eye problems such as proptosis and progressive retinal atrophy.

Puli

Other Names: Hungarian Puli and the Hungarian Water Dog
Color variations: black, white, gray, or a shade known as "fako," which is a kind of yellowish color.
Average Lifespan: 10 to 15 years
Origins: Hungary - 9th century - bred as a herding and livestock guarding dog.
Body Size: Males: 16-17 in. 25-35 lbs. Females: 14-16 in. 20-30 lbs.
Personality/Disposition/Compatibility: This breed is not only striking but also incredibly loyal and protective, making it a fantastic family companion. They shower loved ones with affection and has an uncanny ability to sense when someone needs a bit of extra care. With its natural herding instincts, they might try to round up anything that moves, including kids and other pets, adding a bit of playful excitement to your household.
Grooming Needs: They need regular grooming to keep their corded coat from matting and to keep their skin healthy. Despite their thick coat, they don't shed much.
Training & Exercise Needs: Training these dogs can be an incredibly rewarding journey, though it does come with its share of challenges. Their sharp minds and enthusiasm to please make them quick learners, but their independent and strong-willed personalities may require a bit more patience. These energetic pups love to stay active, so they thrive on activities that stimulate both their bodies and minds. Whether it's agility training, herding exercises, or interactive play, they're always up for the challenge. Regular exercise is a must to keep them content and healthy, and they'll truly appreciate having a job to do or a puzzle to solve.
Possible Health Issues: hip dysplasia, progressive retinal atrophy, and patellar luxation.

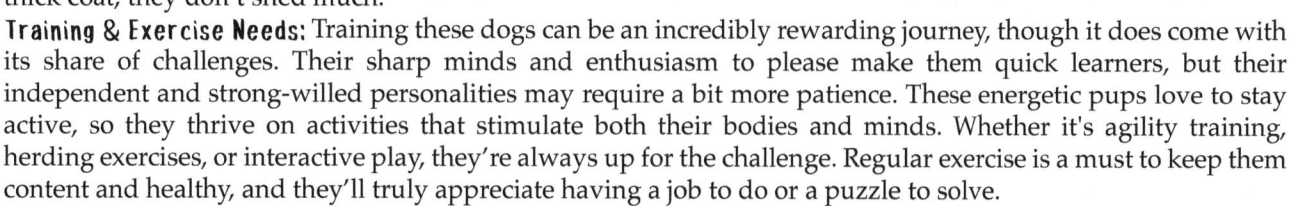

Pumi

Other Names: Hungarian Pumi
Color variations: black, white, gray, and shades of fawn.
Average Lifespan: 12 to 14 years
Origins: Hungary - 17th or 18th century - bred as a herding dog.
Body Size: Males: 16-18.5 in. 22-29 lbs. Females: 15-17.5 in. 18-24 lbs.
Personality/Disposition/Compatibility: With their unique curly coat and boundless energy, the Pumi is as spirited as they come. These dogs are incredibly smart and playful, always ready to turn the ordinary into an exciting adventure. Their mix of enthusiasm and affection makes them fantastic companions for active families. They love being around people, including kids and other pets, especially if they're kept busy with exercise and mental challenges. If you can match their high energy and provide a loving home, this friendly breed will bring a lot of joy to your life.
Grooming Needs: requires regular brushing to prevent matting and occasional trimming to maintain its shape. Bathing should be done as needed to keep the coat clean and healthy.
Training & Exercise Needs: Training them can be a rewarding experience, but it does come with its challenges. These dogs are highly intelligent and eager to please, which can make training easier if you use positive reinforcement techniques. They have high energy levels and need plenty of physical activity to stay happy and healthy. They love activities like running, agility courses, and interactive play. Daily exercise is essential to prevent boredom and to ensure they burn off their abundant energy.
Possible Health Issues: hip dysplasia, patellar luxation, and degenerative myelopathy.

Pyrenean Shepherd
Other Names: Berger des Pyrénées or Pyr Shep.
Color variations: fawn, brindle, grey, merle, and black.
Average Lifespan: 15 to 17 years
Origins: France - early 20th century - bred for herding sheep in the Pyrenees Mountains.
Body Size: Males: 15.5-18.5 in. 25-30 lbs. Females: 15-18 in. 20-25 lbs.
Personality/Disposition/Compatibility: These little dynamo dogs are full of energy and always eager to join in on whatever their family is up to. With their friendly, outgoing personalities, they quickly become beloved family members and show an unwavering loyalty. Their natural herding instincts mean they're always on the job, whether it's corralling the kids or keeping an eye on the household. Their sharp alertness and agility not only make them endearing but also quite handy in various situations. They're great with other pets and thrive on playtime with their canine buddies.
Grooming Needs: They require regular brushing to maintain its coat and prevent matting, particularly for the rough-faced variety. They are moderate shedders and need occasional baths.
Training & Exercise Needs: Training these lively little dogs can be a truly rewarding experience, though it does call for a good dose of consistency and patience. They're smart and eager to please, which makes the training process a bit easier. With their boundless energy, they thrive on plenty of activity to stay happy and healthy. Interactive games and agility exercises are fantastic ways to keep both their minds and bodies stimulated. Just remember, if they don't get enough exercise, they might start to get bored and restless, so be ready to spend some time keeping them entertained!
Possible Health Issues: hip dysplasia, patellar luxation, and progressive retinal atrophy.

Rafeiro de Alentejo
Other Names: Alentejo Mastiff
Color variations: black, fawn, brindle, yellow, and wolf gray. Some may have white markings.
Average Lifespan: 12 to 14 years
Origins: Portugal - the Middle Ages - bred for guarding livestock and property.
Body Size: Males: 25.5-29.5 in. 99-132 lbs. Females: 24-27 in. 77-110 lbs.
Personality/Disposition/Compatibility: These loyal guardians might come across as calm and composed, but don't be fooled by their laid-back attitude, they're fiercely protective of their families and property. They're not the type to constantly seek attention, which is a breath of fresh air if you prefer a dog that's confident and self-assured. While they form strong bonds with their family, they're a bit more reserved with newcomers. They generally get along well with other pets, especially if they've grown up together, but they thrive in homes where their protective nature is truly valued.
Grooming Needs: Regular brushing to remove dead hair and occasional baths are sufficient to keep the coat healthy and clean.
Training & Exercise Needs: Training these dogs can be a bit of a challenge because of their independent streak. They're smart and capable, but they might not always jump at the chance to please or follow commands immediately. They're fairly active and have moderate needs, so they thrive when they have a job to do. Activities that tap into their natural instincts, like guarding or tracking, are especially rewarding for them.
Possible Health Issues: hip dysplasia

Rat Terrier
Other Names: RT, Ratting Terrier, and Decker Giant
Color variations: black, chocolate, tan, blue, isabella, lemon, and apricot, often combined with white.
Average Lifespan: 12 to 18 years
Origins: United States - early 1900s - bred for farm work, hunting and controlling vermin.
Body Size: Males: 13-18 in. 15-25lbs. Females: 10-15 in. 10-18 lbs.
Personality/Disposition/Compatibility: This dog is a bundle of energy and smarts wrapped in a small, spunky package. This little pup will go above and beyond for their family. Their personality strikes a charming balance between playful and serious. They adapt effortlessly to various living situations, thriving just as well in a bustling city apartment as they do on a wide-open farm, provided they get plenty of exercise and mental engagement. With their friendly, outgoing nature, they generally get along well with other pets and children, though their hunting instincts might flare up around smaller critters.
Grooming Needs: Regular brushing and occasional baths are sufficient to keep their coat clean and healthy. Their nails should be trimmed regularly, and their ears checked for debris and infections.
Training & Exercise Needs: These pups are smart and always ready to impress, making training a breeze! They thrive on clear, consistent guidance paired with plenty of praise, so keeping things fun and positive is key. They're pretty flexible when it comes to activity levels. Just be sure to switch things up now and then to keep their curious minds busy and avoid boredom!
Possible Health Issues: generally healthy but can be prone to certain health issues such as patellar luxation, hip dysplasia, allergies, and dental problems

Redbone Coonhound
Other Names: Redbone
Color variations: solid red color, though some may have small white markings on the chest and feet.
Average Lifespan: 12 to 15 years
Origins: United States - 19th century - bred for hunting raccoons and other game animals.
Body Size: Males: 22-27 in. 45-70 lbs. Females: 21-26 in. 40-65 lbs.
Personality/Disposition/Compatibility: With their stunning red coat and those soulful eyes, Redbone Coonhounds are the perfect blend of laid-back charm and boundless energy. These even-tempered and friendly dogs are just as content to snuggle up on the couch with you as they are to follow an intriguing scent on an outdoor adventure. They form strong bonds with their families and have a sweet, affectionate nature without being too clingy. Their easy-going personality makes them a great fit for homes with kids and other dogs, though their hound instincts might occasionally kick in around smaller animals.
Grooming Needs: Their short, smooth coat requires occasional brushing to remove loose hair and maintain shine. Regular ear cleaning and nail trimming are also necessary.
Training & Exercise Needs: Training them is an adventure with a few twists! On the bright side, these dogs are eager to please and naturally friendly, making them a joy to work with. However, their powerful noses tend to take over, and the moment they catch an intriguing scent, their focus can wander. As natural-born hunters, they live for the thrill of following their noses, so incorporating activities like long walks, hikes, or scent-tracking games into their routine will keep them engaged and happy. It's all about finding the balance between their instincts and their willingness to learn!
Possible Health Issues: hip dysplasia, ear infections, and eye problems

Rhodesian Ridgeback
Other Names: African Lion Hound
Color variations: light wheaten to red wheaten
Average Lifespan: 10 to 12 years
Origins: Zimbabwe (formerly Rhodesia) - early 20th century - bred for tracking and holding lions at bay.
Body Size: Males: 25-27 in. 85-90 lbs. Females: 24-26 in. 70-75 lbs.
Personality/Disposition/Compatibility: They may seem like the "strong, silent type," but don't let that fool you, they're all heart when it comes to their loved ones. They're more of the quiet, watchful guardian type, always keeping an eye out without making a scene. While they carry themselves with a calm, dignified air, they've got a playful, fun-loving streak that pops out when the time's right. They're wonderful with kids, though their size and energy mean you might need to keep an eye on them around the little ones. When it comes to other dogs, they can be a bit picky, often preferring to take the lead. And as for cats or small animals, their strong prey drive could make things a little complicated, so that's worth considering.
Grooming Needs: Regular brushing is sufficient to keep its short coat healthy, and it only requires occasional baths.
Training & Exercise Needs: Training these dogs can sometimes feel like a bit of a puzzle, but with patience and consistency, you'll crack the code. They're smart and independent thinkers, but that also means they might have their own ideas now and then! These active pups thrive on both physical and mental challenges, so keeping them busy is key. They love activities like tracking, agility, or any dog sport that works both their mind and body. If they don't get enough exercise, they might get a little creative in how they burn off energy.
Possible Health Issues: hip dysplasia, elbow dysplasia, thyroid problems, and dermoid sinus.

Romanian Carpathian Shepherd
Other Names: Romanian Carpathian Sheepdog, Carpathian Shepherd Dog, Ciobănesc Românesc Carpatin
Color variations: wolf-gray, sandy, and various shades of gray with white markings.
Average Lifespan: 12 to 14 years
Origins: Romania - ancient times - bred for guarding livestock against predators in the Carpathian Mountains.
Body Size: Males: 25-29 in. 70-100 lbs. Females: 23-26 in. 60-90 lbs.
Personality/Disposition/Compatibility: Their calm, confident nature means they like to take a step back and assess a situation before jumping in.They're incredibly dedicated to their families. When it comes to strangers, they might be a little reserved at first, but once they've sized you up and decided you're trustworthy, they'll show off their affectionate, warm side. Around kids, they play the role of gentle protector. If they're socialized from an early age, they're generally easygoing and get along well with other pets. They may not be the life of the dog park, but they make reliable, good-natured companions in the right setting.
Grooming Needs: requires regular grooming to maintain its thick double coat. Brushing a few times a week will help remove loose hair and prevent matting. During shedding seasons, more frequent brushing may be necessary.
Training & Exercise Needs: These dogs are smart and hardworking, but they've got a bit of a stubborn streak. Don't expect them to follow orders without question; they like to think for themselves! That's why training requires a lot of patience and consistency. Give them the right mix of physical and mental stimulation, and you'll have a happy, chilled-out companion by your side. Puzzle toys or training games that get them thinking are perfect to keep their brains busy.
Possible Health Issues: hip dysplasia, elbow dysplasia, and progressive retinal atrophy

Romanian Mioritic Shepherd
Other Names: Mioritic Shepherd Dog and Ciobănesc Românesc Mioritic.
Color variations: white, cream, and gray, often with patches or a mottled appearance.
Average Lifespan: 12 to 14 years
Origins: Romania - several centuries - bred for guarding livestock and property.
Body Size: Males: 27-29 in. 100-130 lbs. Females: 25-28 in. 80-110 lbs.
Personality/Disposition/Compatibility: This is the kind of dog that wins you over with its fierce loyalty and devotion. They're all about family. With its calm and patient nature, they are a wonderful choice for families, especially those with kids, they don't get flustered easily. But don't be fooled by that relaxed vibe. When it comes to guarding its loved ones, this dog means business and won't hesitate to step up if it senses a threat. They're pretty accepting of other pets, especially if they grow up together, though their protective instincts might make them a little cautious around unfamiliar animals at first.
Grooming Needs: requires regular grooming due to its thick, long coat. Brushing several times a week is necessary to prevent matting and remove loose hair. Occasional baths will help keep the coat clean.
Training & Exercise Needs: They've got a mind of their own, so early training is key—and trust me, they'll respond way better to positive reinforcement than anything harsh. At their core, these dogs are true workers, so they need plenty of physical exercise to stay content. They also thrive when they've got a job to do, so keeping their body and mind busy is the best way to prevent boredom and the mischief that can come with it.
Possible Health Issues: hip dysplasia, elbow dysplasia, and bloat (gastric torsion).

Rottweiler
Other Names: Rotties.
Color variations: black coat with clearly defined rust or mahogany markings.
Average Lifespan: 8 to 10 years
Origins: Germany- 74 AD - bred for herding and guarding cattle, protecting the camp, and pulling carts and wagons.
Body Size: Males 24-27 in. 95-135 lbs. Females: 22-25 in. 80-100 lbs.
Personality/Disposition/Compatibility: They're the perfect blend of strength and heart. Sure, they're confident and carry themselves with a sense of responsibility, but once you get past that tough exterior, you'll discover how deeply loyal and loving they are. Their protective nature is undeniable, yet they balance it with a gentle, affectionate side, especially with their family. When raised in a loving environment, they're playful, great with kids, and even get along well with other pets. While they take their role as a guardian seriously, they're not aggressive by nature, just deeply bonded and protective of their people. Proper socialization is key to making sure they're comfortable with strangers and new animals, but with the right upbringing, Rotties are exceptional companions.
Grooming Needs: Their short coat requires weekly brushing to remove loose hair and maintain a healthy shine. Regular nail trimming, ear cleaning, and dental care are also essential.
Training & Exercise Needs: They're sharp and quick learners, always ready to impress, but they've got a bit of a stubborn streak too! They do best with someone who's confident and knows how to set firm, loving boundaries. These pups are full of energy and need regular activity to burn it off—think at least an hour or two of exercise each day. If they don't get enough, they can get a little antsy or bored, so keeping them busy is a must. But with the right mix of training and playtime, Rottweilers make incredible companions, full of love and loyalty.
Possible Health Issues: hip and elbow dysplasia, heart problems, such as aortic stenosis, and certain cancers

K9 Chatter

Russell Terrier

Other Names: Jack Russell Terrier and JRT
Color variations: white, white with black markings, or white with tan markings.
Average Lifespan: 12 to 14 years
Origins: England - early 19th century - developed by Reverend John Russell for hunting foxes.
Body Size: Males and females: 10-12 in. 9-15 lbs.
Personality/Disposition/Compatibility: They're smart, full of energy, and their zest for life is downright infectious. Don't let their small stature fool you; these terriers are fearless and love to think they're in charge. But beneath that lively attitude is a loyal, loving companion who thrives on being part of the family. They adore people, and with their playful spirit, they can be wonderful with kids. As for other dogs, they tend to get along well, but they may not be ideal for homes with small pets unless they're properly socialized.
Grooming Needs: Their short, dense coat requires regular brushing to remove loose hair and keep the coat healthy. Occasional baths are needed, and their nails should be trimmed regularly.
Training & Exercise Needs: Training these lively terriers can be a bit tricky, but with a little patience and consistency, it's absolutely achievable. They're sharp as a tack, but their independent and sometimes stubborn nature means they often prefer to march to the beat of their own drum. These little bundles of energy need plenty of exercise to keep them happy. Without enough physical and mental stimulation, they might find their own fun—and that's when the mischief kicks in! Keep them busy with a good mix of activities and training, and you'll have a content, well-behaved companion by your side.
Possible Health Issues: patellar luxation, deafness, and eye problems such as cataracts and lens luxation

Russian Toy

Other Names: Russian Toy Terrier, Russkiy Toy
Color variations: black and tan, blue and tan, brown and tan, solid red of various shades, and sable.
Average Lifespan: 10 to 12 years
Origins: Russia - early 18th century - bred as a companion dog for Russian nobility.
Body Size: Males and Females: 8-10 in. 3-6 lbs.
Personality/Disposition/Compatibility: These little charmers are full of playful energy and absolutely love being the center of attention. They thrive on human companionship and are perfect for someone who enjoys having a loyal, close-knit buddy by their side. While they're friendly with people they know, they can be a little cautious around new faces, but it doesn't take long for them to warm up once they feel safe. They also do well with other pets, especially if introduced properly, but because of their smaller, more delicate size, it's smart to keep an eye on them around bigger, dogs.
Grooming Needs: The smooth-coated variety requires minimal grooming, while the long-haired variety needs regular brushing to prevent tangles and matting.
Training & Exercise Needs: These little dogs are sharp thinkers, but their independent nature can sometimes lead to a bit of stubbornness. The trick to training them is keeping things fun and engaging to hold their interest. Even though they're small, they've got a surprising amount of energy to burn. They enjoy a good play session but aren't too demanding, making them a great fit for various living situations. Just don't forget to challenge their minds too! They're naturally curious and love to explore, so keeping them mentally stimulated will help avoid any boredom.
Possible Health Issues: patellar luxation, dental problems, and progressive retinal atrophy (PRA).

Russian Tsvetnaya Bolonka
Other Names: Russian Colored Lapdog.
Color variations: black, brown, gray, red, and combinations of these colors with white markings.
Average Lifespan: 12 to 16 years
Origins: Russia - mid-20th century - bred to be a companion dog.
Body Size: Males: 9-11 in. 9-11 lbs. Females: 8-10 in. 7-10 lbs.
Personality/Disposition/Compatibility: Whether it's a silly antic or just snuggling up beside you, they have a special way of brightening your day. They absolutely love being the star of the show, soaking up all the attention they can get. Their sweet and easygoing temperament makes them wonderful companions for anyone, young or old. Plus, their gentle demeanor means they tend to get along well with other pets, blending effortlessly into a multi-pet home. They're not the type to be yappy or demanding. Instead, they prefer a more relaxed vibe but are always up for a fun play session whenever the moment feels right.
Grooming Needs: Their long, curly coat requires regular brushing to prevent matting and tangles, and they may need professional grooming every few months.
Training & Exercise Needs: Training these little pups is a joy! They're eager to make you happy and love being by your side, which makes learning new commands come naturally to them. They catch on quickly, but like all good students, they thrive with a bit of consistency and plenty of praise. They're pretty low-maintenance when it comes to exercise—a couple of walks and some playtime will keep them happy and energized. And if you're heading outdoors, they'll gladly tag along for some fun in the sun!
Possible Health Issues: hip dysplasia, patellar luxation, and eye problems

Saint Bernard
Other Names: St. Bernards or Bernards
Color variations: red and white or brindle and white.
Average Lifespan: 8 to 10 years
Origins: Switzerland - 11th century - bred by monks at the Great St. Bernard Pass for rescues in the harsh Alpine conditions.
Body Size: Males: 28-30 in. 140-180 lbs.
Females: 26-28 in. 120-140 lbs.
Personality/Disposition/Compatibility: They aren't just the stars of rescue tales, they're everyday heroes in the family. Always ready with a comforting presence or a slobbery kiss when you need it. With their gentle and affectionate personalities, they form deep, heartwarming connections with their people. Despite their size, they're surprisingly patient and calm, which makes them wonderful pals for kids and even other pets. They're also natural protectors, keeping an eye on the family without ever being too pushy about it.
Grooming Needs: weekly brushing to manage shedding and prevent matting. Bathing should be done as needed, and routine care for their ears, nails, and teeth is essential.
Training & Exercise Needs: These pups are clever and always happy to make you proud, but their relaxed vibe can sometimes slow things down a bit when it comes to learning commands. They're not the type to leap into action, but with a little patience, they'll get the hang of it. While they're not bouncing off the walls with energy, they still need regular exercise to stay fit and happy. A long run? Probably not their idea of fun, but they do appreciate a nice walk or a chance to stretch out. Just keep an eye on their joints, especially as they age, and make sure they don't overdo it while they're still growing.
Possible Health Issues: hip and elbow dysplasia, heart problems, eye conditions such as entropion and ectropion, and bloat (gastric torsion).

Saluki
Other Names: Persian Greyhound or the Gazelle Hound
Color variations: white, cream, fawn, golden, red, grizzle, tan, black, and tricolor (white, black, and tan).
Average Lifespan: 12 and 14 years
Origins: Ancient Egypt - 2100 B.C. - bred for hunting game such as gazelles due to their speed and endurance.
Body Size: Males: 23-28 in. 40-65 lbs. Females: 23-27 in. 35-60 lbs.
Personality/Disposition/Compatibility: They have earned the nickname "the cats of the dog world," and for good reason! These dogs are fiercely independent and love to do things their own way. Sure, they're smart but don't expect them to follow your every command without question. At home, they're calm and quiet, creating a peaceful vibe, but once they're outside, their speed and agility are a sight to see. They thrive in laid-back households and are great with kids and other dogs, especially when socialized early. Just keep an eye on smaller pets, as their chase instinct might kick in!
Grooming Needs: This includes brushing at least once a week to remove loose hairs and prevent matting, especially on the feathered areas.
Training & Exercise Needs: Training them can feel like trying to convince a free spirit to follow a plan but they've got their own ideas! The key is to keep things fun and upbeat, with plenty of treats and positive reinforcement to keep them engaged. Since they were bred to hunt, they've got a lot of energy to burn, especially when it comes to sprinting. While they love a good nap at home, they absolutely need chances to stretch those long legs. If you enjoy an active lifestyle, a Saluki might just be your perfect jogging or hiking buddy!
Possible Health Issues: hip dysplasia, heart problems, and certain cancers.

Samoyed
Other Names: Smiling Sammy
Color variations: white, cream, and biscuit color variations.
Average Lifespan: 12 to 14 years
Origins: Siberia, Russia - 19th century - bred by the Samoyede people for herding reindeer, pulling sleds, and guarding the tribe.
Body Size: Males: 21-23.5 in. 45-65 lbs. Females: 19-21 in. 35-50 lbs.
Personality/Disposition/Compatibility: They're the life of the party, always ready for fun and family time. These dogs thrive on attention and seem happiest when surrounded by people or other pets. With their famously cheerful expressions, it's no wonder they're often called the "smiling Sammie." They've got a natural herding instinct and a protective streak, but their gentle and affectionate nature shines through. Whether you're a toddler or a grandparent, they will get along with you just fine. And if you're into outdoor adventures, they'll be right there, wagging their tail, ready to hit the trails with you.
Grooming Needs: requires regular brushing to prevent matting and control shedding. They have a thick double coat that needs to be brushed several times a week, with more frequent grooming during the shedding seasons.
Training & Exercise Needs: They're smart and quickly learn new commands, but don't be surprised if their independent nature shines through. A good mix of patience, consistency, and plenty of positive reinforcement will go a long way to keep them focused. These fluffy adventurers need daily activity to stay happy and healthy, so if you're the outdoorsy type, they'll be more than happy to join you. Whether it's a jog, a romp at the park, or some fun agility training, they're natural athletes who thrive on exercise. Keeping them active is the secret to a well-behaved and content companion.
Possible Health Issues: hip dysplasia, progressive retinal atrophy, diabetes, and hypothyroidism.

Schapendoes
Other Names: Dutch Sheepdog
Color variations: black, blue, gray, brown, and white.
Average Lifespan: 12 to 15 years
Origins: Netherlands - late 19th century - bred for herding sheep.
Body Size: Males: 17-19 in. 26-44 lbs. Females: 16-18 in. 26-44 lbs.
Personality/Disposition/Compatibility: This breed is an absolute delight to have in your life. They're like a little spark of energy, always keeping things lively and fun. With their upbeat personality, you'll never have a dull moment when they're around. They're sharp thinkers with just the right touch of independence. They're affectionate without being clingy, forming strong, loving bonds with their family, and they thrive when they feel included in the action. Their social and friendly nature makes them great with other pets, and they're wonderful companions for kids. 
Grooming Needs: They have high grooming needs due to their long, dense coat. Regular brushing is necessary to prevent matting and tangling, and they may require occasional professional grooming.
Training & Exercise Needs: Training these dogs is a breeze most of the time, thanks to their sharp minds and desire to make you happy. That little independent streak can pop up now and then, so don't be surprised if they show a bit of stubbornness. Regular walks, play sessions, and brain-boosting activities like puzzle toys or agility courses will keep them feeling their best. They thrive when given a job, so mixing some training into their exercise is a fun way to help them burn off that extra energy!
Possible Health Issues: hip dysplasia, progressive retinal atrophy (PRA), and ear infections.

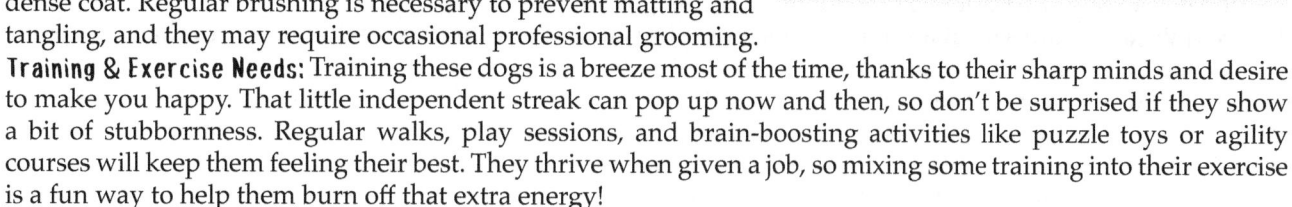

Schipperke
Other Names: Little Black Devil
Color variations: black, though other colors like tan, chocolate, and cream can occasionally be found but are not standard.
Average Lifespan: 12 to 15 years
Origins: Belgium - early 16th century - bred as small watchdogs and ratters on canal boats.
Body Size: Males: 11-13 in. 12-18 lbs. Females: 10-12 in. 10-16 lbs.
Personality/Disposition/Compatibility: They're little bundles of energy and curiosity, always on the go and ready to explore. It's no wonder they've earned the nickname "little black fox" with their sharp features and lively personalities. These mischievous pups have a knack for finding adventure wherever they go, and their independent streak makes them both confident and playful. Despite their spunky nature, they're fiercely loyal to their families and make fantastic companions. They tend to get along with other animals, though their herding instincts can kick in at the sight of anything moving quickly—whether it's a cat or even just a leaf blowing by! 
Grooming Needs: Their double coat requires regular brushing to manage shedding and prevent matting, particularly during seasonal shedding periods.
Training & Exercise Needs: These little pups are smart as a whip and eager to please. They prefer doing things on their terms, so you'll need a good mix of consistency, patience, and plenty of positive vibes to guide them. With all the energy packed into their tiny bodies, they're always up for an adventure. Be prepared, though they've got stamina and will happily keep exploring longer than you might expect! If they don't get enough action, their curious nature might lead them to stir up their own kind of mischief around the house.
Possible Health Issues: hip dysplasia, patellar luxation, Legg-Calvé-Perthes disease, and progressive retinal atrophy (PRA).

Schnauzer
Other Names: Mittelschnauzer
Color variations: salt and pepper, and solid black.
Average Lifespan: 12 to 15 years
Origins: Germany - 15th century - bred for ratting and guarding.
Body Size: Males: 18.5-19.5 in. 35-50 lbs.
Females: 17.5-18.5 in. 30-45 lbs.
Personality/Disposition/Compatibility: These dogs are sharp as a tack and always up for learning something new, making them fantastic companions for active families. They've got a big heart and build strong connections with their people, all while keeping an eye out to make sure everyone's safe. As both a loyal watchdog and a loving buddy, they strike the perfect balance. They're typically great with kids, especially if they've grown up alongside them, and with early socialization, they can get along well with other dogs too. But keep in mind, their natural prey drive means small pets like cats or hamsters might not make the best roommates.
Grooming Needs: requires regular grooming, including brushing several times a week and periodic hand-stripping or clipping to maintain their wiry coat.
Training & Exercise Needs: These dogs are all about making their owners happy, so they're usually quick to learn new things. That said, their smarts come with a dash of independence, so you'll need to stay consistent with training. They thrive on regular exercise—whether it's a long walk, a hike, or a good round of fetch. Keeping their minds active is just as important, so toss in some puzzle toys or fun training games to keep them engaged. If they get bored, you might find them getting into a little trouble, so keeping them busy is key!
Possible Health Issues: hip dysplasia, eye conditions such as cataracts and progressive retinal atrophy, and skin problems like follicular dermatitis.

Schnauzer (Giant)
Other Names: Riesenschnauzer
Color variations: solid black or a salt-and-pepper pattern
Average Lifespan: 12 and 15 years
Origins: Germany - 17th century - bred to drive cattle from farms to markets and to guard breweries, butcher shops, and stockyards.
Body Size: Males: 25.5-27.5 in. 60-85 lbs.
Females: 23.5-25.5 in. 55-75 lbs.
Personality/Disposition/Compatibility: These dogs take their responsibilities seriously, whether it's watching over the home or showing off their skills in training. They're all about family and form strong, loving connections with their people. With the right direction, they're great with kids, but their independent streak makes them a better fit for a confident, experienced owner. Early socialization helps them get along with other pets, but deep down, they kind of like being the center of attention.
Grooming Needs: requires regular grooming to maintain their wiry coat. This includes brushing several times a week and periodic hand-stripping or clipping to keep their coat in good condition.
Training & Exercise Needs: Training these dogs can feel like an adventure of its own, but the payoff is worth every minute. They're sharp learners and pick up new commands in no time. However, their independent streak means you'll need to be a patient, confident leader who sticks to the plan. Keep them active, too—they thrive on regular exercise. Whether it's a hike, a jog, or just a lively game of fetch in the backyard, they're always up for some outdoor fun.
Possible Health Issues: hip dysplasia, elbow dysplasia, hypothyroidism, and certain types of cancer.

Schnauzer (Miniature)

Other Names: Zwergschnauzer
Color variations: salt and pepper, black, black and silver, and white.
Average Lifespan: 12 to 15 years
Origins: Germany - late 19th century - bred to be small farm dogs and ratters.
Body Size: Males & Females: 12-14 in. 11-20 lbs.
Personality/Disposition/Compatibility: These dogs are little bundles of energy with an insatiable curiosity, always eager to check out what's happening around them. Despite their size, they've got bold personalities and are more than happy to play the role of a fearless watchdog, letting you know when someone's at the door with their sharp, attention-grabbing bark. What's even better is how well they get along with the whole family, kids, other dogs, and even cats when given the proper introduction. They're the perfect addition to homes of all kinds!
Grooming Needs: They require regular grooming, including brushing and trimming, to maintain their wiry coat and prevent matting. They should also have their ears checked and nails trimmed regularly.
Training & Exercise Needs: These dogs are quick learners thanks to their smarts, but that independent side of theirs can add a touch of stubbornness now and then. They thrive on regular activity to keep that lively energy balanced. A good mix of daily walks, playtime, and some brain games will work wonders. They're not the type to lounge around all day, but don't worry you won't need to sign up for marathons either. Just enough to keep them content and out of mischief!
Possible Health Issues: cataracts, pancreatitis, and hyperlipidemia.

Scottish Deerhound

Other Names: Deerhound
Color variations: blue-gray, gray, brindle, yellow, sandy red, and red fawn.
Average Lifespan: 8 to 11 years
Origins: Scotland - 15th century - bred for hunting deer.
Body Size: Males: 30-32 in. 85-110 lbs. Females: 28-30 in. 75-95 lbs.
Personality/Disposition/Compatibility: The Scottish Deerhound, often lovingly called a "gentle giant," brings a calm, noble presence to any home. Despite their roots as fierce hunting companions, these dogs are all about affection and forming deep, meaningful connections with their family. Their loyalty is undeniable, but it comes with a quiet, regal charm—they're the kind of dog that's there for you without being clingy. They're fantastic with other dogs and their easy-going nature makes them wonderfully patient with children, though their large size might be a bit much for the tiniest of toddlers. When it comes to strangers, they're more aloof than wary, more likely polite reserve rather than standoffishness.
Grooming Needs: Their harsh coat should be brushed weekly to remove dead hair and prevent matting. Occasional hand-stripping is recommended to maintain the coat's texture.
Training & Exercise Needs: Training these dogs can definitely keep you on your toes. They're smart but that independent streak of theirs can make them a bit stubborn when it comes to following orders. Patience and consistency will be your best friends here. Since they were bred for speed and endurance, they need plenty of exercise. Daily runs or nice long walks will help burn off that energy. If you've got a fenced yard, that's perfect for letting them run, but if not, regular outings to open spaces or a fun dog park should do the job just fine.
Possible Health Issues: cardiomyopathy, osteosarcoma, bloat (gastric torsion), and sensitivity to anesthesia.

Scottish Terrier
Other Names: Scottie
Color variations: black, wheaten, and brindle
Average Lifespan: 12 and 15 years
Origins: Scotland - 19th century - bred to hunt vermin such as rats, foxes, and badgers.
Body Size: Males: 10 in. 19-22 lbs. Females: 10 in. 18-21 lbs.
Personality/Disposition/Compatibility: They have a charming mix of independence and determination that gives them an air of quiet confidence. These little dogs are fiercely loyal, often forming a special bond with one person in the family, making them the perfect devoted companion. Their sharp senses make them excellent watchdogs. While they aren't the type to instantly make friends with everyone they meet, once they decide you're part of their circle, their loyalty is rock solid. With proper socialization, they can coexist happily with other pets, though their strong prey drive might make smaller animals a bit too tempting to resist.
Grooming Needs: They require regular grooming, including brushing their dense coat several times a week and trimming every few months to maintain their characteristic appearance.
Training & Exercise Needs: They're undeniably clever, but their independent nature means they tend to march to the beat of their own drum. This can sometimes be mistaken for stubbornness, but really, they just like to think for themselves. Scotties are quite full of energy! They don't need anything too intense, but regular activity is a must to keep them happy. A good walk each day, paired with some play or mental challenges, will keep them content. And let's not forget their love for digging and chasing! Giving them a chance to tap into these instincts is a great way to keep them entertained and out of trouble!
Possible Health Issues: Von Willebrand's disease, patellar luxation, and certain skin problems

Sealyham Terrier
Other Names: Sealy
Color variations: white, sometimes with lemon, tan, or badger markings on the head and ears.
Average Lifespan: 12 to 14 years
Origins: Wales - mid-19th century - bred for hunting small game such as badgers, foxes, and otters.
Body Size: Males: 10.5 in. 23-24 lbs. Females: 10.5 in. 20-23 lbs.
Personality/Disposition/Compatibility: This little terrier may be small, but it's packed with personality and charm. Always ready to entertain, they're full of playful energy and an attitude that's sure to make you smile. Despite their independent nature, they're total lovebugs when it comes to their families, always wanting to be part of the fun. Unlike some of their more high-energy terrier cousins, these pups have a relaxed side and are often a bit more reserved with new faces but they warm up fast. They usually get along well with other dogs, but watch out for their strong prey drive; smaller animals might trigger their inner chaser!
Grooming Needs: They require regular grooming to maintain its dense, wiry coat. This includes brushing several times a week and professional grooming every few months.
Training & Exercise Needs: These pups are bright and love to make you happy, but their independent side can sometimes lead to a touch of stubbornness. With a bit of patience, a consistent routine, and plenty of praise, they'll catch on to new tricks and commands in no time. While they're not the kind of dog that needs a marathon workout, they do enjoy a fun romp around the yard or a refreshing walk to burn off that lively energy. A couple of walks each day mixed with playtime will keep them content and feeling their best.
Possible Health Issues: lens luxation, retinal dysplasia, hip dysplasia, and allergies

Segugio Italiano
Other Names: Italian Hound
Color variations: fawn, black and tan, and occasionally with white markings.
Average Lifespan: 12 to 14 years
Origins: Italy - ancient times - bred for tracking game.
Body Size: Males: 19-23 in. 40-60 lbs. Females: 18-22 in. 35-55 lbs.
Personality/Disposition/Compatibility: This breed is all about the thrill of the chase, making them a fantastic companion for hunting adventures. They build deep connections with their families and have a naturally kind-hearted nature. While they're loyal and loving, they're also perfectly fine with a little alone time, so you won't have them following you around every minute. At home, they're calm and gentle, fitting in smoothly with families, even those with kids. And when it comes to other dogs, they tend to get along well, especially if introduced early on. Just watch them around smaller pets—those hunting instincts can sneak up!
Grooming Needs: They require minimal grooming due to its short coat. Regular brushing to remove loose hair and occasional baths are sufficient to keep the coat clean and healthy.
Training & Exercise Needs: These dogs are sharp and driven, especially when they're doing what they love. That independent nature, though, can add a little spice to training sessions, so it's all about patience and sticking with it. Using positive reinforcement goes a long way in keeping them motivated. They're happiest when they've got plenty to do, both physically and mentally, so daily exercise is non-negotiable. Don't expect them to be couch potatoes! Without enough activity, they might start to feel restless. Give them long walks, a good run, or some playtime in a secure yard, and you'll have a happy, healthy companion.
Possible Health Issues: hip dysplasia, ear infections, and certain genetic conditions common in hounds.

Shetland Sheepdog
Other Names: Sheltie
Color variations: sable and white, blue merle, black and white, and tricolor.
Average Lifespan: 12 to 14 years
Origins: Shetland Islands, Scotland - early 20th century - bred for herding and guarding sheep on the rugged terrain.
Body Size: Males: 13-16 in. 14-27 lbs. Females: 12-15 in. 12-23 lbs.
Personality/Disposition/Compatibility: These dogs are like the perfect adventure buddy wrapped in loyalty and smarts! They thrive in active families and have a real knack for getting along with other pets, making them a natural fit for homes with multiple animals. And when it comes to kids? They absolutely adore them! While they're affectionate with their loved ones, they might take a little time to warm up to new faces, but once they do, they're all in. With their sensitive nature, they're often right by your side, offering a comforting nuzzle when you need it most.
Grooming Needs: require regular grooming due to their thick double coat. Weekly brushing is essential to prevent matting and reduce shedding, with more frequent grooming needed during shedding seasons.
Training & Exercise Needs: Training these dogs is a joy because they're quick learners with a strong desire to make you happy. They catch on to new commands in no time, but it's important to mix things up to keep them engaged. They are full of energy, they thrive with plenty of exercise. Whether it's a brisk walk, a run, or some fun in the yard, these pups love to stay active. They also enjoy using their brains, so activities like fetch, puzzle games, or agility courses are great ways to keep them mentally sharp and entertained.
Possible Health Issues: hip dysplasia, hypothyroidism, Collie eye anomaly, and von Willebrand's disease.

K9 Chatter

Shiba Inu
Other Names: Shiba and Shiba Ken
Color variations: red, sesame, black and tan, and cream.
Average Lifespan: 12 to 15 years
Origins: Japan - 300 B.C. - bred for hunting small game and birds.
Body Size: Males: 14.5-16.5 in. 20-23 lbs.
Females: 13.5-15.5 in. 17-20 lbs.
Personality/Disposition/Compatibility: These dogs are a little firecracker with a bold spirit, often described as fiercely independent, with a charming confidence that can sometimes come across as aloof. They're incredibly loyal, but they've got a mind of their own; don't expect them to be stuck to your hip. They're surprisingly tidy! Some even have cat-like grooming habits. While they can be picky when it comes to other dogs, often wanting to call the shots, early socialization can help them learn to get along with others.
Grooming Needs: Their double coat requires regular brushing to manage shedding, especially during seasonal changes. They are naturally clean dogs and tend to groom themselves like cats.
Training & Exercise Needs: These clever little dogs have a mind of their own, which can sometimes make them seem a bit stubborn. They're smart, no doubt, but pleasing you isn't always their top priority, so training takes a bit of patience and plenty of positive reinforcement. They love to stay active, but don't worry—they don't need marathon sessions of exercise. A couple of solid walks and some fun activities to keep their brains busy will keep them content. And here's a tip: make sure your yard is escape-proof! These little adventurers have a knack for finding a way out if given the chance.
Possible Health Issues: allergies, glaucoma, hip dysplasia, and patellar luxation

Shih Tzu
Other Names: Chrysanthemum Dog
Color variations: black, white, blue, brindle, gold, liver, red, and silver, often with white markings.
Average Lifespan: 10 to 18 years
Origins: China - 800 B.C. - bred to be a companion dog for Chinese royalty.
Body Size: Males & Females: 9-10.5 in. 9-16 lbs.
Personality/Disposition/Compatibility: These dogs are absolute sweethearts, and it feels like they were made for love and companionship. With their natural charm, they can light up a room without needing to be the center of attention. Whether they're cuddled up in your lap or proudly prancing by your side, they love being with their people. They fit in just as well in a lively family as they do with a solo owner, making them an ideal match for almost anyone. Plus, their laid-back, friendly vibe means they get along wonderfully with kids, other dogs, and even cats!
Grooming Needs: require frequent grooming due to their long coat. Regular brushing, bathing, and trimming are necessary to prevent mats and tangles.
Training & Exercise Needs: Training these little charmers is generally a breeze, thanks to their eager-to-please attitude. They're smart and pick up commands quickly, especially if you use positive reinforcement like treats and praise. They're not high-energy dogs, but they do enjoy short bursts of activity, whether it's a game of fetch or a quick romp around the yard. A couple of daily walks and some playtime will keep them content.
Possible Health Issues: hip dysplasia, patellar luxation, ear infections, and respiratory problems due to their brachycephalic (short-nosed) structure.

Shikoku
Other Names: Kochi-ken and Mikawa Inu
Color Variations: sesame, black and tan, or red.
Average Lifespan: 10 to 12 years
Origins: Shikoku island region, Japan - early 20th century - bred for hunting boar in the mountainous areas.
Body Size: Males: 18-22 in. 35-55 lbs. Females: 17-21 in. 30-50 lbs.
Personality/Disposition/Compatibility: The Shikoku is the perfect mix of independence and loyalty. While they can be a bit reserved around new people, they're all heart when it comes to their family, forming strong, almost unbreakable bonds. Whether they get along with other pets can vary, but with early socialization, they tend to be great companions. Their independent nature means they won't be glued to your side, they appreciate their own space and will happily chill on their own until it's time for the next adventure with you.
Grooming Needs: Regular brushing is necessary to keep their coat healthy and to manage shedding, especially during seasonal changes. Bathing should be done occasionally or when necessary.
Training & Exercise Needs: Training them can be a bit of an adventure, but with some patience and consistency, you'll get there. They love to stay active and need both physical exercise and mental challenges to keep them engaged. They're happiest when they're out exploring or diving into agility training, tapping into those natural instincts. Keep them stimulated, and you'll have a well-balanced, content pup by your side.
Possible Health Issues: generally, a healthy breed but can be prone to certain health issues such as hip dysplasia, patellar luxation, and various eye conditions.

Siberian Husky
Other Names: Husky.
Color variations: black, white, gray, red, sable, and agouti, often with distinct facial markings.
Average Lifespan: 12 to 15 years
Origins: Siberia, Russia - 3,000 years ago - bred by the Chukchi people for sledding and companionship in harsh Arctic conditions.
Body Size: Males: 21-23.5 in. 45-60 lbs. Females: 20-22 in. 35-50 lbs.
Personality/Disposition/Compatibility: Huskies are the dogs that bring excitement to everyday life. With their independent streak, they like to keep you on your toes, but that's part of their charm! Friendly and outgoing, they greet everyone, human or dog, like an old friend. What they might lack in strict obedience, they more than make up for with their loyalty and playful energy. They thrive in homes where they can stay active and engaged, both physically and mentally. While they're far from being couch potatoes, their lively, affectionate personalities make every moment spent with them feel special and fun.
Grooming Needs: They require regular grooming due to their thick double coat. They shed heavily twice a year, and during these periods, more frequent brushing is necessary to manage the shedding and keep their coat healthy.
Training & Exercise Needs: Huskies are undeniably smart, but they've got a independent streak that can keep you on your toes. They like to do things their own way! This makes training a bit of an adventure (and a patience tester). With their boundless energy, they need more than just the usual walk around the block to stay content. A daily workout is a must, and keeping their sharp minds busy with puzzles or engaging training sessions will help them stay happy and healthy.
Possible Health Issues: hip dysplasia, cataracts, progressive retinal atrophy, and hypothyroidism.

Silky Terrier
Other Names: Australian Silky Terrier
Color variations: blue and tan, or grey and white
Average Lifespan: 12 to 15 years
Origins: Australia - late 19th century - bred for companionship and to hunt small vermin.
Body Size: Males & Females: 9-10 in. 8-10 lbs.
Personality/Disposition/Compatibility: Despite their small size, Silkies carry themselves with a fearless confidence, often acting like they're much bigger than they are. You might even catch your little one standing tall against larger dogs, convinced they can take on the world! These pups love being around people and thrive when they have plenty of human companionship, making them perfect for families or anyone who spends a lot of time at home. While they usually get along with other pets, their terrier instincts can sometimes take over. So, if you have small animals or a particularly dominant dog, a little extra supervision might be needed.
Grooming Needs: require regular grooming to maintain their long, silky coat. This includes daily brushing to prevent tangles and matting, as well as regular baths and occasional trimming.
Training & Exercise Needs: Silkies are clever little pups, always eager to make you happy, but don't be surprised if their terrier independence shows up now and then! A bit of patience and consistency will go a long way in training them. Despite their size, Silkies are full of energy and need a good daily dose of activity. Whether it's a walk around the neighborhood or a fun play session, they're always ready to go.
Possible Health Issues: can be prone to certain health issues, including patellar luxation, Legg-Calvé-Perthes disease, tracheal collapse, and dental problems.

Skye Terrier
Other Names: Skye
Color variations: black, blue, dark or light gray, fawn, or cream, often with black points.
Average Lifespan: 12 to 14 years
Origins: Isle of Skye, Scotland - 1500s - bred for hunting and exterminating vermin.
Body Size: Males: 10 in. 35-40 lbs. Females: 10 in. 25-30 lbs.
Personality/Disposition/Compatibility: These little guys are full of personality. They're fiercely loyal, creating tight-knit bonds with their families. They like to think for themselves, which sometimes shows as stubbornness, but really, it's just their way of being sure of their choices. When it comes to strangers, they might play it cool at first, but once you're in their circle, their affection knows no bounds. As for getting along with other animals, it's all about early introductions. They may not hit it off with every dog or cat they meet, but with socialization, peace can be had.
Grooming Needs: They require regular grooming due to their long coat. Weekly brushing is necessary to prevent tangles and matting, and occasional bathing will keep the coat clean. Professional grooming may be needed to maintain the coat's length and shape.
Training & Exercise Needs: These dogs are smart with a bit of a rebellious streak, preferring to do things their way. If you're patient, consistent, and ready with some tasty treats or praise, they'll warm up to training in no time. They don't need marathon exercise sessions, but they do thrive on regular walks and playtime to keep their energy in check. A couple of strolls a day, along with some fun in the backyard or indoor games, will keep them cheerful and content.
Possible Health Issues: orthopedic problems such as hip dysplasia and luxating patellas, as well as allergies and certain genetic conditions like progressive retinal atrophy (PRA).

Sloughi
Other Names: Arabian Greyhound
Color variations: fawn, brindle, and various shades of red
Average Lifespan: 12 to 16 years
Origins: Morocco, North Africa - ancient times - bred for hunting game such as hare and gazelle.
Body Size: Males: 26-29 in. 50-70 lbs. Females: 24-27 in. 40-60 lbs.
Personality/Disposition/Compatibility: Their independent nature gives them a quiet confidence, and while they might seem aloof to strangers, their loyalty and love for their family are incredibly genuine. They have a knack for picking up on their humans' emotions and are very in tune with their surroundings, even though they don't need constant attention. They thrive in a peaceful, balanced home and usually get along well with other pets. With kids, they are patient and gentle, but they do best in a home that matches their calm and steady energy.
Grooming Needs: Regular brushing to remove dead hair and occasional baths are sufficient to keep them clean and healthy.
Training & Exercise Needs: These dogs are smart and always ready to make their families happy. They do have a bit of an independent streak, so a touch of patience and consistency from their owners goes a long way when training. They thrive when they have a job to do, so engaging them with puzzle toys or training exercises can be really rewarding. A daily walk and some playtime usually do the trick to keep them both happy and healthy.
Possible Health Issues: generally, a healthy breed but can be prone to certain health issues such as progressive retinal atrophy (PRA), which affects vision, and hip dysplasia.

Slovak Rough-haired Pointer
Other Names: Slovenský Hrubosrstý Stavač
Color variations: gray, ranging from a light silver-gray to a darker charcoal-gray. Some dogs may have white markings.
Average Lifespan: 12 to 15 years.
Origins: Slovakia - 1950s - bred by crossing the Weimaraner, German Wire-haired Pointer, and Cesky Fousek to create a hunting dog that could work in various terrains and weather conditions.
Body Size: Males: 24-27 in. 66-77 lbs. Females: 22-26 in. 55-66 lbs.
Personality/Disposition/Compatibility: This breed might be known for their versatility in the field, but what really sets them apart is their sweet and steady nature at home. They're not just hunters, they're all about forming strong bonds. With their patient and dependable attitude, they make wonderful family pets, even in households with kids. Don't let their rugged, working-dog look fool you…they're actually big softies when it comes to snuggling. Plus, with the right socialization, they get along well with other dogs and pets.
Grooming Needs: Regular grooming is necessary to maintain their rough coat. Brushing several times a week will help remove loose hairs and prevent matting. Occasional trimming may be needed, particularly around the face and ears.
Training & Exercise Needs: These dogs are super smart and always ready to make you happy, so they learn commands in no time. They've got loads of energy and love staying active. To keep them joyful and in top shape, daily exercise is a must. They're big fans of long walks, play sessions, and even a few brain-teasers to keep their minds sharp.
Possible Health Issues: hip dysplasia, elbow dysplasia, and eye conditions such as cataracts.

Slovensky Cuvac

Other Names: Slovenský Čuvač or Slovak Chuvach
Color variations: white or cream
Average Lifespan: 11 to 13 years
Origins: Slovakia - 17th century - bred for herding and guarding livestock in the mountainous regions.
Body Size: Males: 26-28 in. 77-99 lbs. Females: 23-27 in. 66-88 lbs.
Personality/Disposition/Compatibility: This breed is known for its fierce loyalty and a protective nature that's just right, never too aggressive, but always ready to stand guard. With family, they're the epitome of calm and gentle, making them fantastic companions for kids and other pets. They're natural guardians, always alert and ready to keep their loved ones safe if the need arises. Once you've earned their respect, they're all in, whether it's joining you on exciting adventures or just lounging around the houses. They thrive when they have a job to do, whether it's protecting the home or accompanying you on your hikes.
Grooming Needs: requires regular grooming to maintain its thick coat. Weekly brushing is recommended to prevent matting and reduce shedding. During shedding seasons, more frequent brushing may be necessary.
Training & Exercise Needs: When it comes to training, they thrive on positive reinforcement and clear, firm commands. They might show a bit of stubbornness, so a touch of persistence is helpful. Daily walks, play sessions, and fun activities like puzzle toys or agility training are perfect for them. They're also up for outdoor adventures and will happily join you on hikes or other active outings. Offering a variety of exercises will keep them content and in great shape.
Possible Health Issues: generally, a healthy breed but can be prone to hip dysplasia, elbow dysplasia, and certain eye conditions.

Slovensky Kopov

Other Names: Slovak Hound or the Black Forest Hound
Color variations: black coat with tan markings
Average Lifespan: 12 to 14 years
Origins: Slovakia - 17th century - bred for hunting wild boar and other game due to its excellent tracking abilities and persistence.
Body Size: Males: 16-20 in. 33-44 lbs. Females: 15-19 in. 29-40 lbs.
Personality/Disposition/Compatibility: This breed is full of energy and determination. Their loyalty to their family is unmatched, making them a wonderful and dependable companion. They form strong bonds and are very protective of their loved ones, but they also have a fun, playful side that will light up your home. Ideal for active families who can match their lively pace, they usually get along well with other dogs, especially if they're as energetic as they are. Just keep in mind that their strong hunting instincts might make them a better fit for a home without small pets or very young children, as they could see them as prey or become a bit too excited.
Grooming Needs: Regular brushing to remove dead hair and occasional baths are sufficient to keep their coat healthy and clean.
Training & Exercise Needs: Training this breed can be a truly rewarding journey, but it does call for some consistency and patience. They are bright and eager to please, which is a big plus, though their strong-willed nature means they need a firm but fair hand. These dogs are quite active and thrive on plenty of physical exercise to stay happy and healthy. To keep them content and avoid boredom, regular, vigorous workouts are a must. Daily walks, playtime, and mental challenges are key. Engaging them in activities like agility or obedience training can also be especially beneficial.
Possible Health Issues: generally, a healthy breed, but like all breeds, it can be prone to certain health issues. Potential problems include hip dysplasia, ear infections, and obesity

Soft-Coated Wheaten Terrier

Other Names: Wheaten Terrier or the Wheaten.
Color variations: wheaten-colored coat, ranging from a pale beige to a golden hue.
Average Lifespan: 12 to 15 years
Origins: Ireland - 18th century - bred as all-purpose farm dogs, skilled at herding, hunting vermin, and guarding property.
Body Size: Males: 18-19 in. 35-40 lbs. Females: 17-18 in. 30-35 lbs.
Personality/Disposition/Compatibility: This breed is the epitome of friendliness and charm, making it a fantastic companion for both families and individuals. Their enthusiasm for life is truly infectious, and their wagging tail seems to have a mind of its own. With a natural knack for socializing, they get along wonderfully with children and other pets. They love being part of the family hustle and bustle, often trailing their humans from room to room.
Grooming Needs: They require regular grooming to keep their coats free of mats and tangles. They need to be brushed several times a week and professionally groomed every few months to maintain their coat's softness and prevent matting.
Training & Exercise Needs: They're always eager to please and quick to pick up new tricks, making training a breeze. To keep their enthusiasm high, keep training sessions short and fun. They thrive on regular exercise, so make sure they get plenty of it. Daily walks, playtime in the yard, or even agility courses will help them stay active and burn off their energy. They love interactive play and mental challenges, so finding activities that engage both their mind and body will keep them happy and well-balanced.
Possible Health Issues: prone to certain health issues, including protein-losing nephropathy (PLN), protein-losing enteropathy (PLE), Addison's disease, and hip dysplasia.

Spanish Water Dog

Other Names: Perro de Agua Español, Turco Andaluz, SWD
Color variations: black, beige, brown, and white, as well as bicolor like black and white or brown and white.
Average Lifespan: 12 to 14 years
Origins: Andalusia, Spain - 1100 AD - bred for herding, retrieving, and assisting fishermen.
Body Size: Males: 17.5-20 in. 40-49 lbs.
Females: 15.75-18 in. 31-40 lbs.
Personality/Disposition/Compatibility: This breed is known for its energetic and friendly nature, making it an ideal companion for a lively household. With a personality that combines alertness with affection, they're incredibly loyal to their families and love to play. Their playful antics can bring a lot of fun and a touch of mischief to your home. They generally get along well with children and other dogs. While they might not suit a more relaxed lifestyle, they're a fantastic match for an active family or individual.
Grooming Needs: Their curly coat requires regular brushing to prevent matting and occasional trimming. They should not be bathed too frequently to maintain the natural oils in their coat.
Training & Exercise Needs: These dogs are smart and really eager to make you happy. They respond great to positive reinforcement and clear, consistent commands. They pick up new skills quickly but love a good mental challenge, so adding fun activities to their training routine can make it even more effective. A blend of physical exercise and mental stimulation keeps them engaged and satisfied. Daily exercise is key to their happiness and well-being. They love running, playing fetch, and getting into interactive games with you.
Possible Health Issues: hip dysplasia, progressive retinal atrophy (PRA), hypothyroidism, and allergies.

Spinone Italiano
Other Names: Spinone
Color variations: white, white with orange markings, white with brown markings, orange roan, and brown roan.
Average Lifespan: 12 to 14 years
Origins: Italy - Middle Ages - bred for hunting, serving as an all-purpose gun dog known for its versatility in various terrains.
Body Size: Males: 23-27 in. 70-90 lbs. Females: 22-25 in. 60-80 lbs.
Personality/Disposition/Compatibility: This breed is gentle and friendly, exuding a warm and welcoming vibe that endears them to both families and individuals. They thrive in the middle of the action, whether it's participating in family activities or simply lounging with their favorite people. They're renowned for their patience and calm demeanor, making them wonderful companions for kids and other pets. Their easygoing nature means they get along great with other animals, including dogs and cats.
Grooming Needs: requires regular brushing to prevent matting and tangling. Occasional hand-stripping is recommended to maintain the coat's texture. The breed also needs routine ear cleaning, as its floppy ears can be prone to infections.
Training & Exercise Needs: They're usually pretty easy to train because they're so eager to please and smart. They might show a bit of independence now and then, but with positive reinforcement and steady training, they respond really well. These active pups thrive when they have a purpose, so they benefit from daily exercise like long walks, playtime, or activities that get their minds and bodies working. They're not overly demanding, but they do appreciate regular activity to keep them happy and healthy.
Possible Health Issues: hip dysplasia, elbow dysplasia, and eye conditions such as entropion and ectropion.

Stabyhoun
Other Names: Frisian Pointer
Color variations: black, brown, or orange, often with white markings.
Average Lifespan: 13 to 15 years
Origins: Netherlands - early 1800s - bred for hunting, farm work, and companion.
Body Size: Males: 19-21 in. 45-50 lbs. Females: 18-20 in. 35-45 lbs.
Personality/Disposition/Compatibility: a wonderful breed known for its calm temperament and deep affection for its family. These dogs are incredibly friendly and get along effortlessly with everyone, whether it's kids or other pets. Their easygoing nature makes them an ideal companion for both active families and individuals looking for a loyal, adaptable friend. They're also great with other animals, as long as they've been properly socialized. With them in your home, expect plenty of love and joy. Their balanced temperament and warm personality make them a delightful addition to any household.
Grooming Needs: They require regular brushing to maintain its coat, especially during shedding seasons. Occasional baths and routine care for nails, ears, and teeth are also necessary.
Training & Exercise Needs: These dogs really shine with positive reinforcement, like treats and praise, and they love picking up new tricks. They do best with a consistent and patient approach, thriving on gentle guidance. They're moderately active, so they need regular exercise to stay happy and healthy. This could mean daily walks, playtime, and some mental challenges. A good balance of physical activity and interactive play will keep them engaged and prevent any boredom.
Possible Health Issues: hip dysplasia, elbow dysplasia, and certain eye conditions such as progressive retinal atrophy (PRA)

Staffordshire Bull Terrier
Other Names: Staffy or Staffie
Color variations: brindle, black, white, blue, and fawn. They can also be found with or without white markings.
Average Lifespan: 12 to 14 years
Origins: England - early 19th century - bred for bull-baiting and later for dog fighting, companionship and loyalty.
Body Size: Males: 14-16 in. 28-38 lbs. Females: 14-16 in. 24-34 lbs.
Personality/Disposition/Compatibility: With hearts as big as their playful spirits, these dogs truly shine with loyalty and affection for their families. They're more than just pets; they're little bundles of warmth and charm. Often called Staffies, they are incredibly social and thrive on interaction. Their loving nature makes them fantastic with children, often becoming their best friends and favorite playmates. While they have a natural instinct to protect their loved ones, they're just as likely to greet strangers with a wagging tail. Their compatibility with other animals can vary, so early socialization is important to help them become friendly and well-adjusted companions.
Grooming Needs: Their short, smooth coat requires regular brushing to remove loose hairs and maintain a healthy shine. Regular bathing, nail trimming, and dental care are also important.
Training & Exercise Needs: Training is usually a breeze, especially when you use positive reinforcement. These dogs are smart and eager to please, so teaching them new commands and tricks can be a lot of fun. They're also quite energetic and need regular exercise to stay healthy and happy. Daily walks, playtime in a secure yard, and mental stimulation are essential for them.
Possible Health Issues: hip dysplasia, cataracts, skin allergies, and certain genetic conditions such as L-2-HGA and hereditary cataracts

Sussex Spaniel
Other Names: Sussex
Color variations: rich golden-brown shade
Average Lifespan: 12 to 15 years
Origins: Sussex, England - early 19th century - bred primarily for hunting and flushing game birds in dense undergrowth.
Body Size: Males & Females: 13-15 in. 35-45 lbs.
Personality/Disposition/Compatibility: This breed is a real sweetheart, known for their deep affection and unwavering loyalty. They thrive on companionship and can get a bit restless or anxious if left alone for too long. With their easygoing nature, they adapt well to different living situations, making them a versatile choice for many homes. They're especially great with kids, showing patience and a playful side that makes them wonderful family pets. Friendly by nature, they usually get along well with other dogs and pets, adding a harmonious touch to multi-pet households.
Grooming Needs: require regular grooming to maintain their coat, including brushing several times a week to prevent matting and tangling. They may also need occasional trimming and regular ear cleaning to prevent infections.
Training & Exercise Needs: Training this breed is usually a joyful experience. They're smart and eager to please, so they quickly catch on to commands and new tricks. They thrive on interactive activities like fetch or agility training, which keeps their minds engaged. Regular exercise is key to preventing boredom and maintaining their well-being. A mix of daily walks and playtime is typically enough to keep them happy and healthy.
Possible Health Issues: prone to certain health issues, including hip dysplasia, ear infections, and heart conditions.

K9 Chatter

Swedish Lapphund

Other Names: Lappie
Color variations: black, brown, and bear brown colors
Average Lifespan: 12 to 14 years
Origins: Sweden - 7000 B.C. - bred by the Sami people to herd reindeer.
Body Size: Males: 18-20 in. 40-50 lbs. Females: 16-18 in. 33-44 lbs.
Personality/Disposition/Compatibility: These dogs are cherished for their friendly and affectionate personalities, which make them wonderful family companions. They love being around people and thrive in homes where they can be fully involved in family life. Adaptable and versatile, they fit in seamlessly whether you have a lively household or a more serene environment. They are great with kids and usually get along with other pets, though their herding instincts might prompt them to try and corral anything that moves!
Grooming Needs: requires regular grooming to maintain its thick double coat, including weekly brushing to prevent matting and occasional baths. More frequent grooming may be necessary during shedding seasons.
Training & Exercise Needs: These dogs are not just intelligent but also incredibly eager to make you happy, so they catch on to commands and tricks in no time. To keep them content and healthy, they need plenty of physical activity. Regular walks, play sessions, and chances to run and explore are crucial. They really shine when they have a job or task, so engaging in interactive play or agility training can be a great way to keep them stimulated and satisfied.
Possible Health Issues: hip dysplasia, progressive retinal atrophy (PRA), and autoimmune disorders.

Swedish Vallhund

Other Names: Västgötaspets or Swedish Cattle Dog
Color variations: grey, red, sable, and combinations of these colors, often with darker hairs on the back, neck, and sides.
Average Lifespan: 12 to 15 years
Origins: Sweden - 8th or 9th century - bred as a herding dog.
Body Size: Males: 12.5-13.5 in. 25-35 lbs.
Females: 11.5-12.5 in. 20-30 lbs.
Personality/Disposition/Compatibility: With a cheerful and sociable personality, this breed wins hearts wherever it goes. They easily become friends with kids and other pets, filling the home with their playful and loving spirit. Although they're friendly, Vallhunds have a natural herding instinct, so you might find them trying to herd your kids or even you now and then. They're at their best when they have something to do, so they thrive in environments where they're kept busy and mentally stimulated.
Grooming Needs: requires regular grooming to maintain its double coat. Brushing a few times a week is typically sufficient to manage shedding and keep the coat healthy.
Training & Exercise Needs: Vallhunds are clever and always ready to make their owners happy, which makes training them a rewarding experience. They do have a strong herding instinct, so they might show a bit of stubbornness if they're not given clear guidance. These energetic dogs need plenty of action to stay content and in good shape. They thrive on activities like agility training, herding, or even just long walks. Keeping them active not only keeps them physically fit but also mentally engaged, helping to keep them well-behaved and cheerful.
Possible Health Issues: hip dysplasia, patellar luxation, and progressive retinal atrophy.

Taiwan Dog
Other Names: Formosan Mountain Dog or the Formosan Dog.
Color variations: black, white, brindle, and yellow.
Average Lifespan: 10 to 13 years
Origins: Taiwan - ancient times - bred for hunting and a guard dog.
Body Size: Males: 18-20 in. 31-44 lbs. Females: 16-18 in. 26-39 lbs.
Personality/Disposition/Compatibility: You'll find a loyal and loving companion in them, someone who truly enjoys spending time with people. They're playful and full of energy, always ready for fun and games. Their friendly and gentle demeanor makes them great pets for both families and individuals. They're also quite attentive and protective of their loved ones, serving as excellent watchdogs without being too aggressive. Their easygoing nature means they get along well with everyone, including kids and other pets.
Grooming Needs: Regular brushing to remove loose hair and occasional baths are sufficient to keep them clean and healthy.
Training & Exercise Needs: Training these dogs is a genuinely rewarding experience. They're enthusiastic learners who thrive on pleasing their owners and picking up new commands quickly, making each training session feel like a win. They're full of energy and relish regular physical activity, so daily walks and playtime in the yard or at a dog park are just what they need to stay happy and healthy. They also love engaging in interactive games that challenge their minds. With a good balance of exercise and mental stimulation, these dogs stay content and well-rounded.
Possible Health Issues: generally healthy but can be prone to certain health issues such as hip dysplasia, patellar luxation, and skin allergies.

Teddy Roosevelt Terrier
Other Names: Bench-Legged Feist or the Short-Legged Rat Terrier.
Color variations: black, white, tan, red, blue, chocolate, and lemon, often with various patterns and markings.
Average Lifespan: 12 to 16 years
Origins: United States - early 1900s - bred for hunting small game and as farm dogs to control pests.
Body Size: Males: 10-15 in. 15-25 lbs. Females: 8-13 in. 10-18 lbs.
Personality/Disposition/Compatibility: These lively little dogs are known for their cheerful nature and endless energy. Their personality strikes a delightful balance between playful and affectionate. Teddies are incredibly loyal to their families and absolutely love spending time with people. They get along wonderfully with children, making them fantastic family pets. Their friendly demeanor also extends to other pets, although their terrier heritage might spark a bit of a chase instinct now and then.
Grooming Needs: Regular brushing to remove loose hair and occasional baths to keep them clean are sufficient.
Training & Exercise Needs: Training Teddies is usually a lot of fun, as they're both eager to please and pretty sharp. They can be a bit stubborn at times, so patience and consistency are key. They love their daily walks and playtime to help burn off some energy. While they need regular activity to stay happy and healthy, they're not overly demanding. A good balance of play and walks typically keeps them satisfied and well-exercised.
Possible Health Issues: hip dysplasia, patellar luxation, allergies, and certain heart conditions

K9 Chatter

Thai Bangkaew
Other Names: None
Color variations: base color of white, which is marked with patches of black, gray, red, or fawn.
Average Lifespan: 12 to 14 years
Origins: Phitsanulok Province, Thailand - mid-20th century - bred for its skills as a guard dog and its loyalty to families.
Body Size: Males: 18-20 in. 35-44 lbs. Females: 16-18 in. 30-40 lbs.
Personality/Disposition/Compatibility: These dogs are incredibly loyal and forge deep connections with their families. Their protective nature makes them outstanding watchdogs, always on high alert and ready to spring into action if something seems amiss. They generally get along well with children, especially if they're socialized properly from a young age. While they might be a bit reserved with strangers at first, they warm up quickly as they get to know them. Their strong-willed demeanor means they're best suited for experienced dog owners who appreciate a bit of a dominant personality.
Grooming Needs: Their double coat requires regular brushing to prevent matting and reduce shedding. Occasional baths and routine care, such as nail trimming and ear cleaning, are also necessary.
Training & Exercise Needs: Their strong-willed and independent personality means they thrive with a firm yet gentle approach and lots of positive reinforcement. Start training them early and keep the sessions short but fun to keep their attention and cooperation. They need regular exercise to stay happy and healthy. They love having tasks to do, so activities like agility training or interactive games can be a fantastic way to keep them engaged.
Possible Health Issues: hip dysplasia, eye problems, and skin allergies.

Thai Ridgeback
Other Names: Mah Thai Lung Arn
Color variations: red, black, blue, and fawn.
Average Lifespan: 12 to 13 years
Origins: Thailand - 17th century - bred for hunting and guarding.
Body Size: Males: 22-24 in. 50-75 lbs. Females: 20-22 in. 35-55 lbs.
Personality/Disposition/Compatibility: This breed exudes confidence and independence, carrying itself with a self-assuredness that naturally commands respect. Yet, beneath its tough exterior, they are deeply loyal and protective of their family. While their strong-willed nature might come off as aloof at times, they are loving companions with a knack for clever problem-solving. Their intelligence shines through in their inventive ways of getting what they want. Due to their independent streak and strong personalities, they might not be the ideal choice for first-time dog owners. However, they thrive in families who appreciate their distinctive traits and are ready to engage them in activities that keep their agile minds and bodies stimulated.
Grooming Needs: Regular brushing is sufficient to keep their coat healthy and to remove loose hair.
Training & Exercise Needs: Training a Ridgeback can be a bit of a journey due to their independent and strong-willed nature. While they are smart and quick learners, they also have a stubborn streak that calls for a firm and consistent approach. These dogs are full of energy and need plenty of physical activity to stay healthy and happy. They thrive on engaging activities like agility training or interactive toys that challenge their minds. Keeping them busy and active is key to preventing boredom and ensuring they remain in great shape.
Possible Health Issues: hip dysplasia, dermoid sinus, and hypothyroidism

Tibetan Spaniel
Other Names: Tibbie
Color variations: gold, cream, fawn, red, white, black, and sable, often with white markings.
Average Lifespan: 12 to 15 years
Origins: Tibet - 1100 A.D. - bred as a companion and watchdog for monasteries.
Body Size: Males & Females: 10-11 in. 9-15 lbs.
Personality/Disposition/Compatibility: These little guys are a bundle of joy with their cheerful and confident personalities. Even though they're small, they carry themselves with a touch of royalty and have a charming independence that's hard to resist. Their gentle nature makes them fantastic with kids and other pets, and they'll greet strangers warmly, though they might be a bit shy initially. They're smart and quick to learn, but you might notice a hint of stubbornness now and then.
Grooming Needs: require regular grooming, including weekly brushing to prevent matting and occasional baths. Attention should be given to their ears, teeth, and nails.
Training & Exercise Needs: Training these pups might take a bit of patience because they have a stubborn side, but their smarts and desire to please make it totally doable. They love regular playtime and short walks to stay happy and healthy. They're not too demanding, but a bit of daily activity keeps them fit and content.
Possible Health Issues: prone to certain health issues, including progressive retinal atrophy, hip dysplasia, patellar luxation, and respiratory problems.

Tibetan Terrier
Other Names: Tsang Apso and Dhokhi Apso
Color variations: white, gold, tricolor, brindle, silver, black, and combinations of these.
Average Lifespan: 12 to 15 years
Origins: Tibet - 1000 A.D. - bred by monks in monasteries as companion animals and watchdogs.
Body Size: Males: 14-17 in. 18-30 lbs. Females: 13-16 in. 18-25 lbs.
Personality/Disposition/Compatibility: This breed is known for being incredibly friendly and affectionate. They're always eager to please, yet their touch of independence only adds to their charm. With a strong sense of loyalty, they form deep bonds with their families. They tend to get along well with children and are often quite playful, making them wonderful companions for families. They also mix well with other pets, including both dogs and cats, especially if introductions are handled smoothly. Though they have a gentle nature and aren't typically aggressive, they do have a knack for keeping an eye out, alerting you to any unusual sounds or visitors.
Grooming Needs: require regular grooming due to their long, thick coat. Brushing several times a week is necessary to prevent matting, and professional grooming every few months can help maintain their coat in good condition.
Training & Exercise Needs: Training this breed is often a breeze because they are so eager to please and quick on the uptake. Mixing in interactive activities and games can make training even more fun for them. To keep them happy and healthy, make sure they get daily walks and plenty of playtime. This not only keeps them fit but also keeps their minds engaged.
Possible Health Issues: prone to certain health issues, including hip dysplasia, progressive retinal atrophy, cataracts, hypothyroidism, and allergies.

Tornjak
Other Names: Croatian Shepherd Dog
Color variations: white, black, brown, red, yellow, or a combination of these, often with large patches.
Average Lifespan: 12 to 14 years
Origins: Bosnia and Herzegovina and Croatia - 11th century - bred to guard livestock and property.
Body Size: Males: 25-27 in. 80-110 lbs. Females: 23-25 in. 70-100 lbs.
Personality/Disposition/Compatibility: One of their most charming qualities is their independence. These dogs have a calm, self-assured demeanor that makes them natural guardians of home and family. They are incredibly loyal and loving, forming strong bonds with their human companions and displaying a protective nature. Confident and content, they don't require constant attention, making them ideal for busy families. Though they may appear serious at times, they are surprisingly gentle with children and get along well with other pets, especially if introduced early on.
Grooming Needs: requires regular grooming to maintain its thick, double coat. Brushing several times a week is necessary to prevent matting and remove loose hair.
Training & Exercise Needs: When it comes to training, they really shine with consistent, positive reinforcement and love interactive sessions that keep them engaged. They thrive on activities that challenge their minds, so adding puzzle toys or agility training can be a great idea. With the right amount of exercise, they stay happy and healthy, fitting in perfectly whether you have a bustling household or a more laid-back setting.
Possible Health Issues: generally healthy dogs but can be prone to certain issues such as hip dysplasia, elbow dysplasia, and bloat.

Tosa
Other Names: Tosa Inu, Tosa Ken, and Japanese Mastiff
Color variations: red, fawn, black, brindle, and occasionally with white markings.
Average Lifespan: 10 to 12 years
Origins: Japan - mid-19th century - bred for dog fighting, which was a popular sport at the time.
Body Size: Males: 24-32 in. 100-200 lbs. Females: 22-30 in. 80-170 lbs.
Personality/Disposition/Compatibility: The Tosa is a calm and reserved dog with a naturally gentle demeanor. Despite their impressive size and sturdy build, they have a wonderfully mellow temperament. They form deep bonds with their family and are incredibly loyal, always wanting to be close to their loved ones for both play and relaxation. With a relaxed attitude and a patient nature, they get along well with children and other pets, especially when they've been properly socialized. While their protective instincts might make them a bit reserved around strangers, their loyalty and calmness shine through in their everyday interactions.
Grooming Needs: minimal grooming needs due to their short coats. Regular brushing to remove loose hair and occasional baths are sufficient.
Training & Exercise Needs: These dogs are quite clever and pick up commands and tricks with ease. They thrive best when trained with a firm, calm, and positive approach, and they respond well to gentle encouragement rather than strict discipline. They do have a decent amount of energy, but they're not as demanding as some other breeds. A daily walk and a bit of playtime are usually enough to keep them happy and engaged. They're pretty adaptable to a laid-back lifestyle, as long as their basic exercise needs are taken care of.
Possible Health Issues: prone to certain health issues, including hip dysplasia, elbow dysplasia, bloat, and skin allergies

Transylvanian Hound
Other Names: Erdélyi Kopó
Color variations: black and tan
Average Lifespan: 10 to 14 years
Origins: Transylvania, Hungary - 9th century - bred for hunting, specifically large game in the mountainous regions.
Body Size: Males: 22-26 in. 55-77 lbs. Females: 20-24 in. 44-66 lbs.
Personality/Disposition/Compatibility: This breed offers a wonderful blend of energy and calm, making them a truly delightful companion. They're known for their smarts and alertness, and they absolutely thrive on being part of the family. If you enjoy a dog that's both active and affectionate, this breed will fit right in. They're great with kids and generally get along well with other pets, though their strong prey drive means they might get a bit too excited around smaller animals. Instead of lounging around, they'd much rather be out exploring or playing with enthusiasm.
Grooming Needs: Their short coat requires regular brushing to remove dead hair and occasional baths to keep them clean.
Training & Exercise Needs: They tend to learn commands fast and respond great to positive reinforcement. They really flourish with consistent, encouraging training methods, as they thrive on praise and rewards. Since they're full of energy, daily walks, playtime, and mental challenges are key to keeping them content and in good shape. Games like fetch, agility exercises, and interactive play can help meet their need for both physical and mental stimulation.
Possible Health Issues: hip dysplasia, ear infections, and certain genetic disorders.

Treeing Tennessee Brindle
Other Names: None
Color variations: brindle coloring, ranging from black to brown with varying shades of brindle stripes.
Average Lifespan: 10 to 12 years
Origins: Tennessee, United States - mid-20th century - bred for its treeing ability and to enhance hunting efficiency.
Body Size: Males: 18-24 in. 30-45 lbs. Females: 16-22 in. 25-40 lbs.
Personality/Disposition/Compatibility: This breed is a bundle of enthusiasm, always ready for action and adventure. Loyal and devoted, they build strong connections with their families. While their protective instincts make them fantastic watchdogs, they also have a soft side, showing warmth and affection to those they trust. Their smarts and sharp instincts make them excellent problem-solvers, which can be entertaining but also a bit demanding if they're not kept busy. They generally get along well with kids and can be friendly with other pets, especially if they've had some early socialization to help them become well-rounded companions.
Grooming Needs: Regular brushing to remove loose hair and occasional baths are typically sufficient to maintain its coat in good condition.
Training & Exercise Needs: These dogs are not only smart but also eager to make you happy, which is a fantastic foundation. Regular training sessions and a lot of patience will go a long way in helping them shine. They have high energy levels and need plenty of activity to stay both happy and healthy. Activities like agility training or interactive games are great for keeping their minds sharp and engaged. If they don't get enough exercise, they might get bored or restless, so keeping them active is essential.
Possible Health Issues: hip dysplasia, ear infections, and eye problems.

Treeing Walker Coonhound

Other Names: Walker Hound or Walker.
Color variations: tricolor pattern, which includes white with black and tan markings.
Average Lifespan: 12 to 13 years
Origins: United States - early 19th century - developed from the English and American Foxhounds for hunting & treeing raccoons.
Body Size: Males: 22-27 in. 50-70 lbs. Females: 20-25 in. 45-65 lbs.
Personality/Disposition/Compatibility: One of their most delightful qualities is their keen hunting instinct. This makes them always up for a good chase, so they need lots of exercise to stay content. Known for their endless energy and friendly demeanor, these dogs are a joy to be around. Their affectionate nature makes them a hit with everyone they meet. They do great with kids and get along well with other pets, especially if they've had the chance to socialize early on.
Grooming Needs: requiring only occasional brushing to keep its coat healthy and free of loose hair. Regular ear cleaning is important to prevent infections.
Training & Exercise Needs: Training them can be a bit of a challenge because of their independent nature and strong hunting instincts. To keep them engaged, mix up your training sessions with different activities. These dogs are full of energy and need lots of physical exercise to stay happy. If they don't get enough activity, they might get bored and restless. Make sure they have plenty of chances to run and explore. Daily long walks, runs, or playtime are crucial to keep them satisfied and well-exercised.
Possible Health Issues: hip dysplasia, ear infections, and certain eye conditions.

Vizsla

Other Names: Hungarian Pointer
Color variations: solid golden rust color
Average Lifespan: 12 to 15 years
Origins: Hungary - 10th century - bred for hunting and retrieving.
Body Size: Males: 22-24 in. 55-66 lbs. Females: 21-23 in. 45-55 lbs.
Personality/Disposition/Compatibility: Often called a "velcro dog," they're all about forming close connections with its family. Whether it's cozying up on the couch or diving into outdoor escapades, this breed thrives on being part of the action. With their boundless energy and playful spirit, they make great companions for active individuals or families who love running, hiking, or playing fetch. They're friendly with other pets and kids, and their gentle, fun-loving nature makes them wonderful family dogs. Just keep in mind that their need for companionship means they're not ideal for long periods alone.
Grooming Needs: Regular brushing will help keep their coat healthy, and occasional baths are sufficient. They do not shed excessively.
Training & Exercise Needs: These dogs are usually pretty easy to train because they're both smart and eager to please. They do best with positive reinforcement, so being consistent and patient during training is key. With their high energy levels, they need a lot of activity to stay content and healthy. Try to give them at least an hour of vigorous exercise each day. Whether it's running, hiking, playing fetch, or agility training, they thrive on both physical and mental challenges. Mixing up their routine keeps them engaged and helps avoid boredom.
Possible Health Issues: hip dysplasia, epilepsy, and various eye conditions such as progressive retinal atrophy.

Vizsla (Wire-haired)
Other Names: Drótszőrű Magyar Vizsla
Color variations: golden rust
Average Lifespan: 12-14 years
Origins: Hungary - 1930s - bred as a versatile hunting dog, capable of working in both field and water.
Body Size: Males: 23-25 in. 55-65 lbs. Females: 21.5-23 in. 45-55 lbs.
Personality/Disposition/Compatibility: Just like the smooth coated Vizsla, they have boundless energy but they are also incredibly gentle and affectionate. They form deep connections with their families and are especially great with kids. Their playful spirit makes them ideal companions for active families who can match their energy. They thrive in social environments and generally get along well with other pets, as long as introductions are handled smoothly. Their friendly and outgoing nature means they're usually more than happy to have a buddy, dog or otherwise.
Grooming Needs: regular brushing to maintain its wiry coat and occasional trimming to keep it neat. The coat is relatively low-maintenance, but regular grooming helps keep the dog clean and healthy.
Training & Exercise Needs: They're smart and eager to please, which makes teaching them new commands and behaviors a breeze. Being consistent and using positive reinforcement really helps them pick things up quickly. Because they have lots of energy, they need plenty of physical activity. Daily walks, playtime, and mental stimulation are essential for them. They flourish in environments where they can run and play, so activities like agility training or a good game of fetch are ideal for keeping them happy and healthy.
Possible Health Issues: hip dysplasia, elbow dysplasia, and eye conditions like progressive retinal atrophy (PRA).

Volpino Italiano
Other Names: Volpino
Color variations: white, red, and champagne color variations.
Average Lifespan: 14 to 16 years
Origins: Italy - 1888 - bred primarily as a companion dog and watchdog, valued for its alertness and loyalty
Body Size: Males: 10.5-12 in. 9-11 lbs. Females: 9-11 in. 8-10 lbs.
Personality/Disposition/Compatibility: These little dogs are full of energy and have a playful spirit that makes them a joy to be around. They quickly form close bonds with their families and are particularly great with kids, making them ideal companions in a busy home. They usually get along well with other pets, especially if they're introduced properly. Their keen sense of alertness means they make excellent watchdogs, always ready to let you know if something seems off. Just be ready for their enthusiastic barking, they've got plenty to say and love to make their voices heard!
Grooming Needs: requires regular grooming due to its dense double coat, including brushing several times a week to prevent matting and reduce shedding.
Training & Exercise Needs: They're smart and eager to please, which makes training a breeze. That said, they can be a bit stubborn, so it's important to be consistent and patient. When it comes to exercise, they've got plenty of energy to burn off. Regular walks and playtime are essential to keep them happy and healthy. They love interactive games and mental challenges, so switching up their routine with toys and puzzles is a great idea.
Possible Health Issues: patellar luxation, eye problems like cataracts, and dental issues.

Weimaraner

Other Names: Gray Ghost
Color variations: gray, ranging from mouse-gray to silver-gray.
Average Lifespan: 10 to 13 years
Origins: Germany - early 19th century - bred for hunting large game such as deer, boar, and bear.
Body Size: Males: 25-27 in. 70-90 lbs. Females: 23-25 in. 55-75 lbs.
Personality/Disposition/Compatibility: With their striking silver-gray coats and soulful eyes, these dogs are as charming as they are dynamic. They radiate friendliness and energy, making them perfect companions for active families and individuals. They generally get along well with other dogs and pets, though their high energy and playful nature might overwhelm more laid-back animals. They're also fantastic with kids, especially if the little ones can match their boundless enthusiasm. Though they have a sweet disposition, they can be a bit stubborn, so early training and socialization are essential to help them shine.
Grooming Needs: have low grooming needs due to their short coats. Regular brushing and occasional baths are sufficient to keep their coat in good condition.
Training & Exercise Needs: Training these dogs can be a bit of a challenge because they have a stubborn streak. However, with patience and consistency, they really thrive on positive reinforcement.
These energetic pups need plenty of activity to stay happy and healthy. Playing interactive games or getting involved in dog sports is a fantastic way to meet their exercise needs and keep their minds stimulated.
Possible Health Issues: prone to certain health issues, including hip dysplasia, gastric torsion (bloat), and progressive retinal atrophy.

Welsh Corgi (Cardigan)

Other Names: Cardigan
Color variations: red, sable, brindle, black, blue merle, and occasionally with white markings.
Average Lifespan: 12 and 15 years
Origins: Wales - 1200 BC - bred for herding cattle and driving them to market.
Body Size: Males: 10.5-12.5 in. 30-38 lbs. Females: 10.5-12.5 in. 25-34 lbs.
Personality/Disposition/Compatibility: These little dogs are a bundle of energy and smarts, and it's easy to see why they're so delightful. At home, their affectionate nature really shines. They form strong bonds with their human family members and are known for their loyalty. Socially, they're friendly and enjoy being around people, though they might be a bit shy around newcomers until they get to know them better. They generally get along well with other pets, especially if they're introduced properly, and they're usually good with kids. Just keep in mind their herding instincts might lead them to nip at heels with younger children.
Grooming Needs: require regular grooming to maintain their double coat. This includes brushing several times a week to reduce shedding and occasional baths to keep their coat clean.
Training & Exercise Needs: Their intelligence and eagerness to please make them very trainable. To keep them engaged, it's best to keep training sessions short and fun. These dogs are full of energy and need regular exercise to stay happy and healthy. They thrive on interactive play and enjoy tasks that challenge their problem-solving skills. Adding these elements to their daily routine will help keep them well-rounded and satisfied.
Possible Health Issues: hip dysplasia, progressive retinal atrophy (PRA), intervertebral disc disease, and obesity

Welsh Corgi (Pembroke)
Other Names: Corgi or Pembroke
Color variations: red, sable, fawn, black, and tan, often with white markings.
Average Lifespan: 12 to 15 years
Origins: Pembrokeshire, Wales - 10th century - bred for herding cattle, sheep, and horses.
Body Size: Males: 10-12 in. 25-30 lbs. Females: 10-12 in. 24-28 lbs.
Personality/Disposition/Compatibility: They're bursting with playful energy and sharp intelligence. Their cheerful, can-do attitude makes them delightful companions in any home, as long as they receive the attention and activity they need. With their alert and curious nature, they're always up for an adventure or eager to sniff out the next interesting scent. Affectionate and loyal, they build strong bonds with their families and are especially great with kids. They also get along well with other pets, though their herding instinct might lead them to try and round up other animals or even family members!
Grooming Needs: They shed regularly, particularly during seasonal changes, and benefit from weekly brushing to manage their double coat. Regular ear cleaning, nail trimming, and dental care are also important.
Training & Exercise Needs: They love being rewarded with treats and praise, making positive reinforcement a great training method for them. They really shine with daily walks, playtime, and engaging mental activities. A well-exercised Pembroke is a happy and well-behaved friend. Keeping their minds and bodies active with agility training or interactive toys is a fantastic way to ensure they stay sharp and fit.
Possible Health Issues: prone to certain health issues, including hip dysplasia, progressive retinal atrophy (PRA), intervertebral disc disease (IVDD), and obesity.

Welsh Springer Spaniel
Other Names: Welsh Spaniel
Color variations: red and white
Average Lifespan: 12-15 years
Origins: Wales - 16th century - bred for hunting and retrieving game birds.
Body Size: Males: 18-19 in. 40-45 lbs. Females: 17-18 in. 35-40 lbs.
Personality/Disposition/Compatibility: They're a wonderful mix of friendliness, energy, and affection. With their playful spirit and enthusiasm for outdoor adventures, they're always ready for fun. These dogs are naturally sociable and eager to please, making them great companions whether you're a family or an individual. Their gentle nature and loving temperament make them great with kids and other pets. They truly thrive on social interaction and love being involved in all the family activities.
Grooming Needs: They require regular grooming including brushing several times a week to prevent matting and to keep their coat healthy. Occasional trimming and regular ear cleaning are also necessary.
Training & Exercise Needs: Training these dogs is usually pretty straightforward because they're so eager to make you happy and naturally sociable. They really shine with positive reinforcement, so staying patient and consistent will help a lot. These dogs love to stay active, both physically and mentally. Mixing up their exercise routine with different activities and games will keep them excited and in great shape. They absolutely relish daily walks, play sessions, and any chance to burn off their energy.
Possible Health Issues: hip dysplasia, ear infections, and eye conditions such as progressive retinal atrophy and cataracts.

Welsh Terrier

Other Names: Welshie
Color variations: black and tan, although the black may sometimes be grizzled.
Average Lifespan: 12 to 15 years
Origins: Wales, United Kingdom - 1700s - bred for hunting foxes, rodents, and badgers.
Body Size: Males & Females: 15 in. 20-22 lbs.
Personality/Disposition/Compatibility: These lively little dogs are always up for turning an ordinary day into a fun adventure with their playful antics. Full of courage and determination, they often show a fearless attitude that seems surprising given their size. They are incredibly loyal to their families and make wonderful companions. While they usually get along well with other dogs, their high energy and sometimes stubborn personality might be a bit much for families with very young children.
Grooming Needs: require regular grooming, including brushing several times a week and professional trimming or hand-stripping every few months to maintain the wiry texture of their coat.
Training & Exercise Needs: Training these lively pups can definitely be a bit of a challenge, but with patience and consistency, it's totally doable. The key is to keep training sessions short and enjoyable to hold their attention. They thrive on regular, vigorous activity, so daily walks, playtime, and mental stimulation are a must. These activities help keep them happy, healthy, and out of mischief.
Possible Health Issues: hip dysplasia, allergies, hypothyroidism, and eye problems such as cataracts and glaucoma.

West Highland White Terrier

Other Names: Westie
Color variations: White
Average Lifespan: 12 to 16 years
Origins: Scotland - 19th century - bred for hunting small game like rats and foxes.
Body Size: Males: 10-12 in. 15-22 lbs. Females: 9-11 in. 13-16 lbs.
Personality/Disposition/Compatibility: These dogs are bursting with playfulness and affection. Their loyalty to their families is unwavering. Their sharp intelligence and boundless curiosity keep them constantly on the move, ready to explore every new sight and sound. They also have a surprisingly bold and brave side, often displaying a feisty attitude and a touch of stubbornness, which only adds to their irresistible charm. Their confident nature means they might come off as a bit bossy with other pets, so early socialization is important to help them get along smoothly. They generally do well with kids, as long as the children understand how to treat a small dog with the respect they deserve.
Grooming Needs: including brushing at least once a week to maintain their coat and prevent matting. They also require periodic professional grooming to keep their coat in optimal condition.
Training & Exercise Needs: These dogs are sharp and quick learners, but their spirited and sometimes stubborn nature can present a bit of a challenge. They really enjoy having a purpose, so adding some training or agility exercises to their day is a fantastic way to keep them both happy and healthy. Regular physical activity is key for them, helping manage their boundless energy and keep their minds active. Daily walks, playtime, and interactive games are must-haves for their well-being.
Possible Health Issues: skin allergies, hip dysplasia, patellar luxation, and certain types of cancers.

Wetterhoun
Other Names: Frisian Water Dog
Color variations: solid black or brown, or a black-and-white or brown-and-white bicolor pattern.
Average Lifespan: 12 to 14 years
Origins: Friesland region, Netherlands - 16th century - bred for hunting small game and waterfowl and for guarding property.
Body Size: Males: 21-23 in. 55-77 lbs. Females: 20-22 in. 44-66 lbs.
Personality/Disposition/Compatibility: While they tend to be calm and steady, they also have a playful side that can surprise you with bursts of youthful energy. They're fiercely protective of their family, watching over them with a vigilant eye. Their loyalty is remarkable, creating strong, lasting bonds with their loved ones. They generally get along well with other dogs, especially if they've been socialized early on, and they're great with kids, making them a wonderful addition to any family. Just be mindful of their strong hunting instincts—they might have a higher prey drive, so keeping an eye on them around smaller animals is a good idea.
Grooming Needs: requires regular brushing to maintain its curly coat and prevent matting. The coat is naturally water-resistant, so bathing should be done only when necessary to preserve its natural oils.
Training & Exercise Needs: These dogs are smart and eager to please, which makes training a breeze. They do best in an active environment where they can stay busy, so be ready to give them lots of chances to expend their energy. To keep them happy and healthy, make sure they get regular physical activity. Daily walks, playtime, and brain teasers like puzzle toys are perfect for keeping them fit and content.
Possible Health Issues: generally healthy but can be prone to hip dysplasia, elbow dysplasia, and certain eye conditions.

Whippet
Other Names: Whips
Color variations: black, white, red, fawn, blue, and various shades of brindle. They can also have markings or be a mix of these colors.
Average Lifespan: 12 to 15 years
Origins: England - late 19th century - bred for hunting small game, particularly rabbits, and for racing.
Body Size: Males: 19-22 in. 25-40 lbs. Females: 18-21 in. 20-35 lbs.
Personality/Disposition/Compatibility: This breed is known for its incredibly sweet and affectionate nature. They make loving companions who absolutely thrive on human interaction. These aren't just lap dogs; they're always eager to snuggle up next to you, whether you're relaxing on the couch or taking a leisurely stroll. Their gentle demeanor makes them fantastic family pets, and they usually get along well with kids and other animals, including other dogs. Easygoing and adaptable, they fit comfortably into all kinds of living situations, from cozy apartments to spacious homes.
Grooming Needs: minimal grooming needs due to their short coat. Regular brushing will help keep their coat healthy and shiny. They are low shedders and only require occasional baths.
Training & Exercise Needs: Training this breed is usually a breeze because they're so eager to please and quick to respond to positive reinforcement. They love interactive games, so mixing in some fetch or agility exercises can be a fantastic way to keep them engaged and content. They adapt well to a routine that offers both physical and mental stimulation. Daily walks and a bit of playtime will keep them happy and healthy.
Possible Health Issues: hip dysplasia, deafness, and heart problems. They can also be sensitive to anesthesia and extreme temperatures due to their low body fat.

Wire-haired Pointing Griffon
Other Names: Korthals Griffon
Color variations: steel gray with brown markings, though they can also be seen in chestnut brown, roan, white and brown, or white and orange.
Average Lifespan: 12 to 14 years
Origins: Netherlands - late 19th century - bred by Eduard Korthals for pointing and retrieving game.
Body Size: Males: 22-24 in. 50-70 lbs. Females: 20-22 in. 35-50 lbs.
Personality/Disposition/Compatibility: They have an infectious enthusiasm for life. Their affectionate nature makes them incredibly loyal, and they quickly become devoted members of the family. Known for their gentle and patient temperament, these dogs make fantastic companions for both kids and adults. They get along well with other pets, especially when introduced to them early on. Their friendly attitude often means they're more than happy to share their home with both dogs and cats. Just keep in mind that they have a strong prey drive, so it's wise to supervise them around smaller animals.
Grooming Needs: requires regular brushing to maintain its wiry coat and prevent matting. Occasional hand-stripping may be necessary to remove dead hair and maintain the coat's texture.
Training & Exercise Needs: These dogs are a delight to train, thanks to their smarts and their desire to make you happy. They really shine with positive reinforcement and love training sessions that keep them engaged and interested. To keep them happy and healthy, they need regular exercise. They thrive on activities that challenge both their minds and bodies, so adding some training exercises or interactive play is a great idea. Daily walks, playtime in a secure yard, and chances to run and explore are perfect for keeping them content.
Possible Health Issues: hip dysplasia, elbow dysplasia, progressive retinal atrophy (PRA), and hypothyroidism.

Xoloitzcuintli (show-low-eats-QUEENT-lee)
Other Names: Mexican Hairless Dog
Color variations: black, gray, bronze, red, fawn, and spotted.
Average Lifespan: 13 to 18 years
Origins: Mexico - over 3,000 years - bred for companionship and as a healing dog believed to have mystical healing properties.
Body Size: They comes in three sizes: toy, miniature, and standard. Toy: 9-14 in. 5-15 lbs. Miniature: 15-20 in. 15-30 lbs. Standard: 20-30 in. 25-55 lbs.
Personality/Disposition/Compatibility: They might have a history as a guard dog, but they're incredibly gentle and affectionate. They're a loving and loyal companion who thrives on close family bonds. It's especially great with kids and gets along well with other dogs, particularly if socialized early. Its calm nature makes it a great fit for both active and laid-back households. Just remember, because of its hairless coat, keeping its skin moisturized and protected from the sun will help keep this unique breed happy and healthy.
Grooming Needs: The hairless variety requires regular skin care, including moisturizing and sunscreen to protect against sunburn. The coated variety needs occasional brushing. Both types need regular dental care, nail trimming, and ear cleaning.
Training & Exercise Needs: These dogs really shine with positive reinforcement, so treats and praise work wonders. They're enthusiastic learners, though they might show a bit of stubbornness now and then, so a dash of patience goes a long way. They love their daily walks and play sessions but don't need endless activity. A mix of exercise and mental challenges keeps them content. They're pretty adaptable, happy in both lively and laid-back settings, as long as they get a good dose of regular activity to stay fit and engaged.
Possible Health Issues: generally, a healthy breed but can be prone to skin issues, dental problems, hip dysplasia, and luxating patella.

Yakutian Laika
Other Names: Yakut Laika or Yakutskaya Laika
Color variations: white, black, gray, brown, and piebald, often with distinct markings.
Average Lifespan: 10 to 14 years
Origins: Yakutia region, Russia - Ancient times - bred for sledding, hunting, and herding.
Body Size: Males: 21-23 in. 55-77 lbs. Females: 20-22 in. 50-66 lbs.
Personality/Disposition/Compatibility: These dogs are the ultimate adventurers, designed to conquer the rugged Siberian landscape with their incredible endurance and resilience. Full of spirit and intelligence, they're naturally curious and love to explore. They thrive in active homes where they get plenty of mental and physical stimulation. They generally get along well with kids and other dogs, especially with a proper introduction. Just be aware that their strong prey drive might make them less suited for homes with small pets.
Grooming Needs: requires regular grooming to manage its thick double coat, including brushing several times a week to prevent matting and reduce shedding.
Training & Exercise Needs: These dogs are smart and eager learners, but their strong-willed and curious nature can sometimes make them a bit stubborn. Patience and persistence are essential because they might need a bit more time to stay focused and follow commands. They are bursting with energy and love vigorous physical activities. Keeping them busy with interactive games or activities that challenge both their mind and body will make them happier and better behaved. The more you keep them active and engaged, the more content they'll be.
Possible Health Issues: hip dysplasia, eye problems such as cataracts, and possible allergies.

Yorkshire Terrier
Other Names: Yorkie
Color variations: blue and tan, blue and gold, black and tan, and black and gold.
Average Lifespan: 11 to 15 years
Origins: England - mid-19th century - bred for catching rats in clothing mills and factories.
Body Size: Males & Females: 8-9 in. 7 lbs.
Personality/Disposition/Compatibility: They may be small, but they're full of spirit and confidence, making them charming companions who always let you know they're around. These little bundles of energy are incredibly loving and form close connections with their families. They might be a bit cautious around strangers, but once they get to know you, they're friendly and excited to make new friends. They can usually get along with other pets, but it's a good idea to introduce them slowly to ensure everyone gets along smoothly.
Grooming Needs: require regular grooming due to their long, silky coats. Daily brushing is necessary to prevent tangles and mats, and professional grooming every few weeks is recommended.
Training & Exercise Needs: Training Yorkies can be a bit of a challenge due to their independent and occasionally stubborn streak. Despite their small size, they still need regular activity to keep them happy and healthy. While they don't require as much exercise as larger breeds, they thrive on energetic play sessions and daily walks to burn off some of their lively energy.
Possible Health Issues: dental problems, patellar luxation, tracheal collapse, and hypoglycemia.

FINAL THOUGHTS

As we wrap up this adventure through the world of dog breeds, we at K9 Chatter hope you've found Woof-a-pedia: The Ultimate Dog Breed Guide both insightful and, well, a bit like sitting down with a group of dog-loving friends. Because let's be real—welcoming a dog into your life is a wild ride. Sure, it's full of belly rubs and wagging tails, but also muddy paws on the couch and the occasional chewed-up shoe. Still, ask any dog parent, and they'll tell you it's all worth it, ten times over.I remember when I first brought home my own little tornado, a scruffy mutt named Max. He was a bundle of energy, zipping through the house like he was on a mission, leaving chaos in his wake. But one night, after a particularly rough day of work, Max just sat beside me, resting his head on my knee, as if he knew that's exactly what I needed. That's the magic of dogs—they get you, often better than we get ourselves.

In this guide, we've explored not just the names and looks of each breed, but their histories, personalities, quirks, and yes, their demands. Each dog has a unique backstory, like the proud Border Collie who once herded sheep in the Scottish highlands or the sweet-natured Golden Retriever whose roots trace back to the aristocratic hunting parties of 19th-century England. And let's not forget the feisty little Dachshund, originally bred to hunt badgers! It's these deep dives into their pasts that make their personalities so much more understandable and their needs more relatable.

So, whether you're drawn to the high-energy, always-on-the-go nature of a Border Collie, the laid-back, couch-cuddling vibes of a Basset Hound, or the stubborn yet charming antics of a Bulldog, we hope this guide has helped you figure out which breed best fits your lifestyle, your home, and, most importantly, your heart.

Choosing a dog is not like picking out a new piece of furniture. It's about finding a companion whose personality vibes with yours. Maybe you need a jogging partner, or maybe you're more of a "Netflix and nap" kind of person. Either way, the right breed can make a world of difference in how fulfilling that relationship becomes. After all, you're choosing a friend who's going to be there for the long haul—through thick and thin, rainy days, and sunny hikes, and, let's be honest, probably some stolen food off the counter.

And for those of you who are just dipping your toes into the world of dog ownership, don't worry, we've got more to share. Stay tuned for our upcoming series of breed-specific books. We're talking deep dives here—training tips, nutritional advice, health care, and all the nuances of their quirky little personalities. Ever wonder why your Beagle can't stop sniffing every square inch of the park? Or why your Husky howls like it's auditioning for a role in a werewolf movie? We'll cover all that and more.

At the end of the day, being a dog parent is about more than just making sure your pup gets fed and walked. It's about creating a bond that lasts a lifetime. And trust us, that bond will sneak up on you in the most unexpected ways. One day, you'll look over at your dog, and it'll hit you—you're not just their owner. You're their whole world. They love you with every wag of their tail, every goofy grin, every time they bring you a slobbery toy because they just want to share their joy.
So, here's to the future—one filled with muddy paws, wet noses, and years of unconditional love. We hope this book has given you the tools to make the best possible decision for you and your future four-legged friend. And if you need us, K9 Chatter will be right here, ready to help guide you every step of the way.

Now, go hug your dog (or start planning for one if you're still in the research phase)—and savor the moments. Because they're the ones that make this whole journey truly special.

APPENDICES

APPENDIX A: Resources for Ongoing Support and Education

To provide the best care for your dog, it's important to stay informed and seek support when needed. Here are some valuable resources:

Veterinary Care
Regular Visits: Establish a relationship with a trusted veterinarian for routine care and emergencies.
Specialists: Consult veterinary specialists for specific health concerns, such as orthopedics, dermatology, or behavior.

Training and Behavior
Professional Trainers: Seek professional trainers for obedience training, behavior modification, and specialized training needs.
Online Resources: Utilize reputable websites, videos, and online courses for training tips and techniques.

Support Groups and Communities
Local Clubs and Groups: Join local dog clubs, breed-specific groups, and social media communities to connect with other dog owners and share experiences.
Support Networks: Seek support from friends, family, and fellow dog owners for advice, encouragement, and companionship.

Educational Materials
Books and Magazines: Read books and magazines on dog care, training, and health to stay informed about best practices and new developments.
Websites and Blogs: Follow reputable websites and blogs for expert advice, product reviews, and the latest research in canine health and behavior.

ENCOURAGEMENT TO ENJOY THE JOURNEY WITH YOUR NEW BEST FRIEND

Owning a dog is a rewarding journey filled with joy, companionship, and unconditional love. Here are some tips to make the most of your time with your furry friend:

Embrace the Experience
Cherish Moments: Enjoy the everyday moments, from walks in the park to cuddling on the couch. These simple experiences create lasting memories.
Celebrate Milestones: Celebrate your dog's achievements, birthdays, and special occasions. These celebrations strengthen your bond and add joy to your life.

Create a Fulfilling Life
Active Engagement: Keep your dog mentally and physically stimulated with regular exercise, training, and interactive play.

Explore Together: Take your dog on new adventures, explore different environments, and enjoy activities that you both love.

Foster a Strong Bond
Trust and Respect: Build a relationship based on trust and respect. Understand your dog's needs, communicate effectively, and show consistent love and care.
Quality Time: Spend quality time with your dog every day. This strengthens your bond and enhances your mutual happiness.

Stay Positive
Patience and Understanding: Be patient and understanding, especially during challenging times. Your dog looks to you for guidance and support.
Positive Reinforcement: Use positive reinforcement to encourage good behavior and create a harmonious relationship.

Bringing a dog into your life is a journey filled with challenges and rewards. By committing to their care, seeking ongoing support and education, and embracing the joys of companionship, you can ensure a fulfilling and happy life for both you and your new best friend. Enjoy every moment of this incredible journey and cherish the unconditional love that only a dog can provide.

APPENDIX B:
Breed Group Quick Reference

The American Kennel Club (AKC) sorts purebred dogs into seven main groups, each reflecting their unique traits, roles, and histories. In this appendix, you'll find a handy guide to these breed groups, showcasing their distinctive features and offering examples of breeds within each one. By getting to know these groups, you can better understand which dog traits align with your lifestyle and preferences, making it easier to find the ideal furry friend for you.

Sporting Group
The Sporting Group is like a squad of your favorite adventure buddies—they're always up for an outdoor escapade and have a knack for assisting with hunting, especially when it involves tracking down and retrieving birds. These dogs are bursting with energy, eager for a game of fetch, and they absolutely thrive on being around people. Breeds like the cheerful Labrador Retriever, the ever-loyal Golden Retriever, and the spirited English Springer Spaniel are all in this group. They're not only stellar in the field but also wonderful family companions who fill your home with love and joy.

Hound Group
The Hound Group is made up of dogs that were originally bred for hunting, either by tracking scents or using their sharp eyesight. These breeds are known for their incredible sense of smell or keen vision, and they have a strong instinct to chase and track prey. Take the Beagle, for instance—it's renowned for its amazing ability to track scents. Then there's the Greyhound, famous for its speed and excellent sight-hunting skills. And let's not forget the Bloodhound, whose exceptional sense of smell makes it a top-notch tracker. Hounds tend to be independent, focused, and full of energy, so they need plenty of exercise to keep them happy and healthy.

Working Group
The Working Group is made up of breeds that were originally bred for important jobs like guarding property, pulling sleds, and assisting in search and rescue missions. These dogs are known for their smarts, strength, and stamina, which makes them great partners for tasks that require a lot of energy and dedication. For instance, you have the strong and loyal Rottweiler, the tough and spirited Siberian Husky, and the large but gentle Giant Schnauzer. These breeds are not only brave but also incredibly dependable, thriving in roles that call for both physical might and mental grit.

Terrier Group
The Terrier Group is all about feisty, energetic, and spirited dogs that were originally bred to track down and deal with pesky vermin. These dogs have big personalities packed into small to medium-sized frames, with a knack for digging and chasing that's hard to beat. They often sport wiry or smooth coats that need regular grooming to stay in tip-top shape. Breeds like the Jack Russell Terrier, Scottish Terrier, and Airedale Terrier each bring their own special blend of determination and charm, making them as lovable as they are lively.

Toy Group
The Toy Group is all about small, loving dogs that are perfect for cozy apartment living. Don't let their tiny size fool you—these little furballs come with big personalities and plenty of charm. They're great for anyone looking for a devoted and energetic friend. These breeds are not only easy to carry around but also full of playful energy

and deep connections with their owners. Think of the Chihuahua, Pomeranian, and Maltese, each bringing their own special flair.

Non-Sporting Group
The Non-Sporting Group is a real melting pot of dog breeds that don't quite fit into other categories. From the tiny and feisty to the large and laid-back, these breeds come in all shapes and sizes, each with their own special charm. They're mostly known as fantastic companions, whether they're the dignified Dalmatian, the sturdy Bulldog, the elegant Poodle, or the endearing Shiba Inu. Despite their diverse appearances and personalities, they all have one thing in common: they're loyal and adaptable friends.

Herding Group
The Herding Group is packed with breeds that are not only smart and agile but also have a knack for keeping animals in check. These dogs are real go-getters, known for their incredible trainability and boundless energy. They work seamlessly with humans, making them great companions for those who enjoy an active lifestyle. Think of the Border Collie, Australian Shepherd, and German Shepherd—each of these breeds is famous for their sharp focus and quick response to commands. They absolutely thrive when they have a job to do and need plenty of mental and physical stimulation to keep them happy and healthy.

APPENDIX C:
Glossary of Terms

This glossary covers a range of terms commonly used in the world of dog care, training, and breeding. Understanding these terms will help you navigate the complexities of dog ownership and enhance your ability to communicate effectively with veterinarians, trainers, and other dog professionals.

Autoimmune Skin Disorders (e.g., Discoid Lupus Erythematosus, DLE): These conditions primarily affect the skin, leading to symptoms like hair loss, scaling, crusting, and depigmentation, often around the nose and face.
Baiting: Using food or toys to attract a dog's attention and encourage them to perform specific behaviors during training or in the show ring.
Bladder infections: Also known as urinary tract infections (UTIs), occur when bacteria enter the urinary tract and cause inflammation. This condition is more common in female dogs due to their shorter urethra, which makes it easier for bacteria to travel up into the bladder. Symptoms can include frequent urination, straining to urinate, blood in the urine, and sometimes licking the genital area. Bladder infections can cause discomfort and, if left untreated, may lead to more serious conditions such as kidney infections.
Bladder Stones: Mineral formations in the bladder that can cause pain, difficulty urinating, and infections.
Blepharitis: Inflammation of the eyelids, causing redness, swelling, and discomfort.
Brachycephalic Airway Syndrome: Respiratory issues common in brachycephalic (short-nosed) breeds, causing difficulty breathing due to anatomical abnormalities.
Breed Standard: A written description of the ideal physical and behavioral characteristics of a breed, including size, coat, color, temperament, and movement.
Bronchitis: Inflammation of the bronchi in the lungs, leading to coughing and difficulty breathing.
Canine Brucellosis: A bacterial infection that can cause reproductive issues and other health problems, often spread through breeding.
Canine Distemper: A viral disease that affects the respiratory, gastrointestinal, and central nervous systems, leading to severe symptoms and often death.
Canine Good Citizen (CGC): A certification program by the AKC that promotes responsible dog ownership and basic good manners for dogs.
Canine Influenza: Also known as dog flu, this is a contagious respiratory disease caused by influenza viruses.
Canine Parvovirus (Parvo): A highly contagious viral disease that affects the gastrointestinal tract and can be fatal, especially in puppies.
Cataracts: Clouding of the lens of the eye, leading to blurry vision or blindness.
Cerebellar Abiotrophy (CA): a genetic neurological condition that affects dogs, primarily impacting the cerebellum, the part of the brain responsible for coordinating movement and balance. In dogs with CA, the cerebellar cells, particularly the Purkinje cells, degenerate prematurely, leading to a progressive loss of coordination and motor control.
Cherry Eye: Prolapse of the gland of the third eyelid, resulting in a red, swollen mass in the corner of the eye.
Chronic Kidney Disease: A progressive condition where the kidneys lose their ability to function properly, leading to a buildup of waste products in the blood.
Chylothorax: a rare but serious condition in which chyle, a milky fluid rich in fat and lymphocytes (a type of white blood cell), accumulates in the pleural cavity, the space between the lungs and the chest wall. This accumulation can compress the lungs, making it difficult for the dog to breathe. Chylothorax can result from various underlying causes, including trauma, heart disease, tumors, or abnormalities in the lymphatic system.

Clicker Training: A positive reinforcement training method that uses a clicker to mark desired behaviors, followed by a reward.
Cognitive Dysfunction Syndrome (CDS): Similar to dementia in humans, this condition affects older dogs, leading to confusion, disorientation, and behavioral changes.
Color Dilution Alopecia (CDA): a genetic condition in dogs that affects the coat's pigmentation, particularly in breeds or individuals with a diluted coat color, such as blue, fawn, or isabella. The condition is caused by a defect in the way pigment is deposited in the hair shafts, leading to hair thinning, patchy hair loss, and sometimes complete baldness in affected areas. The skin in these areas can become dry, scaly, and prone to secondary infections. While there is no cure for CDA, management typically involves regular skin care, protection from sun exposure, and addressing any secondary infections that may arise.
Conformation: The physical structure and appearance of a dog as defined by its breed standard. Conformation shows evaluate how well a dog meets these standards.
Congestive Heart Failure (CHF): This is a condition where the heart cannot pump blood efficiently, leading to fluid accumulation in the lungs and other body parts. CHF can be caused by various underlying heart diseases.
Conjunctivitis (Pink Eye): Inflammation of the conjunctiva, causing redness, discharge, and discomfort.
Copper toxicosis: a genetic disorder that leads to the accumulation of excessive amounts of copper in the liver, which can eventually cause liver damage or liver failure. This condition is most commonly seen in certain breeds, such as Bedlington Terriers, West Highland White Terriers, and Doberman Pinschers, though it can occur in other breeds as well. The liver normally stores and processes copper, but in dogs with copper toxicosis, the liver is unable to properly regulate copper levels, leading to toxic buildup.
Corneal Ulcers: Open sores on the cornea of the eye, often caused by injury or infection, leading to pain and vision problems.
Crate Training: The process of teaching a dog to accept a crate as a safe and secure place. Used for house training, travel, and providing a den-like environment.
Cruciate Ligament Injuries: Tears or ruptures of the ligaments in the knee, often requiring surgical repair.
Cryptorchidism: a condition where one or both of the dog's testicles fail to descend into the scrotum and remain in the abdomen or inguinal canal. Normally, a puppy's testicles descend into the scrotum by the time they are a few weeks old, but in cases of cryptorchidism, this process is incomplete. The condition can be unilateral (one testicle undescended) or bilateral (both testicles undescended).
Cushing's Disease: A condition caused by excessive production of cortisol, leading to symptoms such as increased thirst, urination, and a pot-bellied appearance.
Cystinuria: a genetic disorder that affects the kidneys' ability to filter cystine, an amino acid, from the urine. In dogs with this condition, cystine is not reabsorbed properly and instead accumulates in the urine, where it can form crystals or stones (uroliths) in the urinary tract. These stones can cause discomfort, urinary blockages, and potentially life-threatening complications if not treated. Breeds that are more prone to cystinuria include Newfoundlands, Labrador Retrievers, and Dachshunds.
Degenerative Myelopathy (DM): a progressive neurological disease that affects the spinal cord, leading to a gradual loss of coordination and mobility in the hind limbs. It typically occurs in older dogs, often around the age of 8 years or older, and is comparable to amyotrophic lateral sclerosis (ALS) in humans. The disease is caused by the degeneration of the white matter of the spinal cord, which impairs the transmission of nerve signals.
Demodectic Mange: a skin condition in dogs caused by an overpopulation of Demodex mites, which are naturally present in small numbers on a dog's skin. These mites live in the hair follicles and sebaceous glands, usually without causing harm. However, if a dog has a weakened immune system or other underlying health issues, the mite population can grow excessively, leading to skin problems.
Dermatitis: Inflammation of the skin, which can be caused by allergies, infections, or parasites.
Dermatomyositis: An inflammatory condition affecting the skin and muscles, often causing skin lesions and muscle weakness.
Dermoid sinus: a congenital skin condition found in dogs, particularly in certain breeds such as the Rhodesian Ridgeback. It is a neural tube defect that occurs during embryonic development, where a portion of the skin remains connected to the underlying tissues, such as the spinal cord or muscle. This results in a tubular, cyst-like structure that can extend from the skin's surface deep into the tissues. The sinus can sometimes become infected, leading to discomfort, pain, or other complications.
Desensitization: A training technique used to reduce a dog's fear or anxiety by gradually exposing them to the feared object or situation at a level they can tolerate.
Diabetes Mellitus: A condition in which the dog's body cannot properly regulate blood sugar levels, often requiring insulin treatment.
Diabetes: a chronic condition where a dog's body either cannot produce enough insulin or cannot effectively use the insulin it does produce. Insulin is a hormone that regulates blood sugar levels, and without proper insulin

function, glucose cannot enter cells to be used for energy. This leads to high levels of glucose in the bloodstream, a condition known as hyperglycemia.

Dilated Cardiomyopathy (DCM): This condition is characterized by the heart's chambers enlarging and the walls becoming thin, leading to decreased heart function. It's more common in larger breeds such as Doberman Pinschers, Boxers, and Great Danes.

Distichiasis: Abnormal growth of eyelashes that can irritate the eye.

Docking: The surgical removal of a portion of a dog's tail, often done shortly after birth for certain breeds. It is a controversial practice and banned in some countries.

Dog Show (Conformation Show): A competitive event where dogs are judged on how closely they adhere to their breed standard. Categories can include breed, group, and best in show.

Double Coat: A type of coat with two layers: a soft, insulating undercoat and a longer, protective topcoat. Common in breeds like the Siberian Husky and German Shepherd.

Dry Eye (Keratoconjunctivitis Sicca): Insufficient tear production, leading to dry, irritated eyes.

Ear Infections: Common in dogs with floppy ears, ear infections can cause itching, redness, and discharge.

Ectropion: A condition where the eyelids roll outward, exposing the inner eyelid and causing dryness and irritation.

Elbow Dysplasia: a condition characterized by abnormal development of the elbow joint, leading to joint instability, pain, and arthritis. It is a common orthopedic issue, particularly in large and giant breeds. The condition is often caused by a combination of genetic factors and rapid growth during puppyhood, leading to one or more abnormalities in the joint, such as fragmented coronoid process (FCP), osteochondritis dissecans (OCD), or ununited anconeal process (UAP).

Encephalitis: Inflammation of the brain, which can be caused by infections, autoimmune diseases, or other factors, leading to neurological symptoms.

Endocarditis: An infection of the heart's inner lining, usually affecting the heart valves. It can occur due to bacterial infections spreading from other body parts.

Entropion: A condition where the eyelids roll inward, causing the eyelashes to rub against the cornea.

Eosinophilic Granuloma Complex: A group of skin disorders characterized by the presence of eosinophils, a type of white blood cell, causing lesions and itching.

Epilepsy: A neurological disorder causing recurrent seizures.

Esophagitis: Inflammation of the esophagus, often caused by acid reflux, leading to pain and difficulty swallowing.

Exercise-induced collapse (EIC): A condition where the pancreas does not produce enough digestive enzymes, leading to malnutrition and weight loss.

Fanconi syndrome: a rare but serious kidney disorder that affects the renal tubules, leading to the improper reabsorption of essential nutrients, such as glucose, amino acids, and electrolytes, back into the bloodstream. Instead, these nutrients are lost through urine, which can result in symptoms like excessive thirst (polydipsia), frequent urination (polyuria), weight loss, muscle wasting, and weakness. If left untreated, Fanconi syndrome can lead to more severe conditions such as kidney failure.

Fibrosarcoma: A type of cancer affecting the connective tissues, often occurring in the skin or mouth.

Flews: The loose, hanging part of the upper lip on some dog breeds, such as the Bloodhound.

Follicular Dermatitis: an inflammatory condition affecting the hair follicles, often leading to symptoms such as itching, redness, swelling, and hair loss in the affected areas. This condition can result from various underlying causes, including bacterial or fungal infections, allergies, parasites (like mites), or even autoimmune diseases. The inflamed hair follicles can become filled with pus, leading to small, pimple-like bumps on the dog's skin, which may rupture and cause scabs or crusts.

Gastric Cancer: Cancer of the stomach, though relatively rare in dogs.

Gastric dilatation-volvulus (bloat): A life-threatening condition where the stomach twists, cutting off blood supply and causing rapid swelling. also known as gastric torsion.

Giardia: A parasitic infection of the intestines causing diarrhea, weight loss, and dehydration.

Glaucoma: Increased pressure in the eye that can cause pain and lead to blindness if untreated.

Granulomatous Meningoencephalitis (GME): An inflammatory disease affecting the central nervous system, causing neurological symptoms.

Heartworm Disease: Caused by parasitic worms that live in the heart and blood vessels, this disease can lead to severe lung disease, heart failure, and other organ damage. It's transmitted through mosquito bites.

Hemangiosarcoma: A type of cancer that originates in the blood vessels and often affects the spleen, liver, and heart.

Hip Dysplasia: A genetic condition where the hip joint does not fit together properly, leading to arthritis and pain. Common in large breeds like the German Shepherd and Labrador Retriever.

Histiocytoma: A benign skin tumor that often affects young dogs and usually resolves on its own.

Hydrocephalus: a condition characterized by an abnormal accumulation of cerebrospinal fluid (CSF) within the brain's ventricles, leading to increased pressure on the brain tissue. This can cause the skull to enlarge, especially in puppies, and can result in neurological symptoms such as seizures, difficulty walking, blindness, and behavioral changes. The condition can be congenital (present at birth) or acquired due to injury, infection, or tumors.

Hyperadrenocorticism (Cushing's Disease): Overproduction of cortisol by the adrenal glands, causing symptoms such as increased thirst and urination, hair loss, and a pot-bellied appearance.

Hyperlipidemia: a condition characterized by abnormally high levels of lipids, such as cholesterol and triglycerides, in the blood. This can be a primary condition, often due to genetic factors, or secondary to other health issues like hypothyroidism, diabetes mellitus, pancreatitis, or obesity.

Hypertension: High blood pressure, which can lead to organ damage, particularly affecting the kidneys and eyes.

Hypertrophic Cardiomyopathy (HCM): Characterized by the thickening of the heart muscle, leading to decreased heart efficiency. It's less common in dogs compared to cats but can still occur.

Hypertrophic Osteodystrophy (HOD): A bone disease affecting rapidly growing large breed puppies, causing pain and swelling in the growth plates.

Hypoadrenocorticism (Addisonian Crisis): An acute medical emergency caused by a sudden drop in hormone levels produced by the adrenal glands, leading to severe lethargy, vomiting, and collapse.

Hypoglycemia: Low blood sugar, which can be particularly dangerous in small breeds and puppies, leading to weakness, seizures, and even coma.

Hypothyroidism: Often caused by autoimmune thyroiditis, where the immune system attacks the thyroid gland, leading to decreased production of thyroid hormones. Symptoms include lethargy, weight gain, hair loss, and skin issues.

Immune-Mediated Hemolytic Anemia (IMHA): This condition occurs when the immune system destroys red blood cells, leading to anemia. Symptoms include lethargy, pale gums, rapid breathing, and jaundice.

Immune-Mediated Thrombocytopenia (IMT): In IMT, the immune system attacks and destroys platelets, which are essential for blood clotting. Symptoms include bruising, bleeding from the gums, nosebleeds, and blood in the urine or stool.

Immunoproliferative Small Intestinal Disease (IPSID): a rare type of gastrointestinal lymphoma that primarily affects the small intestine. It is characterized by the abnormal proliferation of lymphoid cells in the intestinal lining, leading to chronic inflammation and impaired nutrient absorption.

Inflammatory Bowel Disease (IBD): Chronic inflammation of the gastrointestinal tract, causing symptoms such as vomiting, diarrhea, and weight loss.

Inflammatory Polyps: Non-cancerous growths in the nasal passages or ear canal, causing respiratory or ear issues.

Intervertebral Disc Disease (IVDD): A condition affecting the spinal discs, causing pain, nerve damage, and possible paralysis.

Intestinal Parasites: Various worms, such as roundworms, hookworms, and whipworms, which can cause digestive issues and poor health.

Kennel Cough: Also known as canine infectious tracheobronchitis, this is a highly contagious respiratory disease that causes a persistent cough.

Laryngeal Paralysis: A condition affecting the larynx, leading to breathing difficulties.

Legg-Calvé-Perthes Disease: A condition that affects the hip joint, causing the femoral head to deteriorate due to insufficient blood supply, resulting in pain and lameness.

Lens Luxation: Dislocation of the lens, which can cause pain and vision loss.

Leptospirosis: A bacterial infection that affects the kidneys and liver, often transmitted through contaminated water.

Lipoma: A benign fatty tumor that is generally harmless but can become large and uncomfortable.

Liver Cancer: Hepatocellular carcinoma is the most common form.

Liver Disease: Various conditions can affect the liver, leading to symptoms such as jaundice, weight loss, and vomiting.

Lundehund Syndrome: a serious and complex gastrointestinal disorder that primarily affects the Norwegian Lundehund breed. This syndrome is characterized by a combination of gastrointestinal issues, including protein-losing enteropathy (PLE), which leads to the loss of proteins from the digestive tract, malabsorption, and lymphangiectasia, a condition where the lymphatic vessels in the intestines become enlarged and leaky.

Lung Cancer: Although less common, dogs can develop primary lung tumors.

Lyme Disease: A tick-borne disease caused by the bacterium Borrelia burgdorferi, leading to symptoms such as fever, lameness, and joint swelling.

Lymphangiectasia: A condition where the lymph vessels supplying the intestines become dilated, leading to protein loss and digestive issues.
Lymphoma: A type of cancer that affects the lymphatic system, causing swollen lymph nodes and other symptoms.
Malignant Melanoma: A type of cancer that can occur in the skin, mouth, or other areas, often aggressive and requiring prompt treatment.
Mammary Gland Carcinoma: Breast cancer, which is more common in unspayed female dogs.
Mange: Skin disease caused by mites, leading to itching, hair loss, and skin infections.
Marking: A behavior in which a dog urinates on objects to leave a scent mark, often seen in male dogs to establish territory.
Mast Cell Tumors: A type of skin cancer that can vary in severity and may spread to other parts of the body.
Megaesophagus: A condition where the esophagus loses its ability to move food to the stomach, leading to regurgitation and malnutrition.
Melanoma: A cancer of the pigment-producing cells, commonly found in the skin, mouth, and eyes.
Meningitis: Inflammation of the protective membranes covering the brain and spinal cord, leading to severe pain and neurological issues.
Mitral Valve Disease (MVD): Common in smaller breeds like Cavalier King Charles Spaniels and Dachshunds, MVD involves the degeneration of the mitral valve, leading to heart murmur and heart failure if untreated.
Mixed Breed: A dog whose parents are of different breeds or a combination of multiple breeds, also known as a mutt.
Myasthenia Gravis: This neuromuscular disorder results from an immune attack on the connections between nerves and muscles, causing muscle weakness and fatigue. Symptoms include difficulty swallowing, drooping eyelids, and weakness after exercise.
Nasal Mites: Tiny parasites that live in a dog's nasal passages, causing sneezing, nasal discharge, and irritation.
Nasopharyngeal Polyps: Non-cancerous growths in the nasopharynx, causing respiratory and swallowing difficulties.
Obedience Trial: A competitive event where dogs perform a series of exercises in response to commands, demonstrating their training and responsiveness.
Obesity: Excess weight can lead to a range of health issues, including diabetes, heart disease, and joint problems.
Osteoarthritis: Degenerative joint disease-causing chronic pain and stiffness, especially in older dogs.
Osteosarcoma: A type of bone cancer, most frequently occurring in the long bones of large breed dogs.
Pancreatitis: Inflammation of the pancreas, which can cause severe abdominal pain, vomiting, and diarrhea.
Pannus: A condition where an abnormal layer of tissue grows over the cornea, often seen in German Shepherds.
Panosteitis: A painful condition affecting the long bones of young, growing dogs, often leading to lameness.
Patellar Luxation: This condition occurs when the kneecap dislocates or moves out of its normal position. It can cause pain and difficulty walking.
Patent Ductus Arteriosus (PDA): A congenital defect where the ductus arteriosus fails to close after birth, leading to abnormal blood flow between the aorta and pulmonary artery. It's more common in breeds like Poodles, German Shepherds, and Shetland Sheepdogs.
Pemphigus: This group of autoimmune diseases affects the skin and mucous membranes. There are several types, including pemphigus foliaceus and pemphigus vulgaris. Symptoms include blisters, ulcers, and crusty lesions on the skin.
Perianal Fistulas: Painful, draining sores around the anus, often requiring surgical treatment.
Pericardial Effusion: This is the accumulation of fluid in the pericardial sac surrounding the heart, leading to decreased heart function. It can be caused by tumors, infections, or trauma.
Periodontal Disease: A common dental disease that affects the gums and teeth, leading to pain, infection, and tooth loss.
Plasmacytoma: A type of cancer affecting plasma cells, often found in the skin or mucous membranes.
Pneumonia: Infection or inflammation of the lungs, causing coughing, difficulty breathing, and fever.
Pneumothorax: Air in the chest cavity outside the lungs, causing breathing difficulties and requiring emergency treatment.
Portosystemic shunt (PSS): a congenital or acquired condition where an abnormal blood vessel allows blood from the gastrointestinal tract to bypass the liver, which prevents the liver from properly detoxifying and metabolizing substances before they enter the general circulation.
Primary Ciliary Dyskinesia: A genetic disorder affecting the cilia, leading to respiratory issues due to improper clearance of mucus.
Progressive Retinal Atrophy (PRA): A genetic condition leading to gradual vision loss and blindness.

Prostate Disease: Conditions affecting the prostate gland, including enlargement, infection, and cancer, particularly in older male dogs.

Pulmonic Stenosis: This is a congenital condition where the flow of blood from the right ventricle to the pulmonary artery is obstructed, common in breeds like Bulldogs, Beagles, and Boxers.

Puppy Mill: A commercial breeding operation that prioritizes profit over the health and welfare of the dogs. Often associated with poor living conditions and inadequate care.

Purebred: A dog whose parents are both of the same breed and typically registered with a breed registry.

Pyometra: A serious uterine infection that can occur in unspayed female dogs, often requiring emergency surgery.

Renal cortical hypoplasia: a congenital condition where the outer layer of the kidneys (the cortex) fails to develop properly, leading to an underdeveloped or smaller-than-normal kidney. This condition can result in reduced kidney function because the cortex contains the filtering units (glomeruli) responsible for cleaning the blood.

Renal Dysplasia: A congenital condition where the kidneys do not develop properly, leading to chronic kidney disease.

Respiratory Problems: Due to their short snouts, Affenpinschers can be prone to breathing difficulties and conditions like brachycephalic airway syndrome.

Retinal Dysplasia: a congenital condition characterized by the abnormal development of the retina. This condition can vary in severity and presentation, but it generally involves the retina's layers not forming correctly, leading to visual impairment.

Rheumatoid Arthritis: An autoimmune disease that causes chronic inflammation of the joints. Symptoms include joint pain, swelling, and stiffness.

Rickettsial Infections: Diseases caused by Rickettsia bacteria, such as Rocky Mountain Spotted Fever, which are transmitted by ticks.

Ringworm: A fungal infection affecting the skin, causing circular, hairless patches and is highly contagious.

Scleroderma: An autoimmune disease causing hardening and tightening of the skin and connective tissues.

Seborrhea: A skin condition causing flaky, scaly, and often oily skin, which can be either primary (genetic) or secondary to other conditions.

Separation Anxiety: A behavioral condition where dogs become extremely anxious when left alone, leading to destructive behavior and distress.

Socialization: The process of exposing a dog to various people, animals, environments, and experiences to ensure they are well-adjusted and confident.

Spay/Neuter: Surgical procedures to sterilize a dog, preventing them from reproducing. Spaying refers to females, and neutering refers to males.

Spinal Cord Injuries: Trauma or disease affecting the spinal cord, potentially causing pain, paralysis, or loss of function.

Squamous Cell Carcinoma: A skin cancer that can also affect the mouth, toes, and nails.

Stomatitis: Inflammation of the mouth's mucous membranes, often leading to severe oral pain and difficulty eating.

Sub-aortic Stenosis: A congenital heart defect causing narrowing below the aortic valve, leading to heart issues.

Syringomyelia (SM): a neurological condition where fluid-filled cavities, known as syrinxes, develop within the spinal cord. This condition often occurs due to a malformation at the base of the skull, which obstructs the normal flow of cerebrospinal fluid, leading to the development of these cavities. Syringomyelia is particularly common in certain breeds, such as the Cavalier King Charles Spaniel and the Brussels Griffon, where the skull may be too small to accommodate the brain.

Systemic Lupus Erythematosus (SLE): SLE is a chronic autoimmune disease that can affect multiple organs and systems, including the skin, joints, kidneys, and blood. Symptoms vary widely but may include joint pain, fever, skin lesions, and kidney dysfunction.

Temperament: The inherent personality and behavioral traits of a dog, including factors like friendliness, aggression, and sociability.

Tetanus: A bacterial infection caused by Clostridium tetani, leading to muscle stiffness and spasms, often through wounds.

Tetralogy of Fallot: A complex congenital heart defect involving four abnormalities that result in insufficient oxygenated blood reaching the body. It can be seen in breeds like Keeshonds and Bulldogs.

Therapy Dog: A dog trained to provide comfort and affection to people in hospitals, nursing homes, schools, and other settings. Unlike service dogs, they do not perform specific tasks for individuals with disabilities.

Thrombocytopathy: a condition where the platelets are dysfunctional, leading to problems with blood clotting. This condition can be hereditary or acquired due to diseases or medications.

Thrombocytopenia: Low platelet counts in the blood, leading to increased bleeding and bruising.

Thyroid Tumors: Tumors of the thyroid gland that can cause either hyperthyroidism or hypothyroidism, affecting the dog's metabolism.

Tick-Borne Diseases: Besides Lyme disease, ticks can transmit other diseases like Ehrlichiosis, Anaplasmosis, and Rocky Mountain Spotted Fever.
Topline: The outline of a dog's back from the neck to the tail, used as an indicator of conformation and breed standard adherence.
Toxoplasmosis: A parasitic infection that can cause neurological symptoms, especially in young or immunocompromised dogs.
Tracheal collapse: a condition in dogs where the trachea, or windpipe, becomes flattened and causes airway obstruction. The trachea is composed of rings of cartilage that normally hold it open, but in tracheal collapse, these rings weaken and lose their rigidity, leading to a narrowing of the airway. This condition is most common in small dog breeds.
Transitional Cell Carcinoma (TCC): A type of cancer affecting the urinary bladder, causing urinary issues.
Tremors: Involuntary muscle contractions that can be caused by a variety of factors, including neurological issues or toxins.
Urinary Tract Infections (UTIs): Infections of the urinary system, causing frequent urination, pain, and sometimes blood in the urine.
Uveitis: Inflammation of the uvea, the middle layer of the eye, causing pain and vision problems.
Valley Fever: A fungal infection caused by Coccidioides organisms, leading to respiratory issues and systemic symptoms.
Ventricular Septal Defect (VSD): A congenital heart defect characterized by a hole in the wall separating the heart's ventricles, affecting blood flow.
Von Willebrand's disease: a genetic bleeding disorder found in dogs (and humans) that is caused by a deficiency or dysfunction of von Willebrand factor (vWF), a protein essential for normal blood clotting. This disease affects the blood's ability to clot properly, leading to excessive bleeding.
Weave Poles: A set of upright poles used in agility training and competition, where the dog must weave in and out of the poles in a specific pattern.
Working Dog: A dog bred and trained to perform specific tasks, such as herding, guarding, or search and rescue.
Zinc-Responsive Dermatosis: A condition caused by zinc deficiency, leading to crusting and scaling of the skin, particularly around the face and paws.

APPENDIX D: Resources and Further Reading

Here's a handpicked selection of books, websites, and organizations to guide you on your journey as a dog owner. These resources are brimming with practical advice on dog care, training, health, and behavior. Whether you're looking for tips on training, health guidance, or just some general pointers on how to best care for your furry friend, these recommendations have got you covered.

RECOMMENDED BOOKS

"The Art of Raising a Puppy" by The Monks of New Skete
A comprehensive guide to raising a well-behaved and well-adjusted puppy from one of the most respected dog training groups.

"How to Raise the Perfect Dog: Through Puppyhood and Beyond" by Cesar Millan
Renowned dog behaviorist Cesar Millan offers practical advice and techniques for raising a balanced and happy dog.

"Decoding Your Dog: Explaining Common Dog Behaviors and How to Prevent or Change Unwanted Ones" by the American College of Veterinary Behaviorists
This book provides insights into canine behavior and practical solutions for common behavioral issues.

"The Other End of the Leash: Why We Do What We Do Around Dogs" by Patricia McConnell
A look into the human-canine relationship, emphasizing how our behavior affects our dogs.

"Don't Shoot the Dog!: The New Art of Teaching and Training" by Karen Pryor
A classic on positive reinforcement training techniques from a pioneer in the field.

"Dr. Pitcairn's Complete Guide to Natural Health for Dogs & Cats" by Richard H. Pitcairn and Susan Hubble Pitcairn

A guide to holistic pet care, covering nutrition, health, and natural remedies.

"Canine Nutrigenomics: The New Science of Feeding Your Dog for Optimum Health" by W. Jean Dodds and Diana Laverdure
Insights into how nutrition affects your dog's genetics and overall health.

RECOMMENDED WEBSITES

American Kennel Club (AKC)
Website: www.akc.org
Offers breed information, training tips, and resources for dog owners.

ASPCA (American Society for the Prevention of Cruelty to Animals)
Website: www.aspca.org
Provides resources on pet care, animal behavior, and adoption.

PetMD
Website: www.petmd.com
A comprehensive source for pet health information and veterinary advice.

Whole Dog Journal
Website: www.whole-dog-journal.com
Offers articles on dog training, health, and nutrition with a focus on holistic care.

The Humane Society of the United States
Website: www.humanesociety.org
Resources on pet care, adoption, and animal welfare.

Dogster
Website: www.dogster.com
Provides articles on dog breeds, training, health, and lifestyle.

VetStreet
Website: www.vetstreet.com
Offers pet health information, breed guides, and veterinary advice.

RECOMMENDED ORGANIZATIONS

American Kennel Club (AKC)
Website: www.akc.org
The primary registry for purebred dogs in the United States, offering resources and events for dog owners and breeders.

American Veterinary Medical Association (AVMA)
Website: www.avma.org
Provides veterinary resources, including information on pet health and welfare.

The Humane Society of the United States (HSUS)
Website: www.humanesociety.org
Advocates for animal protection and offers resources for pet owners.

ASPCA (American Society for the Prevention of Cruelty to Animals)
Website: www.aspca.org
Works to prevent animal cruelty and provides resources on pet care and adoption.

Petfinder
Website: www.petfinder.com
A database of adoptable pets from shelters and rescue groups across North America.

Canine Health Foundation (CHF)
Website: www.akcchf.org
Supports research on canine health issues and provides educational resources.

International Association of Canine Professionals (IACP)
Website: www.canineprofessionals.com
Offers resources for dog trainers, behaviorists, and pet care professionals.

BIBLIOGRAPHY

- ABCadmin. (2023, January 16). *Official Bloodhound Website - American Bloodhound Club*. American Bloodhound Club. https://www.americanbloodhoundclub.org/
- *ABMC – American Belgian Malinois Club*. (n.d.). https://www.malinoisclub.com/abmc/
- *About*. (n.d.). PPPA. http://www.portuguesepodengopequeno.org/about.html
- *About - TTCA*. (2024, June 13). TTCA. https://ttca-online.org/ol-about/
- *About American Polish Lowland Sheepdog Club*. (n.d.). http://www.aponc.org/about%20aponc.htm
- *About breed: History — Tisama Tosa Ken — Tosa Inu San Marino*. (n.d.). http://tosainu-sanmarino.com/about-breed-history/
- *About French Spaniels | French Spaniels at Audentastra*. (n.d.). UK French Spaniels. https://www.frenchspaniels.co.uk/about-french-spaniels
- *About Greyhounds*. (2024, May 9). Greyhound Club of America. https://www.greyhoundclubofamericainc.org/greyhounds/
- *About Our Breed | American Shih Tzu Club*. (n.d.). https://shihtzu.org/about_our_breed
- *About Papillons – Papillon Club of America*. (n.d.). https://papillonclub.org/about-papillons/
- *About the American Maltese Association | American Maltese Association*. (n.d.). https://www.americanmaltese.org/site-page/about-american-maltese-association-1
- *About the breed | Stabyhoun UK*. (n.d.). https://stabyhounuk.com/qa/
- *About the Pug — Pug Dog Club of America*. (n.d.). Pug Dog Club of America. https://www.pugdogclubofamerica.com/about
- *ABOUT US | DDBSA Dogue de Bordeaux Society of America*. (n.d.). Ddbsawebsite. https://www.ddbsa.org/
- ACCCAdmin. (2024, February 5). *Breed Standard - American Chinese Crested Club - ACCC*. American Chinese Crested Club - ACCC. https://chinesecrestedclub.info/breed-standard/
- ACDCAadmin. (n.d.). *Australian Cattle Dog Club of America – Australian Cattle Dog Club of America*. Australian Cattle Dog Club of America. https://www.acdca.org/
- Admin. (n.d.). *BEDLINGTON TERRIER CLUB of AMERICA*. BEDLINGTON TERRIER CLUB of AMERICA. https://www.bedlingtonamerica.com/
- Admin. (2024, July 25). *New Home | English Springer Spaniel Club*. English Springer Spaniel Club. https://englishspringer.org/
- Administrator, B. (2024, March 4). *Biewer Terriers | Biewer Terrier Club of America*. Biewer Terrier Club of America. https://biewerterrierclubofamerica.org/
- Administrator, P. (2021, April 13). *About Bichons | Bichon Frise Club of America*. Bichon Frise Club of America. https://bichon.org/about-bichons/
- admin@japanesechinclubofamerica.org. (2023, May 24). *BREED INFO - Japanese Chin Club of America*. Japanese Chin Club of America. https://japanesechinclubofamerica.org/breed-info/
- admin@schipperkeclubofamerica.org. (2023, September 22). *THE BREED - Schipperke Club of America*. Schipperke Club of America. https://schipperkeclubofamerica.org/the-breed/
- *AEDCA | AEDCA Home*. (n.d.). https://aedca.org/home.php
- *Airedale Terrier Club*. (n.d.). https://airedale.org/
- *AKC Breed Standard - The Poodle Club of America*. (2021, June 30). The Poodle Club of America. https://poodleclubofamerica.org/akc-breed-standard/
- *Alaskan Klee Kai Association of America*. (n.d.). AKKAOA. https://www.akkaoa.org/
- America, C. D. C. O. (n.d.). *Canaan Dog Club of America*. Canaan Dog Club of America. https://cdca.org/
- America, N. T. C. O. (2017, June 7). *About Norwich*. Norwich Terrier Club of America. https://norwichterrierclub.org/about-norwich/
- America, Y. L. C. O. (n.d.). *Yakutian Laika Club of America*. Yakutian Laika Club of America. https://yakutianlaikaclubofamerica.org/

- *American Azawakh Association.* (n.d.). American Azawakh Association. https://www.azawakhclub.org/
- *American Belgian Tervuren Club – ABTC.* (n.d.). https://abtc.org/#
- *American Black and Tan Coonhound Club.* (n.d.). https://abtcc.org/
- American Boerboel Club. (n.d.). *American Boerboel Club.* https://americanboerboelclub.org/
- American Bolognese Club. (n.d.). *American Bolognese Club.* https://americanbologneseclub.com/
- American Boxer Club. (2024, May 17). *HOME - American Boxer Club.* https://americanboxerclub.org/
- *American Brittany Club.* (n.d.). Copyright American Brittany Club, Inc. - All Rights Reserved. http://www.theamericanbrittanyclub.org/
- *American Cesky Terrier Fanciers Association (ACTFA).* (n.d.). American Cesky Terrier Fanciers Association (ACTFA). https://www.americanceskyterrierfanciersassociation.org/#/
- American Chesapeake Club. (2024, July 15). *Home - American Chesapeake Club.* https://amchessieclub.org/
- *American Dutch Shepherd Association – Committed to preserving the purebred Dutch Shepherd as the "Jack-of-all-trades" farm dog they are. Learn more about the versatile breed under breed information and consider joining us in our effort.* (n.d.). https://www.dutchshepherd.org/
- *American Hairless Terrier Club of America, Inc.* (n.d.). American Hairless Terrier Club of America. https://ahtca.info/index.html
- *American Karelian Bear Dog Alliance.* (n.d.). http://www.akbda.com/
- American Kennel Club. (n.d.). *Dog Breeds - Types Of Dogs - American Kennel Club.* https://www.akc.org/dog-breeds/
- American Lhasa Apso Club. (2024, January 30). *ABOUT LHASAS - American Lhasa Apso Club.* https://lhasaapso.org/about-lhasas/
- *AMERICAN NORRBOTTENSPETS ASSOCIATION.* (n.d.). AMERICAN NORRBOTTENSPETS ASSOCIATION. https://www.usnorrbottenspets.com/
- *American Pit Bull Terrier – THE AMERICAN BULLY KENNEL CLUB.* (n.d.). https://abkcdogs.net/breeds/american-pit-bull-terrier/
- American Pointer Club. (2024, August 7). *About Pointers - American Pointer Club.* https://www.americanpointerclub.org/about-pointers/
- *American Sealyham Terrier Club.* (n.d.). https://sealyham.org/
- American Sloughi Association. (2023, July 5). *Welcome to the American Sloughi Association - AKC National Parent Club for the Sloughi Welcome to the American Sloughi Association American Sloughi Association- AKC National Parent Club for the Sloughi AKC National Parent Club for the Sloughi.* Welcome to the American Sloughi Association - AKC National Parent Club for the Sloughi. https://sloughi-international.com/
- *Ameri-Can Stabyhoun Association.* (n.d.). Ameri-Can Stabyhoun Association. https://stabyhouns.org/
- *American Teddy Roosevelt Terrier Club.* (n.d.). AMERICAN TEDDY ROOSEVELT TERRIER CLUB. http://www.teddyroosevelterrier.org/
- *American Tibetan Mastiff Association-Photos, Breeder List, Puppies.* (n.d.). https://www.tibetanmastiff.org/
- *American Toy Fox Terrier Club, Toy Fox Terrier, ATFTC.* (n.d.). https://www.atftc.com/
- American Whippet Club Administrator. (2023, September 27). *About Whippets - American Whippet Club.* American Whippet Club. https://www.americanwhippetclub.org/about-whippets/
- *American-Thailand Ridgeback Association (ATRA) - First American Registry of the Rare Breed Thailand Ridgeback Dog.* (n.d.). (C) Copyright 1999 Capt. Jack Sterling. http://www.thaidog.org/
- Andrei, J. (2023a, September 27). *Braque du Bourbonnais.* DogTime. https://dogtime.com/dog-breeds/braque-du-bourbonnais
- Andrei, J. (2023b, October 16). *Bavarian Mountain Scent Hound.* DogTime. https://dogtime.com/dog-breeds/bavarian-mountain-scent-hound
- Andrei, J. (2023c, November 14). *Hanoverian Scenthound.* DogTime. https://dogtime.com/dog-breeds/hanoverian-scenthound
- *Appenzell Mountain Dog Club of America.* (n.d.). AMDCA. https://www.appenzellers.org/
- *Articles | SchubertUS Kennel Bohemian Dogs In America.* (n.d.). SchubertUS Kennel Bohemian Dogs in America. https://www.bohemiandogsinamerica.com/articles
- ASCA. (2024, August 22). *ASCA - Australian Shepherd Club of America.* https://asca.org/
- *ASDCA – ASDCA.* (n.d.). https://asdca.club/
- ASSAAdmin. (n.d.). *American Shetland Sheepdog Association – American Shetland Sheepdog Association.* American Shetland Sheepdog Association. https://www.americanshetlandsheepdogassociation.org/#
- *ASTCDS of America.* (n.d.). ASTCDS of America. https://stumpytailcattledogs.org/welcome
- *ATCA – Australian Terrier Club of America.* (n.d.). https://australianterrier.org/
- *AWSC.* (n.d.). AWSC. https://www.americanwaterspanielclub.org/

- *Barbado da Terceira Club - USA*. (n.d.). Barbado Da Terceira Club - USA. https://barbadousa.com/
- *Barbet Club of America - Official Site*. (n.d.). Barbet Club of America - Official Site. https://www.barbetclubofamerica.com/
- *Basset Bleu de Gascogne UK | Dog Breeder*. (n.d.). Caelestibleu Basset. https://www.bassetbleudegascogne.co.uk/
- *Basset Fauve de Bretagne Club of America*. (n.d.). *Home - Basset Fauve de Bretagne Club of America*. Basset Fauve De Bretagne Club of America. https://bassetfauve.org/
- *Basset Hound Club of America*. (n.d.). Basset Hound Club of America. https://basset-bhca.org/
- *BCA Home | Briard Club America*. (n.d.). Briard Club America. https://www.briardclubofamerica.org/
- *BCSA*. (n.d.). BCSA. https://bordercolliesocietyofamerica.com/
- *Bearded Collie Club of America*. (n.d.). Bearded Collie Club of America. https://beardedcollieclub.us/
- *Belgian Sheepdog Club of America*. (2022, August 29). *Belgian Sheepdog Club of America*. https://bsca.info/
- *Berger Picards - Berger Picard Club of America*. (n.d.). https://bpclubofamerica.org/
- *Bernese Mountain Dog Club of America (BMDCA) a network for Regional Clubs and Owners*. (n.d.). BMDCA. https://www.bmdca.org/
- *BICA Home | Bica*. (n.d.). Bica. https://www.thebraccoclub.org/
- *Black Russian Terrier Club of America*. (n.d.). Black Russian Terrier Club of America. http://www.thebrtca.org/
- *Borzoi Club of America, Inc*. (n.d.). https://www.borzoiclubofamerica.org/
- *Boston Terrier Club of America – The Boston Terrier, a true American Gentleman*. (n.d.). https://bostonterrierclubofamerica.org/
- Boswell, E. (2024a, May 21). *Norwegian Elkhound*. DogTime. https://dogtime.com/dog-breeds/norwegian-elkhound
- Boswell, E. (2024b, June 7). *Tosa Inu*. DogTime. https://dogtime.com/dog-breeds/tosa
- Boswell, E. (2024c, August 12). *Spanish Mastiff*. DogTime. https://dogtime.com/dog-breeds/spanish-mastiff
- Boswell, E. (2024d, September 3). *Porcelaine*. DogTime. https://dogtime.com/dog-breeds/porcelaine
- *Breed - TTCA*. (2024, June 30). TTCA. https://ttca-online.org/ol-home/
- *Breed History | JACA - Japanese Akitainu Club of America*. (n.d.). https://akita-inu.com/breed-history/
- *Breed History | Sussex Spaniels*. (n.d.). https://www.sussexspaniels.org/about-sussex-spaniels/breed-history/
- *Breed History – Lancashire Heelers*. (n.d.). https://unitedstateslancashireheelerclub.com/breed-history/
- *Breed History – The Norfolk Terrier Club*. (n.d.). https://norfolkterrierclub.org/mission-statement/
- *Breed Info*. (n.d.). Korean Jindo Dog Association of America. http://www.jindos.org/breed-info.html
- *Breed Info | Pyrenean Shepherd Club of America*. (n.d.). Pyrenean Shepherd Club of America. https://www.pyrshepclub.org/breed-info
- *BREED INFO | USNMC*. (n.d.). USNMC. https://www.neapolitan.org/breed-info
- *Breed Information*. (2022, January 21). Thai Bangkaew Dog Club of America. https://thaibangkaewclub.com/breed-information/
- *Breed Information | SVCA, Inc*. (n.d.). https://www.swedishvallhund.com/breed-information
- *Breed Standard*. (n.d.). Kromfohrlander Club of America. https://www.kromiclubusa.org/breed-standard.html
- *Breed Standard | MASCUSA*. (n.d.). https://mascusa.org/breed/standard
- *Breed Standard – NSDTRC-USA*. (n.d.). https://www.nsdtrc-usa.org/breed/standard/
- *Bull Terrier Club of America*. (n.d.). BTCA. https://www.btca.com/
- *Cane Corso Association of America*. (n.d.). Cane Corso Association of America. https://www.canecorso.org/
- *Carolina Dog Fanciers of America | The AKC Parent Club for Carolina Dogs*. (n.d.). https://carolinadogfanciers.com/
- *Carpathian Sheepdog Dog Breed Information and Pictures*. (n.d.). https://www.dogbreedinfo.com/carpathian.htm
- Carter, B. (2023, September 10). *About the Breed - Saint Bernard Club of America*. Saint Bernard Club of America. https://saintbernardclubofamerica.club/about-the-breed/
- *Cavalier King Charles Spaniel Club*. (n.d.). Cavalier King Charles Spaniel Club. https://ckcsc.org/
- *Chinese Shar-Pei Club of America, Inc*. (2019, May 21). https://cspca.com/

- *Chinook Club of America Home Page*. (n.d.). Chinook Club of America Inc. https://www.chinookclubofamerica.org/
- Clancy, M. (2023a, October 12). *Belgian Laekenois*. DogTime. https://dogtime.com/dog-breeds/belgian-laekenois
- Clancy, M. (2023b, December 12). *Taiwan Dog*. DogTime. https://dogtime.com/dog-breeds/taiwan-dog
- Clancy, M. (2024, February 20). *Croatian Sheepdog*. DogTime. https://dogtime.com/dog-breeds/croatian-sheepdog
- Clark, M. (2023, October 12). *Caucasian Shepherd Dog*. DogTime. https://dogtime.com/dog-breeds/caucasian-shepherd-dog
- *Club Info — GBGVCA*. (n.d.). GBGVCA. https://www.gbgv.net/about
- Clumber Spaniel Club of America. (2024, May 21). *The Club - Clumber Spaniel Club of America*. https://clumbers.org/the-club/
- *Collie Club of America homepage | CCA*. (n.d.). https://collieclubofamerica.org/
- CyberNewt. (n.d.). *About Manchester Terriers*. https://www.americanmanchester.org/?page_id=209
- *Dachshund Club of America – Founded in 1895*. (n.d.). https://www.dachshundclubofamerica.org/
- *Danish-Swedish Farmdog Club of America home page - Danish-Swedish Farmdog Club of America*. (n.d.). https://dsfca.clubexpress.com/
- Dcwd. (2024a, September 1). *Home Scottish Terrier Club of America -*. Scottish Terrier Club of America. https://stca.biz/
- Dcwd. (2024b, September 2). *About the Breed Scottish Terrier Club of America -*. Scottish Terrier Club of America. https://stca.biz/about-the-breed/
- DDTCA. (2024, March 12). *Dandie Dinmont Club of America | Home*. DDTCA | THE DANDIE DINMONT TERRIER CLUB OF AMERICA. https://www.ddtca.org/
- *Detail*. (n.d.). https://dogsaustralia.org.au/members/breeds/breed-standards/Australian-Kelpie
- *Deutscher Wachtelhund North America Club | DWNA*. (n.d.). DWNA Club. https://www.wachtelhund.info/
- Developer, G. (2024, June 29). *American Brussels Griffon Association - American Brussels Griffon Association*. American Brussels Griffon Association. https://abga.club/
- *Dogo Argentino Club of America*. (2023, July 1). Dogo Argentino Club of America. https://dogousa.org/
- DogTime. (2023a, October 2). *Shetland Sheepdog*. DogTime. https://dogtime.com/dog-breeds/shetland-sheepdog
- DogTime. (2023b, October 12). *English Foxhound*. DogTime. https://dogtime.com/dog-breeds/english-foxhound
- DogTime. (2024a, January 3). *Treeing Tennessee Brindle*. DogTime. https://dogtime.com/dog-breeds/treeing-tennessee-brindle
- DogTime. (2024b, January 17). *Plott*. DogTime. https://dogtime.com/dog-breeds/plott
- DogTime. (2024c, March 11). *Small Munsterlander Pointer*. DogTime. https://dogtime.com/dog-breeds/small-munsterlander-pointer
- DogTime. (2024d, March 19). *Miniature Schnauzer*. DogTime. https://dogtime.com/dog-breeds/miniature-schnauzer
- DogTime. (2024e, June 14). *Welsh Springer Spaniel*. DogTime. https://dogtime.com/dog-breeds/welsh-springer-spaniel
- DogTime. (2024f, June 24). *Shih Tzu*. DogTime. https://dogtime.com/dog-breeds/shih-tzu
- DogTime. (2024g, July 25). *Samoyed*. DogTime. https://dogtime.com/dog-breeds/samoyed
- DogTime. (2024h, August 7). *Shiba Inu*. DogTime. https://dogtime.com/dog-breeds/shiba-inu
- DogTime. (2024i, August 30). *American English Coonhound*. DogTime. https://dogtime.com/dog-breeds/american-english-coonhound
- DogTime. (2024j, September 4). *Treeing Walker Coonhound*. DogTime. https://dogtime.com/dog-breeds/treeing-walker-coonhound
- Dpca. (2024, May 7). *Doberman Pinscher Club of America | Home*. Doberman Pinscher Club of America. https://dpca.org/
- Drever Association of America. (n.d.). *Drever Association of America*. https://dreverusa.org/
- English Cocker Spaniel Club of America. (2024, August 7). *ECSCA-Home-New - ECSCA*. ECSCA. https://englishcocker.org/
- *English Toy Spaniel Club of America – Official Site of English Toy Spaniel Club of America*. (n.d.). https://englishtoyspanielclubofamerica.org/
- Esaa, Esaa, Esaa, Esaa, Esaa, & Esaa. (n.d.). *ESAA*. ESAA. https://www.esaa.com/
- *Events & News - ABdFC*. (n.d.). American Bouvier Des Flandres Club. https://www.bouvier.org/events-news-824429.html

- Fcrsa. (2023, December 26). *Home - Flat-Coated Retriever Society of America*. Flat-Coated Retriever Society of America. https://fcrsa.org/
- Fernandez, J. (2024a, June 10). *Central Asian Shepherd Dog*. DogTime. https://dogtime.com/dog-breeds/central-asian-shepherd-dog
- Fernandez, J. (2024b, June 10). *Portuguese Pointer*. DogTime. https://dogtime.com/dog-breeds/portuguese-pointer
- Fernandez, J. (2024c, June 11). *Broholmer*. DogTime. https://dogtime.com/dog-breeds/broholmer
- FieldSpaniels. (2024, June 6). *Field Spaniel Society of America - Home*. Field Spaniel Society of America. https://www.fieldspanielsocietyofamerica.org/
- *Finnish Lapphund Club of America*. (2023, June 13). Finnish Lapphund Club of America. https://www.finnishlapphund.org/
- *Finnish Spitz Club of America*. (n.d.). Finnish Spitz Club of America. http://www.finnishspitzclub.org/
- German Longhaired Pointer Club. (2024, February 21). *Home Page - German Longhaired Pointer Club*. https://www.glpclub.org.uk/
- *GERMAN SPITZ CLUB OF AMERICA, INC*. (n.d.). GERMAN SPITZ CLUB OF AMERICA, INC. https://www.germanspitzclub.org/
- *German Wirehaired Pointer Club of America*. (n.d.). German Wirehaired Pointer Club of America. https://gwpca.com/
- *GITCA | Glen of Imaal Terrier Club of America*. (n.d.). https://www.glens.org/
- Golden Retriever Club of America. (2018, March 9). *Breed History - Golden Retriever Club of America*. https://grca.org/about-the-breed/breed-history/
- *Gordon Setter Club Of America*. (n.d.). https://gsca.org/
- Great Pyrenees Club of America. (2024, August 23). *HOME - Great Pyrenees Club of America*. https://greatpyrenees.club/
- GSMDCA. (2021, March 19). *Breed Information - GSMDCA*. https://www.gsmdca.org/breed-info/
- *GSPCA German Shorthaired Pointer Club of America | Learn more about this wonderful, versatile dog, the German Shorthaired Pointer*. (n.d.). https://www.gspca.org/
- *Hamiltonstovare Club of America*. (n.d.). Hamiltonstovare Club of America. https://www.hamiltonstovare.org/
- *Harrier Club of America - About The Harrier Club*. (n.d.). http://www.harrierclubofamerica.com/about-the-harrier-club/
- HCAAdmin. (2024, May 14). *ABOUT HAVANESE - Havanese Club of America*. Havanese Club of America. https://havaneseclubofamerica.org/about-havanese/
- Heckert, E. (2024, May 1). *The History of the Pomeranian*. American Pomeranian Club. https://ampomclub.org/the-history-of-the-pomeranian/
- *History*. (n.d.). JAPANESE TERRIER CLUB OF AMERICA. http://www.japaneseterrier.org/history.html
- *History – American Sealyham Terrier Club*. (n.d.). https://sealyham.org/history/
- *History of the Keeshond | KCA*. (n.d.). KCA. https://www.keeshond.org/history-of-the-keeshond
- *History of the Swedish Lapphund — Swedish Lapphund Club of America*. (n.d.). Swedish Lapphund Club of America. https://www.swedishlapphundclub.com/history
- *Hokkaido Association of North America*. (n.d.). https://www.hokkaidoken.org/
- *Home*. (n.d.-a). Hovawart Club of North America (HCNA). https://www.hovawartclub.org/hovawarts.html
- *Home*. (n.d.-b). https://chowclub.org/ccci/
- *Home*. (n.d.-c). https://www.basenji.org/
- *Home*. (n.d.-d). American Bulldog Association. http://www.ababulldogs.com/home.html
- *Home*. (2024a, May 9). Afghan Hound Club of America, Inc. https://afghanhoundclubofamerica.org/
- *Home*. (2024b, August 1). Dalmatian Club of America. https://dalmatianclubofamerica.org/
- *Home*. (2024c, August 21). Affenpinscher Club of America. https://www.affenpinscher.org/
- *Home | AMCA Website*. (n.d.). AMCA Website. https://www.alaskanmalamute.org/
- *Home | Estrela Mountain Dog*. (n.d.). Estrela Mountain Dog. https://www.estrelamountaindogassociation.com/
- *Home | Slovakian Rough Haired Pointer Club*. (n.d.). Slovakian Rough Hair. https://www.slovakianroughhairedpointerclub.org.uk/
- *Home | Wirehaired Vizsla Cl*. (n.d.). Wirehaired Vizsla Cl. https://www.wvca.club/
- *Home - American Beauceron Club*. (n.d.). https://beauce.clubexpress.com/
- *Home - The American Bullmastiff Association*. (2024, September 7). The American Bullmastiff Association. https://bullmastiff.us/

- *Home - Tibetan Spaniel Club of America*. (2023, February 27). Tibetan Spaniel Club of America. https://www.tsca.ws/
- *Home Page*. (n.d.). http://www.giantschnauzerclubofamerica.com/
- *http://www.facebook.com/pages/American-Portuguese-Podengo-MedioGrande-Club/199594486733380*. (n.d.). http://www.podengo-mediogrande.com/
- *Hungarian Pumi Club of America, Inc.* (2001, September 21). https://pumiclub.org/
- Ibizan Hound Club of the United States. (2022, May 23). *Breed History - Ibizan Hound Club of the United States*. https://new.ihcus.org/?page_id=383
- Inc, N. C. O. A. (n.d.). *Official site of the Newfoundland Club of America*. https://www.ncanewfs.org/index.html
- *Irish Terrier Club of America | Irish Terrier Resources*. (n.d.). ITCA. https://www.itca.info/
- *Irish Water Spaniel Club of America Inc - What is an Irish Water Spaniel?* (n.d.). https://iwsca.org/What_is_an_Irish_Water_Spaniel
- Irish Wolfhound Club of America, Inc. (2021, July 11). *Irish Wolfhounds - Introduction*. https://www.iwclubofamerica.org/about-irish-wolfhounds
- *IRWSAA | Home*. (n.d.). https://www.irishredwhitesetterassociation.com/
- Italian Greyhound Club of America. (2023, December 3). *About the Italian Greyhound - IGCA*. IGCA. https://italiangreyhound.org/about-the-italian-greyhound/
- *Jack Russell Terrier JRTCA - Breed Information*. (n.d.). https://www.therealjackrussell.com/breed/index.php
- Johnson, J. (n.d.). *Border Terrier Club of America – The AKC Parent Club for Border Terriers*. Border Terrier Club of America. https://btcoa.org/
- Johnson, J. (2023a, July 4). *Welsh Terrier Club of America*. Welsh Terrier Club of America. https://welshterrier.org/
- Johnson, J. (2023b, August 18). *The Puli - Puli Club of America*. Puli Club of America. https://puliclub.org/wp/the-puli/
- Johnson, J. (2024, July 5). *Akita Club of America - HOME*. Akita Club of America. https://www.akitaclub.org/
- Kai Ken Society of America. (2023, May 9). *History - Kai Ken Society of America*. https://kaisociety.org/history/
- *Klub slovenského kopova*. (2023, October 5). Klub Slovenského Kopova. https://www.slovenskykopov.cz/
- *Komondor Club of America | Official Site of the Komondor Club of America*. (n.d.). https://komondorclubofamerica.org/
- Koshyk, C. (2024, April 17). *Wirehaired Pointing Griffon – Dog Breed Information, Form, Function, History, and More*. Project Upland. https://projectupland.com/hunting-dogs/wirehaired-pointing-griffon/
- Kuvasz Club of America. (2024, June 3). *Kuvasz Club of America • Official Parent Club to the American Kennel Club*. https://kuvaszclubofamerica.org/
- *LA RACE | schapendoes*. (n.d.). Schapendoes. https://en.schapendoesdubouleaublanc.ca/la-race
- *Lagotto Romagnolo Club of America - Breed Information*. (n.d.). https://www.lagottous.com/Breed-Information
- LCA_Admin. (2023, March 28). *A Brief History of the Leonberger*. Leonberger Club of America. https://leonbergerclubofamerica.com/a-brief-history-of-the-leonberger/
- *Löwchen Info | Lowchen Club Of America*. (n.d.). Lowchen Club of Amer. https://www.thelowchenclubofamerica.org/l%C3%B6wchen-info
- LTCAdmin. (2024, February 23). *THE BREED - US Lakeland Terrier Club*. US Lakeland Terrier Club. https://usltc.org/the-breed/
- *Meet the breed | Slovakian Rough Hair*. (n.d.). Slovakian Rough Hair. https://www.slovakianroughhairedpointerclub.org.uk/meet-the-breed
- Michael. (2019, December 2). *About The Breed | The Tibetan Spaniel Club of America*. Tibetan Spaniel Club of America. https://www.tsca.ws/aboutthebreed/
- *Miniature Bull Terrier Club of America*. (n.d.). MBTCA. https://www.mbtca.net/
- Mlynar, P. (2023a, September 27). *Slovensky Kopov*. DogTime. https://dogtime.com/dog-breeds/slovensky-kopov
- Mlynar, P. (2023b, October 6). *Tornjak*. DogTime. https://dogtime.com/dog-breeds/tornjak
- Mlynar, P. (2023c, October 23). *Rafeiro do Alentejo*. DogTime. https://dogtime.com/dog-breeds/rafeiro-do-alentejo
- Mlynar, P. (2024a, January 17). *Romanian Mioritic Shepherd Dog*. DogTime. https://dogtime.com/dog-breeds/romanian-mioritic-shepherd-dog
- Mlynar, P. (2024b, March 11). *Braques Français Pyrenean*. DogTime. https://dogtime.com/dog-breeds/braque-francais-pyrenean
- *MPCA | Miniature Pinscher Club of America*. (n.d.). http://www.minpin.org/
- *Mudi Club Of America*. (2023, July 12). Mudi Club of America. https://www.mudi.us/

- *NAPPA | North American Pudelpointer Alliance | United States.* (n.d.). NAPPA. https://www.pudelpointer-alliance.com/
- *National Association of Louisiana Catahoulas.* (n.d.). National Association of Louisiana Catahoulas. https://www.nalc-inc.org/
- National Bluetick Coonhound Association. (n.d.). *National Bluetick Coonhound Association.* https://nationalblueticks.com/
- *National Entlebucher Mountain Dog Association (NEMDA) - Home.* (n.d.). https://nemda.org/
- National Kennel Club. (2022a, February 18). *English Foxhound | National Kennel Club.* National Kennel Club |. https://nationalkennelclub.com/english-foxhound/
- National Kennel Club. (2022b, June 6). *American Leopard Cur | National Kennel Club.* National Kennel Club |. https://nationalkennelclub.com/american-leopard-cur/
- *National Kishu Ken Club | The Official AKC Parent Club for the Kishu Ken.* (n.d.). National Kishu Ken Club | the Official AKC Parent Club for the Kishu Ken. https://www.kishuclub.com/#kishu
- *National Redbone Coonhound Association.* (n.d.). https://www.nationalredbonecoonhoundassociation.org/
- *National Shiba Club of America.* (n.d.). https://www.shibas.org/about.html
- Nbca. (n.d.). *NBCA.* NBCA. https://buhund.org/about-the-breed
- Niles, A. (2018, October 31). *About the Rottweiler.* American Rottweiler Club. https://www.amrottclub.org/about-the-rottweiler/
- *North American Shikoku Club » The North American Shikoku Ken Club (NASC) | Breed History.* (n.d.). https://shikokuclub.com/history/
- *Norwegian Lundehund Association of America – NLAA, Inc.* (n.d.). https://nlaainc.com/
- NVSW - Nederlandse Vereniging voor Stabij- en Wetterhounen. (n.d.). *Wetterhoun - NVSW.* https://www.nvsw.nl/english/frisian-water-dog-wetterhoun/wetterhoun
- *Overview — Bergamasco Sheepdog Club of America.* (n.d.). Bergamasco Sheepdog Club of America. https://bergamascousa.com/overview
- *Overview — Icelandic Sheepdog Association of America.* (n.d.). Icelandic Sheepdog Association of America. https://www.icelanddogs.com/overview
- *Page 1.* (n.d.). https://www.prtaa.org/the-parson-russell-terrier
- <i>PBGVCA Breeders' Tool Chest ~ The Kennel Club Standard Basset Griffon Vendeen (Petit) Breed Standard. (n.d.). <span class=&qout;url&qout;>https://pbgv.org/tools/standard-kennelclub.shtml
- PCAadmin. (2024, April 2). *HOME - Pekingese Club of America.* Pekingese Club of America. https://pekingeseclubofamerica.com/#
- *Pembroke Welsh Corgi Club of America - Home.* (n.d.). https://pwcca.org/
- *Peruánský Naháč Velký - Peruvian Hairless Dog - Breed.* (n.d.). http://www.hairlessbrno.com/index.php/en/breed
- *Petit Basset Griffon Vendeen Dog Breed Information - Continental Kennel Club.* (n.d.). https://ckcusa.com/breeds/petit-basset-griffon-vendeen/
- Pivoncy, M. (2024, February 8). *Mountain Cur.* DogTime. https://dogtime.com/dog-breeds/mountain-cur
- *PM History | PMAA.* (n.d.). PMAA. https://www.pyreneanmastiffassociation.org/pm-history
- *Portuguese Sheepdog – Clube Português de Canicultura.* (n.d.). https://www.cpc.pt/en/breeds/portuguese-breeds/portuguese-sheepdog/
- <i>Portuguese Water Dog Club of America, Inc. (PWDCA) - Powered by AMO . (n.d.). <span class=&qout;url&qout;>https://www.pwdca.org/site_page.cfm?pk_association_webpage_menu=8853&pk_association_webpage=18266
- Ramsey, J. (2024, June 30). *CdECA - Home of the Cirneco dell'Etna.* 100% Pure Cirneco. https://cirneco.org/
- *Rat Terrier Club of America.* (n.d.). Rat Terrier Club of America. https://ratterrierclubofamerica.org/
- *RED VOLPINO ITALIANO | volpinoitalianoclub.* (n.d.). Volpinoitalianoclub. https://www.volpinoclubofamerica.com/red-volpino-italiano
- *Russian Toy Club of America.* (n.d.). Russian Toy Club of America. https://www.russiantoyclubamerica.org/
- Russian Tsvetnaya Bolonka Club of America. (2023, August 15). *HOME - Russian Tsvetnaya Bolonka Club of America.* https://www.rtbca.com/
- *Saluki Club of America.* (n.d.). Saluki Club of America. https://salukiclub.org/index.html
- *Schapendoes, colette peiffer, dog breeder, Tremblent, Canada.* (n.d.). Schapendoes. https://www.schapendoesduboleaublanc.ca/
- *Segit – Un Cane Tra I Cani.* (n.d.). http://segugioitalianoclubofamerica.com/
- *Siberian Husky Club of America, Inc-Home.* (n.d.). Siberian Husky Club of America, Inc. https://www.shca.org/
- *SilkyTerrierClub.* (n.d.). http://silkyterrierclubofamerica.org/
- Site, S. (n.d.). *STCA Site.* STCA Site. https://amstaff.org/

- *Skye Terrier Club of America*. (n.d.). Skye Terrier Club of America. https://stca.us/
- *Small Munsterlander Breed Club in North America*. (n.d.). https://www.smcna.org/Breed-Info
- *Spanish Water Dog Club of America (SWDCA)*. (n.d.). SPANISH WATER DOG CLUB OF AMERICA. https://www.swdclub.org/
- *Spinone Club of America*. (n.d.). Spinone Club of America. https://www.spinoneclubofamerica.com/
- *SS Breed Information Page*. (n.d.). https://www.standardschnauzer.org/newSSCA/breed_info.html
- Staffordshire Bull Terrier Club of America. (2019, July 5). *The Breed - Staffordshire Bull Terrier Club of America*. https://sbtca.com/the-breed/
- STCAdmin. (2024, July 26). *Silky Terrier Club of America - Your Silky Terrier Resource - Silky Terrier Club of America*. Silky Terrier Club of America. https://silkyterrier.net/#
- Steve. (2020, September 17). *About The Pharaoh Hound Breed - Pharaoh Hound Club of America*. Pharaoh Hound Club of America. https://ph-club.org/about-the-pharaoh-hound/
- *Sussex Spaniels | Sussex Spaniel Club of America*. (n.d.). https://www.sussexspaniels.org/
- *SVCA, Inc. | The official website of the Swedish Vallhund Club of America*. (n.d.). https://www.swedishvallhund.com/
- *Swedish Lapphund Club of America*. (n.d.). Swedish Lapphund Club of America. https://www.swedishlapphundclub.com/
- Szoó, A. (2021, January 8). *Transylvanian Hound, the most endangered Hungarian breed*. Transylvania Now. https://transylvanianow.com/transylvanian-hound-the-most-endangered-hungarian-dog-breed/
- The American Miniature Schnauzer Club. (2024, February 24). *All About Miniature Schnauzers - The American Miniature Schnauzer Club*. https://amsc.us/all-about-miniature-schnauzers/
- *The Boykin Spaniel Club*. (n.d.). http://bscbaa.com/
- *The Breed*. (n.d.). AMERICAN TEDDY ROOSEVELT TERRIER CLUB. http://www.teddyroosevelterrier.org/the-breed.html
- *The Cairn Terrier Club of America | Cairn Terrier Club of America*. (n.d.). https://www.cairnterrier.org/
- *The Cardigan Welsh Corgi Club of America*. (2001, October 5). https://cardigancorgis.com/cwcca/
- *The Chihuahua Club of America | The Official Website of the Chihuahua Club of America*. (n.d.). https://chihuahuaclubofamerica.org/
- *The Czechoslovakian Vlciak Club of America*. (n.d.). The Czechoslovakian. https://www.czechoslovakianvlciak.com/
- *The DJT breed – Deutsche Jagdterrier*. (n.d.). https://djt-jagdterrier.com/en/the-djt-breed/
- *The Drent*. (n.d.). Drentsche Patrijshond Club of America. https://www.dpcna.org/the-drent.html
- *The German Pinscher Club of America | A Member of the American Kennel Club*. (n.d.). https://germanpinscher.org/
- The German Shepherd Dog Club of America. (2024, August 2). *Home - The German Shepherd Dog Club of America*. https://www.gsdca.org/
- *The Great Dane*. (n.d.). https://gdca.org/the-great-dane/
- The Labrador Retriever Club, Inc. (2024, May 10). *Home - The Labrador Retriever Club, Inc.* https://thelabradorclub.com/
- *The National Beagle Club of America, Inc. - Home*. (n.d.). https://www.nationalbeagleclub.org/
- *The Old English Sheepdog Club of America | OESCA*. (2020, July 10). Old English Sheepdog Club of America. https://oldenglishsheepdogclubofamerica.org/
- *The Otterhound Club of America, Inc.* (n.d.). The Otterhound Club of America, Inc. https://otterhound.org/
- *The Presa Canario | Presa Canario Club of America*. (n.d.). Presa Canario Club. https://www.presacanarioclub.net/the-presa-canario
- *The Rhodesian Ridgeback Club of the United States - Breed Standard*. (n.d.). https://www.rrcus.org/The-Standard
- *The Samoyed - Samoyed Club of America*. (2024, August 1). Samoyed Club of America. https://www.samoyedclubofamerica.org/the-samoyed/
- *The Scottish Deerhound Club of America*. (n.d.). The Scottish Deerhound Club of America. https://deerhound.org/
- *The Yorkshire Terrier Club of America*. (n.d.). http://www.theyorkshireterrierclubofamerica.org/
- *UK Picardy Spaniel Club*. (n.d.). https://www.ukpicardyspanielclub.org/the-epagneul-de-pont-audemer
- *United States Eurasier Club*. (n.d.). USEC. https://www.useurasierclub.org/
- *United States Kerry Blue Terrier Club, Inc. - Is a Kerry the Dog for Me?* (n.d.). https://www.uskbtc.com/Is-a-Kerry-the-dog-for-me
- *United States of America Coton de Tulear Club*. (n.d.). https://www.usactc.dog/

- Usa, C. (n.d.). *Cuvac USA*. Cuvac USA. https://cuvacusa.com/the-slovensk%C3%BD-%C4%8Duva%C4%8D
- Vizsla Club of America. (2024, May 2). *Home - Vizsla Club of America*. https://vcaweb.org/
- Webb, D. (2024, September 2). *Bulldog Club of America - Home of the Official AKC Bulldog Breed Club - The Bulldog Club of America*. The Bulldog Club of America. https://bulldogclubofamerica.org/
- Webmaster. (2023, May 10). *About the Breed - Mastiff Club of America*. Mastiff Club of America. https://www.mastiff.org/about-the-breed/
- Webmaster, S. (2001, September 30). *Soft Coated Wheaten Terrier Club of America*. Soft Coated Wheaten Terrier Club of America. https://scwtca.org/
- *Weimaraner Club of America*. (n.d.). https://www.weimaranerclubofamerica.org/
- Weise, C. (2024, April 12). *Thai Bangkaew Dog (character, nutrition, care, tips)*. Hundeo. https://www.hundeo.com/en/dog-breeds/thai-bangkaew-dog/
- *Welcome to the Curly Coated Retriever Club of America*. (n.d.). https://www.ccrca.org/
- *Welcome to the French Bull Dog Club of America!* (n.d.). French Bull Dog Club of America. https://frenchbulldogclub.org/
- *Werken in de kooi*. (n.d.). [Video]. NKCUSA. https://www.nkcusa.org/about-the-breed
- *West Highland White Terrier Club of America*. (n.d.). https://westieclubamerica.com/
- Wilson, J. (n.d.). *Home*. Irish Setter Club of America, Inc. https://irishsetterclub.org/
- *Xoloitzcuintli Club of America*. (n.d.). Xoloitzcuintli Club of America. https://www.xoloitzcuintliclubofamerica.org/
- Zephyr Design. (n.d.). *Japanese Spitz Club of America - Breeders & Puppies*. Copyright Zephyr Design. https://www.japanesespitzamerica.com/

DOG BREED INDEX

A

Affenpinscher	49
Afghan Hound	49
Airedale Terrier	50
Akita (American)	50
Alaskan Husky	51
Alaskan Klee Kai	51
Alaskan Malamute	52
American Bulldog	52
American English Coonhound	53
American Eskimo Dog	53
American Foxhound	54
American Hairless Terrier	54
American Leopard Hound	55
American Pitbull Terrier	55
American Staffordshire Terrier	56
American Water Spaniel	56
Anatolian Shepherd	57
Appenzeller Sennenhund	57
Australian Cattle Dog	58
Australian Kelpie	58
Australian Shepherd	59
Australian Stumpy Tail Cattle Dog	59
Australian Terrier	60
Azawakh	60

B

Barbado da Terceira	61
Barbet	61
Basenji	62
Basset Bleu de Gascogne (Grand)	62
Basset Bleu de Gascogne (Petit)	63
Basset Fauve de Bretagne	63
Basset Griffon Vendeen (Grand)	64
Basset Griffon Vendeen (Petit)	64
Basset Hound	65
Bavarian Mountain Scent Hound	65
Beagle	66
Bearded Collie	66

Beauceron	67
Bedlington Terrier	67
Belgian Laekenois	68
Belgian Malinois	68
Belgian Sheepdog	69
Belgian Tervuren	69
Bergamasco	70
Berger Picard	70
Bernese Mountain Dog	71
Bichon Frise	71
Biewer Terrier	72
Black and Tan Coonhound	72
Black Russian Terrier	73
Bloodhound	73
Bluetick Coonhound	74
Boerboel	74
Bohemian Shepherd	75
Bolognese	75
Border Collie	76
Border Terrier	76
Borzoi	77
Boston Terrier	77
Bouvier des Flandres	78
Boxer	78
Boykin Spaniel	79
Bracco Italiano	79
Braque de Bourbonnais	80
Braque Francais Pyrenean	80
Braque Saint-Germain	81
Brazilian Terrier	81
Briard	82
Brittany	82
Broholmer	83
Brussels Griffon	83
Bull Terrier	84
Bulldog	84
Bullmastiff	85

C

Cairn Terrier	85
Canaan Dog	86
Cane Corso	86
Carolina Dog	87
Catahoula Leopard Dog	87
Caucasian Shepherd Dog	88
Cavalier King Charles Spaniel	88
Central Asian Shepherd Dog	89
Cesky Terrier	89
Chesapeake Bay Retriever	90

Chihuahua — 90
Chinese Crested — 91
Chinese Shar Pei — 91
Chinook — 92
Chow Chow — 92
Cirneco Dell'Etna — 93
Clumber Spaniel — 93
Cocker Spaniel (American) — 94
Cocker Spaniel (English) — 94
Collie — 95
Coton De Tulear — 95
Croatian Sheepdog — 96
Curly-coated Retriever — 96
Czechoslovakian Vlack — 97

D
Dachshund — 97
Dalmatian — 98
Dandie Dinmont Terrier — 98
Danish-Swedish Farmdog — 99
Deutscher Wachtelhund — 99
Doberman Pinscher — 100
Dogo Argentino — 100
Dogue de Bordeaux — 101
Drentsche Patrijshond — 101
Drever — 102
Dutch Shepherd — 102

E
English
Foxhound — 103
English Setter — 103
English Springer Spaniel — 104
English Toy Spaniel — 104
Entlebucher Mountain Dog — 105
Estrela Mountain Dog — 105
Eurasier — 106

F
Field Spaniel — 106
Finnish Lapphund — 107
Finnish Spitz — 107
Flat-Coated Retriever — 108
Fox Terrier (Toy) — 108
Fox Terrier — 109
French Bulldog — 109
French Spaniel — 110

G

German Pinscher — 110
German Long-haired Pointer — 111
German Short-haired Pointer — 111
German Wire-haired Pointer — 112
German Shepherd — 112
German Spitz — 113
Glen of Imaal Terrier — 113
Golden Retriever — 114
Gordon Setter — 114
Great Dane — 115
Great Pyrenees — 115
Greater Swiss Mountain Dog — 116
Greyhound — 116
Greyhound (Italian) — 117

H

Hamiltonstovare — 117
Hanoverian Scenthound — 118
Harrier — 118
Havanese — 119
Hokkaido — 119
Hovawart — 120

I

Ibizan Hound — 120
Icelandic Sheepdog — 121
Irish Red and White Setter — 121
Irish Setter — 122
Irish Terrier — 122
Irish Water Spaniel — 123
Irish Wolfhound — 123

J

Jagdterrier — 124
Japanese Akita Inu — 124
Japanese Chin — 125
Japanese Spitz — 125
Japanese Terrier — 126

K

Kai Ken — 126
Karelian Bear Dog — 127
Keeshond — 127
Kerry Blue Terrier — 128
Kishu Ken — 128
Komondor — 129
Korean Jindo Dog — 129

Kromfohrlander 130
Kuvasz 130

L

Labrador Retriever 131
Lagotto Romagnolo 131
Lakeland Terrier 132
Lancashire Heeler 132
Lapponian Herder 133
Leonberger 133
Lhasa Apso 134
Lowchen 134

M

Maltese 135
Manchester Terrier (Standard) 135
Manchester Terrier (Toy) 136
Mastiff (English) 136
Mastiff (Pyrenean) 137
Mastiff (Neapolitan) 137
Mastiff (Spanish) 138
Mastiff (Tibetan) 138
Miniature American Shepherd 139
Miniature Bull Terrier 139
Miniature Pinscher 140
Mountain Cur 140
Mudi 141
Musterlander Pointer (Large) 141
Musterlander Pointer (Small) 142

N

Nederlandse Kooikerhondje 142
Newfoundland 143
Norfolk Terrier 143
Norrbottenspets 144
Norwegian Buhund 144
Norwegian Elkhound 145
Norwegian Lundhund 145
Norwich Terrier 146
Nova Scotia Duck Tolling Retriever 146

O

Old English Sheepdog 147
Otterhound 147

P

Papillon 148

Parson Russell Terrier _____148
Pekingese _____149
Peruvian Inca Orchid _____149
Pharaoh Hound _____150
Plott Hound _____150
Pointer _____151
Polish Lowland Sheepdog _____151
Pomeranian _____152
Pont-Audemer Spaniel _____152
Poodle _____153
Poodle (Miniature) _____153
Poodle (Toy) _____154
Porcelaine _____154
Portuguese Podengo (Medio) _____155
Portuguese Podengo (Pequeno) _____155
Portuguese Pointer _____156
Portuguese Sheepdog _____156
Portuguese Water Dog _____157
Presa Canario _____157
Pudelpointer _____158
Pug _____158
Puli _____159
Pumi _____159
Pyrenean Shepherd _____160

R

Rafeiro de Alentejo _____160
Rat Terrier _____161
Redbone Coonhound _____161
Rhodesian Ridgeback _____162
Romanian Carpathian Shepherd _____162
Romanian Mioritic Shepherd _____163
Rottweiler _____163
Russell Terrier _____164
Russian Toy _____164
Russian Tsvetnaya Bolonka _____165

S

Saint Bernard _____165
Saluki _____166
Samoyed _____166
Schapendoes _____167
Schipperke _____167
Schnauzer _____168
Schnauzer (Giant) _____168
Schnauzer (Miniature) _____169
Scottish Deerhound _____169
Scottish Terrier _____170
Sealyham Terrier _____170

Segugio Italiano	171
Shetland Sheepdog	171
Shiba Inu	172
Shih Tzu	172
Shikoku	173
Siberian Husky	173
Silky Terrier	174
Skye Terrier	174
Sloughi	175
Slovak Rough-haired Pointer	175
Slovensky Cuvac	176
Slovensky Kopov	176
Soft-Coated Wheaten Terrier	177
Spanish Water Dog	177
Spinone Italiano	178
Stabyhoun	178
Staffordshire Bull Terrier	179
Sussex Spaniel	179
Swedish Lapphund	180
Swedish Vallhund	180

T

Taiwan Dog	181
Teddy Roosevelt Terrier	181
Thai Bangkaew	182
Thai Ridgeback	182
Tibetan Spaniel	183
Tibetan Terrier	183
Tornjak	184
Tosa	184
Transylvanian Hound	185
Treeing Tennessee Brindle	185
Treeing Walker Coonhound	186

V

Vizsla	186
Vizsla (Wire-haired)	187
Volpino Italiano	187

W

Weimaraner	188
Welsh Corgi (Cardigan)	188
Welsh Corgi (Pembroke)	189
Welsh Springer Spaniel	189
Welsh Terrier	190
West Highland White Terrier	190
Wetterhoun	191
Whippet	191

Wire-haired Pointing Griffon _____ 192

X
Xoloitzcuintli _____ 192

Y
Yakutian Laika _____ 193
Yorkshire Terrier _____ 193

Milton Keynes UK
Ingram Content Group UK Ltd.
UKHW010724131124
451037UK00012B/243